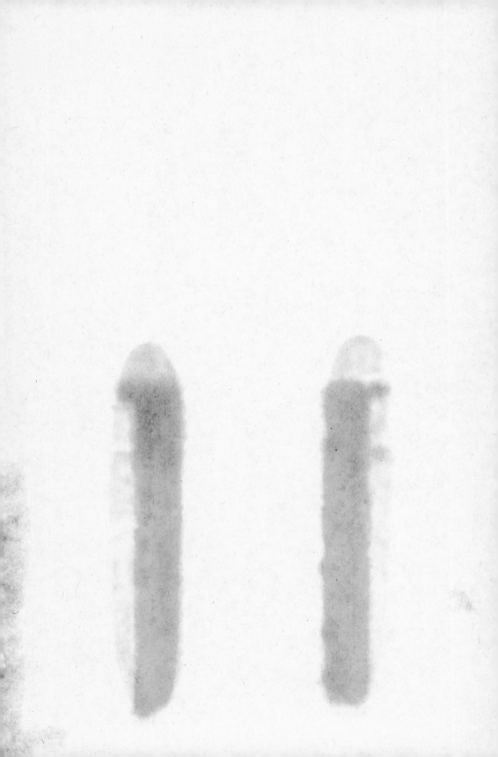

The Joy of Sports

MICHAEL NOVAK

THE JOY OF

SPORTS

End Zones, Bases,

Baskets, Balls,

and the Consecration

of the American Spirit

Basic Books, Inc., Publishers   New York

Library of Congress Cataloging in Publication Data

Novak, Michael.
   The joy of sports.

   1. Sports—United States.   I. Title.
GN583.N68   796'.0973   75-36383
ISBN 0-465-03679-1

This book is dedicated

to

Richard, Tanya, and Jana

and to their cousins

Joshua, Joseph, and PeiPei

Acknowledgments

I AM GRATEFUL to the following for permission to re-print some of the materials in this book.

The *Washington Post,* for items from the front page of October 11, 1924.

The editors of *Harvard Magazine* for "Crimson Lines of Appreciation to Philips Andover Academy," by Francis Whiting Hatch. Copyright © 1975 Harvard magazine.

The Los Angeles Dodgers and Vince Scully for the tran-script of the broadcast of the last inning of the game of September 9, 1965.

The *Notre Dame Observer,* for "Letters to a Lonely God," by the Reverend Robert Griffin, C.S.C.

The *Intellectual Digest* for selections from "I Experience a Kind of Clarity," by John Brodie and Michael Mur-phy.

Harper & Row, for a passage from *The City Game,* by Peter Axthelm. Copyright © 1970 by Peter Axthelm.

GV
583
.N68

Contents

Introduction:
Faith Seeks Understanding

THE TOWN in Pennsylvania where I grew up has some of the loveliest baseball diamonds of any city in the nation. Each summer, twenty-four teams from as far away as New Orleans, Boston, Brooklyn, and Baltimore arrive in town: eighteen-year-olds, playing before a score of big league scouts, scoop grounders out of the infield dust, throw sharply, hit the white ball across the cut green grass. Down at the ancient Point Stadium, near the stone bridge where the flood of '89 backed up and swirled backward on the city, Babe Ruth once lined a home run that was still rising in the night air when it cleared the wall over the huge, blocked yellow "415" in right center, near the scoreboard. Al Kaline played there. Just after he pitched a one-hitter, I once got Joe Torre's autograph in the Dairy Dell, and marveled at his Brooklynese.

I must have been six when I first heard the name "Brooklyn Dodgers." Dodge ball? Dodge the police? Dodging traffic? I imagined risks, tricks, zany errors. I didn't know then the Dodgers' reputation, only that the Johnstown Johnnies in those balmy days had a class-C farm club for them. They played in the Middle Atlantic League, where scores like 16–9 were ordinary. As I grew older, names like Pee Wee Reese and Pete Reiser filtered through the distance. My father told me Ducky Medwick played in Johnstown before he went to Brooklyn; Joe Cronin, too.

In 1946 my family moved 60 miles across the Laurel Mountains. We lived in McKeesport, a trolley ride from Forbes Field. Suddenly, the next summer, I could *see* the Dodgers. How proud I was that they hired Jackie Robinson. The Dodgers meant not only victory to me and heartbreak, but goodness; they were a cut above ordinary human life. I saw Jackie steal home on two different occasions, bluffing the steal so credibly for three or four attempts before he actually stole it that he had me and all the black folks and half the white folks laughing out loud at the bafflement of Pirate pitchers. "Night games," a steelworker told me in the bleachers, "can't even see the spook. Uniform, is all. Go! ya goddamn ghost!" I also saw him dive through the air to knock down a line drive behind first base, shove himself up off the ground in a marine pushup, and throw underneath his body to nail Ralph Kiner a step from the bag. Jackie Robinson was a magician, a performer, and in his person took the images I had had of blacks as Step'n'fetchits, spoofs, and put-on artists and tied them to athletic excellence. His grace, power, cunning, and deception were to me distinctly black; the man's fluidity stays with my memory still, as silken as a Georgia accent, as nightlike as the humid air.

So, in 1973, in my fortieth year, I am riding on the 5:29 from my job in Manhattan to my home on Long Island, one of 90 million workers weary with the Monday blues. It is early in September, my birthday is half a week away. The Scotch is swaying restlessly in my paper cup. Suddenly, I remember. Monday night: television. The Dodgers are at Montreal. My spirits lift. Tonight there is a treat.

That hot September night, the Dodgers lost. I was three days shy of forty, and their loss depressed me. I didn't even know, in advance, six of the nine players on the team—young guys, far away in Los Angeles, and in this busy summer of my life beyond the range of my perception. The Dodgers had been winning; they lost in the ninth. Saturday and Sunday they had blown an important series to Cincinnati. They were going to blow first place, lose the pennant—and later in the month that's exactly what they did. I was angry at the Dodgers: blowing it.

My wife lives in some other world at such times of private suffering. I sat there vacantly.

How could I be forty years old and still care what happens to the Dodgers? How could I have thrown away three hours of an evaporating life, watching a ritual, an inferior dance, a competition without a socially redeeming point? About the age of forty, almost everything about one's life comes into question. There is so little time to grasp and hold, it slides through fingers like the sand. It seems important, now, to concentrate. And so I asked myself: Is it time for sports to be discarded? Is it time to put away the things of childhood?

Quietly, I knew the answer. What I had just seen was somehow more important than my other work, was deeper in my being than most of what I did, spoke to me of beauty, excellence, imagination, and animal vitality— was *true* in a way few things in life are true. My love for sports was deeper than any theory that I had. The reality is better than its intellectual defense.

So I knew I had an obligation to work on this book.

I love sports, and I want to bequeath that love to my children—to that stranger with the mitt who is ten, and the two girls who are eight and three. It seems a precious gift to give. But why? Why do I love sports? How can I explain it to myself, let alone to others, especially to those who are skeptical unbelievers?

Sports is, somehow, a religion. You either see or you don't see what the excitement is. I wish wives were not so often unbelievers; but, then, many of the male sex are agnostic, too. Often I feel sorry for them. I smart, as well, under their transmitted belief in their own superiority.

James Wechsler expressed on New Year's 1974 my own sentiments: "The country seems divided between those caught up in the frenzy and those who could not care less. In many places, the latter must feel like aliens." Wechsler himself was at a New Year's party, serious and contemplative, and when he asked his hosts if he could slip into the study to watch the end of the Notre Dame–Alabama game, he felt a cold condescension circle out from the others and noticed the "fatalistic expression" on the countenance of his wife. The conversation had been intelligent and somber: the state of the nation, Watergate, etc. Wechsler had felt the contest sliding by, unwatched. Heroically, he had not referred to it, wondering all the

while how anybody could be so insensitive as to schedule
dinner during the hours of such a game. His secret desire
voiced, the others turned on him. A journalist snapped:
"It's the most *American* thing you can do!" Wechsler knew
what he meant by that: "How could an allegedly mature
man squander time watching pros claw at each other for
pay, or give a damn whether Notre Dame beats Alabama?"

But it *is* so important whether Notre Dame beats Alabama. Can't unbelievers understand?

The accusation made against Wechsler is a prejudice all
believers live under: "To love sports is to love the lowest
common denominator, to be lower-class, adolescent, patriotic in a corny way." The *intellectual* thing, the *liberal*
thing, the *mature* thing is to set sports aside.

This severe prejudice is not usually fatal, not at least to
persons of goodwill; but it *is* evidence of insufficiently developed perception. The basic reality of all human life is
play, games, sport; these are the realities from which the
basic metaphors for all that is important in the rest of life
are drawn. Work, politics, and history are the illusory,
misleading, false world. *Being, beauty, truth, excellence,
transcendence*—these words, grown in the soil of play,
wither in the sand of work. Art, prayer, worship, love,
civilization: these thrive in the field of play. Play belongs
to the Kingdom of Ends, work to the Kingdom of Means.
Barbarians play in order to work; the civilized work in
order to play.

The severe Puritan bias of America leads us to under-
value sports. America took root in Protestant culture, and
as de Tocqueville noted in 1836, Americans did not play,
had no sports, centered their lives in work. As America
has grown more Catholic, more Jewish, more various, the
world of play has acquired intellectual traditions here.
The nation needs a post-Protestant understanding of itself. At the heart of its rejuvenation may lie sports.

When John F. Kennedy wished to underline the
seriousness of some impending decision, he made certain
that the news media showed pictures of him playing
touch football or walking on the beach. The most important things are in the hands of God, so to speak, and the
appropriate human attitude is to enjoy the combat.

When Richard M. Nixon wished to underline the seriousness of some impending decision, he made sure the news media learned that he was staying up all night, asking for a fresh supply of yellow legal pads, sending out for cottage cheese and catsup. The most important crises, so to speak, require that God's suffering servants *suffer*. The appropriate human attitude is seriousness, suffering, self-discipline. Nixon talked about sports but played little. Sports were part of his work; he made them lessons in morality, rather than in liberty and joy.

To care about the Notre Dame–Alabama game during an evening of discussion is—take your pick—A sign of grace? Machismo? Regression? Humanism?

Faith in sports, I have discovered, seeks understanding. I cannot forever split my life in two, half in love with sports, half in love with serious thought. Life seeks unity. This book is an attempt by a believer to explore his belief, to find some useful words for it, to give his head reasons for what his heart already knows. Next New Year's Day, again, I will watch three football games. But why? Why is sports a good love, worthy of the best men have to give it?

Other believers know how hard it is to put in words what they so deeply and obscurely know. They have also argued with their wives and friends, and even in their own heads. All around this land there is a faith without an explanation, a love without a rationale. This book is written to fill a void among the faithful.

It is also written for unbelievers. Perhaps they will gain a larger, ecumenical understanding of those who partake of religions not their own. Perhaps they will learn, vicariously, even if the gift of faith is not given them, what others feel and love.

An unbeliever might think that anyone who has seen one football game has seen them all, and that anyone who has seen a hundred, or a thousand, games has seen everything there is to see in them. I know it isn't true, but I have to ask myself, "What grabs me? *Why* do I keep coming back?"

I hope the reader enjoys bringing experience into consciousness. This book is not complete if only the author searches memory; the readers must join the game as well.

When a sentence hits the mark, let the reader call a strike; when it misses, let the reader hit the corner I was aiming at. Putting things in words is a sport as difficult as any other. I would be happy if this little essay gets others playing it with excellence.

There is not much competition in the field at present. Most books about sports are hagiography, "lives of the saints," hero worship. Other books debunk sports, exposing their corruptions and pretensions. Still others are social science ideologies and theories. In philosophy, a book by Paul Weiss, *The Philosophy of Sports,* stands virtually alone. Considering the importance of sports to humankind—considering the eminence of stadia and gyms and playing fields on university campuses, comparing the size of the sports section to any other in the paper—our intellectual negligence is inexcusable. Only prejudice, or unbelief, can account for it.

What "grabs" so many millions? What is the secret power of attraction? How can we care so much?

I concentrate on baseball, football, and basketball because these are the three sports I love best, a holy trinity. They are also the three that seem to be most powerful in our nation's consciousness. All three were invented in the last hundred years or so. Despite some debts to other games in other lands, all three were invented in America, for Americans. Of the hundreds of sports that might have grown up here, these are the ones that have captured the imagination, energies, and hard work of many millions. What sort of religions are they?

I can't say I follow every game with passion. But I am always aware of the Dodgers' fate; it is on some track parallel to mine. And likewise the fate of Notre Dame, the Knicks, the Jets. When they are up, I am up; when they lose, I must learn to tolerate defeat. Many hours of comfort, peace, wisdom, community, and courage these mythic clubs have given me! A belief in miracles (the Franco Harris catch in the last six seconds of a game given up as lost to Oakland in the playoffs of 1972). A sense of continuity. Respect for the brilliant fairness—and unfairness—of the Fates.

Sports is part of my religion, like Christianity, or "Western civilization," or poetry, or politics. Philosophers speak of "language games"; their games do not satisfy parts of the human spirit which football reaches. Not that football satisfies everything. It doesn't offer much guidance in how to understand a woman. The emotions it dramatizes, deeper and more mystical than doubters will ever understand, are not the most complex. They are, however, basic, and often starved for notice. "Of armaments and men I sing," Vergil wrote. If war is the teacher men have turned to in order to learn teamwork, discipline, coolness under fire, respect for contingency and fate, football is my moral equivalent of war.

Say, if you like, that men *ought* to be less primitive, less violent, less mesmerized by pain and injury. Say, if you like, that football dramatizes what is worst in the human breast and ought, like pornography, to be refused public benediction. Football makes conscious to me part of what I am. And what football says about me, and about millions of others like me, is not half so ugly as it is beautiful. Seeing myself reflected in the dance, the agony and the ritual of a heated contest, I am at peace.

So, sitting there that Monday night in September, three days before my fortieth birthday, I watched what I had watched hundreds of times. What gripped me to the set for three hours of a rapidly passing life? It was not novelty. It was some mythic form, some mystic struggle, which the drama of baseball in a million variations game by game portrays. Like football, baseball is a game of aesthetic form, a ritual elaborating some music of the human spirit. Done well, it is as satisfying as a symphony, as moving as *Swan Lake* or *Madame Butterfly*. People who respond aesthetically to sports are sane. Those who do not may be teachable.

There is no substitute for the squeak of sneakers on the court and the sound of the ball slipping through the cords. No words are as adequate as the cool sheen of a baseball fresh from its paper wrapper, tossed to the pitcher at the height of the last game of the World Series. No analysis does justice to the instantaneous decision of a quarterback, trapped on his goal line in the waning seconds of a game, to snap the pigskin toward a blurred target at his distant 30-yard line. To talk about sports without recreating their drama, feel, and excitement

would render one worthy of death by continuous committee meetings, from which fate God spare us all.

Sports are bursts of dust, squeaky wood, infield grass,
collisions at second base, an explosive tackle—they are
vivid, concrete, swift, and fun. If this book is to mirror
the reality of sports, it must be vivid and concrete; it must
be tense with action, switch from scene to scene as swiftly
as a television camera. The sections I have called
"Sportsreel" may help to do that.

The writer should enjoy it with the reader, and perhaps
a little more. In all my life I have loved few things as much
as sports, found few as faithful and as satisfying. To
linger over a book on sports is, for a philosopher, almost
too much pleasure; for a theologian, sinful. But delicious.

MICHAEL NOVAK

Part One

ONE
NATION
UNDER
SPORTS

"Next to religion, baseball has furnished a greater impact on American life than any other institution."

—HERBERT HOOVER

"Whoever wants to know the heart and mind of America had better learn baseball."

—JACQUES BARZUN

IN THE STUDY of civil religions, our thinkers have too much neglected sports. It is the fashion, nowadays, to swing out wildly at all established institutions, including sports. It is true that sports often tell us a great deal about a people—but almost as tea leaves tell us about the future. Much depends on how we read the leaves.

Sports are an almost universal language binding our diverse nation, especially its men, together. Not all our citizens have the gift of faith. The religion, even so, is an ample one, and it allows great freedom for diverse experiences, diverse interpretations, and mutual dissents. Our sports are liturgies—but do not have dogmatic creeds. There is no long bill of doctrines all of us recite. We bring the hungers of our spirits, and many of them, not all, are filled—filled with a beauty, excellence, and grace few other institutions now afford. Our sports need to be reformed—*Ecclesia semper reformanda.* Let not too much be claimed for them. But what they do so superbly needs our thanks, our watchfulness, our intellect, and our acerbic love.

1

Homeric Deeds

ON SUNDAY, October 25, 1970, clouds of drizzle lift from San Francisco Bay. Against the gray horizon, white buildings burst into light. Gulls dip and rise on the undulating air. Fifty-four thousand fans stream from their shimmering automobiles toward the gates of the Oakland–Alameda County Coliseum. They cannot know they will witness a legend being born.

The air smells of soaked grass and warming sun, of shiny-slick programs fresh with ink, new angora sweaters, popcorn, beer, cigars, plastic raincoats, coffee, peanut shells, mustard, hot dogs, the alkaline of new concrete. An uncertain day, brisk, windy, fresh: Indian summer, after a week of rain.

Down on the green oval floor of the amphitheater, George Frederick Blanda, forty-three years old, takes the new Spalding football and sets his fingers on its strings, cocks the ball behind the longish gray hair around his ears, and snaps it forward in a slightly wobbly spiral. He spits, digs his cleats at the drying turf, receives the pigskin back at groin level, grips it, pulls it back, snaps. The spiral sings true as an arrow feathered through the air. The football slaps his partner's hands, comes back. Blanda likes the sting of it, likes the blood warming in his arm, likes the calisthenics, likes the work and sweat, likes the combat.

The Pittsburgh Steelers are a big team, rough, without finesse or explosive power. In the mud, they will try to halt the Oakland Raiders cold, pummel them, weary them, and with brute force push across enough points to win. Oakland is an electric team, counting on surprise and suddenness; above all, on Daryle Lamonica's ability to hit the mark on swiftly conceived passes far downfield. Sun is good for Oakland; mud for Pittsburgh.

As October 25 began, George Blanda was just another professional, older, wiser, a minor legend because of his longevity. He had played ball amost a decade longer than many of his peers. (Sid Luckman said when *he* retired that no quarterback should play past the age of thirty-one.) Blanda had often played brilliantly, but he had been the subject of only two national stories, both minor, both in the *Sporting News,* one in 1956 when he was suffering daily insults under owner-coach George Halas of the Chicago Bears, and one in 1964 when he starred with the struggling Houston Oilers. After October 25, 1970, George Blanda suddenly became the most sought-after news copy in sports; and yet that is merely an accident of recognition. What is significant is what he *did,* and how his deeds—and Fate—lifted him into a realm apart, excited the imagination, touched some central strand in the texture of myth that surrounds accomplishment in football.

Tens of thousands of passes are thrown every year, thousands of games are played in grammar schools, high schools, colleges, and professional stadia; all the routines are thoroughly known. Occasionally, however, often enough to stir the heart, a player or a team executes a play so beautifully, achieves such classic perfection, that it is as though they cease for a moment to be pedestrian and leap into a realm of precision as lovely as a statue of Praxiteles. Athletic achievement, like the achievements of the heroes and the gods of Greece, is the momentary attainment of perfect form—as though there were, hidden away from mortal eyes, a perfect way to execute a play, and suddenly a player or a team has found it and sneaked a demonstration down to earth. A great play is a revelation. The curtains of ordinary life part, and perfection flashes for an instant before the eye.

True lovers of sport respond to beauty. And beauty, as James Joyce once defined it, is the light that shines from form: the naked simplicity in things. Those who are starting out in sports can seldom respond to beauty; to excitement and pageantry, perhaps, but not to beauty. Too much novelty confronts them; they can't discern the form. For them, a game is a gibberish of actions, incoherent, meaningless. That one team has to get the ball over the other's goal, *that* they understand. And they can understand suspense—that there are two minutes left to play, and the losing team has the ball for a last try, and the signals are being called . . . .

If you have not played the game, you may not recognize how difficult it is to launch a successful play, how much more difficult to sustain a series of successful plays without mistake. But even if you do not understand the game, a willing suspension of skepticism in the closing minutes of a hard-fought contest communicates, at least, a sense of dramatic resolution. Will is pitted against will; skill against skill; one team emerges the victor. The drama—beginning, middle, end—is resolved.

So on October 25, 1970, a coin is flipped in full view of the spectators in the center of the field (after having previously been tossed for the coaches underneath the stands). The coin toss is a ritual of Fate, the unseen god of sports events. Fate presides over sports, as over life. The turf of the Oakland–Alameda County Coliseum is soaked, but the sun is drying it: signs of favor, signs of doom. Sea gulls swoop against the clouds; ducks honk in the air. The wind blows in basketfuls, from time to time, through the Golden Gate Bridge less than 7 miles away.

George Blanda pulls at his black jersey; he observes this ritual for his 261st professional game with some dispassion. His career, his wife, Betty Blanda, says, is Death and Resurrection, again and again. A senior in college in 1949 before some of his new teammates were born, he has played with football greats of the past, like Steve Van Buren and Sid Luckman, whom some of his teammates never saw in action. He was being called "Old George" in 1960. Once, in 1965, George Blanda engineered 38 points in a single afternoon against Kansas City; he didn't even enter the game until the second half, and started out trailing 17–0. He passed for five touchdowns and won 38–36. His career is governed by Fate, beyond his control. He has never had a serious injury. He has had great days, amassed records, been overlooked.

The Coliseum—that hackneyed name from ancient Rome—is a grim oval, new, not yet rich with memories. The Oakland Raiders are a business organization created, and extremely tightly run, with the sole purpose of producing winning football. The Oakland record for 1970 stands at 2–2–1 (two wins, two losses, one tie)—a disgrace. The players have something like pregnancy jitters; they are nervous, some are gray and pokerfaced—many wear their "game faces." Sixty minutes of action is all they will be allowed, no more than a half-dozen plays for some of them, and in every moment each will be expected to play perfectly. The teams line up. Sacred time begins.

Daryle Lamonica, the premier Oakland passer, throws to Raymond Chester for a 37-yard touchdown. The sun stays out. The field has drained well, the fleet and mobile Oakland team uses good footing methodically. The slower, heavier, tougher Pittsburgh Steelers aim their attack at the passer. Lamonica is hit hard; in the crunching fall, a nerve is pinched. Lamonica has to leave the game.

Heavy John Madden, puffing up and down the sidelines, hesitates between sending in young Ken Stabler, his number two quarterback, and George Blanda. He chooses the veteran. Lamonica is so good and so reliable, and young Kenny Stabler so promising, that for four years Blanda has thrown the ball, on the average, only thirty times a year. Behind the bench Blanda licks the tips of his fingers, throws a last practice toss, feels the pigskin curl sharply off his fingertips, lifts his helmet, and jams it over his bushy gray hair and ears. Jogging out to the huddle, Blanda likes the tang of Indian summer in the air. The hills of the western Pennsylvania mining town where he was born have already turned a stunning scarlet and yellow. The University of Kentucky, where, naïve and totally unknowing about the outside world, he had ended up his college days, was more than half a continent and more than half his lifetime away. He bent over in the huddle, surrounded by ten hulking Raiders, and called a play.

Play begins at the Pittsburgh 35-yard line. At the center of the black-clad Oakland line the ball is snapped into Blanda's hands, he backs up rhythmically, fakes, throws.

The fleet, smooth Raymond Chester is in the open; the ball is there. Touchdown! Even as the fans are leaping to their feet, a yellow flag flutters to the field. The play is nullified; Oakland, holding. Moments later, Pittsburgh scores to tie the game. Fate is only testing faith.

The Pittsburgh defense remains keyed on the Oakland quarterback. The Steelers abandon caution and on every pass send extra men crashing through the line to knock Blanda down. Blanda loves the challenge. He sets up Warren Wells against a single defender, pulls a fake on that defender, and sets Wells free. Later he sets up Raymond Chester against another defensive back. One after the other, only minutes apart, Wells and Chester run with fluid simplicity, fake, gain a step, look up, and there arrives the perfectly feathered spiral just within their reach—touchdowns of 44 and 19 yards. Between the touchdowns, Blanda puts his toe into the ball and lifts it, turning, through the goalposts 27 yards away. By the end of the afternoon, throwing only twelve times, Blanda has hit his streaking targets seven times, thrice for touchdowns. Oakland wins.

Blanda's past weighs heavily with evidence of skill. So on October 25, 1970, it isn't statistics that impress. It is precision, beauty, reliability. And, perhaps more than that, unaccountable public surprise. For Blanda's good performance is routine; after twenty-one years, he expects no fuss. Repetition, however, is beginning to affect public consciousness. Called upon suddenly, the man delivers. With stubborn, directive grace. As he crouches in the huddle, one can sense intelligence at work. Mind commands, body obeys. So do ten other men, a team.

The situations in which destiny places him soon become more trying, more impossible. Struggle is the classic form of human life: the voyages of Ulysses, the trials of Hercules, the great deeds of defenders and attackers at the siege of Troy, *Pilgrim's Progress,* the trials of a platoon of soldiers in Norman Mailer's *The Naked and the Dead.* The hero is placed in a situation foredooming him to failure, and just as he succeeds new obstacles arise. The hero's enemies determine to defeat him. His friends may, or may not, fail him. His body is afflicted. There are countless reasons to be embittered, to cry out against injustice, to allow self-pity to demand release. Against the odds, the hero concentrates. He seeks the single open pathway through the maze. Thus the exaltation, when out of the labyrinth of failure a man suddenly breaks clear, "runs for daylight" as the cliché puts it, scores a sudden touchdown. It is a victory of Light over Darkness. An almost Persian imagination of reality.

But a single football game is not a final drama. It has a beginning, a middle, and an end, yet in a larger sense is inconclusive. It is a single battle in a year's campaign, and in the warfare of a man's career—or of a team's existence—it is a unit in a long series of campaigns. Perhaps that is why some find the games of sports "meaningless"—next week, they say, it starts again. (Is not life itself meaningless? Its purpose, at least, is not transparent.) One Sunday's game *is* replaced by another. Over the years they blend together. In human life, repetition is a universal law. In a single lifetime, how many times do a reader's eyes move back and forth, cover to cover, following the straight lines of a book? How many books do we read in a lifetime? Each book has been given form. Each is different. In memory they blur.

So October 25 is followed by November 1. Winter is coming to Kansas City. Around old Municipal Stadium, darkness seems to gather early. Kansas City was the American Football League representative in the first Super Bowl; Oakland went to the second. They are bitter rivals. Oilman Lamar Hunt started his team as the Dallas "Texans," and from the beginning his organization hated George Blanda and the Houston Oilers. Now in Kansas City—where at first Hunt wanted to keep right on calling them the "Texans"—they hate George Blanda and the Oakland Raiders. The first period score is 0–0.

One of the two or three coolest passers in football is Len Dawson of the Chiefs, and Otis Taylor, his favorite target, is one of the silkiest receivers. Before the second period is minutes old, Dawson hits Taylor for 56 yards, and a moment later the fullback scores. Then Lamonica counters with a short pass to Raymond Chester and, in the third quarter, with yet another: 14–7, Oakland. Jan Stenerud

kicks his special instep floater, end-over-end, and the
Chiefs close to 14–10.

With 5:14 left in the game, Otis Taylor bumps Kent
McCloughan to the ground in a struggle for position and
dances alone, tall and slender, as a soft pass floats into his
hands: 17–14, Kansas City.

With 1:08 left, Kansas City has the ball on the Oakland
40-yard line. The Chiefs have one chance to gain 11 yards,
and then, if that fails, to call on blond Stenerud for a
clinching field goal, or else to punt. Use up the clock, take
the ball deeper into Oakland territory—the strategy is
simple. Kansas City sends its best receivers into pass formation. Dawson fades back deceptively and then races
downfield and gets past his target: 11 yards. That should
clinch the game. Ben Davidson, the moody Oakland
giant, is so frustrated that he throws himself late at Dawson's prone body. Unthinkingly, the Chiefs blaze, fists
swing, at least eight Chiefs try to get at Davidson. Otis
Taylor is outraged by the assault upon his quarterback.
Emotions churn in Taylor in the quietest of times; even
after the melee has begun to calm, he focuses on Davidson
with rage and runs at him with fists circling in the air.

Taylor is ejected from the game. Oakland is penalized
15 yards. The ball is moved to the Oakland 14.

And then erupts a furious argument about rules and
facts. Back and forth go the officials. Gestures in football
are not restrained. Arms wave; lips yield transparent ex-
pletives. Watching national television, millions wait for
chaos to be dissipated—and strain, too, to see, for winter
twilight is falling on the Great Plain, staved off by struggling stadium lights.

The Raiders argue that since Taylor was banished from
the game, the Chiefs must also be assessed a penalty. The
two penalties then offset each other. The play should be
nullified and the ball moved back to the Oakland 40. The
Kansas City crowd dares the referee to move the ball from
its resting place near the Oakland goal.

Finally, the officials realize they must move the ball, all
the way back to the original line of scrimmage. Boos bay
across the Plains. In the gloom, a running play goes nowhere. The Chiefs punt, driving Oakland back to their
own 20 with only 40 seconds left. Daryle Lamonica hur-

ries his team, and passes to Fred Biletnikoff for 33 yards to
the Kansas City 47. There are 23 seconds left; the Raiders
can only take a single time-out.

A million viewers know the classic moves: (1) Throw at
least two short passes, toward the out-of-bounds lines, to
stop the clock; (2) save one time-out to be sure Blanda can
come in to try a field goal for the tie. The Raiders would
like to move at least to the 30; a successful kick from the 47
is improbable.

Lamonica sets up. When he finally finds Biletnikoff in
the gray and hanging air, the lanky receiver can gain a
mere 4 yards and can't get out of bounds. A Kansas City
player lies twitching on the ground; he is not seriously
hurt but, luckily for Oakland, the pain makes him neglect
to hurry off the field. The clock is stopped: 12 seconds
remain. Lamonica racks his brain, stoops in the huddle.
Again, he tries to find Wells and Biletnikoff. He looks. He
can only find Chester, short. Two paltry yards.

The ball is not in the center of the field; it rests on the
grass to the right. Lamonica kneels at the 48, where the
ball will be centered back to him. He will twist it so the
laces face the goal, and hold it to the tee with his index
finger. In red and white, Buck Buchanan, six-foot-seven,
glowers across the line a few yards away; the kick will
have to rise over Buchanan's charging, outstretched
hands. Blanda measures two steps back from Lamonica,
concentrates upon the space where the ball will be, on the
feeling his leg should have if he swings it with the correct
force. The white goalposts half a field away look like pen-
cils. Blanda has already told Coach Madden: "No problem. We've got it."

The ball is snapped, twirled, and Blanda starts stepping
forward instinctively, before Lamonica has placed the
pigskin at the proper angle—no delay to benefit Buchanan. By the time the sound of toe on leather floats to
the broadcasting booth, the trajectory of the ball is crystal
clear: "It's good. It's good. It is good. George Blanda has
kicked a 48-yard field goal. . . . Holy Toledo! Holy Toledo!" Three seconds show on the clock.

And then November 1 becomes November 8. George
Blanda has never played on a team that beat the Cleveland
Browns. Out in Oakland, the radio announcer for station

KNEW has developed a series of spots called "The Perils
of George Blanda." Taped replays of Blanda's feats are introduced by futuristic music and a voice intones, as it
were, from the netherworld: "Can George do it again?
Tune in and hear: Can George Blanda do it again?" For six
Sundays in a row, Blanda will perform a "miracle." So
now it is not only athletic myths as old as the Greeks that
George Blanda, stoic and fatalist, evokes but picaresque
adventures of the American frontier, of Hollywood, of
damsels in distress and knights confronted with a thousand obstacles. The tall stories of Texas and the Canadian
northwest, Gold Rush days, and the age of the golden
West. There are villains, ritual settings, overpowering obstacles, the almost tangible signals of intervening Fate.
And there is a hero cut from the ancient mold: tough,
strong, cunning, enduring, lacking all self-pity. He is not
a celebrity; he does not seek headlines; he is solid and or-
nery and true; he does his job. His six brothers and four
sisters back in Youngwood, Pennsylvania, like his aged
mother, are said to be as hale and tough as he. Three of
his brothers are said to be better football players. Injured
only once in twenty-one years of play, Blanda puts it less
than straight: "You can't hurt a Polack." In the luggage of
the Slavs is Fate. Fate gives and takes away: Death and
Resurrection, again, again.

   November 8 is muggy and humid in Oakland. And it
doesn't look like a day for miracles. Even Blanda makes
mistakes, as though to prove his stars are in no especially
favorable conjunction. The game opens well enough. The
Raiders lead the orange-helmeted Cleveland Browns 13–0.
They relax. Suddenly the score is 17–13, Browns. Blanda
has never beaten the Browns, and it seems the jinx will be
continued. He has twice in his life been roughed up by
Browns tacklers. He doesn't like that team.

   With 10:05 to play, Ron Snidow hits Daryle Lamonica
so hard that the doctors who gather around the latter's
limp, throbbing left arm fear that the ligaments of his
shoulder have been torn from the bone. With 8:17 to play,
Blanda gets his first chance at the ball. Three straight completed passes. Then he throws an interception; a curse of
Fate, an evil omen, a stroke of helplessness. Cleveland

once again contains the Oakland offense. And moves the ball close enough to kick a field goal: 20–13, with 4:11 left. So Blanda, watching from the bench, gathers strength for what the press will call Miracle III.

Blanda's pass to Warren Wells, cutting to the center of the field, carries from the Oakland 31 to the Cleveland 38. Then orange helmets collide with silver, and Blanda is pushed down into the muck at the 48—loss of 10. Chester is covered on the next play, so Blanda, as he is again falling into the mud, under Cleveland shirts and muscles, throws short to Biletnikoff. Coach Madden talks to Blanda, who is down on one knee trying to get his heaving breath under control. Madden wants a running play. Blanda wants to pass for the distance. The coach concedes.

Blanda runs slowly out to his teammates, testing the mud. Rubbing his hands, he calls their favorite pass play, 99-in-Y-in. Chester breaks down the middle. Wells goes for the cornerback one-on-one. Blanda warns Wells to look for the ball low and fast, because an interception would mean the game. Wells has a bruised shoulder, but as Chester clears the center, Wells cuts, looks, bends, scoops the speeding ball into the solid wall of his stomach to stop its momentum, and falls across the goal line. Blanda kicks the point: 20–20. He goes to the bench, sucks on the oxygen mask, rests.

That would have been enough, at 1:39. But Oakland intercepts a Cleveland pass. No time-outs are left. Blanda has the ball on the Cleveland 46 with seven seconds to go, fourth down. Lamonica, hurt, cannot hold the ball; Stabler comes in, his jersey fresh and clean, as Blanda walks back to a spot 52 yards from the goalpost. He says later: "I knew I was going to kick it. I'm thinking, just do it like you always do. . . . I'm going over the fundamentals of kicking in my mind. Hell, I know I've got this field goal. I know I've finally got the Cleveland Browns right where I want them. . . ."

In bars and homes and college dormitories, they are listening to broadcaster Bill King: "Waiting for the snap . . . fourth down . . . here it is . . . snap! spotted down! It's kicked. That's got a *chance!* That is—good. It's good!

Holy Toledo! Holy Toledo! This place has gone wild.
Wheeeeee-U! I don't believe it! I do not believe it! There
are three seconds left in the game. If you can hear me, this
place has gone wild . . . The Oakland Raiders 23! . . .
the Cleveland Browns . . . 20. George Blanda has just
been elected King of the World! I don't believe it! Holy
Toledo! It went 53 . . . 52 yards! . . ."

It is George Blanda's 251st field goal. The touchdown
before it was his 228th. "You know, John," he tells Madden later, rubbing ice on the back of his 43-year-old neck,
"that wasn't my longest field goal. I got a 55-yarder once
in Houston."

By this time, the national press begins sending extra
staff to Oakland. The phones are ringing.

On November 15, 1970, the plane carries the Raiders
over the snowy peaks and purple valleys to Denver.
Blanda is playing poker. "It comes from my childhood,"
he says of his coolness, his love of difficulties. "Hell, first
thing you wanted to do was escape the mines and that
image of being a drunken, stupid, dirty Polish miner. So
you'd concentrate hard as you could, so you could grow
up and do something different. . . . I had six brothers
and four sisters . . . you get all these hands reaching for
the eggs at breakfast. If you're slow you don't eat. . . ."
He gives some perspective on Youngwood, where many
men went away all week to work on their knees in the
pitch-black corridors of the mines, coming home only on
weekends. "We had a warm house," Blanda says, "and
we had food, but if my old man made more than $2,000 it
was one hell of a year. I didn't even know we were poor
for a hell of a long time."

In the Denver game, the young Broncos are shocking
Oakland 19–17 with only 4:01 on the stadium clock. Madden calls for Blanda, who somehow already has his helmet
on, as if he knew. Madden does not usually call on him,
except for kicking. Stabler is preferred. But who can resist
the tides of Fate?

The fans throw snowballs at the field. They boo. They
have been drinking, in order to keep warm and in order
to drink.

Hewritt Dixon, the big black fullback, is hit before he
can control a swing pass; he almost loses it and is thrown

for a loss. Then Blanda misses Wells. So he calls long to George Sherman on the 99-in-Y-in. Blanda fixes his eyes on one defender's eyes for two seconds, holding him transfixed. (After the game, he admits that Blanda froze him.) The defender closest to Sherman can't cover him alone. The air is mountain cold. The leather slips into Sherman's hands: 27 yards. The clock reads 2:47. Blanda in his old man's strut advances, shouts, takes the snap between his center's tight silver pants, backs up, bumps Hewritt Dixon accidentally, is forced to retreat, throws the ball by memory and concentration to an empty place short of where Warren Wells is supposed to be. Wells, alert, races to the spot, snatches the falling ball and twists to the Denver 20. Blanda, on the ground, never saw him catch it, but knew he would.

Then Blanda calls Biletnikoff's number. The rush is hard; Biletnikoff is covered. Rising from the hard ground, Blanda ruminates. He decides, and in the huddle calls exactly the same play. He feels the familiar leather hit his fingers, backs up six steps, spins the ball forward in a smart spiral, and places it a yard in front of Biletnikoff, who is a yard in front of his defender. Biletnikoff reaches forward, holds it, and needs only one stride to score. Blanda has taken less than two minutes to move his ten players 80 yards. For 58 minutes, the Broncos had held Oakland; now they could not. Six passes, four completions. 24–19, Oakland.

Miracle V may be told in simpler terms. Daryle Lamonica did most of the work. Early in the season at San Diego, Blanda had missed an easy field goal and lost the game. Now San Diego is at Oakland, and with 4:35 to play the score is 17–17. Lamonica has the ball and starts using up the clock. Trapped on third down, his receivers covered, Lamonica ducks under a rusher's padded arm and runs from the 41 to the 27. The league lead is at stake. Kansas City will be tied with Oakland if Oakland fails to win. Lamonica keeps his backs running the ball, using up the clock. Some fans hope he hasn't forgotten how little time is left, hope there is no mistake on the stadium clock. Finally, with only seven seconds left, Lamonica calls timeout. Blanda trots across the chalk lines, calmly finds the spot on which he wants the ball held, on the 16, and rhythmically swings his foot through the pigskin, sending it hurtling between the thin white bars toward the crowd. Another last-second victory. It has become routine.

They go on that way. In the postseason All-Star game, Blanda kicks another in front of New York fans. In 1971, the following season, at least two similar dramas arise out of the unpredictable patterns each game takes. On Halloween, losing 20–10 to Kansas City with 8:38 to play, Coach Madden calls Blanda off the bench with the ball at the Oakland 34. In 37 seconds, Blanda has passed to Chester, then to Biletnikoff, for a touchdown. Oakland gets the ball next time on the Chiefs' 45. Blanda fools the Chiefs by *not* passing, handing off to Highsmith up the middle for 26 yards. The Chiefs stop Oakland at the goal line with fourth down coming up. Blanda wants to run. Madden says kick. The angle is very bad—too close, off to the side. Blanda argues, shrugs, trots back, kicks, and ties the game at 20–20, to keep Oakland in first place. It is his 1,609th point, more than any other player has ever scored.

Later in the year, Kansas City keeps the Raiders out of the playoffs by beating them 16–14 in the Midwest. Losing 10–0, the Raiders call on Blanda before the first half is over. He outscores Kansas City from then on, 14–6, but it isn't enough. He misses a 47-yard field goal. Another attempt is blocked. Huge Buck Buchanan flings the 44-year-old to the ground in a great bear hug and knocks Blanda out. Blanda finally stirs, rises slowly, shakes his head, is helped off. The miracles don't happen as they did in 1970. The games don't fall into the same close patterns every week, and when they do, Blanda doesn't win them all.

To be at the right place at the right time—all the truisms leap to mind. To keep cool, to handle hundreds of details and call exactly the plays that work, to fight one's way through opposition to do what one wills to do, against odds, against probabilities—these are to practice a very high art, to achieve a few moments of beauty that will delight the memory of those who watched, or listened, or read, for all their lives. What we mean by "legend" is what we mean by "art": the reaching of a form, a perfection, which ordinarily the flesh masks, a form eternal in its beauty. It is as though muscle and nerves and spirit

and comrades were working together as flawlessly as God
once imagined human beings might.

NOTE

Sources include "George Blanda Is Alive and Kicking," *Time;* "A Kick in Time," *Newsweek;* and Tex Maule's "Let George Do It—and He Does," *Sports Illustrated,* all dated November 23, 1970; B. Bruns, "Tale of Two Quarterbacks," *Life,* Dec. 4, 1970; George Blanda with Jack Olsen, "I Keep Getting My Kicks," "A Decade of Revenge," and "That Impossible Season," *Sports Illustrated,* July 19, July 26, and August 2, 1971; and Wells Twombly, *Blanda: Alive and Kicking* (New York-Avon, 1973).

2

The Natural Religion

THE SAGA of George Blanda had further games to run. Yet its elements already exhibit the ways in which sports are a religion.

A sport is not a religion in the same way that Methodism, Presbyterianism, or Catholicism is a religion. But these are not the only kinds of religion. There are secular religions, civil religions. The United States of America has sacred documents to guide and to inspire it: The Constitution, the Declaration of Independence, Washington's Farewell Address, Lincoln's Gettysburg Address, and other solemn presidential documents. The President of the United States is spoken to with respect, is expected to exert "moral leadership"; and when he walks among crowds, hands reach out to touch his garments. Citizens are expected to die for the nation, and our flag symbolizes vivid memories, from Fort Sumter to Iwo Jima, from the Indian Wars to Normandy: memories that moved hardhats in New York to break up a march that was "desecrating" the flag. Citizens regard the American way of life as though it were somehow chosen by God, special, uniquely important to the history of the human race. "Love it or leave it," the guardians of orthodoxy say. Those on the left, who do not like the old-time patriotism, have a new kind: they evince unusual outrage when this nation is less than fully just, free, compassionate, or good—in short, when it is like all the other nations of human history. America should be *better*. Why?

The institutions of the state generate a civil religion; so do the institutions of sport. The ancient Olympic games used to be both festivals in honor of the gods and festivals in honor of the state—and that has been the classical position of sports ever since. The ceremonies of sports overlap those of the state on one side, and those of the churches on the other. At the Super Bowl in 1970, clouds of military jets flew in formation, American flags and patriotic bunting flapped in the wind, ceremonies honored prisoners of war, clergymen solemnly prayed, thousands sang the national anthem. Going to a stadium is half like going to a political rally, half like going to church. Even today, the Olympics are constructed around high ceremonies, rituals, and symbols. The Olympics are not barebones athletic events, but religion and politics as well.

Most men and women don't separate the sections of their mind. They honor their country, go to church, and also enjoy sports. All parts of their lives meld together.

Nor am I indulging in metaphor when I say that nearly every writer about sports lapses into watery religious metaphor. So do writers on politics and sex. Larry Merchant says television treated the Super Bowl "as though it were a solemn high mass." Words like *sacred, devotion, faith, ritual, immortality,* and *love* figure often in the language of sports. Cries like "You gotta believe!" and "life and death" and "sacrifice" are frequently heard.

But that is not what I mean. I am arguing a considerably stronger point. I am saying that sports flow outward into action from a deep natural impulse that is radically religious: an impulse of freedom, respect for ritual limits, a zest for symbolic meaning, and a longing for perfection. The athlete may of course be pagan, but sports are, as it were, natural religions. There are many ways to express this radical impulse: by the asceticism and dedication of preparation; by a sense of respect for the mysteries of one's own body and soul, and for powers not in one's own control; by a sense of awe for the place and time of competition; by a sense of fate; by a felt sense of comradeship and destiny; by a sense of participation in the rhythms and tides of nature itself.

Sports, in the second place, are organized and dramatized in a religious way. Not only do the origins of sports, like the origins of drama, lie in religious celebrations; not only are the rituals, vestments, and tremor of anticipation involved in sports events like those of religions. Even in our own secular age and for quite sophisticated and agnostic persons, the rituals of sports really work. They do serve a religious function: they feed a deep human hunger, place humans in touch with certain dimly perceived features of human life within this cosmos, and provide an experience of at least a pagan sense of godliness.

Among the godward signs in contemporary life, sports may be the single most powerful manifestation. I don't mean that participation in sports, as athlete or fan, makes one a believer in "God," under whatever concept, image, experience, or drive to which one attaches the name. Rather, sports drive one in some dark and generic sense "godward." In the language of Paul Tillich, sports are manifestations of concern, of will and intellect and passion. In fidelity to that concern, one submits oneself to great bodily dangers, even to the danger of death. Symbolically, too, to lose is a kind of death.

Sports are not the highest form of religion. They do not exclude other forms. Jews, Christians, and others will want to put sports in second place, within a scheme of greater ultimacy. It is quite natural and normal to envisage human life and responsibilities as falling within schedules of ultimacy. Each "world" can be ultimate of its own kind, yet subsumed within a larger circle. The family is a good in itself, not derivative from the state. It is "ultimate" in its responsibilities. Yet the individual has claims against the family. So does the common good. A sport, like the family, can be in its own sphere an ultimate concern and a good in itself, while yet being subject to other and greater claims on the part of individuals and the common good.

For some, it may require a kind of conversion to grasp the religiousness at the heart of sports. Our society has become secular, and personal advancement obliges us to become pragmatic, glib, superficial, and cynical. Our spirits often wither. Eyes cannot see; ears cannot hear. The soil of our culture is not always fertile for religious life. Americans must read religious messages in foreign languages. And so many will, at first, be tempted to read what I am saying as mere familiar metaphor. A change of perspective, and of heart, may be necessary.

Sports are religious in the sense that they are organized institutions, disciplines, and liturgies; and also in the sense that they teach religious qualities of heart and soul. In particular, they recreate symbols of cosmic struggle, in which human survival and moral courage are not assured. To this extent, they are not mere games, diversions, pastimes. Their power to exhilarate or depress is far greater than that. To say "It was only a game" is the psyche's best defense against the cosmic symbolic meaning of sports events. And it is partly true. For a game is a symbol; it is not precisely identified with what it symbolizes. To lose symbolizes death, and it certainly feels like dying; but it is not death. The same is true of religious symbols like Baptism or the Eucharist; in both, the communicants experience death, symbolically, and are reborn, symbolically. If you give your heart to the ritual, its effects upon your inner life can be far-reaching. Of course, in all religions many merely go through the motions. Yet even they, unaware, are surprised by grace. A Hunter pursues us everywhere, in churches and stadia alike, in the pews and bleachers, and occasionally in the pulpit and the press box.

Something has gone wrong in sports today. It went wrong in medieval Christendom, too. A proverb in Chaucer expresses it: *Radix malorum cupiditas* (The root of all evils is greed). True in the fourteenth century, it is as modern as television: Money corrupts. Nothing much changes down the centuries, only the props and the circumstances. With every day that passes, the "new" world recreates the "old." The ancient sources of corruption in Athens, Constantinople, Alexandria, and Rome are as vigorous in New York, Boston, and Washington as the preparations for Olympic games. Then as now, the hunger for excellence, for perfection-in-act, for form and beauty, is expressed in the straining muscles and fiercely determined wills of heroes of the spirit: of athletes, artists, and even, sometimes, political giants like a Pericles or Cicero. In the corruption of a slave state, a fleshpot, Homer wrote of deeds of beauty. Through his writing, pieces from the flames were salvaged. So it is in every age. Rise and fall are as steady as the seasons of our sports.

But Homer seems to be nodding nowadays. Larry
Merchant of the New York *Post,* no Homer he, called his
column "Fun and Games" and has been called the pioneer
"of modern skepticism and irreverence toward sports."
Merchant modestly replies to praise: "I must state for pos-
terity that I was merely part of a broad-based movement.
. . . We were irreverent, debunking heroes and myths
that didn't stand up to scrutiny." Shucks, folks. Sportswriting "has changed conceptually." His own self-image
isn't bad: "We were humanistic. . . . We saw ballparks as
funhouses, not temples. We . . . [dug] for the hows and
whys and whos." The intellectually fearless skeptics.
Sports isn't religion. It's entertainment. "A baseball
game," writes Robert Lipsyte, formerly a New York *Times*
sportswriter and the author of *SportsWorld,* "is a staged
entertainment, and baseball players are paid performers."

Jewish and Protestant writers draw on different intellectual traditions from mine, of course, but from my point
of view, Catholic that I was born, any religion worthy of
the name thrives on irreverence, skepticism, and high an-
ticlericalism. A religion without skeptics is like a bosom
never noticed (which isn't entirely farfetched, since at
least one writer has said that covering sports for the New
York *Times* is like being Raquel Welch's elbow). When
Catholicism goes sour, as periodically down the centuries
it does, almost always the reason is a dearth of critics or,
worse, the death of heretics. A nonprophet church de-
cays. When things go well, it is because critics condemn
what is going ill. A decent religion needs irreverence as
meat needs salt.

Temples do not require whispering. Jesus knocked
temple tables over, jangling metal coins on the stones.
The root of the religious sense is not the stifling of questions. It lies in asking so many questions that the true
dimensions of reality begin to work their own mysterious
awe. No one is less religious than the pleasantly con-
tented pragmatist after lunch. Nothing is more religious
than fidelity to the drive to understand. For that drive is
endless, and satisfied by nothing on earth. It is the
clearest sign in our natures that our home is not here; that
we are out of place; and that to be restless, and seeking, is
to be what we most are.

Sports are not merely fun and games, not merely diversions, not merely entertainment. A ballpark is not a temple, but it isn't a fun house either. A baseball game is not an entertainment, and a ballplayer is considerably more than a paid performer. No one can explain the passion, commitment, discipline, and dedication involved in sports by evasions like these. Many otherwise intelligent people attempt to do so. Some sportswriters call sports the "toy department." Howard Cosell goes out of his way, when he isn't making money from them, to pronounce sports "essentially entertainment," apart from "the serious issues" of our time. A new fashion among sports journalists, like the new fashion among clergymen, is to be ashamed of their own profession and to believe that the important issues lie in social and political concerns. The dominant myth among our elites, at least since the ascension of John F. Kennedy and the evocation of Camelot, is that politics is the home of true morality. Yet politics is mainly machinery; necessary machinery, with some moral implications. "Politics begins in mysticism, and mysticism always ends in politics," Charles Péguy wrote. *Mystique* is larger than *politique,* more original, deeper, longer-lived.

The new sports journalists misunderstand their subject. They lust for politics, for *implications;* they covet power and wealth and social significance. They seem uninterested in sports. In the modern sports pages where the new skeptics perform, it is difficult to find coverage of actual sports events. Having failed in their attempt to find a place on the first page, or in the financial pages, it seems, they choose second-best by changing the nature of the sports page. "Sportswriting has changed conceptually" seems to mean "the only thing we will never describe is an actual sports event." From having been the best, most lively, most significant, exciting, and revealing pages in the paper, the new sports pages repeat the issues on page one, more boringly. Over a third of readers buy papers chiefly for the sports; nowadays they are cheated. (On this subject, more will be said in Chapter 14.)

The motive for regarding sports as entertainment is to take the magic, mystification, and falsehood out of sports. A great deal of sentimentality has grown up around our national contests. Things are not always what they seem. Corruptions of various sorts need to be exposed. Yet in the desire to be honest and to tell it like it is, many of our commentators have overreacted. They falsify the deep springs of sports. They offer a vision not deep enough for the reality, a vision that is simply not true. They do not explain to me the substance of my own love for sports. If they are trying to account for me, they miss.

At a sports event, there may be spectators, just as some people come to church to hear the music. But a participant is not a spectator merely, even if he does not walk among the clergy. At a liturgy, elected representatives perform the formal acts, but all believers put their hearts into the ritual. It is considered inadequate, almost blasphemous, to be a mere spectator. Fans are not mere spectators. If they wanted no more than to pass the time, to find diversion, there are cheaper and less internally exhausting ways. Believers in sport do not go to sports to be entertained; to plays and dramas, maybe, but not to sports. Sports are far more serious than the dramatic arts, much closer to primal symbols, metaphors, and acts, much more ancient and more frightening. Sports are mysteries of youth and aging, perfect action and decay, fortune and misfortune, strategy and contingency. Sports are rituals concerning human survival on this planet: liturgical enactments of animal perfection and the struggles of the human spirit to prevail.

To put on a great liturgical performance, enormous funding is required. Commerce finds its way into the temple—into its very building. Almost certainly, bribes were passed to obtain the permit for the Roman Colosseum, for the site of the Parthenon, and for the negotiation of the land on which the cathedral of Notre Dame of Paris was erected. It is naive to believe that commerce makes religion less religious. Is there an earthier religious imperative than to put up buildings?

Cynicism, skepticism, and irreverence are not only compatible with sports; without them, sports would choke us with their cloying. They are preconditions for sports. Cynicism, skepticism, and irreverence with regard to the "serious things" in life give rise to sports. Athletes and fans know that entire industries are born

and obsolesce, that governments come and go, that economic cycles ebb and flow, that empires rise and fall. The
British Empire has not outlived cricket, after all. Soccer
will be played when China, Russia, and the United States
no longer dominate the planet. A certain cynicism about
the "real world" may be permitted those who live brief
lives, enjoying the clear, cold taste of the combats of
sports. The lessons here are eternal ones.

The news departments of our newspapers and television studios are constructed to attract consumers. Each
day they give us headlines, tell of manufactured crises,
and report on events created so they can report them.
They pretend that in the last few hours something has
happened in the world worth knowing. Like commercial
sports, they are involved in selling. Buying a newspaper
or a television station is a little like buying a franchise.
The political myths and stories reported on the news may
have less substance than the sports account of the local
team's fifty-seventh loss this year. Who tells a more
mythic story, the White House correspondent giving us
sixty seconds on the president's day, or the local radio announcer calling the play-by-play, his sympathies clearly
with the locals? The statistics of the business reporter may
be less reliable than the seasonal statistics on the pitchers,
hitters, fielders. Which world is more "real"?

There are difficulties for the journalist in this unique
field of sports, to which a later chapter must be set aside.
Here it is only necessary to assert the central proposition
forcefully: Those who think sports are merely entertainment have been bemused by an entertainment culture.
Television did not make sports possible—not even great,
highly organized sports. College football and major
league baseball thrived for decades without benefit of
television. Sports made television commercially successful. No other motive is so frequently cited as a reason for
shelling out money for a set. (Non-sports fans, it appears,
are the least likely Americans to have sets.)

In order to be entertained, I watch television: prime-
time shows. They slide effortlessly by. I am amused, or
distracted, or engrossed. Good or bad, they help to pass
the time pleasantly enough. Watching football on television is totally different. I don't watch football to pass the

time. The outcome of the games affects me. I care. Afterward, the emotion I have lived through continues to affect me. Football is not entertainment. It is far more important than that. If you observe the passivity of television viewers being entertained, and the animation of fans watching a game on television, the difference between entertainment and involvement of spirit becomes transparent. Sports are more like religion than like entertainment. Indeed, at a contest in the stadium, the "entertainment"—the bands, singers, comedians, balloons, floats, fireworks, jets screaming overhead—pales before the impact of the contest itself, like lemonade served to ladies while the men are drinking whiskey.

Television is peculiarly suited to football, and vice versa; the case is special. But football, whether in the fresh air of the stadium, in the foul air of a sawdust tavern, or in the private corner of one's home, is far more than *Mary Tyler Moore*. The animation on the faces of the fans, the groans, the yells will show you that while televised entertainment may leave its watchers passive, football doesn't. Wives can tell, rather quickly, whether their husbands' teams have won or lost. Sports affect people, and their lives, far more deeply and for a longer time than mere diversion would.

On Monday nights, when television carries football games, police officers around the nation know that crime rates will fall to low levels otherwise reached only on Mother's Day and Christmas.

We are, as I said, too close to sports to appreciate their power. Besides, our education is rigorously pragmatic and factual: those things are real which can be counted. It teaches us nothing about play, or myth, or spirit. So we are totally unprepared to speak about the things we love the most. Our novelists write poorly of women, of love, of tragedy. Our religious sensibilities, which in some are warm with fervor, in our major publicists are chill. Grown men among us are virtually inarticulate about anything that touches our souls. Grunts, groans, and silence. Being cool. Taciturn like Bogart, Grant, Fonda, Newman, Brando, Hoffman, the American male responds to beauty by seeing, by participating, by ritual acts, but not by speaking. Our women can get nothing important out of us. Women talk one language, men another. Our nation lacks cultural institutions, rituals, and art forms that would bridge the sexes. We have no truly popular operas, or suitably complex literature, or plays in which our entire population shares. The streets of America, unlike the streets of Europe, do not involve us in stories and anecdotes rich with a thousand years of human struggle. Sports are our chief civilizing agent. Sports are our most universal art form. Sports tutor us in the basic lived experiences of the humanist tradition.

The hunger for perfection in sports cleaves closely to the driving core of the human spirit. It is the experience of this driving force that has perennially led human beings to break forth in religious language. This force is in us, it is ours. Yet we did not will its existence, nor do we command it, nor is it under our power. It is there unbidden. It is greater than we, driving us beyond our present selves. "Be ye perfect," Jesus said, "as your heavenly Father is perfect." The root of human dissatisfaction and restlessness goes as deep into the spirit as any human drive— deeper than any other drive. It *is* the human spirit. Nothing stills it. Nothing fulfills it. It is not a need like a hunger, a thirst, or an itch, for such needs are easily satisfied. It is a need even greater than sex; orgasmic satisfaction does not quiet it. "Desire" is the word by which coaches call it. A drivenness. Distorted, the drive for perfection can propel an ugly and considerably less than perfect human development. True, straight, and well targeted, it soars like an arrow toward the proper beauty of humanity. Sports nourish this drive as well as any other institution in our society. If this drive is often distorted, as it is, even its distortions testify to its power, as liars mark out the boundaries of truth.

Sports, in a word, are a form of godliness. That is why the corruptions of sports in our day, by corporations and television and glib journalism and cheap public relations, are so hateful. If sports were entertainment, why should we care? They are far more than that. So when we see them abused, our natural response is the rise of vomit in the throat.

It may be useful to list some of the elements of religions, to see how they are imitated in the world of sports.

If our anthropologists discovered in some other culture the elements they can plainly see in our own world of sports, they would be obliged to write monographs on the religions of the tribes they were studying. Two experiments in thought may make this plain.

Imagine that you are walking near your home and come upon a colony of ants. They move in extraordinary busy lines, a trail of brown bodies across the whitish soil like a highway underneath the blades of grass. The lanes of ants abut on a constructed mudbank oval; there the ants gather, 100,000 strong, sitting in a circle. Down below, in a small open place, eleven ants on one side and eleven on the other contest bitterly between two lines. From time to time a buzz arises from the 100,000 ants gathered in their sacred oval. When the game is over, the long lines of ants begin their traffic-dense return to their colonies. In one observation, you didn't have time to discover the rules of their ritual. Or who made them up, or when. Or what they mean to the ants. Is the gathering mere "escape"? Does it mirror other facets in the life of ants? Do all ants everywhere take part? Do the ants "understand" what they are doing, or do they only do it by rote, one of the things that ants do on a lovely afternoon? Do ants practice, and stay in shape, and perfect their arts?

Or suppose you are an anthropologist from Mars. You come suddenly upon some wild, adolescent tribes living in territories called the "United States of America." You try to understand their way of life, but their society does not make sense to you. Flying over the land in a rocket, you notice great ovals near every city. You descend and observe. You learn that an oval is called a "stadium." It is used, roughly, once a week in certain seasons. Weekly, regularly, millions of citizens stream into these concrete doughnuts, pay handsomely, are alternately hushed and awed and outraged and screaming mad. (They demand from time to time that certain sacrificial personages be "killed.") You see that the figures in the rituals have trained themselves superbly for their performances. The combatants are dedicated. So are the dancers and musicians in tribal dress who occupy the arena before, during, and after the combat. You note that, in millions of homes, at corner shrines in every household's sacred room, other citizens are bound by invisible attraction to the same events. At critical moments, the most intense worshipers demand of the less attentive silence. Virtually an entire nation is united in a central public rite. Afterward, you note exultation or depression among hundreds of thousands, and animation almost everywhere.

Some of the elements of a religion may be enumerated. A religion, first of all, is organized and structured. Culture is built on cult. Accordingly, a religion begins with ceremonies. At these ceremonies, a few surrogates perform for all. They need not even believe what they are doing. As professionals, they may perform so often that they have lost all religious instinct; they may have less faith than any of the participants. In the official ceremonies, sacred vestments are employed and rituals are prescribed. Customs develop. Actions are highly formalized. Right ways and wrong ways are plainly marked out; illicit behaviors are distinguished from licit ones. Professional watchdogs supervise formal correctness. Moments of silence are observed. Concentration and intensity are indispensable. To attain them, drugs or special disciplines of spirit might be employed; ordinary humans, in the ordinary ups and downs of daily experience, cannot be expected to perform routinely at the highest levels of awareness.

Religions are built upon *ascesis,* a word that derives from the disciplines Greek athletes imposed upon themselves to give their wills and instincts command of their bodies; the word was borrowed by Christian monks and hermits. It signifies the development of character, through patterns of self-denial, repetition, and experiment. The type of character celebrated in the central rituals, more likely than not, reveals the unconscious needs of the civilization—extols the very qualities that more highly conscious formulations are likely to deny. Thus, the cults have a revelatory quality; they dramatize what otherwise goes unspoken.

Religions also channel the feeling most humans have of danger, contingency, and chance—in a word, Fate.

Human plans involve ironies. Our choices are made with so little insight into their eventual effects that what we desire is often not the path to what we want. The decisions we make with little attention turn out to be major turning points. What we prepare for with exquisite detail never happens. Religions place us in the presence of powers greater than ourselves, and seek to reconcile us to them. The rituals of religion give these powers almost human shape, forms that give these powers visibility and tangible effect. Sports events in baseball, basketball, and football are structured so that "the breaks" may intervene and become central components in the action.

Religions make explicit the almost nameless dreads of daily human life: aging, dying, failure under pressure, cowardice, betrayal, guilt. Competitive sports embody these in every combat.

Religions, howsoever universal in imperative, do not treat rootedness, particularity, and local belonging as unworthy. On the contrary, they normally begin by blessing the local turf, the local tribe, and the local instinct of belonging—and use these as paradigms for the development of larger loyalties. "Charity begins at home." "Whoever says that he loves God, whom he does not see, but hates his neighbor, whom he does see, is a liar and the truth is not in him."

Religions consecrate certain days and hours. Sacred time is a block of time lifted out of everyday normal routines, a time that is different, in which different laws apply, a time within which one forgets ordinary time. Sacred time is intended to suggest an "eternal return," a fundamental repetition like the circulation of the human blood, or the eternal turning of the seasons, or the wheeling of the stars and planets in their cycles: the sense that things repeat themselves, over and over, and yet are always a little different. Sacred time is more like eternity than like history, more like cycles of recurrence than like progress, more like a celebration of repetition than like a celebration of novelty. Yet sacred time is full of exhilaration, excitement, and peace, as though it were more real and more joyous than the activities of everyday life—as though it were *really living* to be in sacred time (wrapped up in a close game during the last two minutes), and comparatively boring to suffer the daily jading of work, progress, history.

To have a religion, you need to have heroic forms to try to live up to: patterns of excellence so high that human beings live up to them only rarely, even when they strive to do so; and images of perfection so beautiful that, living up to them or seeing someone else live up to them, produces a kind of *"ah!"*

You need to have a pattern of symbols and myths that a person can grow old with, with a kind of resignation, wisdom, and illumination. Do what we will, the human body ages. Moves we once could make our minds will but our bodies cannot implement; disciplines we once endured with suppressed animal desire are no longer worth the effort; heroes that once seemed to us immortal now age, become enfeebled, die, just as we do. The "boys of summer" become the aging men of winter. A religion celebrates the passing of all things: youth, skill, grace, heroic deeds.

To have a religion, you need to have a way to exhilarate the human body, and desire, and will, and the sense of beauty, and a sense of oneness with the universe and other humans. You need chants and songs, the rhythm of bodies in unison, the indescribable feeling of many who together "will one thing" as if they were each members of a single body.

All these things you have in sports.

Sports are not Christianity, or Judaism, or Islam, or Buddhism, or any other of the world religions. Sports are not the civil religion of the United States of America, or Great Britain, or Germany, or the Union of Soviet Socialist Republics, or Ghana, or any other nation.

But sports are a form of religion. This aspect of sports has seldom been discussed. Consequently, we find it hard to express just what it is that gives sports their spirit and their power.

Athletes are not merely entertainers. Their role is far more powerful than that. People identify with them in a much more priestly way. Athletes exemplify something of deep meaning—frightening meaning, even. Once they become superstars, they do not quite belong to themselves. Great passions are invested in them. They are no

longer treated as ordinary humans or even as mere celebrities. Their exploits and their failures have great power
to exult—or to depress. When people talk about athletes'
performances, it is almost as though they are talking
about a secret part of themselves. As if the stars had some
secret bonding, some Siamese intertwining with their
own psyches.

Thus, George Blanda in his exploits in 1970 was not
simply a curiosity, like a carnival figure with two long
hands or seven ears. He touched something vulnerable in
the breasts of millions. He seemed to acquire some form
of magic, some miraculous power, some beautiful
achievement like the deeds of dreams. He also exemplified the wish of all who grow old that they might retain their powers down the years, against the harsh
weathering of time. Some truth about life, some deep
vein of ancient emotion and human imagination—this is
the chord George Blanda's performances happened to
strike. His own body and ordinary self became, as it
were, inwardly suffused with a power not his own. Naturally, he made little of the sudden attention; he was doing
just what he had always done. Part of his glory was simply the result of modern communications, ballyhoo, and
publicity. But for those who saw the actual deeds, their
beauty spoke for themselves; their excellence pleased;
something true shone out. The tales of *Gawain and the
Green Knight,* the *Song of Roland,* the exploits of Ivanhoe—
these are the ancient games in which human beings have
for centuries found refreshment. The crowds who
watched the jousts of old are still cheering, still quenching
the dust in their throats with cold drinks between the
acts, and still seeing enacted before their naked eyes
myths of courage, brains, and skill.

We are so close to sports, so enmeshed in them, that we
do not truly *see* them, we do not marvel. We overlook the
wonder even the existence of sports should cause, let
alone their persistence and their power. Long after the
Democratic Party has passed into history, long after the
United States has disappeared, human beings will still be
making play fundamental to their lives.

Play is the most human activity. It is the first act of
freedom. It is the first origin of law. (Watch even an infant

at play, whose first act is marking out the limits, the rules, the roles: "This is the road. . . ." The first free act of the human is to assign limits within which freedom can be at play.) Play is not tied to necessity, except to the necessity of the human spirit to exercise its freedom, to enjoy something that is not practical, or productive, or required for gaining food or shelter. Play is human intelligence, and intuition, and love of challenge and contest and struggle; it is respect for limits and laws and rules, and high animal spirits, and a lust to develop the art of doing things perfectly. Play is what only humans truly develop. Humans could live as animals (and often we do, governed by instinct), envying what seems to be the freedom of the wild, the soaring aloft of birds, the unfettered wanderings of jungle felines "born free." But animals are not free, not as humans are. Animals do not multiply cultures and languages, and forms of play, and organizational patterns. Animals play as they have for centuries, while humans ceaselessly invent, produce the multiple varieties of religion and play that establish on the soil of nature the realm of culture, the field of liberty. The religions we have, like the games we have, have issued forth from the historical response of humans to their own liberty.

In all these ways, religions and sports have much in common. Sports belong in the category of religion.

One of the most sensitive of the European professors driven to America by Hitler, Eugen Rosenstock-Huessy, observed at Harvard that his references to European stories, historical or legendary, did not illuminate for Americans the points he was making, as they did for his students in Germany. He tried for several years to find a field of examples of which his American students would have vivid personal experience. Later he wrote: "The world in which the American student who comes to me at about twenty years of age really has confidence in is the world of sport. This world encompasses all of his virtues and experiences, affection and interests; therefore, I have built my entire sociology around the experiences an American has in athletics and games." When he wanted to talk about discipline, excellence, failure, contingency, community, the sacred, dedication, spirit, a recognition of limits, asceticism, concentration, mysticism, will, insight, the relation between body and emotion and intelligence, and so on, he chose his examples from experiences his students had already had with sports. Almost always they could get the point exactly. Since their attention was turned upon their own experiences, sometimes they could notice elements in those experiences which had eluded him.

Sports constitute the primary lived world of the vast majority of Americans. The holy trinity—baseball, basketball, and football—together with tennis, bowling, skiing, golf, hiking, swimming, climbing (not to mention gambling, Monopoly, cards, and other forms of play), are not simply interludes but the basic substratum of our intellectual and emotional lives. Play provides the fundamental metaphors and the paradigmatic experiences for understanding the other elements of life. "People preserve their thousand-year-old experiences," Rosenstock-Huessy writes, "in the world of play."

SPORTSREEL

The Conversion of Robert Griffin

Many years ago, about 1948 or so, I remember Bob Griffin entering the seminary across St. Mary's Lake from the Notre Dame grotto. A huge, gentle, kindly, Chestertonian figure, it would be difficult to imagine a less athletic man. He wrote even then in elegant and witty prose, and either literature or theology would, it was clear to his fellows, be his chosen fields. And he went on, through some struggling years, to become a priest of Holy Cross, the community that established Notre Dame in 1841. Eventually, he came back to the campus as a professor and one of the rectors of Keenan Hall. He is still a Chestertonian figure, bulky, round, merry, abstracted, like some monk misplaced from medieval England in this rowdy contemporary world. And, in 1975, he was asked, rather against his will, to fill in as chaplain to the Notre Dame team on its visit to Boston for *Monday Night Football* in the first meeting of Notre Dame and Boston College.

Father Griffin himself confessed that prior to 1975 he was not altogether certain whether football was played with a wicket, a wedge, or a racquet. His finest athletic muscles, he has written, "were developed on the challenger's side of a Chinese checkers board." He went to Boston innocent of Notre Dame football. (Not *all* Notre Dame professors, let alone priests, lift their attention to what occurs at Cartier field; for some it is part of the background that they never notice, like residents nearest a thruway who never hear the traffic.)

Griff said Mass for the players, lived with them for approximately three days, and learned to love it. He had no way of knowing—facts like these do not normally exist in the world of his perception—that Notre Dame and Boston College had never played before; that Boston College, with the number one passer of 1974, thought itself on the threshold of the "big time"; that Boston, an Irish city deeply torn in 1975 over busing, was in a mania of excitement over the clash of these two great Irish symbols in American life: Notre Dame and B.C. Catholic New England seemed to be afire for the game. In the sellout crowd, alcohol fed team spirit.

With a new coach, a brand-new quarterback, and an almost entirely new offensive team, Notre Dame played a shaky and then increasingly self-confident and internally controlled game. It looked as though they might lose. But they won 17–3.

Best of all, Notre Dame won a convert to the religion of football; the team converted its chaplain. Such stories are best told in the convert's words, and I quote from the Notre Dame *Observer* of September 19, 1975:

"The last time I went to a [Notre Dame] football game, there was a drunk sitting next to me, cheering for the Mishawaka fire department. My leg was in a cast, my arm was in a sling, from a minor skirmish I had had with clumsiness. It was a bitter, cold November afternoon, and we were playing some Protestants who spoke disrespectfully of the Pope. The score was something like ninety-nine to nothing, in favor of the Vatican. That was ten years ago, and I haven't been to a game since. Needless to say, thrilled as I was to go to Boston with the team, I wasn't prepared to open myself up to football as a semireligious experience. But, hate me for saying it if you will, the B.C. game turned out to be something like a semireligious experience. Afterwards, I felt like an agnostic who has attended Mass; and after the service, finds himself reciting the Creed.

"I don't remember whether Hemingway ever wrote about football; but he admired the ritualistic sports, like fishing and bullfighting; sports that involve the use of proper skills and techniques, if you don't want to be destroyed by what you are doing. For Hemingway, there was a *nada*, a nothingness, confronting man, instead of the grace that a religious man feels. A man has only his own strength, and his own courage, to rely on. If order is to be found in a meaningless universe, a man has to impose that order; a way of doing it was through the ritual of sports. There was a right way and many wrong ways of catching a fish or killing a bull. If you did it well, with dignity and courage, though you might get badly battered, you were a kind of hero; even, as in the case of Santiago, the old man of the sea, you were a kind of secular Christ, and you, by being pretty good, defeated the *nada*, the nothingness. Sometimes there was a brotherhood you felt with other creatures, but you didn't rely on outside help. A bullfighter might pray for the Virgin's aid; but he prayed with restraint. A bullfighter who prayed too much for heaven's help showed that he was really a coward. This, at least, is how I now remember Hemingway's code, but it's been a long time since I read him. I hope the freshmen won't quote me in their term papers.

"I think Hemingway would have appreciated the Notre Dame team on Monday evening. From the first moment of the Sunday practice until the final moment in the dressing room on Monday, when the final scratch was Mercurochromed, you could feel the discipline underlying randomness, the order that seemed a ritual—and all of it was a ritual: the travel, the meals, the conversations, the warm-ups, and certainly, the game itself. There are techniques and skills indispensable to football, I guess, if you are going to win the game and avoid being physically destroyed. But in Boston, all of it was done with an ease and casual grace that hid the hard work, as when dancers are choreographed to perform the ballet.

"Religion, of course, is a part of the football liturgy; Mass was said and prayers were offered; in the dressing room, a player or coach might kneel down and ask the priest for his blessing. It was a reverent worship, and the blessings were asked against accidents that skills cannot be trained against. The priest knew he was blessing courage and poise and hard work and a hope of victory that superb form and conditioning have a right to expect. The Mass, the prayers, the blessings seemed as terse and to the point as a final score with no sense of sentimentality or wasted gesture, so that when the game was over and won, the priest who said the Mass felt it was his victory as much as the team's. What is more, by God, he felt he was part of the team, and as necessary to the touchdowns as the kids in the padded suits.

"There has always been, for me, a beauty surrounding Notre Dame and her people so that if one had only this experience, with neither hope of heaven nor expectation of glory, it would be enough, as much of goodness and beauty as a man inheriting the earth would really need. Now, for me, the football experience is, in a different way from before, part of that beauty. I do not think I shall forget the two days in September in an Irish town: being on the field, under the lights, at game-time; the meals shared with the gentlemen, the really great gentlemen, who give such class to the Notre Dame game; the coaches, the doctors, the trainers, the managers, the office personnel; the quiet, thoughtful young men dressing for the game, tense and sweating at half-time, slapping each other on the back as part of the language of congratulations and encouragement for plays well made or challenges about to be faced; the calm, sensible words of the coaches in the dressing rooms and the instructions of the head coach at half-time; the final Hail Mary after the game was over; the ride back to the Marriott, when judging from the conversations and the appetites, life seemed to have resumed rhythms once again.

"Beneath the pleasant pageantry, I had a sense of sharing in one of those fundamental human experiences, where the primal energies have been channelled into symbolic action that gives a dignity to the suffering and fight. The world is out there, waiting to defeat you: because you are not alone in a hostile universe, you ritualize the battle. The nameless forces seem arrayed against you on a single field, but you face it as a team trained in the stratagems of victory. But the enemy is a team of decent lads like yourself, and you admire and respect them, even while overcoming them. Keeping their decencies and yours intact, you struggle against them as stand-ins for principalities and powers.

"In the end, of course, it is only a game, and I don't know whether football players ever elevate their Armageddons to the cosmic level. But for a little while, on September fifteenth, a football game seemed, as the bull fights and fishing in Hemingway do, like one of the rituals of courage that affirm the dignity of being human.

"As Chesterton wrote in a poem on Notre Dame foot-

ball, in images contrasting it to the games in the pagan
amphitheatre:

> *And I saw them shock the whirlwind*
> *Of the world of dust and dazzle:*
> *And thrice the sand-wheel swirled:*
> *And thrice they cried like thunder*
> *On Our Lady of the Victories,*
> *The Mother of the Master of the Masterers*
>   *of the world*
>
> *Queen of Death and Life undying*
> *Those about to live salute thee.*

"On Monday evening after the game, as I was following
the team off the field, a nine year old boy called me over to
the stands; handing me a football—his own football—he
asked me to sign it. My autograph didn't do much for that
football; eventually, the boy will wonder why he both-
ered with a priest's signature rather than the captain's.
But, for a while, I was identified with greatness. As rector
emeritus of Keenan, I have often been associated with
greatness at Notre Dame, and Mardelle didn't launch me as
the Glee Club chaplain without some of their greatness
rubbing off. But I've [never] been a football hero before in
anybody's eyes. . . ."

3

The Metaphysics
of Sports

SOME HOLD that sports are childish, at best adolescent. "When one becomes a man, one ought to put aside the things of childhood." But what if participation in sports is the mark of a civilized person? What if it deepens and mellows the soul?

Play, not work, is the end of life. To participate in the rites of play is to dwell in the Kingdom of Ends. To participate in work, career, and the making of history is to labor in the Kingdom of Means. The modern age, the age of history, nourishes illusions. In a Protestant culture, as in Marxist cultures, work is serious, important, adult. Its essential insignificance is overlooked. Work, of course, must be done. But we should be wise enough to distinguish necessity from reality. Play is reality. Work is diversion and escape.

Work is justified by myth: that the essential human task is to improve the world. The vision of history this ideology drums into us, with accompanying trumpet flourish, is the "march of time." *Progress.* Our ancestors were inferior to ourselves in knowledge, virtue, and civilization. Our present task is to advance the human condition beyond the state in which we find it. That the reality of human life contradicts this myth does not usually disabuse us of it, at least in our conscious minds. What we call progress should, perhaps, be interpreted in exactly the reverse way: *Decline.* Each year of our labors, it may be, hastens the destruction of this planet. I do not assert these propositions; they do bring to light the optimistic myth we tend to accept as reality itself.

It seems naïve to believe in the reality of progress, at least in the sense that humans become more moral generation by generation. Today there is television, and thirty years ago there was not. Today medicine saves lives that at the beginning of this century would have been lost. Today American society is by some degrees and in certain respects more just and egalitarian than twenty years ago, or forty, or sixty, or eighty, etc. Of course, changes do occur. But the enduring struggles of the human race do not seem to disappear. Death still claims us. The universe, despite us, steadily "does its thing." That we will survive all other species on this planet, or survive as long as there is a universe, it may be permissible to doubt. Now, as in the days when humans lived in caves, people sometimes love each other, sometimes cruelly kill each other; sometimes are honest, sometimes dishonest; sometimes are heroic and excellent in achievement, sometimes cowardly and mediocre.

Historical changes, social changes, cultural changes seem not to alter moral difficulties. They do displace them, rearrange them, distribute them differently. History does not much alter the quantum of good or evil in social structures or in individuals. In every age, in every culture, in every circumstance, it is difficult to be all that one ought to be as a human being. On the face of it, I do not consider myself and my brothers and sister higher human types than our parents or grandparents or our ancestors of a thousand years ago. Allowing for changes in circumstances, I do not think we are more independent of mind, courageous, truthful, and sensitive, or more capable of deep and true love. What we have gained along some lines of development—mobility of mind and travel and education, for example—we seem to have lost along others: a concentration of energy, simplicity, inner definition. We seem to be as lost as any generation in the long history of our people. I would not want to stand before God and claim to be better than my ancestors.

In a word, it has for some time struck me that those matters the newspapers treat as serious and important (national news, international news, financial news, and so forth), are like shadows dancing on the walls of a cave; like the grass of the field that alternately is green, brown, and covered by snow; like dreams; and cyclical, repetitive, and spiraling now upward and now downward. It is not that history stands still: *Eppur, si muove!* It is, rather, that if one is absent from the news for a month, or a year, or three years, the world still seems to turn. Economic crises come and go. So do nations and elections. It is all fascinating. Each day is different. Each social process, each trend, each historical movement is unique. Still, there is a remarkable sameness deep down in things.

For this reason, I have sometimes thought the sports pages print the critical dispatches from the realm of permanent reality. They celebrate the essential human qualities. They sing of the sameness, the cycles, of reality. They tell the truth about human life. They carry minimal illusion. It is the good sense of most humans that leads them to look first at the sports pages, second at the news from the world of image and shadow. It is their good sense that leads them to demand that the sports sections of the papers be longer, fuller, and more complete than the pages of international news, national news, local news, financial news. Sports are at the heart of the matter. Sports are the high point of civilization—along with the arts, but more powerfully than the arts, which are special in taste and execution and appeal. Only a very few books or folktales reach the same metaphysical levels as sports can. Very few philosophical-religious texts have as clear a ring of truth as a baseball smacked from the fat, true center of a willow bat.

The serious ones say that sports are escape. It seems far more true to the eye, the ear, the heart, and the mind that history is an escape. Work is an escape. Causes are an escape. Historical movements are an escape. All these escapes must be attempted; I take part in as many as I can. But the heart of human reality is courage, honesty, freedom, community, excellence: the heart is sports.

Sports are not, of course, all of life. What good are courage, honesty, freedom, community, and excellence if they do not inform one's family life, civic life, political life, work life? Sports do not celebrate such qualities in order to contain them, but in order to hold them clearly before the aspiring heart. No one can live a life wholly within sports. For professional athletes, sports themselves may become work, not sports; just as for a professional academic, studies may become work, not liberal arts; just as for a professional clergyman, religion may become work, not spirit.

It is fashionable to put down "jocks." Others, of course, put down businessmen, or do-gooders, or beatniks, or artists, or theologians, or secularists, or saints. It is part of the human comedy for everyone to put down someone.

What the person of wisdom needs to derive from every sphere of life is its inherent beauty, attraction, power, force.

What I have learned from sports is respect for authenticity and individuality (each player learning his own true instincts, capacities, style); for courage and perseverance and stamina; for the ability to enter into defeat in order to suck dry its power to destroy; for harmony of body and emotions and spirit. Sports are as old as the human race. Sports are the highest products of civilization and the most accessible, lived, experiential sources of the civilizing spirit. In sports, law was born and also liberty, and the nexus of their interrelation. In sports, honesty and excellence are caught, captured, nourished, held in trust for the generations. Without rules, there are no sports. Without limits, a sport cannot begin to exist. Within the rules, within the limits, freedom is given form. Play is the essence of freedom: "The free play of ideas." Play is the fundamental structure of the human mind. Of the body, too. The mind at play, the body at play—these furnish our imaginations with the highest achievements of beauty the human race attains. Symphonies, statues, novels, poems, dances, essays, philosophical treatises—these are transpositions of the world of sports into the exercises of higher civilization. Sports are their fundament, their never-failing life source. Cease play, cease civilization. Work is the diversion necessary for play to survive.

Those who have contempt for sports, our serious citizens, are a danger to the human race, ants among men, drones in the honeycomb. There are many reasons for not participating in sports, or even for not liking certain sports. No one can do, or like, everything. Still, those of us who love sports are obliged to hear many taunts about the human inadequacies of "jocks." We disregard many taunts because of their transparent base in envy. The human body was meant to aspire to excellence, and the spirit to perfection. So when some refer to sports as an "animal occupation," they cause us to become aware of biases of our own. Allow me to mention one of my own, not one in which I judge myself correct, but one which I confess haunts my unconscious responses.

I have never met a person who disliked sports, or who absented himself or herself entirely from them, who did not at the same time seem to me deficient in humanity. I don't only mean that all work and no play makes Jack a dull boy, or Jill a dull ms. I mean that a quality of sensitivity, an organ of perception, an access to certain significant truths appear to be missing. Such persons seem to me a danger to civilization. I do not, on the whole, like to work with them. In their presence I find myself on guard, often unconsciously. I expect from them a certain softness of mind, from their not having known a sufficient number of defeats. Unless they have compensated for it elsewhere, I anticipate that they will underestimate the practice and discipline required for execution, or the role of chance and Fate in human outcomes. I expect them to have a view of the world far too rational and mechanical.

Many women, I believe, who have had less access to sports, have been denied heroic modes of behavior. Many men, traumatized by early failures in sports, often grow up warped by the trauma. Reconciliation to their own limits, submission to the disciplines necessary for accomplishment, submission to the humiliation involved in failure in the presence of their fellows, delight in whatever measure of talent God gave them—these are too often absent. Millions of men were as boys poorly coordinated, lacked strength, suffered from some disease or infirmity that prevented athletic accomplishment, were too sensitive to bear the sting of public failure. Those who were "good sports" lived within their limits and prospered spiritually. Those who grew embittered turned their backs, not on something petty and mean, but on something that would have enriched them. Since sports are so much of boyhood, boys who turn away from sports frequently seem crippled in humanity, poisoned against their peers, driven to a competitiveness in intellect or lost in the acquisition of power and wealth, never graced by the liberty of play.

Machismo—frequently identified with sports—is a vice, a distortion of sports, as manipulation, lust, or self-enclosure are corruptions of love. To diagnose sports as the source of machismo is like diagnosing love as the source of selfishness. By "machismo" I understand the fear of failure, the fear of cutting a *brutta figura*. Machismo is a diseased sense of honor, and it flourishes in cultures where honor—external appearance, style—is prized. It has its own glories: without it, the race would be much poorer, and the beau geste would not exist. Those who attack it do not weigh how much its loss to humanity would cost. I would hope that more women would learn to share in it, as many already do. But machismo is not an athletic ideal. It is, in sports, a deficiency.

A very few athletes are born so richly talented that every action and instinct in their chosen game comes easily to them. Even those of great talent must war against the softness of the body, the slackness of instinct, the slowing of mental reaction, the dispersion of attention. And most must practice for scores of thousands of hours to sharpen their skills; most must painstakingly identify weaknesses and compensate for them; most must learn the humiliations and intricacies of team play, and of that fierce competition with the self in which one is measured against the achieved standards of the sport. All must every day face failure and defeat. Every contest is a risk of loss of face. In sports, machismo dies a thousand deaths. In the experience of most athletes, from earliest ages onward, the youngsters afflicted with machismo are soon identified as quitters. In the thousands of practice sessions, in the hazing and teasing of one's peers, in the countless series of injuries, frustrations, failures, and losses, machismo is burned like dross from maturity. It is true that some splendidly gifted athletes, whose peers cannot contain them, do not early enough or deeply enough know failure; and they, it is true, are sometimes insufferable. (Sometimes, too, they are the most surpassingly gentle among men.)

Yet millions of men look back nostalgically on their days in active athletics precisely because they experienced there, as at few other points in their lives, a quality of tenderness, a stream of caring and concern from and toward others, such as would make the most ardent imaginers of the androgynous ideal envious. Male bonding is one of the most paradoxical forms of human tenderness: harsh, hazing, sweet, gentle, abrupt, soft. Blows are exchanged. Pretenses are painfully lanced. The form of compliment is, often as not, an insult. There is daily, hourly probing as to whether one can take it as well as dish it out. It is sweet preparation for a world less rational, less liberal, than childhood dreams imagine. Among men, sports help to form a brotherhood for which, alas, sisterhood has no similar equivalent, and which it is a high human imperative to invent.

Androgynous? Why do critics so often leer that "jocks" are secret homosexuals, patting one another's buttocks, showing off their well-angled forearms and thighs, affectionately joshing one another in the showers? Sports bring out in every ideal team a form of gentleness and tenderness so intense that it is no misnomer to call it love; and coaches commonly speak to their supposed macho males like golden-tongued preachers of love, brotherhood, comradeship. Tears, burning throats, and raw love of male for male are not unknown among athletes in the daily heat of preparation, in the humiliation of doing plays over and over because the coach does not yet see sufficient perfection, and in the solemn battle. In the working world, such tears must normally await the testimonial dinner upon retirement. They are wrong who think the "brains" are androgynous and the jocks afflicted with machismo. For gentleness of demeanor, I will take the athlete eight times out of ten. For hardness of heart, I have learned to fear the man who has always hated sports.

Indeed, the contempt for machismo in sports that one meets in such men is, on inspection, almost always a form of what it condemns. Those who were ashamed to fail, who needed to protect their dignity rather than risk being laughed at, live out the essence of machismo. As a young-ster of no great bodily talent but of fierce competitiveness, I recall vividly dozens of struggles with my own ma-chismo: reluctance to enter new forms of competition for fear of losing face; the need to learn that humiliation does not bring death, and that failure distills a sweetness of its own.

For the underlying metaphysic of sports entails over-coming the fear of death. In every contest, one side is de-feated. Defeat hurts. No use saying "It's only a game." It doesn't feel like a game. The anguish and depression that seize one's psyche in defeat are far deeper than a mere comparative failure—deeper than recognition of the op-ponent's superiority. That would be a simple emotion to handle. Even before a game, one might be willing to con-cede that much; one might already *know* that the other is better. But in a game, the more talented do not always win. A game tests considerably more than talent. A game tests, somehow, one's entire life. It tests one's standing with fortune and the gods. Defeat is too like death. Defeat hurts like death. It can put one almost in a coma, slow up all of one's reactions, make the tongue cleave to the mouth, exhaust every fount of life and joy, make one *wish* one were dead, so as to be attuned to one's feelings.

How can that be? How can a mere game be a combat with death? But it is. One knows it. One's body knows it. One's psyche knows it. Consolation and comfort from others do not touch the depths of one's feelings. In de-cency, announcers do not usually visit the locker rooms of the losers. It takes enormous efforts of will for the dead to pretend to be alive, congratulating those in whom Life still flows triumphant.

A contest like a baseball, basketball, or football game is in some as yet unexplored way a ritual conducted under the sight and power of the gods. Thumbs up, or thumbs down. One side will live, one will die. When one's team is losing, it is too painful to keep on watching. Sports are not diversion. Entertainment diverts. A contest rivets the energies of life on a struggle for survival. The conflict is absolute. No holds barred. To win an athletic contest is to feel as though the gods are on one's side, as though one is Fate's darling, as if the powers of being course through

one's veins and radiate from one's action—powers
stronger than nonbeing, powers over ill fortune, powers
over death. Victory is abundant life, vivacity, bubbling
over. Defeat is silence, withdrawal, passivity, glumness.

Each time one enters a contest, one's unseen antagonist
is death. Not one's visible opponent, who is only the occasion for the struggle. But the Negative Spirit, the De-
nier. That is why the image of the aging athlete is so poignant: it begins to mix the ritual contest with the actual
contest, ritual death with the coming of real death. In the
aging athlete, the ultimate reality of sports breaks through
the symbol, becomes explicit. Death advances on us all.
Not even our vitality, not even our beauty of form, not
even our heroic acts can hold it back. "The boys of summer" fade away. The ritual goes on, young men testing
themselves against the terror without a name. Human life
is essentially a defeat; we die. The victories of sport are
ritual triumphs of grace, agility, perfection, beauty over
death.

In these respects, sports owe more to the ritual grammar of religion than to the laws and forms of entertainment. Millions become involved in the rituals of sport to a
depth of seriousness never elicited by entertainment. Millions do not care about comedians, or variety shows, or
films, or books—to these they turn for diversion. But they
are deeply affected by participation in the ritual struggle
of a football game. Such a game has the power to depress
or to elate. To the unconscious rather than the conscious
self (for few athletes or fans think such matters out in
words), it offers signals ancient, disturbing, fundamental:
I'm on the slope of life, or I am on the slope of death.
Being, or nonbeing. Only by some such formula can we
explain the seriousness of the depression caused by losing, the vitality of the elation caused by winning. It is not
the mere game, not the mere pride, not the vaunting of
self over others; it is the sense of one's inflation by power
not one's own that makes victory so sweet. The victor has
been chosen. Unsought strength sweeps through him. He
is more than self. The elation of victory must be experienced to be understood; one is lifted, raised, infused with
more than abundant life.

"Winning," said Vince Lombard, "isn't everything; it's

the only thing." It isn't the thought of lording it over number two or number three that brings satisfaction; in one's heart, one may know that in some way one's competitors are superior. But finishing first is to have destiny blowing out one's sails. Let the other teams be better on the books; today, Fate has spoken, darling and beloved Fate.

Those who have been rejected relive the struggle to detect precisely where they showed themselves unworthy. They vow not to fail the gods, next time. They renew their faith that the gods are really on their side, as the contest coming up will show.

When Alabama loses seven bowl games in a row; when for months until the spell is broken the Boston Red Sox cannot win a game in Oakland; when the Dallas Cowboys lose the "big ones" year after year, indescribable anxiety descends. The jinx may be no fluke, no accident, but inescapably disastrous. The flaw within the heart may be incurable. The prognostication may be ultimate.

SPORTSREEL

World Series, 1924

A generation ago, "the sports-writers were absolutely the best writers in the papers." So says Marshall Hunt, who was one of them. In their words, unofficial America was recreated: the idiom of its many regions, the look and feel of the small prairie towns and big city slums, its enthusiasms and terrors, its conflicts and ecstasies.

The headlines and the front page of the Washington *Post* on Saturday morning, October 11, 1924, may stand as a sampling from our past:

JOHNSON IS HERO AS NATIONALS WIN
DECISIVE GAME OF WORLD SERIES, 4–3;
CITY IN CARNIVAL, CELEBRATES VICTORY

The right-hand column carried no less than six subheads:

GRIFFMEN TRIUMPH
IN 12-INNING BATTLE
AS CITY GOES WILD

Walter Johnson Pitches
to Victory in Last
Four Innings.

HE AND HARRIS BEAT
M'GRAW STRATEGY

Barney Wins Gamble in
Passing Young Twice to
Get Kelly.

BUCKY GETS HOME RUN
AND LATER TIES SCORE

Desperate Fighting Spirit of
Boy Manager Wins
for Mates.

The story by N. W. Baxter, sports editor, runs full-column as follows:

Washington won; so did Walter Johnson—baseball world's champions both—but the man who made possible the victory—over which thousands of Washington enthusiasts yesterday afternoon went into paroxysms of joy—was Stanley Raymond Harris.

The heart of a lion: the soul of a leader: the nerve of a born gambler: the tact of a diplomat: the brain of a master tactician and the courage of a great fighter carried the youthful manager to the great finish of a great world's series yesterday in the twelfth inning where with one man down, Earl McNeely singled and made the score Washington 4; New York, 3.

Harris was the rock that would not yield. He stood in the breach while his infield crumbled about him and white of face brought back within his halting colleagues the courage and skill that seemed about to desert them for the first time since late in June.

Harris's Will Wins.

With virtually no aid from his teammates and supported mainly by his will to win, he drove three runs across the plate—one with a homer—when these runs meant the game, $50,000 and the title of world's champions.

He met "The Master Mind" of baseball, John McGraw, on his favorite chess board and outguessed and outgeneraled him.

Who is this Harris? Is he the man who but five short years ago played his first game of major-league baseball? Is he the man upon whom the baseball experts smiled when Clark Griffith announced his choice of manager for 1924? Is he the youth of 27 who had the effrontery and audacity to take his club to the head of the American league and keep it there against the assault of older, wiser and presumably better men?

He was.

Today he sits on baseball's throne with no man possessed of the right or power to challenge his position. He succeeded where almost the whole world predicted he would fail. The fruits of glory can not be refused him.

Fought Desperately.

Yesterday upon his chosen battlefield he fought for all these things that now he has. He fought with all the desperation of a man about to die and all the calmness of the man who will not lose. The greater the crisis and the longer the odds the higher was the wall which his determination erected against the enemy. He tossed the dice with fate and sternly shut his eyes to the possibility that the cast fortune might betray him. A man who gambles thus with human elements deserves to win and Harris did. . . .

Even President Coolidge was less than cool, and after his attendance at the game issued this statement to the press:

Of course I am not speaking as an expert or as a historian of baseball, but I do not recollect a more exciting world's series than that which has finished this afternoon. The championship was not won until the twelfth inning of the last game. This shows how evenly the teams were matched. I have only the heartiest of praise to bestow upon the individual players of both teams.

Naturally, in Washington, we were pleased to see Walter Johnson finish the game, pitching for our home team, and make a hit in the last inning that helped win the series. It has to be kept in mind that though he was not successful in the two games which he pitched, that it was his skill that had won the pennant and put Washington into the world's series. Every one was pleased to see him come back at the close of the last game.

The three contests which I witnessed maintained throughout a high degree of skill and every evidence of a high-class sportsmanship that will bring to every observer an increased respect for and confidence in our national game. It would be difficult to conceive a finer example of true sport.

At the left, another story broke downwards from the headlines:

WHIRLWIND OF JOY
SWEEPS CAPITAL IN
BIG DEMONSTRATION

Milling Crowds Combine
Armistice and Mardi
Gras Outburst.

PRESIDENT VOICES JOY
AT RESULT OF SERIES

Observance Starts as Soon
as Word Is Flashed of
McNeely's Hit.

WORKERS IN BUILDINGS RAIN
CONFETTI STORM

City Heads Today Will Plan
Formal Celebration of
Championships.

The whirlwind of joy which swept over Washington yesterday immediately after Earl McNeely had driven in the run that made the Nationals world champions continued to rage until well after midnight. It subsided then only because a baseball-crazed city had yelled itself hoarse and stopped from sheer exhaustion.

In spontaneity and unadulterated enthusiasm the demonstration yesterday afternoon and last night exceeded anything of its kind in the history of Washington. It was an armistice day and mardi gras blended into one. It was wonderful.

Every one of the more than 400,000 men, women and children who make Washington their home took part in the celebration. Every noise-making device that hands could reach was used to produce a mighty din that continued unchecked for hours.

Streets Jammed by Throng.

Not since the first armistice day celebration had Washington been so happy. It was joy and happiness raised to the nth degree and it caused tens of thousands to forget everything except that "Bucky" Harris and his gallant, fighting team had been crowned kings of baseball.

Street scenes in the downtown section defy description. It seemed that the entire population and 100,000 automobiles were jammed into the few blocks between Pennsylvania avenue, F street and Ninth and Fifteenth streets. They pushed

aimlessly up and down the thoroughfares, shouting and yell-
ing the greatest acclaim ever given a baseball team.

At times it seemed that there were such jams of humanity
that they would never untangle. But there would be a break
some place and the swirling mass would move on to the ac-
companiment of honking horns, bursting torpedoes, cut-
outs, backfires and the shrill screams of a delirious fandom.

City Drunk With Happiness.

The cup of joy had bubbled over and the whole town was
drunk with happiness. Gray-haired men who had never expected to see the day when Washington could boast of a
world championship, marched beside their grandsons whose
lessons remained undone. Gray-haired women took their
places alongside bobbed flappers. And when the more en-
thusiastic of the wild young men threw great handfuls of
confetti into their faces the old ladies only smiled.

The carnival spirit held full sway. How could anyone be
angry at anything? Surely if a young man wanted to say
something nice to a pretty girl, certainly the mere fact that he
didn't know her never entered his mind. And, for that matter, it didn't enter her mind either. Washington had won and
that's all anyone cared about.

Another thing. The demonstration was by no means confined to baseball fans. Many who yelled with the others had
never seen a ball game. . . .

In the left column, we read "POST-SCRIPTS" by
George Rothwell Brown:

> *What news, what news? . . .*
> *It is a reeling world, indeed, my lord.*
> *And I believe will never stand upright.*
> *Some news!*
> *Some reels!*

*   *   *   *

Congratulations to Coolidge and Dawes upon having their
nomination already sewed up, otherwise the ticket of Johnson and Harris would sweep the country:

> " 'Tis a lesson you should heed
> Try, try again.
> If at first you don't succeed,
> Try, try again."

This thing of turning certain defeat into sure victory is a typical American attribute, inherited from our Trojan ancestors, via Brutus the Phoenician King of Britain. Business of taking the laurels from Washington, Jackson, Scott, Grant, Sherman, Lee and Pershing, and weaving a diadem for the Champions of this and other charted and uncharted worlds. A universal celebration—even the moon got full.

* * * *

In a word, the Washington boys win the world series by the score of $148,991.63 to $99,327.75.

* * * *

And now, hats off to the Giants! Confronting seven hostile audiences, and laboring under the handicap of suspicion, they battled to the last 4-to-3 score with steady nerves, clear heads, and, can we now doubt, with clear conscience! As Ella Wheeler Wilcox—or was it Col. John A. Joyce—says,

> *"But the man worth while is the*
> *man who will smile,*
> *When everything goes dead wrong."*

* * * *

4

The Rural Anglo-
American Myth: Baseball

THE NEW YORK METS are playing at Shea Stadium on a
hot Monday night in 1975. The flag in left-center field is
listless. The friendly animation of the crowd emits quiet
currents of electricity. The crack of the bat is a precious
sound, unlike auto horns or machinery, the hum of air-
conditioners or the babble of voices: authoritative, clear,
clean, woodsmanlike. Ash wood meets the white sphere
(a sphere comfortable in the human hand, human size)
and sends it ringing like a shot where will directs. A ball
so smooth that sensuousness awakens at the touch, the
grip of it; its angled stitching rubs across one's fingers,
pads resting on its cool, taut sheen. A baseball has a delicious heft, solid, heavy and light at the same time, a joy to
take in hand and flip lightly in the air to catch again: so
within one's control, designed to please. Anyone who has
searched out rocks at the beach to skip across a lake
knows how satisfying it is to find a rock of proper
smoothness and weight; a baseball yields exultant
pleasure.

Entering the stadium, one's children in tow, is like
walking, almost, through some ancient catacomb, up un-
painted concrete stairs, suddenly bursting into light, the
cool vista of green grass etched in lime-white boundaries
far below. Blue-clad players glide effortlessly across the
green in classic motions, pulling down line drives, pivot-
ing, each cocking his arm and unsheathing a throw

straight as a sword to the infield. The crack of the bat is swollen now by the amphitheater. The visual beauty, and the smells, and the restlessness in the rapidly filling shiny seats fill the senses. Already, before the game begins, satisfaction lifts the spirit. Here is a world, a universe, neat and lovely as a painting in a frame or a sonnet in its fourteen lines, designed for high accomplishment.

Against the night air, the flag waves. Business is represented by the clearly designed billboards along the walls. Kids from the ghettos race around the aisles shouting, quarreling, barely holding their churning energy. The place pulses with emotion, is tutored in restraint by the flawless smooth lawn and geometric boundaries. Second base, like a square white punctuation mark, sits in isolation in the smooth brown dust of the infield.

The visiting team tonight is the Los Angeles Dodgers, and the crowd anticipates a close duel between Andy Messersmith, who with Don Sutton is the ace of the Dodger staff, and John Matlack, later in the summer to share the Most Valuable Player award at the All-Star game. Binoculars help the children focus on the faces of those who were only names to them before, if that, and they begin linking the numbers on the back of jerseys with names, putting together a puzzle not complete until everyone is known, identified, placed. Richie, 9, already knows his favorites' numbers by heart and calls out each accomplishment. Tanya, 7, nervously tries to decide on favorites of her own, switching from one to another with the flow of events as the warm-up period ends.

The grounds crew swarms over the field, damping down the dust, smoothing out every cut and cleat mark, raking gently at the mound, fastidious as barbers, freshening the clean white lines of chalk. One dusts off the sacred "home," starting place, keystone, source and touchstone of triumph: those who cross it most often, according to the classic and almost immemorial rules, carry off the victory. "Around the world" is the myth: batter after batter trying to nudge forward his predecessor in this most American of games until the whole universe is circled, base by base, and runners can come "home." One imagines Yankee Clipper ships blown silently across the sparkling sea, sails creaking in the wind (the canvas that covers the diamond when it rains), the sounds of wood, the silence and isolation of each sailor at his post, encircling the world for trade. Baseball is a voyage. It is also a game of individualists, often taciturn, plying each his special craft, collaborating, but at each crucial point facing events alone, solving the mathematical possibilities of each task in the reflective quiet of his own trained hunches, instincts, and lightning moves.

Baseball is as close a liturgical enactment of the white Anglo-Saxon Protestant myth as the nation has. It is a cerebral game, designed as geometrically as the city of Washington itself, born out of the Enlightenment and the philosophes so beloved of Jefferson, Madison, and Hamilton. It is to games what the *Federalist Papers* are to books: orderly, reasoned, judiciously balanced, incorporating segments of violence and collision in a larger plan of rationality, absolutely dependent on an interiorization of public rules. It also depends on a balance of power between pitchers and hitters, on the delicate interplay between fielders at each position, and on the heights and distances relating every object of interest in the game (fences, pitcher's mound, bases, stands, obstructions). A slight change in the weight of the ball or its composition, in the material used for bats, in heights or distances, can alter the character of the game dramatically, giving decisive edge to one factor or another.

The game depends, besides, on a very high sense of individual dignity and honor. The batter faces the pitcher in utter solitude, depending on no one but himself and on every resource of free-flowing instinct he can draw upon. The most cutting accusation player can make against player is "choke"; that is, standing there alone, the individual panics under pressure, blocks, can't get instinct, will, body, and execution in single harmony. Baseball is a game of magnificent self-control, of cool, of passion transmuted into unruffled instinctual perfection.

In football, on each play eleven men act in unison, and in each action not the individual but the corporate unit acts. When Bart Starr completed a pass for the Green Bay Packers, all the Packers could be said to share the deed; one man alone is quite helpless. When Joe DiMaggio stepped to the plate in Yankee Stadium with his unforgettable stance and fluid swing, DiMaggio stood in spot-lighted solitude, and none of his teammates could act in his behalf. Football is corporate, baseball an association of individuals.

Baseball is a Lockean game, a kind of contract theory in ritual form, a set of atomic individuals who assent to patterns of limited cooperation in their mutual interest. "Fair play" characterizes baseball more than it does football. In football, contact between individuals and teams is infinitely more complex and offers much greater possibilities for sneak advantage. Baseball is early America, and we should not be surprised if the bicentennial outburst sends attendance figures upward. (In 1973–1975, attendance figures reached an all-time three-year level: 89,946,476. A record-tying total of 17 teams drew over 1 million each in 1975.)

In these respects, baseball is not a game that has appeal in every culture. The myth it embodies does not express the inner sense of reality of all peoples. In those nations where, in various forms, individualism and personal honor and the dignity of a man alone are deeply cherished, baseball elicits a responsive chord: in Latin nations, in Japan, in the United States. (Cricket is, one supposes, the British equivalent.) One would have expected the French to take to it, with their *ésprit géometrique* and their famous fiery individualism. But perhaps the French are also too anarchic, too passionate, to accept the rules, boundaries, and coolness of baseball; it must seem to them a bore. Tennis arose as a diversion at the king's courts in France, but for the French populace there has never been an equivalent to tennis in rule-abidingness, disciplined individuality, and serial action. What baseball satisfies in the psyche is restraint in bodily movements, law, grace, swiftness of judgment, poise, respect for order—even enormous love for order. Baseball feeds delight in numbers through quantification of every aspect of the game: runs, hits, errors, hitting percentages, earned-run averages. For Americans, nothing is real until it's counted. The French, I believe, love in games of action the unpredictable, the complex, the flashing outburst, as in repose they love precision and control (French gardens). Baseball would not seem to suit the French.

Such matters, perhaps, do not go exactly into words. Too rich, too elusive, they exceed verbal articulation, appearing more clearly in the actual rituals and dramatized cultural expressions the various nations take into their hearts. It is difficult to imagine a French existentialist, or phenomenologist, or structuralist playing baseball: the symbols are discordant. With American philosophy, or even sociology, the consonance is remarkable.

Baseball is symbolically white and Protestant—not that blacks, Catholics, Jews, Latins, and Japanese cannot play it superbly. Baseball's heroes, clearly, are often neither white nor Protestant, yet there is an elusive, widely felt sense that the naming of a black *manager* for a baseball team represented a vast symbolic breakthrough, worthy of lengthy notice on the national television news. In basketball, the naming of a black coach had no such symbolic repercussions. A black coach feels entirely in harmony with the game of basketball, but not a black manager with baseball. Why? Bigotry is not a sufficient answer, for presumably the same fans have two quite separate sets of symbolic feelings. Part of the answer must await a fuller discussion of basketball, but at least one or two explorations of the mythic content of baseball may shed some light.

The image one has of cultures not white and Protestant, reinforced by many anthropological details, suggests in them patterns of communality and corporateness foreign to the British world. Persons in other cultures may be to every degree as highly individuated as persons in America. Yet Anglo-Saxon culture remains, almost uniquely among the cultures that populate America, the mythic world of the solitary, lone individual. The businessman, the philosopher, the cowboy, the preacher, the publicist, the politician: all exalt the "individual," all celebrate the commitment of individuals to the internalization of social rules and the dictates of rationality. The carriage of the Anglo-Saxon body, its gestures, its need for physical space and for emotional space are quite distinctive among the peoples of the world. These features are almost perfectly dramatized in the rules, distribution of positions, and actions of baseball.

Anyone can learn to operate within the Anglo-Saxon

mythic world; humans everywhere can, and do, imitate and assimilate a mythos not initially their own. While the spiritual world of baseball, acted out in a public arena, exhibits almost perfectly the myths of the white Anglo-Saxon population that settled the towns, prairies, and southlands of America, all Americans can share in the "national pastime." It is a form of Americanization. Those who appreciate the rules and formality of the bull ring and the toreadors can see how Latins would like the order and the nerve called upon in baseball, and similarly with the Japanese.

Eddie Stanky spiking the ankles of his opponents at second base; Leo Durocher's "Nice guys finish last"; the temper of Pete Rose exploding against Bud Harrelson of the Mets; the "beanballs" of Juan Marichal and other Giant and Dodger pitchers down the years and, on one of those occasions, John Roseboro's bat swinging in retaliation; the emptying of both dugouts in an occasional fist-swinging melee—such outbreaks serve to indicate that, even in baseball, humankind cannot bear too much rationality and must break Anglo-American bounds.

The game is exceedingly orderly. Exact scorecards must be kept concerning who may bat when. Tradition fixes each defensive position. Before each game, the ground rules are gone over in detail. The limits of the game are drawn with care, but within those limits the variations are endless, almost like the spins of a few pieces of colored glass in a kaleidoscope, never resulting in the same configuration. Baseball is a festival of angles and inches. A trigonometer's delight.

Each hit that breaks from the bat speeds outward at a different velocity and angle. The pitcher tries to mix up his pitches, throwing them at different angles, speeds, and targets, putting on the ball a variety of spins and turns. Given the limits of the game, its possibilities are subjected to exceedingly refined study and experiment. Whoever can invent a new grip, stance, or motion, gains—or tries to gain—a slight advantage. Given such slight advantages, a team can play the "percentages." Knowing the limits, the team can hope that repeated advantages will propel them inexorably to the best record over the long, exhausting 162-game season.

It is considered a high achievement for a team to win 100 games. At least a third of the time, therefore, even the most exalted and talent-laden teams are bound to lose. So closely balanced are the elements of the game and the strengths and weaknesses of the combatants that even the worst teams in the major leagues rarely fail to win a third of their games. Most of the teams fall somewhere between these two extremes, winning and losing about half their games.

Look, for example, at the final standings for 1975:

THE FINAL STANDINGS
AMERICAN LEAGUE

EAST	W	L	GB	WEST	W	L	GB
Boston	95	65	——	Oakland	98	64	——
Baltimore	90	69	4½	Kansas City	91	71	7
New York	83	77	12	Texas	79	83	19
Cleveland	79	80	15½	Minnesota	76	83	20½
Milwaukee	68	94	28	Chicago	75	86	22½
Detroit	57	102	37½	California	72	89	25½

NATIONAL LEAGUE

EAST	W	L	GB	WEST	W	L	GB
Pittsburgh	92	69	——	Cincinnati	108	54	——
Philadelphia	86	76	6½	Los Angeles	88	74	20
New York	82	80	10½	San Francisco	80	81	27½
St. Louis	82	80	10½	San Diego	71	91	37
Chicago	75	87	17½	Atlanta	67	94	40½
Montreal	75	87	17½	Houston	64	97	43½

Baseball conveys a kind of mysticism of numbers. (It was just such a mysticism that amazed the South Vietnamese in their contacts with Americans; the Americans had a passion for counting *everything*, for understanding reality through numbers.) To circle the bases is to traverse exactly 360 feet, the precise number of degrees in a circle. Each base is 90 feet away from the preceding, a distance that leaves almost an exact balance between runners and fielders when a player hits a deep infield grounder or tries to steal a base; another 2 feet in either direction might settle the issue decisively between them and leave no doubt about the outcome. Baseball has three strikes; three outs; three players in the outfield, six in the infield, nine players in all; nine innings; 90 feet between bases; 360 feet around the world—it is suffused with a gentle Trinitarian mysticism.

The *Reach Baseball Guide* for 1887 calls baseball the "froth and foam and chalice of life." It argues that "when the Pilgrim Fathers landed in America they brought with them the English national game of cricket . . . too slow a sport for the blood of young America." In the first centuries of our national life, of course, as de Tocqueville reports, there were relatively few organized sports in America; the United States was distinctive in the West in this respect. In the 1840s, Alexander Cartwright, a surveyor and member of the New York Knickerbocker Club, laid out the geometry of the diamond. Within two generations, Henry Chadwick had developed the precise mathematical coding of the game's every action that became the box score. "Whoever wants to know the heart and mind of America," Jacques Barzun was to write, "had better learn baseball." Our public image is activist, but a writer in *Harper's Weekly* stresses the contemplative and leisurely side of our national ideal: "A great beauty of baseball is that it contains just the right proportion of action and inaction. That is one of its chief charms. Nothing palls so quickly as continuous action. The times between innings in baseball, bringing relaxation amid the whirl and excitement, are restful and pleasant."

Baseball is designed like the federal system of checks and balances. This is a conceit, to be sure, but the umpires provide a kind of judiciary; the offensive players, stepping to the plate one by one, learn like our executive that "the buck stops here"; the defense attempts to play in concert, a congress checking the power of the hitters. The parallel is far from exact. But the balance of the game mirrors an intellectual psychic love of equilibrium that is also exemplified in our form of government.

Most of the injuries that occur in baseball are strains and sprains, pulled muscles, jammed thumbs, and blistered fingers—injuries that are the revenge the human body takes upon the spirit. Comparatively few injuries result from the violence of contact with opposing players. Only when a base runner tries to crash his way through a defensive player who is unavoidably in his path is physical contact licit. A pitcher who hits a batter with a pitched ball gives the batter first base automatically. While a little intimidation is permissible (a high hard fastball in the vicinity of the head), the rules of the game, and its traditions, oblige the pitcher to avoid hitting the batter and to concentrate on the impersonal target of the strike zone. What would the lawless territory of this continent have been without a little intimidation? And yet it is a triumph of law over the lawless spirit—and hence a vast satisfaction to the national psyche—that so civilized, orderly, and lawful a game could have arisen from the plains, the southlands, and the eastern cities of the nineteenth century, when the frontier and the badlands still loomed on the horizon. The author of the Frank Merriwell books, Burt L. Standish, edited a magazine for "Top-Notch Fellows" and expressed their credo in 1910: "I have no word of praise for the tricky, treacherous, contemptible fellow who wins at anything by underhand methods. Play Fair! Win on the Level!"

There is also in baseball that spirit of equality that de Tocqueville said was so pervasive in the land. While there are, for some practical purposes, "captains" appointed for each team, and while the team manager rules from the dugout with an iron hand, within the confines of actual play the function of authority is severely limited. The manager can tell his players to adjust their defensive positions and can dictate the sequence in which, if circumstances permit, they are to coordinate their moves; and the opposing manager can instruct a batter to swing or not to swing, to swing hard or to bunt, to hit behind the runner, and so forth. Yet, essentially, baseball is each man for himself. The game is associational. It requires joint timing and coordination, and so the individual is not entirely antisocial; a certain public-spiritedness, so to speak, is highly valued. Indeed, the early ambience of the game is described by a Reverend Sawyer of New York in *Baseball Magazine:*

> At the baseball match, we encounter real democracy of spirit; one thing in common absorbs us; we rub shoulders high and low; we speak without waiting for an introduction;

we forget everything clannish—all the pretty conventionalities being laid aside; individual experiences submerge in union of human feeling; we are swayed by a common impulse; we are all equal; the pressure of the crowd makes us one—the office boy who has stolen away, the businessman from the counting room, the clergyman from his study, the clerk from his desk, the girl from the factory, the wife from the home—all are on equal footing. Barriers are forgotten and how good it seems for us to be human beings. It was just this experience which must have moved Ernest Howard Crosby of New York to explain: "I find more genuine religion at the baseball match than I do at my father's church on Fifth Avenue."

Baseball is also exquisite in fairness. Achievement is unambiguous, earned, recorded. Look it up. The box score is printed for every game, registering the abstract, mathematical equivalent of nearly every significant action of every player. No one is perfect. The record shows every error, every strikeout, every wild pitch—and every hit, run, and run batted in. Excuses fall limp. Family fame, status, and connections do not hit home runs or pitch no-hitters; only the man alone is responsible for success or failure.

"The structure of baseball," Marvin Cohen writes in his poetic *Baseball the Beautiful*

is its art. It's a structure that admits of infinitely complicated possibilities and combinations, within the rigid framework of rules in common, of distances to fences, of worked-out angles, of human proportions. Man is the measure of all things. The Major League ballplayer is the measure of the distances on his field of trade. Given these, he must do or die, win or lose. It's the majesty that dignity imparts.

Proportions and measurements are the poet's tool, the sculptor's trade. And they rule in baseball.

Baseball, Cohen argues, is objective, verifiable; it holds up crystalline standards and keeps alive the myth of absolute values and the vision of an ideal harmony. Its "intricate possibilities of clarity" give the mind and heart a form by which one may seek manifestations of the beautiful in the more anarchic, muddled, relativistic realms of modern urban life.

In all these ways, baseball is a mirror held to Anglo-

American aspirations. It is as dry and clean and confident as John Dewey. It is almost a parody of the linguistic analysis of the Cambridge school. One can imagine Ludwig Wittgenstein breaking up its "actions" into "elements" and "units." One can imagine A. J. Ayer applying to it a "verifiability principle." Clean, chaste, nonsubjective, geometric, objective, baseball is of all sports the most suited to the scientific, analytic, empirical temper.

It is also an optimistic game. Under the lights or in the full heat of the August sun, it offers an arena, a universe, a world in which reason and individual action rule, in which the elements are known and planned for, in which balances, fairness, and public-spiritedness reign. "Nice guys finish last," Leo Durocher said, but in this game the reverse is true. Aggressive, pressing, active, chafing at the limits, yes; dirty play, no. The game has too much balance; retribution is too easy, too systematic. In football, "Mean" Joe Greene is intended as a compliment. The world of football is more pessimistic, tougher, more familiar with injustice. Baseball is like a do-gooder's dream of order and individual accomplishment, precisely measured. Mean guys are, inexorably, driven from the game. Their presence jars. They create scandal. Baseball could have been invented by John Rawls: *A Theory of Justice, Exemplified,* could be the title of his book.

In baseball, the fan is constantly invited to shift his point of view. Concentration is essential; minute adjustments foretell dramatic changes yet to come. So one concentrates on the pitcher—or, rather, *with* the pitcher. Tries to think with him, feel his muscles pull, recognize where his body hurts or is tiring, diagnose what the hitter is expecting and how to fool him. (Pitchers face the same hitters four or five times a game, twenty or thirty times a season; each time, they must remember every pitch they've tried before, remember how the batter reacted.) Baseball is the most acute intensifier of memory. Concrete, vivid images abound in the minds of players and fans—exact etchings of history going back as far as anyone can remember. A grandfather recalls Pie Traynor's gait, or exactly how he swung at the fourth pitch offered him in the eighth inning in a game in Pittsburgh in 1923. . . . And then the fan can take the perspective of the runner on first base, wheeling the angles of the field as the stars wheel in the heavens, studying the pitcher's every muscular ripple, trying to judge whether the runner dares to break for second and gain a half-step start by detecting, hawklike, that the pitcher's body has committed itself.

Roger Angell catches this precisely in *The Summer Game:*

> I have watched many other sports, and I have followed some—football, hockey, tennis—with eagerness, but none of them yields these permanent interior pictures, these ancient and precise excitements. Baseball, I must conclude, is intensely remembered because only baseball is so intensely watched. The game forces intensity upon us. In the ball-park, scattered across an immense green, each player is isolated in our attention, utterly visible. . . . what is certain in baseball is that someone, perhaps several people, will fail. They will be searched out, caught in the open, and defeated, and there will be no confusion about it or sharing of the blame. This is sure to happen, because what baseball requires of its athletes, of course, is nothing less than perfection, and perfection cannot be eased or divided. Every movement of every game, from first pitch to last out, is measured and recorded against an absolute standard, and thus each success is also a failure. Credit that strikeout to the pitcher, but also count it against the batter's average; mark his run unearned, because the left fielder bobbled the ball for an instant and a runner moved up. . . . Tension is screwed tighter and tighter as *the certain downfall* is postponed again and again, so that when disaster does come—a half-topped infield hit, a walk on a close three-and-two call, a low drive up the middle that just eludes the diving shortstop—we rise and cry out. It is a spontaneous, inevitable, irresistible reaction. (p. 311, italics added)

Baseball is a game of rural cunning. Musical names from the forgotten, unknown, and unstudied parts of America roll across its rosters: Pie, Ty, Hy, Nap, Preacher, Virgil, Enos, Bobo, Nolan, Rube, Catfish, Stan, Horace, Jesus, Duke, Dizzy, Luke, Thurmond, Vida, Casey, Satchel; and the last names roll unfamiliarly as honor rolls to the dead in all our wars, names seldom met in daily commerce, particular and belonging to an America many others know not of: Mantle, Aaron, Piersall, Hrabosky, Gullett, Kluszewski, Petrocelli, Humperdinck, Wynn, Score, Marichal, Hooton, Bando, Greenberg, Blue, Rose,

Swoboda, Stargell, Cepeda. If the game is mathematical and analytic, the players and the coaches and the managers (not to say the fans) are intelligent, not as Cornell and Berkeley philosophers, but with practiced hunch and instinct, shrewd and tutored eye, tobacco-chewing cunning. One imagines the shock of college-trained Americans meeting the intelligence of V.C. peasants in Vietnam: so in baseball, the masterminds view the "perfessors."

And rural religion, too. The game is as orderly as ever Spinoza would have made the universe, had he been God; as orderly as acres tilled and plotted, precisely measured out; as regular as the sunrise and the seasons. And yet as in agriculture so in baseball: chance rules. Within this well-defined world, human control reaches limits. Care and cunning do not in the end suffice. The gods mock human fairness. And so of all athletes, baseball players are the most religious. Rituals and fetishes grow like jungle weeds, keep their minds at rest, assist their concentration, keep their doubts from unsteadying their hands. Timing is so essential, requiring instantaneous, instinctive judgment in situations in which reasoning or control by will is utterly impossible, that baseball players know their actions are not entirely under their control—not conscious control, at least. They are thrown back on inner mysteries. A slump arises, a hitter cannot get a hit, goes game after game doing as he has always done, then systematically adjusts and reviews every muscle and every angle of his stance, and then despairs, waiting like the Israelites in the desert for the return of a fruitful rain of hits. As it left, so grace returns, unbidden. The athlete is the human achiever par excellence (body, mind, and spirit harmonized as one), and yet achievement, every athlete knows, is in hands other than his, escapes the reaches of his will.

Baseball is unlike football or basketball in not being governed by a clock. Until the last out has been registered, anything can happen. Even in the last of the ninth, with two out, a team can suddenly, surprisingly, score 5 or 7 or 9 or 11 runs. It is part of the brilliant fairness of the game. You must, in the end, defeat yourself, use up in vain your own equal chances. The game can be as placid, smooth, and orderly as you please, three up, three down, for inning after inning; then, suddenly, amazingly, the earth may open up and swallow an entire team. The Dodgers, in their first years in Los Angeles, depended on tight control over such eventualities. They lacked the bats for a big inning. When the great-hitting lineups like Chicago, Pittsburgh, Cincinnati, or San Francisco came to town, the Dodgers had to hold the string taut. One waited every moment for a snap. And one held one's breath until the Dodgers, scratching and bunting and perhaps pulling a double down the line, could give their pitchers a tiny lead. There followed the defensive struggle to maintain it. The classic Dodger victory was by a single run.

In this respect, baseball is an antidote to the national passion for bigness. It is a slow, careful, judicious game. Southerners have made up 60 percent of the major leagues during many seasons. From year to year, the big cities yield a Joe DiMaggio, Joe Torre, Sandy Koufax, or Al Kaline, but the small towns present the great players in profusion. You can put brightly colored uniforms on players, have them grow mustaches, and give out free bats to all comers; the game itself resists jazzing up. If baseball holds the secret to the national character, that character is far removed from Hollywood, or Broadway, or Madison Avenue. It is a quiet game of fairness and precision, of control and discipline, of private hurt and aching limbs.

In baseball, then, the form of Anglo-American culture, particularly of rural culture, is almost perfectly reflected. The fundamental unit is the individual; the most highly developed state of the individual is to be a good "team player," to encourage and assist his fellows. He must try to "hold up his end," "not let them down." It is as though the team were a federation of states, an association of individuals. Players in baseball are like the links in a chain, the chain being no stronger than its weakest link. They perform their actions not so much in unison as serially. Basketball and football are considerably more corporate, require a far higher degree of unity, represent a quite different vision of America.

SPORTSREEL

The Dodgers, the Bums

How lucky one is to have Dodger memories: Al Gionfriddo's impossible catch of a Joe DiMaggio home-run ball in one World Series, Sandy Amoros's hard run toward the corner wall to save another Series game, and the heartbreak of Ralph Branca's second pitch to Bobby Thompson that lost the playoff to the Giants. To have been psychologically rooted in the Dodgers from the time I was old enough to know of baseball has been a gift unmerited. Dodgers! Since 1941, the most tumultuous team in baseball. From Ebbets Field to Chavez Ravine, up and down. Often winning or losing at the last possible moment, in the craziest possible way.

Consider: Since 1940, the Dodgers have won the National League pennant in 1941, 1947, 1949*, 1952*, 1953*, 1955*, 1956*, 1959*, 1963*, 1965*, 1966*, and 1974. They finished second in the National League in 1940, 1942, 1946, 1950*, 1951*, 1954*, 1961*, 1962*, 1970*, 1971*, and 1973*. The asterisk indicates the year they won or lost the pennant on the last two days of the season or in a playoff—the breathtaking years.

In twelve tries, the Dodgers won the World Series but four times. Not until 1955 did they win their first World Series, beating the Yankees in the seventh game. They won the World Series again in 1959, 1963, and 1965 (in the seventh game). They lost in the seventh game in 1947, 1952 and 1956.

Consider, also, the cast of characters that came to populate one's life as a Dodger fan these last thirty-five years: Billy Cox, Duke Snider, Cookie Lavagetto, Erv Palica, Preacher Roe, Roy Campanella, Johnny Roseboro, Willie Davis, Don Drysdale, Pete Reiser, Pee Wee Reese, Leo Durocher, Geno Cimoli, Carl Furillo, Gil Hodges, Carl

Erskine, Joe Ferguson, Mike Marshall, Junior Gilliam, Tommy Davis, Ron Fairly, Charley Dressen, Wes Parker, Steve Garvey, Hugh Casey, Ralph Branca, Bill Grabarkewitz, Ron Perranoski, Billy Herman, Dixie Walker, Von Joshua, Clem Labine, Jim Lefevre, Dolph Camilli, Eddie Miksis, Pete Mikkelsen, Dick Tracewski, Tom Paciorek, Bill Singer, Jeff Torborg, Andy Messersmith, Ron Cey, Chris Van Cuyk, Arky Vaughan, Ed Roebuck, Burt Shotton, Schoolboy Rowe, Mickey Owen, Phil Ortega, Joe Moeller, Don Newcombe, Sal Maglie, Bill Sudakis, Rube Walker, Don Zimmer, Whitlow Wyatt, Phil Regan, and Jackie Robinson. Among others.

My own greatest moment in baseball (actually, in softball) came in a Dodger-like way. I was in the sixth grade, in a new school, St. Bernard's in the town of Indiana, Pennsylvania, and the bigger, tougher boys already had me pegged as a "brain," which wasn't good. I hadn't been as good an athlete as other boys until that time; I was just beginning, suddenly, to grow. I had been a little too gentle, a little too worried about getting hurt. We played softball down at the muddy bottom of the hillside outside the school every lunchtime. My habit of waiting for a perfect knee-high pitch hadn't been working out too well, so I watched the better hitters. Out in left field was the schoolyard fence, and occasionally two or three of the older fellows (plus my friend Barry) could drill a shot over it. They seemed to favor shoulder-high pitches. That seemed too high to me, but I decided to try. A good one came the first time I came to bat after formulating my new strategy. *Pow!* I didn't even feel it, the bat hit the center of the ball so cleanly. Out over the fence it soared. How wonderful that felt. What a joy it was to run the bases. What deep satisfaction the look in the eyes of others gave me. From then on, life in sports became almost purely pleasure. I don't remember many more hits of that sort, but that single shot changed my image of myself; and from then on, respect from others came easily. It was a fluke. But how could a Dodger fan knock flukes? Flukes in Bumsville are the daily substance of the game.

For what one enjoyed most about the Dodgers was that they weren't, like the Yankees, a machine. There was no room for arrogance. One couldn't expect the highest level of excellence every day. Often they failed you when you needed them most. They lost when they should have won. They loafed, or sauntered, or seemed so dreadfully mediocre. Yet watch out! Jackie Robinson would dive so hard to snare a low line drive, as he did to force a tie for the league lead in the twelfth inning of the last day against the Phillies in 1951, that he collapsed and had to be helped off the field; but he had held the ball, and in the fourteenth inning he homered to win the game. They could be such sudden heroes. They could be greater than the greatest. Only just don't demand it every day.

You will say that Sandy Koufax gives the lie to this description. Who could have been more consistent? But everyone forgets the first four years of Sandy Koufax; forgets, as well, his sudden decision to retire at age 31, lest he destroy his arm forever. In true Dodger fashion, Koufax blazed in brilliance like a comet, for six years establishing himself as a reasonable candidate for the greatest pitcher who ever lived. It was as much consistent excellence as a Dodger should supply. Don Drysdale could be the greatest pitcher in the world on Monday and surrender a dozen hits on Thursday. Don Newcombe was incomparable on some days—he could even pitch in both games of a doubleheader, or two days in a row—and on others pass out runs like massage-parlor leafleters on Forty-second Street. Duke Snider was the greatest outfielder in the history of the game for days at a time, and then would seem to fall back in the crowd. The Dodgers were reliable in unreliability. "Dodgers," "Bums," their names suited them, those lovers' names.

When our new family moved to Palo Alto for my first teaching job, in 1965, one hidden benefit was fresh proximity to the Dodgers. My childhood passion was rekindled. I'd watch them battle the winds (and the bits of paper, candy wrappers, sandwich cellophane, whipping and swirling across the grass) at Candlestick Park. I could see them on San Francisco television. On my car radio, I could catch Vince Scully from Los Angeles. No doubt, he is the best baseball announcer in the country: fair, accurate, clear, cool, with a true sense of baseball drama (avoiding extraneous color). He knew the players' woes and struggles. He made no excuses for them. Our indoor radio, with antenna, couldn't reach Los Angeles; the car radio could. In the close pennant races of those years, to my wife's dismay, I would retreat to the car in the driveway and listen to the radio. I felt silly. But I wanted to hear. More than once I took my dinner to the car to hear the end of a game; even now, years later, she can barely believe I did it, or that she tolerated it.

Nothing was ever automatic for the Dodgers. When a game or a pennant race got close, that was just when they might rise to unbelievable heroics. If you didn't listen, you would never know. The newspapers never told you what happened. You had to listen yourself. These were the great days of Koufax and Maury Wills. No great hitting power for the Dodgers in that huge stadium, those miles of grass; only great pitching, and swiftness on the base paths. The Dodgers planned to win with brains and grit, scoring one run more than they would allow to the opposition. Every day was another drama.

The image of baseball that haunts me most is Sandy Koufax soaking his arthritic arm in ice water for more hours than he played on the field; taking cortisone in the arm to keep the pain and the swelling down; suffering one season from the splitting of the skin on the fingers that grasped the cords of the ball—and yet, day after day, hurling with such brilliant steadiness and control that no pitcher before or since can ever be called the greatest without comparison with him. In the six years of his maturity, he hurled a no-hitter once in each of four years (one of them a perfect game), struck out almost as many batters as the number of innings he pitched, and won 129 of 176 games; one out of four of his lifetime victories (40 of 165) were shutouts.

He spoke so eloquently of how he trained, how he thought through what he would do on every pitch, and how he aimed at each moment for exactly the perfect solution to the many possibilities confronting him that he provided one of the highlights of my teaching career. Lecturing on Aristotle's conception of the highest moral habit of mind, *phronesis*, the skill of "hitting the mark" at every shifting moment, I brought a radio to class, and we listened to Sandy Koufax pitch in the World Series. It was the best commentary on *The Nichomachean Ethics,* and the most fun, since Thomas Aquinas, about 1205, got his hands on the first Latin translation from manuscripts that had been lost for 1,400 years.

5

The Immigrant Myth and the Corporate Myth: Football

IMAGINE that you work for an organization in which an annual goal is clearly set before you. The hell of it is that eleven committees have been established to make it difficult for you to move forward toward your goal. The rules of procedure are fairly well established. You have only finite time and finite energy. How do you break through the maze?

You look over the opposition. You figure out a strategy: if you can get through three or four of the committees at once, by the same move, that would be exciting. You recognize early that a certain amount of feinting and disguise will be essential; there is no point in alarming a bureaucracy before you spring surprises. Some of the committees can be moved by nothing short of sheer power; either you will have the votes or you won't. One or more may be your nemeses; you'd like to isolate them until the end, or catch them going for something they want that falls perfectly in line with what you want. You test the opposition little by little, day by day, probing, trying out your strengths against theirs. Possibly, you soon realize that strengths are evenly matched, and you lower your head, as they do at Ohio State, and take the long, steady route: "Three yards and a cloud of dust." But perhaps you spot a weakness; the opposing committees cancel one another out. You drop back and heave a "long bomb." Before anybody realizes it, "Touchdown!" It is marvelously satisfying.

Since 1900, life in the United States for more and more men and women has become corporate. Most of us work in large corporations, firms, bureaucracies, universities, institutes, or centers. Fewer and fewer can afford to be in business solely for themselves. Even free-lance writers work for others part of the time; the few who don't face agents, publishers, merchandisers, publicity agents. The cowboy has been machined away by agribusiness; the local druggist works for a chain. The son of the maker of a superb family ice cream can't resist opening one new franchise, then another; now he needs a board of directors.

In this new America, football has gained in mythic power. Football dramatizes, on a well-defined grid, the psychic contest in which those who work for corporations are engaged. In various places in the corporate network, we push ahead, we "run for daylight." Phalanxes of bureaucracies block everything we try to do. Football exemplifies the strategies, the tactics, the crushing disappointments and the explosive "scores" that constitute our working lives. Football more than baseball has become the mythic form most illuminative of the way we live. It is the liturgy of a bureaucratic world.

Football today is preeminently the sport of the new white-collar and professional class, of the statesmen, bureau chiefs, managers, executives, admen, consultants, professors, journalists, engineers, technicians, pilots, air traffic controllers, secret service men, insurance agents, managers of retail chains, bank officers, and investment analysts. The editors of the Washington *Post* wouldn't miss a game.

But football is also the social liturgy of the working classes, the immigrants, the rednecks. The first amateur football clubs in western Pennsylvania derived from Princeton, Rutgers, and other university clubs and were composed of the young scions of the steel industry. As competition intensified, the young tycoons brought in "ringers" from the mines and mills—even a poor Indian boy, Jim Thorpe, from Carlisle. Soon the working class appropriated the game, with its inherent conflict, contact, and physical violence, and made it their own.

For the immigrants as for modern corporate managers, two features of football made it an apt mirror of life. Football is essentially a corporate game, a game of solidarity, an almost socialistic experience; and it represents the obstructions, fierce denials, and violence the immigrants have faced, and still face, at every step in our society. These obstructions are not always polite and gentle; they are often cruel and violent. Each week, 2,000 workers die or suffer serious permanent injury in American industry, more than in any weekly war toll in any war. Bribes and corruption, uneven police protection, and unfairness in hiring and promotion are matters of daily experience. Hardly a Slavic family in western Pennsylvania has not lost at least one member either to death in the mines or mills, or to clubbings or jail or death in the long struggle both to build and to democratize the unions. (The murder of the Yablonskis was only a recent episode in a 100-year war in Pennsylvania.) Football's ritualized, well-controlled violence is a more accurate picture of the actual experience of American life than the pastoral peace of baseball. Baseball may be the longing; football is the daily reality.

Compared to life in Russia, or Poland, or Czechoslovakia, life in America is free, bountiful, and creative; few are not immensely grateful for the haven and the opportunity America uniquely provides. Yet most are not misled by American propaganda and ideology. America never was as innocent as its boosters proclaimed.

Today, many of the privileged claim that they are "losing faith" in America; many others never shared that sort of faith. Many have always known the crueler, meaner, more avaricious faith of America—the hot steel ovens that baked their skins and burned through the thick soles of their shoes; the cramped darkness and flinty edges of rock that cut their knees as they swung short swings in the pitch-black mines; the lung diseases and persistent coughs; the painful long hours in assembly plants. In the beginning, the immigrants had to bribe the foremen even to be put on the line in mill or mine; for many, the first transaction in America was a bribe. All fine talk about honesty in government has a hollow ring to them. Revelations that shock the privileged strike them as elementary. The workers understand America, as the elite do not.

If in their eyes no nation offers a more worthy, beautiful, and free home, it is not because they believe America is innocent. How could they? They have often been its victims. From the redneck in Texas to the barber in Birmingham, from the miner in Youngville, Pennsylvania, to the farmer in Decorah, Iowa, from the black in Hough to the chicano in Los Angeles, ordinary working people know a great deal about dishonesty, unfairness, and that indirect, intangible, institutional violence that great wealth and power inflict upon all, even while providing all with a greater measure of justice and liberty than their ancestral families had ever known. There is no need either to "have faith" in America or to deride it as "Amerika"; it is a just-unjust nation, a free-unfree land, quite human in its dimensions, not at all innocent (unless by innocent one means, as the privileged so often seem to be, naïve). Football is a perfect celebration of this land.

Football is a violent game. So far as possible, the body is protected; the kinds and forms of violence are surrounded by rules and regulations, closely policed; the violence is so far as possible ritualized, contained, limited, canonized. But physical violence is essential to the game. One of the game's greatest satisfactions, indeed, is that it violates the illusion of the enlightened, educated person that violence has been, is, or will be exorcised from human life. Football obliges one to confront the daily reality of force, pressure, and coercion.

To be sure, in the higher circles of bureaucracy, violence is driven far from sight by rationality, courtesy, proper forms. Liberals prefer economic to physical pressures, for the former seem to them less violent, less messy, less incriminating; only their victims feel the force. Here, too, is one of the sources of football's mythic power. In the office, one must be relatively polite to bosses, authorities, and those with power to do one in. They expect what they call loyalty, cooperation, and teamwork, even when they stand between you and your goals. Your inner emotions are often out of line with your outward behavior; you had better keep your cool. By contrast, football allows you to use your body in harmony with your mind. You not only have an inward attitude toward your opponent; you must also physically hit him as hard, as cleanly, as devastatingly as you can. There is intense joy in using one's body as the language of emotion—a kind of serenity and honesty.

Besides, in a culture in which the sentimental virtues are praised, in which Pollyanna sweetness and light are recognized forms of goodness, it is necessary to find tutors who can bring one's hate and rage to light. For every love is made of hate; without rage, love has no life. The source of love, hate, anger, and rage is uniform: deep concern with another, the opposite to indifference. American men, particularly in the more Americanized and educated classes, have a great advantage over women in being allowed swifter and more open access to rage, so that as an emotion it becomes familiar, manageable, creative. ("I'll cut his balls off . . ." expresses the emotion; wisdom, then, is free to find a law-abiding method.) Football ventilates our rage. It is a game built dramatically upon love and solidarity with one's fellows, and on rage mixed with wary respect for one's opponents. As one's own team is solitary, so also is one's enemy. A magnificent concentration of energy is possible. In simple form, one lives out what one must learn to do in more complex form in other phases of one's life: diagnose the patterns, bide one's time, and strike. One reason men are thought to be cool, and women emotional, may be that men's bodies and emotions have been tutored by games like football to carry the energies of rage with patience and familiarity. While girls were being good, boys were beating the shit out of each other. Women lack direct access to part of their own natures. Their rage is no less real; many have been educated away from it.

Much has been written in recent years in contempt (or envy) of machismo. Properly, machismo is an attitude of Latin males. In Northern and Eastern European countries, models of courtesy and gentleness grew up, as in the codes of the knights of England and France. To this day, many athletes are startling in their gentleness and even childlikeness of heart: intelligent, softspoken, quiet, graceful. Think of Frank Gifford, Roger Staubach, Steve Garvey, Sandy Koufax, Hank Aaron, Willie Mays, and hundreds of others. Sports like baseball, football, and basketball *do* demand boldness, daring, risk, and courage. They *do* demand all the images we derive from the male genitalia: balls, getting it up, thrust, holding, driving onward, and so forth. They demand as well the capacity to feel all the powerful emotions of the agon—hatred, agony, distrust, confidence, humiliation, rage, outraged justice, comradeship, contempt, fear, cunning, joy, ecstasy—and to channel these emotions, whatever they may be, into the next task at hand. The male athletic hero is obliged to feel much, and to learn how to be united to his feelings, how to let them flow from the loins or the guts or the bowels (as the Bible puts it) outward through legs, arms, fingers, torso, knees, until the whole person boils with the energies of inner-outer unity.

When your body feels such juices, victory is within grasp; the opposition seems incapable of halting you; the feeling of invincibility oozes up, quiet, strong, and peaceful. Often, seeming miracles take place: fantastic catches, uncannily placed throws or hits, impossible and never before practiced or executed moves. Even the ball seems sometimes to be guided by mystic beams: to jump over, or somehow to get through, an opponent's perfectly placed hands, to defy gravity or physical opposition, to obey pure will.

What is the opposite of machismo? One meets it often among nonathletic males. They seek revenge in later life for the supposed injustices they suffered at the hands of Fate for their earlier athletic inabilities. While they won the lavish praise of parents and teachers, and basked in the successes of the classroom, they had to accept some humane measure of humiliation on the ball field and could not bear it. Others who felt panic when the teacher asked questions they could not understand, whose tongues were tied in knots, whose necks reddened at the implicit accusations of stupidity they felt in the superior glances of so many girls, redeemed their self-respect in sports. Sometimes in life—in the army, perhaps—the athletic gain revenge upon the unathletic. But, mostly, in later life, the nonathletic, nursing childhood injuries to their self-esteem, get even with the athletes, becoming their bosses, managers, paymasters, commanders, civilizers, preachers, and instructors. The non-macho spirit is seldom the spirit of androgynous generosity and gentleness celebrated by our newest visionaries; it is seldom the spirit of a Socrates, a Christ, a Goethe (to name Nietzsche's three chosen "Supermen"). It is most often the spirit of envy, resentment, pettiness, and revenge. The grudging nonathlete is the opposite of Aristotle's "large-souled man." Some recent books attacking the male ideal have roots in envy and spite, in a rage hidden from their authors' consciousness. Football might have lanced such boils earlier, and let the pus pour out before it festered into words.

What is it about football that grabs the soul and makes it pay attention, even though one has seen, perhaps, 400 games already? For one thing, it is the sheer beauty of the uniforms, the color; the surge of energy that runs and crackles through an entire team, four or five dozen men carrying electricity as though they were a single charged circuit. And the contrast of the uniforms with the almost sacred green, that patch of earth for which one feels a certain awe, not knowing what great deeds and excitements have been and yet will be enacted upon it, that piece of soil in some stadium saved from all other use, consecrated, bloodied, focal point of the interventions of the Fates. Then there is the beauty of the choreography, the patterns, the formations, the variations. It is a ballet for knights, for warriors, for athletes, rather than for artists or dancers; but the same mathematical and musical principles underlie it. There is no difficulty in matching music to the perfect formal expressions of the human body exhibited in the grace of football; television does it all the time now, but the heart did it from the beginning.

Finally, there is the intellectual pleasure of the strategy and the aesthetic pleasure of the execution. I find I cannot bear to have someone talk to me when I am concentrating on a game. At first I couldn't understand my own irritation; my nine-year-old would ask a question, a sensible question, and I'd hiss him into silence. Embarrassed, I later realized that what I do in watching football is to call the game myself, like a chess neophyte following Spassky

and Fischer and trying to anticipate each move. My eye
tries to catch injury, fatigue, or slowness on the other
side; intuitively, I am guessing which sorts of plays have
not been working; I look for defensive lines of force and
patterns of response; I focus my eyes abstractly, looking
for zones not adequately defended. Impossible to do, I
know, for one must be on the field to feel the tempo of will
and strength, to see how the lines of instinct and tactics
are flowing at a given time, to sense the tiny differences
that open up unsuspected possibilities. Still, I match my
wits with those of the quarterbacks and coaches. During
the game, my wife has noted, my palms sweat; impossible to gain my attention seriously. (I playact.) After the
game, I am exhausted. Entertainment? It is more like an
ordeal, an exercise, a struggle lived through. And not exactly vicariously.

One of the great mistakes of superficial observers is to
believe that players do all the work while fans merely sit
passive and "vicariously" have things done for them. Not
true. Football, like other arts, awakens what Tony
Schwartz has called "responsive chords." It reaches people differently, awakening in them what is already there.
If you allow football to touch you deeply, and to probe
further and further in the depths of your psyche, you will
find that it can go far more deeply than you ever had
imagined. It is a rich, a truly profound, a stunningly satisfying game. It is deep enough for a mouse to wade in or
an elephant to drown in.

Basketball is continuous action, but football is played as
a set piece, like chess. In chess, opponents alternate single
moves. In football, each side gets four moves in a row,
with a limited goal of 10 yards; if the team can reach that
goal, it gets another four. So football is essentially a game
of strategic and sustained advance; contrariwise, of sustained containment and maneuver for return-strike position. The action is brief, almost instantaneous; the time
for tactical and strategic reflection is three or four, perhaps even ten or twenty times, longer than the time for
action. After each play, the teams again assume formal
distributions. The game advances play by play, as inexorably as chess.

Moreover, action that to the casual eye locks random

and merely brute—huge linemen clashing with huge linemen in a test of strength—is also highly rationalized. Seldom do defenders and aggressors meet merely head to
head. Blocking patterns are worked out with great mathematical sophistication: *from which angle* to hit a defender
(or to loop past him), *at which part of his body* to apply the
counterbalancing or the unbalancing force, *in which lanes
or angles of activity* an opponent may be disregarded as irrelevant to the course of the play being run. Once, in a
critical championship game, a defensive back of the
Cleveland Browns, Bernie Parrish, made charts of a certain pass play that was a favorite of the opposition. For
each occasion the opponent had used that play all year, he
drew a chart on blocked paper such that each block represented a square yard. Then he superimposed all his
graphs over a very strong light, so that the angle and the
distance between the passer and the receiver could be
clearly measured. Since this play was done by instinct
and precision timing, by memory rather than by observation, the pattern turned out to be precisely measurable.
When the actual game began, by pacing off the distance
mentally when he assumed position (not revealing that he
knew the precise set of spaces into which a successful
pass had to go), Bernie Parrish had only to think along
with the opposing quarterback to guess when the favorite
play would be called. When at last it was, as it was sure to
be, he made two interceptions and knocked another pass
down. Thus, on three separate occasions he was in-
strumental in taking the ball away from the opposition
and giving it to his own team. Cleveland won the game.

Often, it is by such discriminations and precise adjustments that a team gains an advantage over well-matched
(or even superior) opposition and carries off an improbable victory. Notre Dame's brilliant defensive adjustment
against Alabama in the 1975 Orange Bowl, bringing an
extra defensive player up to the line to halt the Alabama
option run and daring the quarterback to pass into the
undefended spaces left downfield, enabled a weaker and
even slower team to defeat a great, amazingly fast, and
considerably more talented team. It is a basic error to
think that bigger teams, or faster teams, or more talented
teams always win. Football is a game of many factors—

wind, field conditions, the bounces of the erratic ball (purposely designed to be an instrument of Fate), a skillful job of diagnosis, sharper or harder-hitting execution, an insuperable *will* to win, psychological readiness to perform each play perfectly, concentration. The brilliance of victory seldom derives simply from what is visible to a casual observer. Football bears mathematical and geometric analysis in terms of lines, angles, spaces, flows; psychological analysis in terms of attitudes and energies; and military analysis in terms of feints, envelopments, and strategic designs. Football weds to a clash of forces as colorful as a medieval joust the pleasures of chess or military tactics.

Each formation on the field has its strengths and weaknesses, its possibilities and limits. Some players excel in one range of possibilities but do not execute well in another. So marrying the talent to the design, and the execution to the psychological and physical occasion, is half the skill. Intelligence counts in football more than brawn. Even when two hulking giants battle each other on the line, their contest is not so much one of brute strength— although strength and endurance are critical—as of cunning, speed, and tactical design. Those bruising giants learn by experience and instinct and even by studying game films how to feint, trick, and surprise their opponents, and how to protect themselves against being tricked. Football is very much a game of angles. Even a huge strong man cannot bring down a smaller man unless he hits him in a proper vector of force; from some angles, force is expended without effect. Thus, lighter men use speed, timing, agility, and changes of direction to baffle forces they could not successfully attack directly. The play of wit in football is perhaps the greatest of its pleasures. Such play is dangerous; the danger heightens achievement because miscalculation, inattention, carelessness, or sheer chance can bring broken bones and snapped sinews, bruised flesh and muscles torn from their native resting place.

Football is a fitting insult to the illusions of an enlightened, liberal age, an age as cruel as, or crueler than, any in history, but eager to maintain a public image of reason, nonviolence, and democratic process (as if these were the opposite to violence, not simply its more civil and corrigible forms). Football announces the continuity between contemporary man and his most ancient ancestors. It is a scandal to the enlightened, whose hypocrisy it exposes. As there is no rage like that of the pacifist insisting on nonviolence, so in football there is no peace and resolution and harmony like that of the men who fashion from violence, rage, and even hatred a dance of utter beauty, a triumph, a redemption.

Some there are who add that football is authoritarian or fascist. Usually they are themselves exponents of socialism, planning, interdependence, federal regulation, federal intervention, and the full enforcement of their own vision of the liberal and humane life. Often they are in the managerial class, the top 10 percent of the population, the effective rulers of both the United States and large portions of the planet. Since they seldom experience in their own flesh the bite of their own plans and laws and ordinances, they do not see the covert violence millions experience at their hands. They therefore do not recognize that millions of those who love football see *them* as the authorities, the enforcers of culture and social forms, the brass, the coaches. They do not see that in hitting an opposing linesman with bone-reverberating blocks, the combatants are vicariously hitting back at *them*.

Football is no more authoritarian than publishing or the television news. In a shake-up on a magazine or in a publishing house, half the staff may be fired on the spot; it has been known to happen. (Careers in such professions do not average a mere five years; and sudden trades without notice rarely occur. The business side of professional football—rather than the game itself—leaves much to be desired, as we must note in chapters sixteen and seventeen.) Like any corporate group, a team must move with a single will, composed voluntarily and eagerly of the strength of each individual will. Football coaches speak often of love, team play, fellowship, solidarity. An aggregate of individuals, however talented, is not yet a team; when the *click* of community occurs, when the many grains become one bread, the transformation is tangible. To live in a community is one of the most precious human achievements. Men have always rejoiced in it, especially in sports.

Looking back on their experience in athletics—and sometimes, too, at the camaraderie of war, of fellows in danger of their lives—many men find that nothing in their lives has since equaled that pure and high imbibing of the communitarian ideal. For many Americans, as for the Greeks, athletics remain the field of experience closest attuned to human perfection, where *beauty* of formal action meets the form of the *good*, where the utmost *individual achievement* is linked to perfect *solidarity* with others, where the word for "good" means at once beautiful, true, and brotherly. He who has not drunk deep of the virtues of football has missed one of the closest brushes with transcendence that humans are allowed.

A word should also be added about coaches. The vision coaches have of football is not that of the players. Coaches are hired to produce winning teams, not to play the game. If they are sensitive to the materials of their art, their viewpoint may approximate the players'. In general, however, their angle of vision is and must be different. It is true that for coaches "winning is the only thing." No matter how much they enjoy the game, coaches are fired if they do not produce winners. But players go on playing, win or lose; and on the average, all lose as often as they win. There is no such thing in football as an athlete or a coach who has never lost; and for as long as a man never loses, he fails to comprehend half the strength of the game. Over a lifetime, playing for different teams, subject to the vicissitudes of favor, attention, and chance, a player has no alternative but to count finally on himself, to measure his performance in his own terms, to learn to identify accurately his own achievements and limits, to find pleasure in meeting his own goals.

Often, in victory, a player will know that his own performance was beneath his ideals; in defeat, that he never played better. Victory tastes sweet; defeat is like death. But the seasons march on, next week is another game. Winning is a priceless and lovely thing, but for players it cannot be the only thing, for losing is a very large part of every career. At its depth, indeed, football like other sports is a confrontation with death, whose athletic shape is defeat, part of whose point is that life is stronger than death. One *must* lose in order to know the game well, just as one must learn how to live in the midst of the death that daily pulls all of us down, drags with the weight of flesh upon our striving bones.

In football, excellence is everything. Winning is a crown the Fates alone decide. It is good to be smiled upon by the Fates. But many champions have known the more solid satisfaction of having spent every ounce of one's energy in reaching one's own highest pitch of excellence—one could have done no better. Millions play football with pleasure; only a few make the team, are drafted by the pros, become stars. Millions find satisfaction in their own level of excellence. The game is large and spacious, and even the most humble player has known the pleasure of a block well laid, a surprise well designed, a single impossible one-handed catch, the recovery of a fumble in the opponent's end zone. In football, everyone is a hero for at least a moment. Football is an equal opportunity occasion.

Some have tried to see the myth of football as essentially capitalist, possessive, colonialist. The myth, as they see it, is a myth of acquiring territory, gaining yards. But one does not win a football game by gaining yards or squatting on territory. One wins in one way only: by breaking through to score. After a score, every yard gained is relinquished and play resumes, with the other side given an equal chance. Many teams outgain their opponents, or hold the ball longer, but lose.

The game requires two different sets of skills: a defense to contain the other team, and an offense to solve the other's defenses and to score. One could imagine a game in which the most highly prized value were suppression. In that case, the team with the most impenetrable defense during an entire year would be awarded the national championship. But what enlivens fans and players, what awakens their symbolic love, is not defense but offense: scoring frequently enough to win each game in succession, however narrowly. The "Four Horsemen" of Notre Dame were extravagantly praised; it was necessary to work overtime to win attention for the "Seven Blocks of

Granite." The fans are excited by offensive play, especially of the sort that exhibits sudden and explosive liberation—swift and total breakthrough, overcoming as many obstacles as possible. Praise for offensive stars comes easily; defensive work lacks glamour.

Because football has a strategic side, like chess, it is spoken of in military metaphor. The hostility of many to the war in Vietnam, to the military generally, and to capitalism led some to fix on football as the symbol of their own self-hatred as Americans. "Dehumanizing" has come to be their favorite word for football.

What is human? What has the human experience been in history? A fully "humanized" world, gentle and sweet and equitable, has never yet been seen on earth. It has been approximated best, perhaps, in the gentle, lawned, peaceful suburbs of the American professional class and in the quiet groves of lawn-carpeted campuses. Here hunger, violence, illiteracy, poverty, and catastrophe have been kept out by neat hedges—and by the rational, peaceful, liberal, and utopian dreams of a generation that had known the Depression. For this world, or at least for its most sensitive spirits, football is a flagrant contradiction. Neanderthal, they say. Beef on the hoof. Military. Authoritarian.

The discovery that this world is an evil place, marked by an egregious lack of fairness, by violence and greed, has come as a late-arriving shock to many who never grasped the meaning of the ancient symbol of "original sin"—that you should not trust anybody, over or under thirty years of age, and least of all yourself. Football is a celebration of a not innocent and not rational and not liberal human condition. That is its attraction. William Phillips caught part of this point in *Commentary* magazine:

> Football is not only the most popular sport, it is the most intellectual one. It is in fact the intellectuals' secret vice. Not politics, not sex, not pornography, but football, and not college football, but the real thing. Pro ball is the opium of the intellectuals. . . . Much of its popularity is due to the fact that it makes respectable the most primitive feelings about violence, patriotism, manhood. The similarity to war is unmistakable: each game is a battle with its own game-plan, each season a campaign, the whole thing a series of wars.

Football strategy is like military strategy. The different positions, each with its own function but coordinated with the rest of the team, are like the various branches of the armed services. There is even a general draft. And one is loyal to one's country—according to geography and the accident of birth. . . . Pro football legitimizes untamed feelings. . . .

To which Larry Merchant replied that football is one of the least intelligible and, therefore, least intellectual of games known to man (he prefers baseball), and that fans grow callous to the violence.

It is not, I think, that fans grow callous; what they love in football is precisely what the soft part of the liberal world will not admit into consciousness: that human life, in Hegel's phrase, is a butcher's bench. Think what happened to the Son of God, the Prince of Peace; what happened in the Holocaust; what has happened in recent wars, revolutions, floods, and famines in South Vietnam, Indonesia, Bangladesh, Cambodia, and Nigeria. The human animal suffers enormous daily violence. Football is an attempt to harness violence, to formalize it, to confine it within certain canonical limits, and then to release it in order to wrest from it a measure of wit, beauty, and redemption. Phillips's stress on the military metaphors is, I think, too heavy. Military analogs are present, as they are in chess (the Russian national sport). But the violence of the mines, the mills, the factories, the ghettos, the corporations, and of nature itself is also present.

We do not need to believe the rhetoric of the National Football League. We do not, after all, believe the advertising of any corporation, or the propaganda of "peace-loving" liberation armies (or imperial armies) of the world. It is not likely that attendance at the liturgies of football purges violence from the human breast. It is not likely that anything known to man or God can do that, so long as human beings are free to do their will, howsoever unenlightened or enlightened it may be. No liberal has exorcised violence from life. Neither has any radical. Nor did Gandhi, or Tolstoy, or A. J. Muste, or any other bold spirit of pacifism. Moreover, football is essentially socialist in structure, not capitalist; it is built on solidarity, and team play, on planning and computer analysis. It is the symbolic expression of a corporate society, in which the individual plays a chastened, checked, and disciplined role. It is its *socialism* that offends the hedonists, not its laissez-faire or rugged individualism.

George Sauer of the New York Jets spoke after his premature retirement of the intolerable disciplines of football life—and many in socialist Eastern Europe might grasp his meaning clearly. "There is little freedom. The system molds you into something easy to manipulate. It is a sad thing to see a forty-year-old man being checked into bed at night. It is personally embarrassing to realize you are part of this." Individual choice is better, of course. Football has become so competitive that coaches are loath to take chances, loath to allow players to live any way they choose. They try to control every possible contingency. They try to legislate against every possible abuse. Few wink at even a top pro's carousings as Knute Rockne did at George Gipp's. No doubt, the authority of the "system" has become too heavy. No doubt, even in the colleges, the game has become work rather than play; it is now, for the players, a profession rather than a sport. About all these things, we may have our own reservations. The point is that football hardly celebrates the capitalist virtues exalted in the pages of the *Wall Street Journal*. Its virtues are those of the early unions: brotherhood, lovely when voluntary, and enforced by clubbing scabs and strikebreakers when it wasn't.

Sauer himself recognizes the spiritual beauties of socialism, if not the disciplines:

> I like football. It is a framework around which you can see the dynamics of a player working together with other players, which can be a beautiful thing to watch. When people enjoy what they're doing it can be ecstatic. But the way it's structured, the intrinsic values of sport are choked off. It has been despiritualized, the profane applied to the sacred. Its inherent worth—doing it for itself, meeting challenges, the brotherhood on a team—is denied by treating the opponent as an enemy, not an antagonist. The game can touch you as a human being if you are permitted to touch others as human beings. But this is difficult when you have a Vince Lombardi type of coach hollering at you to hate the other guy, who's really just like you in a different colored uniform.

An immigrant type of coach like Vince Lombardi knows the other guy is just like Sauer, and indeed he may try to trade for him. But for the purposes of *this* game, it is important to make one's hatred and one's rage conscious, to draw energy from them, to channel them, to focus them upon one's opponent. It would be a lie to block and tackle viciously out of love. There is, of course, a difference in the psychological demands the game makes on deep receivers like Sauer, whose task is to break free and keep away from others, and on interior linemen faced with equivalent physical energy opposing them on every play. The latter need to find emotion stronger than their opponents'. Within this formal ritual, hatred is permitted, even nourished. That is half the game's forbidden pleasure. The other half is to have the fellows in the other shirts just where you want them, and then, like George Blanda facing Cleveland, to boot the ball right through the uprights, and watch them eat their hearts out. Life is unfair, and symbolic victories do not really right all its injustices. They are no less sweet.

No doubt, in heaven, football will seem a little lacking in peace, harmony, gentleness, and love. It is not likely to be the sport most favored by the Almighty. But in this vale of tears, this world of struggle and strife, football is an almost revelatory liturgy. It externalizes the warfare in our hearts and offers us a means of knowing ourselves and wresting some grace from our true natures.

If you think football is a violent liturgy, reflect upon the Eucharist.

SPORTSREEL

From Ice to Sun: Hockey, Soccer

Year: 1933. George Preston Marshall has made a fortune in the laundry business in Washington, D.C., and has purchased ownership of the Redskins. Professional football does not yet amount to much. The college game has the nation's loyalty. Marshall persuades the other owners to make three basic changes in the league rules: (1) Have a championship game; focus the season's ending. (2) The old rule says that passers must stand at least 5 yards behind the line of scrimmage; allow them to pass from any point behind the line of scrimmage. (3) Move the goalposts to the goal line, 10 yards closer than in the college game, and back to their original location.

On December 17, 1933, the Chicago Bears played the New York Giants in the first championship game, under the new rules. "Automatic Jack" Manders kicked three field goals, aided by the change. Bronko Nagurski twice faked his crushing assault into the line, leapt up at the last moment, and passed over the line to Bill Karr for touchdowns (once the pass went to Bill Hewitt, who lateraled to Karr). All 23 Bear points benefited by the new rules. In a seesaw game, playing more conventionally, the Giants scored 21 points, the Bears winning in the last minutes on Nagurski's jump pass.

"The way I look at it," Mr. Marshall told the owners, "we're in show business. I want to give the public the kind of show they want."

But what kind of show does the public want? And why? In different cultures, people find different skills exciting. There is nothing inherently spectacular in catching a ball or swinging a bat (or in running, tackling, shooting a ball in a basket). Jugglers in Hungary, Jim Murray notes, show greater skills. Watching a practice isn't much fun.

What adds the magic, the attraction, the excitement? The form given to the individual activities, the symbolic echoes awakened by the form of the contest itself.

Marshall thought that long runs, sudden passes, options and surprises, and frequent scores would give the public greater pleasure. Some publics might find these boring; they might enjoy straight, grinding line play. But in the United States, one hypothesis goes, the essence of the symbolic form of football is liberation: breaking away, running for daylight, escaping containment.

The defensive team tries to hold tight. The pleasure of the game comes from breaking through. It is like breaking through the frustrations of one's own life. Football is the liturgy of liberation. One key to winning football, of course, is strong defensive play—less glamorous, less exciting, but indispensable. One must prevent the other side from dominating play. There are no "innings" in football; one team might control the ball for most of the game. Defense is critical. A defensive unit can score on interceptions, fumbles, a safety; ordinarily, the offensive team must score the points. Only the team that scores can win. For victory does not consist in holding the opposition to zero (although it might so consist, if that were the symbolic value). Breaking through to score is the primary pleasure of football; containing the other side is secondary. One can be flawless in defense without winning. To win one must score. To ring the symbolic bell with fully satisfying reverberation, one must break from containment and be free. Across the goal line comes a dance of liberation.

In this sense, football has long been the favorite of the poor and the oppressed; its symbols are theirs. Moreover, the sheer physicality of the game also favors them. In physical nature, there is an equality that in language, status, culture, and sophisticated legal technique seldom obtains. The dominant classes have invented the law and the system. To make them work for outsiders is difficult, doubly difficult because they are outsiders and because they do not know the style or the technique. But if the contest pits antagonists together man-to-man, as football does, there is hope of symbolic victory.

The white race, in particular, seems to relish games of

direct physical combat, as in football, rugby, Irish football, and hockey. Whites of the American South and
white immigrants from Southern and Eastern Europe
have rejoiced in football as few others have. The occasion
in the 1920s when a team from Alabama went to Washington State and earned a victory is still remembered in a
state consistently put down by its supposed betters.
Blacks in America have also found the game satisfying—
black players, perhaps, more than fans, whose allegiance
to basketball seems unchallenged. One of the special pleasures of football for the oppressed has been its deep imperative to hit back with one's entire body, to express
one's rage with total physical intensity, or to outsmart
and to evade, against odds. After its upper-class begin-
nings, football soon became the game of the poor rather
than of the privileged. It best suits the tough, the hungry,
the repressed.

If we ask, though, why hockey, an equally physical
game, still has not caught on in the United States, contrasting symbolic values come to light. What is the basic
underlying myth dramatized in hockey? It is a much more
violent game than football. Watching a game with an eye
for its dramatic line, one can't help noticing hockey's
speed, its *teamwork,* its *formal* plays, its *violent contact* and
exceptionally hot *temper tantrums*—and, finally, the exhilaration of *slapping a tiny rubber puck into a narrow, low net.*
In some ways, the dramatic lines are like those of basketball: the speed, the team play, the blending of formal pattern and improvisation. Yet in hockey a team scores seldom; the reinforcement of success is infrequent.
Deprivation is protracted. A score of 6–4 would constitute
a high-scoring game. One notes the death mask on the
face of the goalie, guardian of the net. The game is played
on ice. Its symbolic matrix lies in the lands of snows, bliz-
zards, and dark freezing nights. Hockey is a Slavic sport,
Eastern European, Scandinavian, Canadian. One gets
suggestions of an Ice Age once again smothering the
planet. One senses the sheer celebration of hot blood
holding out against the cold, of the vitality of the warm
human body, of exuberant speed rejoicing in its own
heat, of violence and even the sight of red blood on white

ice as a sign of animal endurance. There are stories about young hockey players saving as trophies the stitches pulled from their own healed wounds. "Twelve more stitches, dad!" the teenager boasts, entering home after a bloody game. Against the possibility of freezing, against the omnipresent threat to human survival, hockey celebrates the heat and passion of survival. *Take the worst, accept, and conquer. Give as well as get. Take it to them.* If hockey is, with chess, the national sport of Russia, let the world recognize the fierce physical resolve of peoples toughened by their climate: let them remember Stalingrad.

The symbolism of hockey, in America, is regional. Yet the game has such excitements and so many parallels to other, already familiar games that one can sense the possibility of its attracting large American participation. Ice rinks, now available all year round, are going up even in regions where it never snows. Youngsters everywhere, for six seasons at least, were exposed to the game's excellence through television, and began to imitate it, sometimes as street hockey on roller skates. One may expect their suburban parents to want to remove some of the "violence" and "brutality" from the game, exactly those qualities that have made hockey a symbol of endurance, passion, warmth, and humanity elsewhere.

Hockey is rather like another game played with a net, the most widely played game in the world, the game par excellence of the southern hemisphere and of Europe, soccer. The soccer field is somewhat larger than a football field; it suggests an almost infinite flat plain. The net is very large. The goaltender cannot possibly cover all of it; like all the other players, he must run and leap. Except for his, the use of hands is virtually outlawed. Agility on one's feet is the essence of the game. Football, basketball, and baseball are games of manual dexterity, as befits societies in which manufacture and the arts of the hand have for centuries been crucial to economic progress. *Homo faber*—man the maker—has built the northern hemisphere with hands. The game of the southern hemisphere (played with passion also in Holland, Germany, Great Britain, Italy, and other nations of Europe) is a game of the feet. (Did their colonies abroad whet the European appetite for soccer? or the surviving passion of Caesar's Roman legions?)

The images surrounding soccer are those of Africa, Brazil, Pakistan, and India: green fields, leisure, space, effortless running and grace, freedom, an almost total absence of violence or force, an almost total commitment to fluid form, to kinesis, to the patterns in motion of a unit of runners. Running and passing are the steady pleasures of the game; the sudden appearance of the great players just as they are needed, flashing in from out of nowhere to execute a perfect kick, suggests the intelligence and instinct of anticipation. Soccer is freedom and flow, and it weaves its graceful tension back and forth, up and down the field, resolving it only infrequently with sudden charges upon the goal and the slashing, spinning projection of the ball, by head or foot, into the large net.

Hockey is swift, soccer graceful. Hockey is physical, brutal, violent; soccer evasive, flowing, quietly impassioned. The net in hockey is small and narrow, almost entirely blocked by the goalie, and the puck whizzes toward it almost as swiftly and invisibly as a bullet; the net in soccer is larger than a mother's arms, ample, the goaltender small in comparison, and the slower flight of the large, black-white ball leaves a visual image almost as permanent as the trail of a jet.

Soccer is an almost birdlike game; its players all but fly, their movements are so graceful, silken, almost leisurely across the expanse from which one watches them. It is an altogether poetic game. Men and women alike can play it. It seems to be growing in America. Yet it has never quite caught on.

For one thing, soccer lacks the physical satisfactions of the harsh body contact of football and basketball (which is only in fiction a noncontact sport). Unlike football and baseball, which proceed from formal play to formal play, soccer flows steadily. Basketball, which flows almost as relentlessly as soccer, requires in its way a higher component of precise strategy and timing, because floor space is so limited and because scores are fifty times more frequent than in soccer. Americans seem attracted to games with greater physical aggression than soccer calls for, with closer tactical control of movements, and with a greater number of small and detailed physical activities—the blocking patterns in football, the grips and precise acts of baseball, the stationary and moving picks in basketball. Soccer requires dozens of skillful moves with feet and head and arms, but the fluidity and spaciousness of the game allow, it seems, for wider scope of initiative and judgment. In American sports, the margin of error seems narrower and the degree of control seems tighter; soccer could not be called a "game of inches" in the way all three American games might be. It is, so to say, a game of feet.

Perhaps Americans too little value feet. Perhaps soccer might become a sport in which American women excel, taking it to themselves as their own. In California and elsewhere, the primary schools seem to be seeing that the game has special values for the young. It could grow very quickly.

6

The Black Myth:
Basketball as Jazz

THE INNER LIFE of baseball is chamber music, slow, pastoral, each instrument distinct, intensely grasped. As Roger Angell notes, one recalls years later each physical detail of every player, each characteristic motion: the curious waddle of Babe Ruth; Maury Wills racing short and swift down to second; the long, loping, watery strides of Willie Davis. Baseball players are watched one by one. Those who are not connoisseurs of every individual are bored by the (to them) tedious tempo of baseball. They want grand opera, not a string quartet. The game of baseball is civilized, mathematical, and operates upon the tiny watchlike springs of infinite detail—a step covertly taken to the left here, a batter choking up just an inch there, a pitcher shortening his step upon delivery by 2 or 3 inches. One must have a passion for detail to appreciate baseball. One must love the interchange of various rhythms, the slow hot rustic pace of a long afternoon, the *adagio* of a hit, the *furioso* of a double steal. Millions who never go to concert halls hear concerts in their hearts. Vivaldi is not a rightfielder for the Mets; all the Mets absorb his music in their veins as the long hot season wends its ancient rural way through training camp, 162 games (not counting the All-Star game and two or three for charity), the playoffs, and the *finale* of the Series. A music that returns, year after year, with the generations.

Football is the *Overture of 1812*; it is Berlioz's *The Dam-*

nation of Faust, Ravel's *Bolero*, Beethoven's Fifth. It builds in great heavy tones like a full orchestra; its plays are as measured and as carefully diagramed as movements in a conductor's concert book. Blocks; tackles; sweeping counters left and right; the emergence of a one on one and counterpoint; the overriding melody first of the violins, then flutes, or perhaps bassoons. Football games build like symphonies toward climactic resolution. The quarters of the game each have their tempo. Nothing is easier than to synchronize the score of a full-bodied, orchestrated concert with the drama of the one-and-many swelling and contracting of a football game.

Basketball, a game of constant movement and a thousand actions, is a difficult game to remember; Leonard Koppett makes this and other excellent points in *All About Basketball*. Football is a series of set plays, as clear in our minds as moves in chess; and the high drama of a baseball game is often distilled in a single pitch, catch, throw, or hit. We remember baseball and football actions as though the players were etched upon our minds like figures on a distant green. In basketball, by contrast, we remember movement, style, flair, but only occasionally a single play. Perhaps we recall the seventh game of the Lakers-Knicks playoff on May 8, 1970, after the Lakers had pounded the Knicks in the sixth game. Willis Reed was injured and out, it seemed, for the season; and we may remember Reed walking stiffly to the floor for that final game just minutes before warm-ups were concluded; remember the sustained ovation; remember his stiff jumps as he put the first two shots of the game through and then had to leave the game in pain; remember that the Knicks, lifted high by his courage, went on to win game seven, bringing to New York basketball a new perspective. But it is hardly ever, even here, individual plays one remembers. A basketball game flows past like a river, like a song.

In basketball as in no other sport, Koppett also notes, the referee is part of the drama. Decisions of the scorer and the timer are critical and affect the outcomes of countless games every year. But the referee is an agent, an actor; he affects the changing tissue of the drama every instant. He cannot call every infraction, but he must control the game. He needs to gain the players' and the crowds' attention, respect, and emotional cohesion. Thus, referees like Pat Kennedy, Sid Borgia, and Mendy Rudolph in the NBA became better known than many of the players. Each blew the whistle in a range of different tones and styles; each had a repertoire of operatic gestures; each had an energy and physical exuberance that added to the total drama. All won respect for coolness under withering emotion.

Basketball players are visible in every action, Koppett notes, and easily singled out by the spectators as football players are not. They handle the ball scores of times and are physically involved in every moment of offense and defense, as baseball players are not. They are subject to many more flukes than baseball or football players, for they pass and run at high speed constantly, forcing dozens of errors, breaks, and opportunities. "Don't shoot!" the coach screams in despair, his voice trailing off to "Nice shot" as he sits down.

Basketball is a difficult game to report in the paper. Too many plays are "decisive." The tempo and flavor of the game—each game having its own character—are difficult to catch succinctly. The highest scorer may not have made the major contribution. Spot defensive play by substitutes may have changed the flow—a credit difficult to verify. Small adjustments made by the two teams to change the character of play may seem too boring to recount. Music critics covering jazz or rock face similar difficulties, without having to cover 82 performances a season, or being assigned 400 words to cover each.

Basketball, like football, is team play; it is of the essence of the game to develop a unit that moves like a single person, like five fingers on a hand. "Hit the open man!" the cry of the Knicks, is an injunction to a single consciousness. Teams move in patterns, in rhythms, at high velocity; one must watch the game abstractly, not focusing on any single individual alone, but upon, as it were, the blurred and intricate designs woven by the paths through which all five together cast a spell upon the opposition. The eye watches five men at once, delighting in their unity, groaning at their lapses of concentration. Yet basketball moves so rapidly and so depends on the versatility of each individual in escaping from the defense intended to contain him that the game cannot be choreographed in advance. Twelve men are constantly in movement (counting two referees), the rebounds of the ball are unpredictable, the occasions for passing or dribbling or shooting must be decided instantaneously; basketball players must be improvisers. They have a score, a melody; each team has its own appropriate tempo, a style of game best suited to its talents; but within and around that general score, each individual is free to elaborate as the spirit moves him. Basketball is jazz: improvisatory, free, individualistic, corporate, sweaty, fast, exulting, screeching, torrid, explosive, exquisitely designed for letting first the trumpet, then the sax, then the drummer, then the trombonist soar away in virtuoso excellence. It was not always so.

Basketball was originally invented as a white man's game, indeed as a game of Scottish Calvinist inspiration, at a college for Presbyterian missionaries in Springfield, Massachusetts. It was a winter game, an indoor game, invented in New England as a means to keep young men at the YMCA gymnasium interested in their daily exercises, when the weather drove them indoors. The idea behind the game was moral, Christian, and hygienic: active clean living through vigorous exercise, played "for fun." The game's inventor, the Reverend James Naismith, did not believe in playing to win. He used basketball as a means of indulging the desire of the restless young males in his gym class for "pleasures and thrills." They were bored with exercises. Exercise was good for them. They *should* exercise. So he spent some days in December 1891 dreaming up a game to sweeten their moral duty.

He began with two simple notions. Almost all team games required a ball. A small ball requires some other instrument—bat, racquet, stick, club—to propel it. A large ball would be safer. Next, he decided against allowing players to run with the ball; he wanted no blocking, tackling, or physical aggression. He wanted a game as free of passion, as clean, as healthful as he could invent. Bodily contact would constitute a "foul" and would be penalized. But what to do with the ball? Thinking of the dramatic line at the heart of every other sport he knew,

Naismith knew he wanted a clear objective, a goal the young men could work for. To remove the influence of force from the game, he decided against a goal that touched the ground vertically, as in football or soccer. He would put the goal on a horizontal plane, so the ball would have to enter it in an arc—by grace rather than by force. Almost immediately, he recognized that placing the goal about 10 feet high would prevent defenders from using force to keep the ball away. He put up two goals, so that each side would both defend and attack, like armies. At first, he allowed as many persons on a side as anyone wanted; he thought nine ideal, but more were "more fun." He imagined the nine distributed, as it were, in zones of defense and offense. The first game was played January 20, 1892. By the fall of 1892, after only ten months, the game had spread all across the United States, from Maine to San Francisco. Girls played it from the very first year—Dr. Naismith married the first woman to play it, Maude Sherman of Springfield. The missionaries spread it within a year to at least a dozen countries. Never did a game grow so fast.

Naismith's original thirteen rules, and their slow modification down the years, envisaged a game of passing, calculation, and team strategy. Even after five players were seen to be the optimal number, game action was slow, deliberate, stolid; like chess. The shot was careful, feet planted, two-handed, set. Scores of 14–11 and 17–13 were typical; seldom did a team exceed 30 points. By 1914, Frank McCormack of New York organized the first professional team, the Original Celtics; "World Champions" was emblazoned on their green jerseys. After World War I, the Original Celtics—a German, a Pole, a Dutchman, a Jew, and an Irishman—played a traveling schedule of 150 games a year, taking on all comers anywhere. They offered to yield their jerseys to any team that could beat them twice. No team could. They seldom lost ten in a year. They were so good, from 1921 to 1929, that fans lost interest in seeing them always win. Their star, Nat Holman, introduced a degree of trickiness, fakes, and feints that the game had never seen; he averaged 10 points a game, phenomenal at the time.

Three other players were to have a decisive impact

upon the underlying possibilities of the game, all of them sons of immigrants: Angelo Luisetti of Stanford, George Mikan of the Minneapolis Lakers, and Bob Cousy of the Boston Celtics. All three started out unwanted or made fun of. They saw and realized possibilities in basketball no one had ever seen. They changed the *mythos* of the game.

On December 30, 1936, Long Island University carried a 43-game winning streak into Madison Square Garden. Eighteen thousand startled fans saw a whole new conception of the game. For Hank Luisetti of Stanford shot with one hand, a method the Eastern press and coaches had ridiculed—until they saw it. Luisetti overwhelmed LIU. His precision was startling; his quick shot was almost impossible to block. Coaches and players all around the country buzzed. Luisetti later scored 50 points in a single game. The game was never to be the same. Experiment after experiment broke out. Running and feinting became more important.

Beginning in 1947, a six-foot-ten, 250-pound center led professional basketball into a new era. Rejected by Notre Dame as "too clumsy," Big George Mikan went to De Paul. During the National Invitational Tournament in Madison Square Garden he scored 53 points against Rhode Island State, the exact number managed by the entire opposition. In the pros, Mikan's pivots, strength, deadly hook shot, and conception of movement so dominated the game that the rules had to be changed to contain him. The lane under the basket in which an offensive player could remain for only three seconds was widened from 6 to 12 feet, to keep the big man farther from the basket. Mikan's accuracy was so great that the change hardly affected his performance. Mikan revolutionized the game because he not only scored with authority but pivoted, faked, and set up other teammates in plays of breathtaking complexity. The game became more and more a game of running, feinting, contriving—and scoring. The tempo quickened.

But what basketball was most waiting for was Bob Cousy. Cousy, son of a New York taxi driver who had immigrated from France, had unusually long and supple arms, long fingers, extraordinary peripheral vision, and the fastest reflexes the game had ever seen. Only 6' 1", he left crowds breathless with his feinting, faking, deception, and ball control while leading Holy Cross College in Worcester to national prominence. Cousy spent hour after hour learning to make a basketball obey his will. He could dribble it behind his back or between his legs; he could pass behind his back or behind his neck (in a move not seen before or since); he could leap in the air and make four or five fakes before passing, shooting, or spinning the ball precisely where he chose. It seemed that he could see behind him and could think with lightning rapidity. His self-possession—the base of all deception—was unsurpassed. He played his best under pressure and in the last few seconds. Once he scored 5 points in eight seconds, to send a game into overtime. Countless times he took—and made—a game's deciding shot. His forte was threading brilliant passes to open teammates for easy scores. For years he led the league in assists.

At first, pulling Cousy's name in a draw, the Boston Celtics felt cheated. Mikan had made teams conscious of the need for big men. But soon Cousy showed a new way to win the game. Joe Lapchick, one of the Original Celtics and then coach of the New York Knicks when Cousy played, said "Bob Cousy is the best I've ever seen. He always shows you something new, something you've never seen before. Any mistake against him and you pay the full price. He's quick, he's smart, he's tireless, he has spirit, and he is probably the best finisher in sports." In 1962, a poll of sports editors of 100 major daily papers named Cousy the National Basketball Association's all-time top player. "Cousy saved pro basketball," one veteran nodded. "Until he came along, the game followed a rigid pattern. It was the practice of every team to work the ball into the giant pivot man and he turned around and hooked a basket. Cousy changed all that; he inserted an extra something. The fans ate up his razzle-dazzle and all the clubs took the hint."

No one taught Cousy his tricks. For years, to develop equal skills with both hands, he did everything left-handed, carrying books, opening doors, turning keys. He studied, thought, experimented, practiced endlessly. He learned new moves before others could learn his old. Everyone who saw him leap, spin, dribble, pass, or shoot in every imaginable position could never watch, or play, the game the same way again. And thus basketball, once a game of artillery, became a game of cavalry. From stationary strategy and deliberation, it unleashed the individual player for improvisation and virtuosity. The music of the game was discovered to be jazz. Leonard Koppett writes: "Black players were still few, so it was Cousy who displayed a truth that was already a cultural norm among the blacks and would be, eventually throughout the game: that in basketball, style is as important to the fan as sheer result."

Cousy was soon joined in Boston by Bill Russell, a great, agile, and high-spirited black who had played at San Francisco State. The team play of the Celtics set a standard for speed and brilliance that still stands. Russell's swiftness, leaps, shot blocking, and offensive rebounding strength and Cousy's magical assists paced the team to a record of five out of six annual national championships. The Celtics did not dominate the game; their competition was equal to them. But in the clutch, few teams could prevail against them. Elgin Baylor of the Los Angeles Lakers—the best forward in the history of the game—did score 63 points against the Celtics in a championship game.

Soon more and more blacks were entering the game at every level, perhaps in part because of the great urban migration of blacks after World War II. The game came to be thought of as the "city game." The tempo was now the tempo of the city. The 24-second rule forced teams to shoot quickly or to surrender the ball. The style was the style of the city: sophisticated, cool, deceptive, swift, spectacular, flashy, smooth. But the mythos became more than urban. It became in a symbolic and ritual way uniquely black.

For basketball, although neither invented by blacks nor played only by blacks, came to allow the mythic world of the black experience to enter directly, with minimal change, into American life. The game is corporate like black life; improvisatory like black life; formal and yet casual; swift and defiant; held back, contained, and then exploding; full of leaps and breakaway fluid sprints.

No one can mistake the difference in cultural running styles between, say, Ernie DiGregorio, John Havlicek, Walt Frazier, Bill Bradley, Jo Jo White, Walt Bellamy, Earl (the Pearl) Monroe, and David Thompson. The Swedes, the Germans, the Poles, the Anglo-Saxons—each carry the body differently, come down harder on toe or heel, have a different line from head through shoulders to hips and heels, move in a different gait with a different grace or stiffness. And so with those sprung from African histories, in several different cultural streams.

I first noticed this watching UCLA and USC play Oregon and Oregon State back-to-back on consecutive nights. At all times, at least eight of the players on the court were black. The contrasts in style were unmistakable. The movement from the hips is wholly different for black runners; bodies sometimes seem to float, without effort; chests and heads do not seem to carry weight, nor to lean, nor to struggle; only the lithe legs sweep across the shining varnished boards. Leaps and jumps follow different parabolas. I thought I could detect, indeed, more than one black running style: (1) as described above; (2) head and shoulders back, feet seeming to be out in front, as in the style of the long-distance runners of Kenya and Uganda; (3) a supple turning from side to side, weaving from the hips, as it were, left to right, even as the weight shifts from leg to leg, so that abrupt changes in direction seem not to be changes at all but only the instantaneous decision to follow through on one of the angles in the swirling arc the forward motion of the body is constantly describing. Recall, in the mind's eye, Julius Erving; Adrian Dantley of Notre Dame; Earl Monroe. One watches basketball as one watches dance, occasionally half-closing the eye to blur out the detail and to fasten upon the essential abstract pattern of the movement, to catch its inner ecstasy.

Basketball represents the black experience in yet another way. Basketball is, as more than one connoisseur has noted, a game of feint, deception: put-on. The very word is a ghetto word. One "puts on" the man. One "puts a move on" him. The man has no right to know one's inner thoughts, desires, plans, schemes, intentions. Face to face with him, one maintains a constant, cool, shaded mask, slipping it to him at the chosen moment. Self-possession is indispensable, a condition for success. Every motion in basketball is disguise for yet another. Fakery, head feints, changes of direction, dribbles between one's legs, false breaks to the basket, picks, back-door plays, steals, deceptive wriggles and deliberately begun but interrupted motions to pass or throw or run— this is more than half the substance of the game. There are more fake passes than passes; more feinted shots than shots (three or four times under the basket a man may pump before he actually lets go). Like the stories and legends of black literature, the hero does not let his antagonist guess his intentions; he strings him along; he keeps his inner life to himself until the decisive moment. The other must commit himself first; only then dare the hero strike.

There is more than one way to play basketball. New York rooters think it is in a special way their game, and New York high schools are studied by scouts as are no others (save the large black ghettos of Chicago, Washington, Philadelphia, and Los Angeles) for the most highly prized talents. But drive slowly through the farmlands of Indiana, Illinois, Iowa, the Dakotas—here, too, one will find backboards nailed and bolted to anything that will hold them. Here, too, as in the city, one will find the most accessible game. Teams of two men each are quite enough; even one-on-one is fiercely satisfying. For countless solitary hours, competing against oneself, one can master new shots, teach oneself new moves, learn by infinite repetition to do smoothly what at first one could not do at all, and observe with satisfaction and confidence the climbing percentages of one's success. Thus, in Crystal City, Missouri, Bill Bradley practiced on some days for seven hours at a time.

In the Midwest, however, the game lacks some sense of deception and subtlety; it is played straight-out, man-on-man, team to team. It is a game of the head, stolid, deliberate, strategic, grinding. The teams are disciplined to plans, patterns, concepts. Improvisation, of necessity, occurs. Yet Midwesterners play almost as the Russians play, not jazz, but rapid and heavy chess. Power, size, sheer running count for more. The game is exciting and well played, but somehow falls short of the potential aesthetic of the game, the virtuoso individual performances of a syncopated group of five deceivers. Watching the New York Knicks in action—or a college team composed of eight or nine blacks out of the top ten or twelve varsity and subs—is to watch a rhythmic beat that seems to have caught the highest ideal possibilities hidden in the game; as though, all unknowing, it was for this the game had been invented. (The Knicks at their greatest were not all black; but the essence of their game combined the solidarity and deception of the black experience with the grinding defense of the rugged Middle West: DeBusschere, Bradley, Reed, with the silkiness of Frazier and Barnett.)

No wonder the game becomes more black with every passing year. There are some who argue that the black body, genetics, or perhaps the fruits of a thousand years of culture yield the black player decisive advantages in running and especially in leaping, in malleability and suppleness of movement. Some think, as well, that the cultural psyche and instincts, fashioned by hundreds of years of black experience, suit blacks peculiarly well for excellence in basketball. To these, the counterargument is that other immigrant groups, usually on the lowest economic ladder, once predominated; now it is the blacks' turn. In boxing, perhaps, or football, one might grant such a point; the upper classes ordinarily lack incentive to endure the physical rigor of sports like those. In basketball, however, something else seems to be at stake.

The resonance and nuances of the game offer absolutely no symbolic conflict to the idea of a black coach. No one comments, even in privacy, that a black might not be "ready" to diagnose, plan, and guide, or that black intelligence might not be up to solving the intricacies of both the tactics and the personalities inherent in the game. One often hears, even in respectable circles, symbolic resistance on these matters in baseball or in football. But not in basketball. This fact needs explanation. The essence of the game affords it, as seems to be implicitly grasped by players, fans, and philosophers alike.

Even phenomenal white players like Jerry West, John Havlicek, Bill Bradley, Rich Barry, Dave DeBusschere, Dave Cowens, and Bob Cousy (the most magical and blacklike of the whites) seem to represent consistency, competitiveness, drive, will, rugged determination, ability in the clutch—but not at all, or hardly so, the potential grace and coolness and fluidity of the game. Once one has seen black athletes shape the game, one must defer to them; a new and indelible stamp has been placed upon it. Elgin Baylor, Oscar Robertson, Bill Russell, "Dr. J.," David Thompson, Wilt Chamberlain, Walt Frazier, Earl Monroe, Kareem Abdul-Jabbar give the mind's eye a vision of possibility the white style does not afford. On this brief list are five or six of the greatest players ever to play the game.

The point to stress is the mythic line of basketball: a game of fake and feint and false intention; a game of run, run, run; a game of feet, of swift decision, instantaneous reversal, catlike "moves," cool accuracy, spring and jump. The pace is hot. The rhythm of the game beats with the seconds: a three-second rule, a ten-second rule, a rule to shoot in twenty-four seconds. Only when the ball goes out of bounds, or a point is scored, or a foul is called does the clock stop; the play flows on. Teams do not move by timeless innings as in baseball, nor by set, formal, single plays as in football. Even when a play is called or a pattern established, the game flows on until a whistle blows, moving relentlessly as lungs heave and legs weary. It is like jazz.

At the end of a game, when time-outs may be used to stop the clock, short bursts of strategy can be designed in a huddle at the sidelines. Play becomes as deliberate, brief, and formal as in football. Otherwise, the teams must adapt to (or change) the game's rhythm, its inner flow, and make it work for them according to their prepared, familiar plays, or improvise at opportunity. The mythic line commands frequent reinforcement: professional basketball scores are always far higher than in baseball or football, often exceeding 100 points per team. Rapid scoring races with the clock: more than a basket a minute is now typical.

Cultural resistance to the dominance of blacks within the game is already marked. Once, five years ago, when Notre Dame fielded five blacks at once in a home game, the student body of the "Fighting Irish" booed and hooted; the student body president later apologized publicly. A team plays a representative role, a symbolic role. The gross booing of the students was, apparently, spontaneous and genuine. Symbolically, the presence of five blacks seemed to them discordant in a student body almost wholly white. The same phenomenon is observable in cities like Chicago, where audiences for basketball have become increasingly black while audiences for hockey are almost wholly white.

There are three separate points to be made in interpretation. First, there has always been racism in American life, and also in sports. Bill Russell used to say that the rule for using blacks in basketball was *two* at home, *three* on the road, *four* if you're behind, and *five* if you need to win the playoffs. Harry Edwards argues that blacks are being used as mercenaries for white America, like paid performers. But the growing resistance of whites to black dominance, particularly in basketball, seems to show that Russell is more correct than Edwards. Athletes are not merely mercenaries; they are symbolic representatives. Teams normally do all they can to recruit representatives of the major ethnic groups in their locality; the early New York Knicks looked eagerly for Jewish players. Quotas would be silly. But so is a wholly mercenary outlook. The subject is certain to be debated in the future, because it seems that blacks could totally dominate basketball in years to come, accounting for 70 or 80 percent of the players. Like it or not, the audience response will almost certainly change.

For, secondly, the symbols of sports depend on rootedness. Everyone can admire excellence wherever it is found. But the human being is an embodied spirit, maintaining attachment to his or her finite roots. There is a special intensity to admiration and affection when excellence is found in one's own family, or neighborhood, or town, or culture. Willie Mays in Harlem generated intensity of an order that Joe DiMaggio or Ted Williams or Stan Musial could not touch; Joe DiMaggio in Flatbush wins smiles of recognition from *paesani* the others could not raise. Muhammad Ali trades on such primordial loyalties by portraying Joe Frazier and George Foreman—outrageously, unfairly—as "white men's niggers." Each place has its local gods; *fanum,* the local temple, is the word from which "fan" derives. Identification is crucial.

There is a problem here of a special order for basketball, unlike that of any other sport. It is certain to cause increasing argument, to bring out charges and countercharges. So long as any American citizen, or any student at a college, plays the game with excellence, his talents alone should commend him to all. In an age in which talent is recruited everywhere, it may be that it is only the black skin of blacks that makes them alone visible as recruits from far away. It could be a familiar form of racism.

Objections to this line of thought will usually assume that cultures do not have special characteristics, allowing them to resonate in special ways to certain symbolic values. Clearly, however, games differ in their appeal in different cultures. Not all communities nourish equally in every area of life the foundations of basic skills and attitudes that lead to excellence.

Another objection is that basketball may be a "city game," a "street game," and the mythic line in the sport may be more proper to urban than to black life. One has only to compare the playing styles of urban whites and urban blacks to see that this is not true. The fluidity and grace of the black players are both distinctive and more in tune with the genius of the game. Look and see.

Pete Axthelm, in his book *The City Game,* lets one of the black heroes of Harlem's Rucker Tournament describe a distinctive style of basketball, a game in which the best competed: Clinton Robinson, a local hero; Wilt Chamberlain; and Connie ("The Hawk") Hawkins, the best, they say, ever to come out of Harlem. The Hawk

"got the ball, picked up speed, and started his first move. Chamberlain came right out to stop him. The Hawk went up—he was still way out beyond the foul line—and started floating toward the basket. Wilt, taller and stronger, stayed right with him—but then The Hawk hook-dunked the ball right over Chamberlain. He *hook*-dunked! Nobody had ever done anything like that to Wilt. The crowd went so crazy that they had to stop the game for five minutes. And I almost fell out of the tree.

"But you didn't get away with just one spectacular move in

those games. So the other guys came right back at The Hawk. Clinton Robinson charged in, drove around him, and laid one up so high that it hit the top of the backboard. The Hawk went way up, but he couldn't quite reach it, and it went down into the basket. Clinton Robinson was about six feet tall and The Hawk was six feet eight—so the crowd went wild again. In fact, Clinton had thrown some of the greatest moves I'd ever seen, shaking guys left and right before he even reached The Hawk.

"Then it was Chamberlain's turn to get back. Wilt usually took it pretty easy in summer games, walking up and down the court and doing just enough to intimidate his opponents with his seven-foot body. But now his pride was hurt, his manhood was wounded. And you can't let that happen in a tough street game. So he came down, drove directly at the hoop, and went up over The Hawk. Wilt stuffed the ball with two hands, and he did it so hard that he almost ripped the backboard off the pole.

"By then everybody on the court was fired up—and it was time for The Hawk to take charge again. Clinton Robinson came toward him with the ball, throwing those crazy moves on anyone who tried to stop him, and then he tried to loft a lay-up way up onto the board, the way he had done before. Only this time The Hawk was up there waiting for it. He was up so high that he blocked the shot with his *chest*. Still in midair, he kind of swept his hands down across his chest as if he were wiping his shirt—and slammed the ball down at Robinson's feet. The play seemed to turn the whole game around, and The Hawk's team came from behind to win. That was The Hawk. Just beautiful. I don't think anybody who was in that crowd could ever forget that game."

In football, as well, blacks have made their greatest inroads—and most enhanced the game—at those positions which most closely resemble the positions in basketball: as wide receivers, flankers, halfbacks, and defensive backs. These are positions in which fleetness of foot, deception, and swift moves are the most highly prized talents. Blacks have played well at every other position, too: at fullback, tackle, guard, and recently at quarterback. Linebackers, however, still tend to be disproportionately from Southern or Eastern European or whites from the American South—men like Butkus, Buoniconti, Nobis, Curry. Tight ends, too, tend to be white, but great defensive tackles (Roosevelt Greer, Mean Joe Greene, Merlin Olsen, Bubba Smith) tend to be black. The speedsters, the outside runners, the slashing halfbacks, and the smoothest long receivers tend to be black: Hayes, Jefferson, Taylor, Washington, Morris, Simpson, Armstrong, Barkum, Caster, and a host of others.

The inherent action of basketball, to resume the point, is more elusive than one at first imagines. Ten feet above the floor, the orange rims of the baskets wait in silence at each end. No sound in sports is sweeter than the clean *twang* and *snap* of the corded nets when the ball spins exactly through. The sexual metaphor of penetration has often been called upon; a neat, perfect, and cleanly dropped shot brings an ecstasy and inner pleasure analogous to the release of high sexual tension. The game proceeds, indeed, by rapid exchanges of "baskets"—the ball dropping through the hoop as often as 100 times a game. It is a long intercourse.

Skill makes the difficult seem easy, and at times it seems that the inherent conflict is a race against the clock—to drop in more baskets than the opposition before time expires. More than in football, the clock is vital; not occasionally, but in virtually every game, the final race is against the clock. The two teams try to stay within range of each other until the end. Then, in the last four or five minutes, perfection is in order; each error becomes a gift to the other side; only so many errors can be borne. Often enough, ecstasy or despair is decided only in the final five or ten seconds, perhaps in overtime. Standing at the foul line, or putting up the last decisive shot, a man will often drive his fist against the air, driving the ball home in exultation.

As in love, the game should not become too easy; intense and long resistance must be applied. And so *de*-fense has come to be the heart of the game. So practiced and skillful are the pros that shooting percentages are as near perfection as one might imagine—as high as .890 for free throws and .630 for field goals. Almost every other time the ball goes up, it goes in. Thus the emphasis in modern basketball has shifted to make each thrust for the basket as laden as possible with friction, difficulty, obstruction, and reluctance to yield. Crowds love the new

pressing defenses, the sweat, the toll they take on blister-
ing feet, the pounding up and down the floor, hawking,
falling, leaping, tangling, pushing, shoving for position.
Each team in basketball is like a single living body: the
two organisms clinging to each other up and down the
floor like giant wrestlers, locked in high-velocity and
sweating contact at every point of movement. Warily, at
times, the dribbling guards approach the other team's
embrace; like arms, the defensive guards swing loosely
right and left, circling, before clapping tightly into the
foe's line of movement. Each team is a mystical body,
one, united. Enormous feats of concentration, enormous
bursts of energy, vast reservoirs of habit and instinct are
required.

The solidarity of basketball makes it appealing in many
cultures; slowly, it is beginning to spread. Europeans,
with feet trained by soccer but hands and arms lacking in
speed or subtlety, take a little while to reverse their development. The game is capable of many different cultural
styles. The plodding, chesslike Russian juggernaut has
proved successful against the individual talents of American All-Star teams; virtuoso excellence is not sufficient in
this game, for solidarity is everything. But the deepest
possibilities of the game are so embedded in the American experience, especially through the black experience,
that it is difficult to believe that any other nation could
consistently present teams that might outplay our own. A
part of our deepest identity is uttered in this game. Those
of us not black are taught possibilities we might otherwise have never known or emulated.

SPORTSREEL

Hooping It

I grew up in an era when basketball was constantly changing. Luisetti introduced the one-hand shot when I was three years old; from my first memories of playing basketball, about age eight or nine, I remember almost *everybody* shooting one-handed. I don't remember seeing baskets in the Slovak section of Johnstown where I grew up. When we moved to a suburban neighborhood, I remember being made to dribble a ball in the gymnasium for the first time. It was a humiliating effort. I remember being awkward and stiff for those early years. My family moved around a lot; I attended five different schools in the first eight grades. By the time I was twelve, I remember feeling determined and adequate and getting better. Anticipation, quickness, attentiveness could make up for lack of special skills. Spirit reaps rewards in basketball. We played until we could scarcely see, throwing up the ball against a backboard nailed to a telephone pole on the corner in McKeesport. The games were rough, brutal even. The bodily contact was as heavy as in football. One learned not to be intimidated.

In the seminary, I grew to love the game with a passion bordering on my love for football. At Notre Dame, in high school, several of us raced during our brief hour for recreation to the smooth cement courts to shovel off the snow, scatter rock salt on the ice, and brush the slush away. We played outdoors all winter. Our hands were red and raw; the skin of our fingers split from the salt; we would bandage them. We slid, jumped over piled snow out of bounds, slapped the slush out of our tennis shoes on the pavement. Occasionally, Notre Dame varsity players dropped by to shoot a few. Leroy ("Axle") Leslie, at that time the highest scorer in Notre Dame history and a lithe, brave young man from Johnstown (a polio victim, he had never played the game until his junior year in high school, and at six-foot-two, playing center, made All-State) put on a show for us once. I had only one small pleasure: dropping in an over-the-head shot I had practiced by the hour, although Axle only laughed when it went in.

In those years, Bob Cousy was graduating from Holy Cross in Worcester. Occasionally, we high school seminarians would get a game with one or another local team and play in a real gym—for example, with the Brothers at Dujarie Hall or the college seminarians at Moreau Seminary. Our coach didn't like my two "junk" shots—a running hook and an underhand drive—and used me as the sixth man. "Cut the cute stuff, Novak!" he would shout. "Play ball!" My greatest satisfaction was entering one game in the second quarter and hitting, by the end, for 19 points. Still, he wouldn't start me. The next time I hit 26. (All these years later, I remember the exact totals; they surprised me and pleased me so much then. I never thought of myself as a player able to score that much; several of my friends were better players. Scoring well, I felt as though I were living out forbidden fantasies, doing exactly what I had always wanted to but never thought I would. Entering the seminary had meant saying no to an athletic career.)

In college, near Brockton, Massachusetts, where we could watch Cousy on television, my cousin Jim Bresnicki and I used to stand any comers, two-on-two, every evening after dinner, no matter how hot or cold it was. Our favorite opposition were Brothers Richard, Peter, and William, religious like ourselves; we even let them have the third man. We seldom lost. "Bres" could hit from anywhere; he shot like an angel, consistent as the day was long. He loved the game more than I. He used to wink: "Wanna hoop?" I never resisted. We played at every possible free moment. We were almost insane about the game. I think it's true that I reached my peak in my sophomore year, and never again was so good. I loved, above all, to be on the weaker side, against odds, and to be losing near the end. The final rush of intensity at the end of the game was even more demanding, relentless, and exhausting than football. We used to play toward a target: 15 baskets, winner has to win by 2. Often our games went to 21–19 or 19–17. We played much more often on a half-court, with two or three on a side. I never did master the intricacies of the full-court team game. Fire the ball up, tight defense, twist and shoot. The cold scent of wintry air, or the mugginess of a summer evening, often prod my memory with images from those days.

On March 17, 1963, by now three years out of the seminary and a graduate student at Harvard, I finally persuaded my future wife to marry me. We counted the day as our engagement. I blush to recall it a little, but after dinner at Durgin Park we went to Boston Garden to see Bob Cousy's farewell game. The Garden lies in the part of the city that always made me wary, a white ghetto, rather like some scenes in novels of Boston's seedy underworld. Basketball is an indoor game, and the emotions of the crowds, on this occasion 13,000 strong, reverberate off the walls and rafters. Shouts and yells fill one's brain, seem to penetrate inside and to be heard not through the ears but through the cells within. That night, the feeling was overpowering. At the final presentation to Cousy, everyone was standing. For minute after minute, the chant was unendurably affectionate, loud, nostalgic, throbbing: "We love Cooz! We love Cooz! We love Cooz!" I shouted myself hoarse. Karen covered her ears. In the end, Cousy broke into tears. I doubt if there was a dry eye in the house. That was the first time Karen pointed out to me that during the game my hand was moist; I might as well have been playing for all I put into the game, she said. I don't think she was envious then, although with all the research "necessary for this book," she may have changed her mind.

The championship games between the Los Angeles Lakers and the Celtics in those years must constitute, it seems, the most perfectly balanced, intense, and sustained championship rivalry in the history of sports. Every year, in the midst of heavy studies and endless duties, I found myself setting aside seven entire evenings or afternoons to hear or watch every game. Unbelievably, against all odds, the Celtics won almost every time.

In the seminary, I had gone to Mass every day. We used

to see many of the championship games there, too. But now sports events rivaled churchgoing in the frequency of my religious liturgies. The liturgies do not have the same worldview, of course, nor celebrate the same way of life. Yet as Aquinas said, so I found it to be true: grace exceeds, but does not cancel, nature.

Part Two

THE
SEVEN
SEALS

THERE ARE PRIESTS who mumble through the Mass, lovers who read letters over a naked shoulder in love's embrace, teachers who detest students, pedants who shrink from original ideas. So also there are athletes, fans, and sportswriters who never grasp the beauty or the treasure entrusted them. It must not be imagined that the mysteries of sport are directly penetrated. Much depends on the qualities of heart of the pursuer. A hundred young men tugged at Excalibur; only Arthur could pull it from the rock. There are, in suitable proportion, vulgar, sotted, and distasteful men in sports. There are minimal perceptions, manipulations, deals, and compromises. There are hucksters, profiteers, and egomaniacs. It is not required by sports, whether in fan, in athlete, or in journalist, that one be virtuous; if that were so, so many millions could not love the game. But the failures of human flesh to measure up to the beauties possible in sports should not deter us from pursuing what it is in them that draws so on our love.

Seven seals lock the inner life of sports. They may be broken, one by one.

7

The First Two Seals: Sacred Space, Sacred Time

THE FIRST SEAL: SACRED SPACE

THE FEELING athletes have for the arena in which they struggle is a secret feeling not often voiced. If you have ever walked on Paratroopers' Hill in Jerusalem, in the trenches and in the dugouts, recalling the fierce nighttime chaos in the barbed wire where men's bodies were shredded by rockets and automatic weapons, and where the liberation of the city was made possible; or if you have walked the fields of Gettysburg, reconstructing in imagination the movements and the courage; perhaps then you understand how certain places are hallowed by deeds.

An athlete trains everywhere he can: boys shoot baskets by the hour in the driveways, in playgrounds, in scores of gyms. Yet there is a special awe that arises when one enters for the first time—or at any time—one's high school gym, or Madison Square Garden, or Pauley Pavilion, or wherever the symbolic center of achievement may be. Each arena is a little different: one concrete place, one patch of earth, one England. The athlete needs to internalize the ambience, to dig his cleats at the turf, to root his senses and instincts there, to bounce the ball experimentally on the floor, to learn by sixth sense the slightest fixtures, signs, and contours of the place. Baseball, basketball, and football do not take place just anywhere. There are consecrated places.

It is a stirring occasion to walk in Notre Dame stadium when no other soul is present. One feels the proximity of every seat. Even when the place is packed, so perfect is the oval that the most distant fan can hear a coach shout from the bench. The drainage slope gives the visitor an upward lift as he walks across the well-kept grass. Images and voices arise from the past. The mind's eye sees Johnny Lujack, Emil Sitko, George Connors, Leon Hart, imagines the Gipper.

Each time I pass the stadium at any of the universities where I sometimes lecture, I feel the presence of such ghosts. I may not know the local traditions, but I know, at Nebraska, at Missouri, at Michigan, at Harvard, at Princeton, that great tales await my learning. Vividness, color, injury, impossible catches, courage, crushing disappointments (Michigan's two devastating ties with Ohio State in 1973 and 1974) await attention.

Sports arenas are storied places. Universes of tales. One sits in them surrounded by ghostly ancestors, as at the Mass one is surrounded by the hosts who have since Abraham celebrated a Eucharist. Even a new stadium, as at Oakland, is a place where tradition instantaneously begins. Impoverished in memory, a new arena is a tabula rasa for new impressions. Records are set. Achievements are fixed in memory.

Three religions in the world, especially, are religions of place; perhaps all religions are, each in its different way. For Judaism, one land is holy. Not a rich land, mainly desert. Not a clearly defined land with sharp natural borders, and not an especially beautiful land—except in its starkness, in the sheer power of hostile nature that one feels in its hills and deserts, and in the extraordinary lucidity of its air and light. Yet all of the longing of the religious tradition focuses upon this land as the symbol of the Divine Presence for the Jewish people and a symbol for the transcendence of God. Judaism is concrete and thisworldly. It is a religion of particularity, of universality *through* particularity. God chose a people, for his own reasons, in his own way. This singular people is a people gathered around a land and a city: Jerusalem. For Catholics, Rome is a special city, but *historically* special, not holy in itself. The Vatican could be located anywhere; only tradition would be violated. But Jerusalem is valued not only for historical reasons, or as a traditional place; it is, as it were, a sacrament of longing and unique graciousness.

Christianity, too, is a religion of particulars, a religion of pilgrimages. God is everywhere, but certain places are especially alive with His presence. From early times, to enter a church was to enter a territory no longer part of the state, a sanctuary which soldiers of the state could not penetrate; the roots of notions of the separation of church and state arose from this sense of sacred space.

In Islam, too, Mecca is a holy city, and toward it all the faithful turn in prayer (just as Christian churches point toward Jerusalem). In a subordinate way, Medina and Jerusalem are also holy places. Because Muhammad is believed to have ascended into heaven from the Tomb of Abraham in Jerusalem, that place is held to be the "center of the world," the "navel of the universe." The place is universal, touching all humans, but locatable, finite, particular—and sacred.

So it is with many national monuments and historical homes, battlegrounds, meetinghouses, and so forth. Where great deeds have been done, places are lifted out of ordinary life and gain a certain aura. It is like that for athletic arenas. Players often feel it. Places where they struggle, where they may suffer injury, where opportunity comes and their careers blossom or, on the other hand, suddenly decline or fail to materialize—places where they meet their trial and testing—have a certain fascination over them. A ball field, a court, a gridiron are, after all, such small and finite spaces, and the thought that within these confined precincts so much that affects their personal destiny will occur presses itself deep in the cells of their flesh and organs. Being traded, going to another place, sometimes tears the unconscious self more than the mind allows; the feeling vibrates in the body more than in the mind. The spirit belongs anywhere, but the body belongs in particular spaces and grows accustomed to them. The body sometimes has an almost physical dread about being transplanted, almost like the dread the body feels in being forced by rational will to enter through an airplane door. The mind says it is as safe as any other kind of travel, no reason to worry, but the body dreads the unnatural environment.

The space in which athletic events occur is not only familiar but also awesome. Not just rookies feel it, in their first entrance onto the playing surface, but even veterans. Deeds done here depend so much on Fate. For one thing, opportunities for the sort of dramatic play that marks greatness come at their own time; the individual cannot control either their advent or their frequency. For another, his response is as much a matter of instinct, chance, timing, and placement as of intention or will. Most great athletic deeds are not thought through or entirely foreseen. One must react to opportunity, however it presents itself, from whatever stance in which one finds oneself. The Fates that govern this one small space have a great deal to do with one's own deeds. There are players who dread, who hate certain arenas in which they must play, because their showing there is consistently unflattering; and others who for some odd reason seem to prosper in certain parks or on certain fields, who play there with a lightness and brilliance they seldom achieve anywhere else. Being unable to control such factors, athletes often harbor feelings about particular arenas which they cannot describe coherently or with secular matter-of-factness.

Sports are carriers of traditions, of rituals. They war against traditionless modernity. They satisfy the most persistent hungers of the human heart—for repetition (how many cocktail parties have you attended? how many dinners?) and for solemn ritual, for pageantry and for uncertain outcomes. For centuries, human beings have gathered so. Sports are our brotherhood with ancient and medieval times. Sports are religions of place, of particulars, of deeds done *here* and at a concrete hour.

When an athlete kicks at the dust of the infield, or digs his cleats into turf or carpet, or squeaks his sneakers on the reflection-yielding floorboards, he gains a sense of concentration: all the hours of practice, all the years of discipline, all the frustrations of getting ready, have their focus here. The arena draws inward the multiplicities of life and weaves them into a tapestry. Once woven, the threads remain entwined forever. Arenas are like monasteries; individual games imprint on memory single images blazing as if from an illuminated text. Awesome places, a familiar, quiet sort of awe. Our cathedrals.

THE SECOND SEAL: SACRED TIME

Baseball is unlike basketball or football in its relationship to time. Baseball pays no attention to the clock. However long an inning takes, it takes; games may last two hours or five. The game should last 9 innings, but anything over 4½ will count (if the home team is winning), in case of rain; and games as long as 17 or 19 or 24 innings have not infrequently occurred. In baseball, clock time does not exist. Time is measured by outs—three outs for each side per inning. Baseball is more intent on equality and fairness than on the clock. From each according to his abilities; to each according to an equal number of outs and innings. "Well, we had our innings," the combatants can say. As nearly as possible, baseball is free of alibis. The bounces of the ball are part of the game.

Still, the time of a baseball game is a special time, measured in outs rather than in minutes. The clock time required to play a game is always listed in the box score, as though to assist one in translating one time measure into another. Every baseball game has its own distinctive clock time. Each *is* its own distinctive unit of time: "One complete game." One hundred and sixty-two complete games constitute a year (not counting exhibition games or playoffs)—the baseball year.

It is almost like being a Catholic and living according to the calendar of the liturgy, or being Jewish and counting the seasons and years along another axis of memory. For Catholics, the year begins four Sundays preceding Christmas, and then day by day the life of Jesus is relived until Good Friday, Easter, and Ascension. Ten days later comes Pentecost, Sunday of Sundays, and then for twenty-odd Sundays the public preaching of Jesus is recounted, until Advent comes again. The secular calendar, January to December, is an abstract convenience, a tool of measurement; it does not recount the inner life of memory and identification—not for Catholics (or Christians generally), not for Jews, and not for devotees of baseball or the other sports. (I knew an Irish Catholic priest once, a friend of Whitey Ford and chaplain to the football Giants; his friends tease him that *his* liturgy begins with the football season, is moved along by basketball, and hits the high holy days when baseballs begin to fly in Florida.)

In basketball, sacred time is measured parsimoniously by two clocks: the stopwatch ticking off the seconds of the game, halted when whistles blow or the ball goes out of bounds; and the 24-second clock (in professional basketball) ticking off the number of seconds allowed before the offensive team must put the ball up toward the basket. Ordinary, secular time is disregarded. Especially toward the end of the game, when classic strategies have been developed for stopping the clock and setting up the final crucial plays, three minutes of sacred time may last as long as fifteen minutes on the pagan clock. The basketball player must be alert, then, to four separate times: profane time, game time, shooting time, and the end time.

In football, there is as in basketball a special game clock, stopped on canonized occasions: a ball out-of-bounds, a signal from the referee. There is, as well, a timer to speed up the offensive team: twenty-five seconds from the end of one play to the snapping of the ball for another. The sixty minutes of official playing time take more than two hours of pagan time. Since play is not continuous, but requires changes of personnel and special units, huddles and conferences, the actual time of action is very short. The execution of each play from the time the ball is snapped until the ballcarrier is driven out of bounds or tackled may last three to ten seconds, seldom much longer. There may be, perhaps, 120 plays a game. Only ten or twelve minutes out of sixty are spent in actual contact. Yet so furious and intense is the physical exertion in these few minutes that exhaustion, even of the most splendidly conditioned athletes, is apparent. Years of practice and preparation are funneled toward these highly charged and limited moments. However well one has performed in practice, only here in these sacred moments does performance count. A quarterback may complete a given pass play thousands of times in practice, and try it three times in a game and miss each one; the preceding thousand do not matter. The pressures under sacred time invite perfection-on-demand. A tight end may be called upon for only three or four passes; a half back may carry the ball but six times; a defensive tackle may have a real shot at only five tackles. Years of training focus tightly down to narrow opportunities.

In this sense, football is far more intense than either basketball or baseball. In baseball, each batter gets his turns at bat, usually four or five per game; and a batted ball is handled by each defender singly, or in discrete sequence. In basketball, each of the five players is absorbed with duties every second, whether on offense or on defense. In football, not only are substitutions more frequent, and not only are specialists called upon in continuous rotation, but also the shifting directions and demands of the game allow some players on virtually every play to commit themselves only partially to action: to carry out feints or fakes, to engage in only brush blocks or tentative charges, on the ready, but not necessarily called upon. Only when the action directly engages them are they in a spotlight where their deeds are critical to success or failure. Some players, of course, carry the brunt of duty on almost every play: the quarterback, the offensive front line, the most frequently called upon runners or receivers, the defensive front four, and the linebackers. But football is so corporate an effort that one player's performance alone can be singled out from others' only by abstraction. Most observers of the game cannot keep track of the efforts of all eleven men, or even of more than three or four on any single play. In baseball and basketball, the individual performer is almost constantly in the spotlight of attention. In this sense, they are sports of greater intensity than football.

The final two minutes of a football game are among the most dramatic in any sport. They take a long time—in secular time—to play. Time-outs have commonly been hoarded (each team is allowed three per half). The offensive team, if it is behind, tries to run each play out-of-bounds, to stop the clock, forcing the game clock to record only the three to ten seconds of concentrated action required for each play. Enormous amounts of action can be compressed into two minutes. Harvard, losing 20–3 to Yale in one recent game, scored three times in the last minutes and won.

A feature of sacred time is its emphasis on life and possibility. As long as there are seconds on the clock, anything can happen; maximal efforts may be crowned with success. Athletes probe the forces and the sources of life, press against them, court them to their uttermost. "With a score of 6–0, two outs, two strikes, nobody on, only an average batter at bat, bottom of the ninth," William Saroyan has written of baseball, "it is still possible, and sometimes necessary, to believe that something can still happen—for the simple reason that it *has* happened before, and very probably will again. And when it does, won't that be the day? Isn't that alone almost enough to live for, assuming there might just be little else? To witness so pure a demonstration of the unaccountable way by which the human spirit achieves stunning, unbelievable grandeur?"

Sacred time is sacred because it stores up possibilities of the heroic; so long as sacred time exists, the heroic is in incubation. Sacred time teaches humans never to quit, to count upon and to entrust themselves to the potencies of life, redemption, beauty. One never knows. Deep in the resources of each of us may be ripening at least one supremely lovely act. Attentive, alert, ever pressing, we may allow it, when the circumstances most desperately call upon it, to flower into being, like a night watchman, a judge, a congressman lifted by the Fates to sudden vindication of their long careers.

I recall vividly, when my son was four or five, just old enough to watch football with me, how discouraged he became when Stanford fell far behind Michigan in the Rose Bowl. "I quit," he said. "This is a lousy game. They lost it. They lost." He had been born in Stanford hospital. He was too young to relish identifying himself, risking himself, and losing. I told him, a little angrily, not to quit, to stay and watch: "You never know. There's lots of time. You cannot be a quitter." Randy Vataha and Jim Plunkett of Stanford made at least one father in America feel a little less pompous, for they stormed back in the second half and devastated the bigger, stronger, crisper Big Ten team.

Ever since, when I hear my son tell me, or his friends, or himself, "You never know, there's still lots of time," I am grateful to football. (The memory in his mind is vivid; I have heard him cite that game—and he remembers that Plunkett's first name was Jim, and that it was Michigan, not Ohio State, as I had written in my first draft, which he corrected.)

In certain African religions, a distinction is drawn between profane time, real time, and the time of the heroes. These times are not so much spoken of in words as observed in practice. Profane time is practical time, time spent in work and utilitarian necessities. Real time is time aware of the swiftness and uncertainty of life, of the illussoriness of practical time (which, indeed, "kills" real time, allows one to forget). For the time of the heroes, one imagines that in every human life is cocooned an ideal form, the ideal beauty of which the human race is capable. By their deeds, the heroes of the past raised their lives to these high, clear, stirring forms at least momentarily; they broke from the daily mediocrity and jading of events and revealed the true possibilities of human life, beyond the veils. These higher levels always beckon human beings. Imagine that we walk through our days on hidden tracks, in cycles round and round, and at foreordained moments we are lifted out of the ordinary sphere and allowed to live momentarily in the eternal "time of the heroes." The true form of humanity then radiates briefly from our deeds: this is what we are truly like, what our usually unfulfilled possibilities dimly point to.

In the sacred time of sports, the time of the heroes occasionally breaks through. No one dictates the moment. It comes when it comes. But by preparing oneself, by laboring steadily, by forcing one's attention and concentration to the highest pitch possible, one may not lose the opportunities which suddenly and surprisingly appear. Such moments do not come frequently. Unhappy is the one whose mind is drifting when the instant comes—the defensive back who drops an easy interception, the touchdown lost because the mind made it before the hands held the ball. Living in the time of the heroes requires intensity. One must often practice raising the quality of one's attention to every instant as it arises, staccato-like, from the void.

Both the real time and the time of the heroes in sports are tokens of eternal life. At moments of high intensity, there seem to be no past, no future. One experiences a complete immersion in the present, absorption in an instantaneous and abundant now. In what seems like an instant, hours of profane time elapse unnoticed. From this experience, the descent into ordinary time is like exchanging one form of life for another. The most acute and disturbing pointer to the form of life high traditions have spoken of as "eternal life"—life in a different mode from that of the life we normally lead in time—arises for saints in contemplation, for artists in the joy and intensity of creation, and for all of us ordinary sinners in the festivals of sport.

It is from experiences like these that the myth of eternity arises. While some, especially among the educated, are properly skeptical, many human beings trust these intimations in themselves of another form of life: butterfly in a cocoon, longing to break free. To live at such instantaneous intensity forever, all gathered up like the sweetness of a plum at peak of ripeness, would be joy indeed. It would be cowardly of me not to say that such life seems to me the truth of human destiny, more credible than its opposite. Yet if it is not true, then the intensities of sports, and art, and love have been enough. If these fail as signs, in themselves they do not fail.

8

The Third Seal: Bond of Brothers

PULLING ON the uniform of a team one admires is a ritual of election. One has been accepted. More than that, it signifies an opportunity to act in a special kind of world: a world of record and legend and cherished significance.

Most of the actions of one's life go unnoticed. An ex-football player on a college campus, no longer recognized, no longer assisted and upheld by coaches and authorities, has resumed the anonymity in which nature places most of us. Being an active player is like living in the select circle of the gods, of the chosen ones who act out liturgically the anxieties of the human race and are sacrificed as ritual victims. The contests of sports—at least, of the trinity of sports we are studying in this book—are eucharists.

The athlete is sometimes spoken of as a star, superstar, or celebrity. The analogies are with show business. But these analogies do not explain some of the peculiar powers and duties of an athlete. Bill Bradley, for example, was once walking the streets of Manhattan on a Sunday morning in April. The air was soft and his mood was meditative, restful. The Knicks had lost badly to Boston the night before, in an important game. Bradley, who tends to be morose after a poor performance or a loss, was trying to heal the pain he felt by drinking deeply of the spring air. He wanted to restore himself. Then, a short, ugly, bespectacled man walked toward him in the street, staring at

Bradley's face. When the man and his wife had passed by, Bradley heard a commotion and felt someone grab his arm. The man pulled him around and with a face full of venom swore at him: "You're Bill Bradley, aren't you? Son of a bitch! What did you mean, throwing that game away last night? You son of a bitch!" The man's embarrassed wife pulled him away. Bradley couldn't understand what right this man had to assault him, why basketball meant so much to this man, why Bradley had to carry the hopes and the venoms of millions around with him. Why couldn't it just be a sport?

But it isn't. Once an athlete accepts the uniform, he is in effect donning priestly vestments. It is the function of priests to offer sacrifices. As at the Christian Mass, in athletics the priest is also the victim: he who offers and he who is offered are one and the same. Often the sacrifice is literal: smashed knees, torn muscles, injury-abbreviated careers. Always the sacrifice is ritual: the athlete bears the burden of identification. He is no longer living his own life only. Others are living in him, by him, with him. They hate him, they love him, they berate him, they glory in him. He has given up his private persona and assumed a liturgical persona. That is, he is now a representative of others. His actions are vicariously theirs. His sufferings and his triumphs, his cowardice and his courage, his good fortune and his ill fortune all become theirs. If the Fates favor him, they also favor *them.* His deeds become messages from beyond, revelations of the favor of the gods. Only by some such an interpretation can we explain the dynamics of the psychic bond between an athlete and the fans.

Nowadays, people identify with all public figures, in fascinating paroxysms of love and hate. (Think of the pleasures of hatred and rage that Richard Nixon has given the liberals of our generation since 1949.) Yet the relationship between fans and athletes is sui generis. For athletes enter a regular series of liturgical struggles, through which their followers suffer with them. Again and again, the bond between athlete and those he represents is put to the test; again and again, he and they risk themselves against death. When the athlete's failure to attain perfection leads them all to defeat, of course they hate him.

Even if they forgive him, they hate him. He let them down, not in a trivial matter, but in their insistent desire for ideal perfection, in their desperate struggle to live and be proved dear in the sight of the gods. He has been the instrument of their rejection. So they reject him.

Athletes may complain about the fickleness of fans. But at least they should understand the dynamics of what they have undertaken. It is *not* just a game. Far more is invested in it than that. The deepest springs of human life are engaged in these ritual contests.

There is no use despising part of our own natures. We are of earth, earthy; descended, so they say, from the other hominids; linked by neurons and cells and organisms to the teeming chemical and biological life of this luxuriant planet. We are not pure minds, nor rational animals, nor separate individuals. The life of earth courses through us like the air we breathe, the sunlight that permeates us, the molecules of water and food that we ingest. We are part of earth. And in sports, earth makes visible to the human mind the great struggle of being and nonbeing that constitutes every living thing. To be alive is to lose, for everything living dies. We protest, of course. We hate the messengers who bring the bad news. From the bottoms of our heart, the hate is murderous. As if we could slay Death.

Thus, sports are a bond of brotherhood in an elemental sense. All the brothers die. Against death, we wrestle for at least the momentary victories of brilliant form, which live in memory. Immortal deeds.

Sports are celebrations of brotherhood in yet a second way. There are sports of solitude: hiking, swimming, running. And all sports drive one into one's resources of solitude: in the end, either the solitary individual heart has courage and stamina or it has not. Deep in the recesses of the solitary heart the most intense conflict of the agon is played out. The outward body is only this inner struggle's sacrament, its expression in fleshly acts.

But team sports introduce another factor altogether. At birth, while totally dependent upon a mother, incapable of sustaining life alone, the human infant is egocentric. What pleases or displeases, what warms or chills, pains or pleasures—these are the infantile preoccupations. Only with difficulty does a child learn to consider others. Often, indeed, such consideration is yielded only as a quid pro quo. In order to survive, one makes deals. Josiah Royce, the great Harvard philosopher, believed that not all human beings, even when they have attained physical maturity, attain moral maturity, or even its precondition, "a moral point of view." That point of view, he said, consists in displacing the self from the center of one's affections and concerns; in allowing other human beings to stand with the self at the center of one's perceptions and one's actions; to become many-centered rather than self-centered; to concede to other humans the same standing as one yields oneself. To be morally mature, the human being must learn to pivot his life upon community, not upon the solitary self. It is, Royce opined, a very difficult lesson, rarely learned.

For millions of youths in America, at least, this lesson is first lived out in sports. Even if its moral implications are not abstracted out from the experience, expressed in words, stated in propositions, and tested in laws of logic, the indispensable moral experience is offered to the reflective mind. Better to have the experience than to form the propositions. Better to have lived community than to know how to define it. On the other hand, to define it is not necessarily to injure it. Those who have known the experience can test the philosopher's words against what they have known; he may, or may not, be capable of grasping it. Philosophers are engaged in a game as well, a serious game, a game of putting experience into words, and many suffer defeat.

When a collection of individuals first jells as a team, truly begins to react as a five-headed or eleven-headed unit rather than as an aggregate of five or eleven individuals, you can almost hear the *click:* a new kind of reality comes into existence at a new level of human development. A basketball team, for example, can click into and out of this reality many times during the same game; and each player, as well as the coach and the fans, can detect the difference. "We were at the top of our profession," Dave DeBusschere wrote in his *The Open Man: A Championship Diary:* "We had shown that, without the best individuals, we could be the best team. We were a unit, a

beautiful, cohesive unit. . . ." Yet there were nights that
1970–1971 season—once, for example, when the Knicks
played the Bucks in Milwaukee—when the Knicks fell
back into playing individual basketball, each one doing
his thing, using the others but not really playing with
them, not one with them. Play would begin to be ragged.
Brilliant individual efforts would flash out, but the magic
of unity was gone. The spell the team could weave on its
opponents and the beauty of five playing as one, as if
with a single swift intelligence, a single generous heart, a
single reflexive system in five sets of arms, legs, leaps,
cuts, and shots, were dissipated. The human race itself is
not merely an aggregate of individuals; thus, images of
human unity excite some hidden longing in the heart,
some long-forgotten memory or expectation. For those
who have participated on a team that has known the click
of communality, the experience is unforgettable, like that
of having attained, for a while at least, a higher level of
existence: existence as it ought to be.

There is, I think, nothing mystical or anti-individual in
this high form of community. It is not a community that
diminishes each individual, or demands the submersion
of the individual. Quite the contrary. Each feels himself to
be acting at his very best, better than his individual best;
and not submerged but uplifted, beyond the limits of the
single self. It is true that the fellow who tends to shoot a
lot, or perhaps to be a prima donna, has to find a different
mode of action; and the change may be painful, its proper
vein difficult to locate. Some tensions, sulking, disappointments, battles, and frustrations may be necessary.
But the new mode, once discovered, does not feel like
subjection; it feels like liberation. One's defenses no
longer need to be held high; one can give and receive easily, ebb and flow with the rhythms of the team; and one
finds new capacities, new energies.

Walt Frazier did not lose any skills, or glory, or achievement when he modified his play for the championship
year, shot less, and became the mainspring of the team; it
was Walt Frazier's most sensational year. His sudden
steals, magnificent passes, and superb feints no longer
seemed capricious and diversionary; they now seemed to

have existence on a higher and more lustrous plane. One marveled at his individual talent, yes, but also at his ability to feel the inner necessities of the team, and at the way his brain seemed to be in harmony with four other brains. There are plenty of brilliant showmen in basketball; there are few who succeed in being so close to the inner instincts of a team as Frazier was. In later years, the Knicks could not sustain that higher music. It was not so much that their opposition grew better. In the loss of Reed, they lost essential music. The perfect balance and flow could return momentarily—and then the Knicks became briefly great again—but could not be sustained.

In football, the feeling of community is a little different. Its critics talk about fascism, authoritarianism, lockstep discipline. Football is a series of set plays, and split-second execution is essential. Concentration must be extremely high, for even in practice, without opposition, the plays fail a high percentage of the time. For perfect execution in the game, intense concentration and extreme alertness to the unexpected are indispensable. Thus, even when players are standing on the sidelines, they must maintain a high level of attention. Indeed, concentration on the game begins on Tuesday and hits a high pitch the evening before the game is played. In the game itself, each individual has only a few opportunities to act; each act must be perfect. Lapses of attention, a reflex only an instant slow, a failure to anticipate a feint, a fake, or a sudden turn of events—these cause perfection to be lost. To play football well, one must school one's attention to the highest possible levels of awareness; to play football wholeheartedly is to live a higher form of life, beyond the ordinary, to drink deep of possibilities of consciousness heretofore neglected. What to the casual observer seems accidental, fortuitous, reflexive is more often than not the fruit of highly tutored consciousness, the eyes constantly taking in multitudes of signals concerning possibilities yet to be realized. Out of the corner of his eye, the defensive halfback spots an unfamiliar stride on the part of an opponent, sets his own body muscles in a new pattern without yet moving outwardly, leaves the receiver open enough to attract the pass, and then breaks in on it in time to knock it down or intercept it. It is a game of intense calculation—a difference of inches separates perfect offense from perfect defense.

In football, no one offensive player can execute a play, and no one defensive player can cover the entire field. In the rapidly changing patterns of play, each player must recognize instinctively what each of his teammates will do; were two of them to converge on the same spot in the same way, one would be leaving undone something else that needed to be done. Indeed, one of the great features of the game is the harmony between a runner and his blockers, as each shifts his angles so as to trap the defenders into futile movements; if either the blocker or the runner miscalculates, the attempted block drives the defenders into, instead of away from, the runner. No coach, no system of authority, can command the instinctive, instantaneous reactions of players on the field; but for a winning team a thorough system of tutoring the instincts (by devising practice sessions that make the fundamentals second nature) can eliminate habitual mistakes and alert the players to variations they are likely to face.

In football, as in politics or business, everything depends on execution. However superior the talent, however excellent the strategy and the preparation, football is fundamentally a game of intense exertion, intelligence, and rapid violent force. If one side hits harder and more swiftly than the other, the best-laid plans are disrupted. Here, too, a team depends on its every member. Each must accept the high intensity and the pain of hitting harder than the opposition. If only two or three do so, the opposition will take the game to the weak spots. Contrariwise, if a team can take the game to their opponents' most highly motivated players, and beat them, its feeling of invincibility—and the dismay of its opponents—is bound to spread. Confidence affects one's ability to dare, one's timing, one's poise, one's feints. Confidence—and here, indeed, is a mystical component—somehow flows like an electrical charge not only into one's own hands and legs but into the ball itself, and like an icy dagger into the heart of one's opponents. A pass thrown with conviction somehow finds the 8-inch hole in the fingers of the defense, and a pass totally desired by a receiver somehow sticks in his fingers no matter what the difficulties. Not always so, of course; but it does happen.

Dave Meggyesy, the young man whose deference to father figures led him from football coaches to gurus, describes one of his own most satisfying playing moments: he was lined up opposite the opponent he admired most, John Mackey of the Baltimore Colts, when the Colts had the ball on the Cardinal 1-inch line. Mackey was the best blocker in the league. Meggysey's restless eye noted two tiny signals in Mackey's demeanor. As the quarterback began his count, Mackey would lower into position and his right arm would tremble slightly as it touched the earth. Meggysey correctly interpreted the nervous reflex as the buildup of tension in Mackey's body, and knew the play would come directly at him. Earlier, Meggysey had noted that a split-second before the snap of the ball, Mackey would dip his helmet slightly to begin his charge. The secret to a successful block in such combat is to get underneath the opponent's head and to apply one's entire force a fraction of a second earlier than he applies the counterforce. The offensive player has the split-second advantage of knowing exactly when the play will begin. Mackey's dropping head gave away that advantage. Meggysey, risking an offsides, started his own forward movement the instant Mackey dipped his helmet. He leapt across the line, swinging his forearm up under Mackey's head with all the force he could muster. The charge halted Mackey in place; the running back was stopped short of the goal. Meggysey executed this swift defense twice. Mackey, surprised, later congratulated him.

In football, each man at each position must execute in this way on every play. No one can, of course; one man's perfection is his opponent's failure. A team gains intensity and confidence from each success on the part of one member—one man's courage inspires the others. If some are playing well, but not with zest, the others tend to shepherd their own resources. A team depends on equal intensity on the part of all. If some slack off, the efforts of the others are canceled out. If all apply equal pressure, a bond of loyalty hardens the resolve of each: *I* will not be the one to let the others down. Each inspires the others to heights they otherwise would never climb.

No wonder, then, that football coaches look so eagerly for signs of *spirit, will, desire.* When teams are reasonably matched, intensity of execution makes the difference. The pain, weariness, danger, and exhaustion of the action discourage everyone. So individual morale is critical; more critical still is team morale. This is the secret behind that mystic word "momentum," so beloved of commentators. The intensity of football is so high that no team can maintain its highest levels indefinitely. A reversal of fortunes, the weariness of a key player, a sudden spasm of self-doubt, a brilliant play by the opposition against one's own best efforts—all these can momentarily take the edge off one's own certainty, confuse one's instincts. Sheer steady talent can hold off the deluge. But the difference between acting at one's peak and becoming cautious is a very fine one. A team that can sense, or diagnose, the opposition's letdowns and exploit them quickly is well on its way to victory. Some teams explicitly incorporate such diagnosis into their strategy. When their opponents are playing at their peak they try to hold them to a standoff. They wait for a sign of weakness, then turn up the pressure. They "play for the breaks," capitalize on weakness, exploit opportunities. It requires a very high degree of self-possession, a corporate self-confidence, for a team to play like that.

Teams, indeed, soon develop their own particular character. Some are unpredictable, stunning, erratic; some are grinding, steady, mistake-proof; some are high-spirited, some cool and professional; some never give up, never concede, while others unaccountably falter when the opposition is tougher than they were led to expect. Those who have played on various sorts of teams learn to adapt themselves to—or to counterbalance—the tendencies of their fellows. You can't make silk out of a sow's ear. Similarly, you can't play one kind of game with another kind of team. Learning how to respect the highest corporate possibility of a collection of individuals, who may walk and talk and look like any other crowd of individuals, is one of the highest communal arts a team and its coaches must master. Somewhere there is a formula that might unite and inspire them all; somewhere there is the secret of how all might play "way over their heads," be better than they normally would be. The great USC squad in 1974 was such a team, particularly in its amazing second-half comeback against Notre Dame. Losing decisively a minute before the half, 24–0, they followed Coach McKay's injunction to "score and score and score," and they won overwhelmingly, 55–24.

Some men remember with frustration teams that failed them in this ideal; some remember with joy its partial achievement. For all, this is the ideal that fires the imagination, becoming a standard for subsequent accomplishment. Even a team not talented enough to win every game can know this pleasure. The point of team sports is to afford access to a level of being not available to the solitary individual, a form of life ablaze with communal possibility.

9

The Fourth and Fifth
Seals: Rooting, Agon

THE FAN "roots." Yet in the tradition of rationalism and the Enlightenment, the highest stage of human development is to attain universality. Particularism is a scandal. Loyalties to a particular tradition, religion, region, group, or place are considered inferior and also immoral, as if they were the root of prejudice and conflict. Can an "enlightened person" be a fan? In this respect, the traditions of rationalism and of the Enlightenment seem at least partly antihuman. The metaphor of enlightenment itself seems pretentious. Human beings are not filled with pure light, are not angels. Their heads are firmly attached to solid, all-too-solid bodies. Enlightenment seems a trifle Manichean: dividing the world into light and darkness, making many pretend to a reasonableness they do not possess.

A human goal more accurate than enlightenment is "enhumanment." Sports like baseball, basketball, and football are already practiced as express liturgies of such a goal. One religion's sins are another's glories. Some "enlightened" persons feel slightly guilty about their love for sports; it seems less rational, less universal, than their ideals; they feel a twinge of weakness. The "enhumaned" believe that man is a rooted beast, feet planted on one patch of soil, and that it is perfectly expressive of his nature to "root." To be a fan is totally in keeping with being a man. To have particular loyalties is not to be deficient in universality, but to be faithful to the laws of human finitude.

A team is not only *assembled* in one place; it also *represents* a place. Location is not merely a bodily necessity; it gives rise to a new psychological reality. Miami, Florida, is a different sort of city now that it has the Dolphins; Denver carries a new identity as the home of the Broncos. New teams in such cities needed a place to play, a stadium, colors, a name. But the cities gained a new persona. Thousands of their citizens gained a focal point for their affections and despairs.

In sports cities around the nation, millions of lives are affected by whether in the days of their youth they were privileged to cheer for winners or, good-naturedly, groaningly, grew up with perennial losers. Around Pittsburgh we went for decades without a winner in anything; inferiority matched the mood of the region. When the Pirates burst through as world champions, followed later by the Steelers, their success released pleasant feelings of vindication, and grounded a rectification of reality: it *was* a good region in which to grow up; national recognition was long overdue. In Detroit, in a year of predicted riots, the Tigers raced toward the championship and brought the city a unity of spirit, a cooling off of hostilities, and even a diminishment of crime no federal programs had been able to accomplish.

It is true that America is steadily being nationalized; the great television networks and the commercial giants require, and help to effect, a unification of consciousness. National sportscasts alternate the teams they telecast; the viewers sometimes cannot see their own teams but must accept the "game of the week." In fact, of course, since a third of the population is highly mobile, the game of the week gives fans who have moved away a chance to see their old hometown squad. That is how I get to see the Dodgers, for example, now that they have moved way out to California. To watch teams I hardly know sometimes satisfies a certain tepid curiosity; I'm glad to catch a glimpse of Yastrzemski, Vida Blue, and others I have heard of. But unless I have a personal stake in a team, a game between two teams unknown to me rarely grabs my attention. Sometimes the sheer drama and perfection of the game holds me at the set; sometimes there is nothing better to do; but for the most part, I depend for excitement on team loyalties.

One effect of contemporary mobility, however, is to have given me multiple loyalties, at various levels of identification. At different times, I have lived near, or learned to love, five or six professional teams: Green Bay, Oakland, Pittsburgh, New York (the Jets), Washington, Minnesota. I like Don Shula, followed the Giants because I once met Fran Tarkenton, liked Baltimore because of John Unitas, kept an eye on the Bears because so many Notre Damers went there. When one or the other of these teams is playing, I have one or another peg on which to fix my affections. But that is the essential point. To watch a sports event is not like watching a set of abstract patterns. It is to take a risk, to root and to be rooted. Some people, it is true, remain detached; they seem like mere voyeurs. The mode of observation proper to a sports event is *to participate*—that is, to extend one's own identification to one side, and to absorb with it the blows of fortune, to join with that team in testing the favors of the Fates. The root of the word "fan" is not only "fanatic" but also "fantastic"; we have already noted its relation to the word for temple, *fanum*, the temple of the god of the place: by an exercise of imagination one places oneself under the fate of a particular group, becomes other than oneself, and risks thereby one's security. When Notre Dame loses, there is no reason for me to have allowed my security to be vulnerable; in rooting for Notre Dame, I open myself to their bad fortune as well as to their good. (Since, as David Hume says, there is a higher proportion of unhappiness than of happiness in every life, identification with another increases one's risks more than one's rewards. This was his argument against marriage; it also holds for sports fans.) A fan dies a thousand deaths. No team is, or can be, always perfect.

To the unbeliever, it is foolish to invest one's fortunes in a team, in a mere *game*. "How," they say, "can you care what happens to a group of silly men doing silly things?" Like attending cabinet meetings? I reply. Like attending press conferences? When I hear serious people talk about really Serious Things (a passion which I also indulge), my heart sometimes wanders in the middle of the conversation, particularly if at that very hour the Dodgers are playing. It is, I know, proper, well-behaved, mature, and adult to take seriously Summits, Diplomatic Shuttles, Crises of the Dollar, Get Out the Vote Campaigns, Riots in the Cities, Peace, War, Justice, Hunger, Dirty Air. It is not true, however, that these adult things are complex, and sports simple. On the contrary, the only difficult point on Serious Issues is to discern which is the More Moral Side. As they say in Congress, look to see how Bella Abzug votes, since at least 30 others will use her as a flag to vote against. The older one gets, the more the Serious Issues seem to be the highest comedy of all. And the more basic and fundamental seem to be the realities of sport: community, courage, harmony of mind and body, beauty, excellence. Let the world burn, these realities endure. Let New Moralities come, and Old Moralities be despised; still, three strikes and you're out, and a base hit when your buddies need it is a deed of beauty.

In sports is reality; not all of it, but a great deal of everything important. In politics and social action is illusion; not all of it, but a great deal of what Serious People today think important. Last year's Big Reform is this year's simpleminded gaffe.

I do not want to overstate the case. Business must go on. For the sake of the Ship of State, someone has to get dirty hands down in the boiler room. I only want to assert that rooting for politicians, movements, and causes is not a simple moral matter; it is full of irony, disappointment, bitterness, and, most of all, illusion. (Read Henry Adams. It doesn't change.) The rabid partisans of right, left, and center seem to me no freer from illusions than the partisans of Gehrig, DiMaggio, and Mays. Political and social commentary seem amazingly simplistic, the more so as one learns of the difficulties inherent in politics and statecraft. Moreover, in politics and social thought, partisans seem to me too little enamored of excellence, too quick in praise solely of their own companions, too rabid in their denunciation of their opposition. In sports fans, I detect a richer and more sophisticated appreciation of excellence. I have watched ovations for a player on the other side. Even at the height of their rivalries, antagonists in sports commonly reflect more respect for each other than do Republicans for Democrats, or radicals for liberals. In terms of civility and an ability to see the virtues on the other side, I prefer the company of sports fans to the company of Activists in the Constituency of Conscience.

The most universal experience in America, historians say, is to have been uprooted. Rooting is a pressing national need. The human being needs roots, because the pretense of infinity, the search for total universality, may be proper to the spirit but not to the body; and whoever commits himself to such a search dooms himself to the disintegration of the embodied self, which is death.

In *Easy Rider*, the moment Captain America commits himself to absolute freedom (just as in *Anna Karenina*, when Anna commits herself to total love), one's dreading heart knows that the ending must be death; suspense is released only when, bloodily, death comes. The human body cannot bear infinity. It is not made to be universal. The human body is of a specific color, sex, bone and neural structure, weight, shape, height, genetic heritage, cultural location, point in time and space. Although we walk on legs, we are as rooted in the long spinning structure of history as an ivy plant in earth.

The mobility of the superculture of the United States (i.e., those who identify with no subculture) is our national version of the pursuit of romantic love. We try to be free in total liberty, for total love. If observers watch with dread, it is because they know the narrative laws of such a story. Our national ideal is antihuman. Resisting the rooting ties, we cut our spirits free from discipline; they grow too large, misshapen, distended, anomic, puffs of gas, figures by Goya and Bosch. Divorce, abortion, abandoned children, greed, power, mobility, affluence—we live in a kind of middle-aged pursuit of the unfettered life, fettered by the realities of the jagged walls up which we climb.

The liturgies of sports counter, though poorly, the national pursuit of rootlessness. Even though the national madness uproots teams from city to city, leading them to hopscotch across the continent like drunks pursuing dollars; even though trades and deals result in tearing heroes out of one field and replanting them in others; still, through it all, the Dodgers, even in Los Angeles, break one's heart in as many ways today as thirty years ago, and Notre Dame is still visited by miracles and plunged into that "vale of tears" the *Salve Regina* of the grotto warns us of. God knows, our families and marriages are even more discontinuous than our national sports. Brothers and sisters, spread out across the globe, learn of nieces and nephews by dittograph at Christmas time. Second and third spouses, and children of various parentage, may seem more distant, even, than the teams of memory and youth. Compared to most American affections, the teams of sports have roots of oak.

To root, to be a fan, is to identify oneself with an organism that in every contest faces death. That is why steady winners become so arrogant, so out of tune with reality, and why losing teams see a decline in patronage. Yet when Ralph Kiner played for Pittsburgh and led the National League in homers every year for seven years, the fans came out, over a million every year, even though the Pirates lost more games than they could win. The spirit and the excellence of Kiner drew them, even in defeat. The bumbling, stumbling Mets of the early years became the darling princes of defeat. In general, however, defeat is death; losing is too painful for the fans. The beauty of the game may still attract them, and the possibility that odds-on losers may pull a grand surprise. But most in adversity dim their identification with a team. Being a steady loser hurts too much. Christianity may teach that a fruitful grain of wheat must die; the religions of sport, less paradoxical and less transcendent, fear death considerably more.

To root is not necessarily to be incapable of larger visions. Sports belong to the Kingdom of Ends, but are not the End. They are foretastes of the End, little ends before the End.

Of course, there are fanatic fans, fans who eat and sleep and drink (above all, drink) their sports. Their lives become defined by sports. So some politicians are devoured by politics, pedants by pedantry, pederasts by pederasty, drunks by drink, compulsive worshipers by worship, nymphomaniacs by phalluses, and so forth. All good things have their perversions, good swollen into Good, idols into God. Every religion has its excess. Sports, as well.

The good is always helpless before corruption, and yet outlasts it. Richard Nixon, a great perverter of sports metaphors, tried to stretch a double, missed a base, bluffed, was caught in the most exciting rundown the nation has ever seen, was lightly tagged on a flapping bit of tape, and then thrown out in a call perfectly clear to everyone in the stadium, just before he slid home lamely. The national liturgy was vindicated. The decision of the judge was final. He was out. The game went on. The people, having seen it all before in metaphor, calmly turned to watch the hitter after him.

THE FIFTH SEAL: AGON

According to rationalists, the form of life is reason. In sports, the form of life is conflict. What grabs us in sports—grabs those, at least, who have the faith—is conflict. An athletic event is an agon. In the ideal event, the antagonists are closely matched and the stakes are as nearly final as possible. Even in an early season meeting, a contest between two top contenders has more significance than other contests because it sets the stage for later meetings; a kind of intimidation, a kind of momentum, is a factor. The winner will gain a later edge, if he can sow in the loser a sneaky fear that, do what he will, victory is impossible. The loser, on the other hand, hopes the winner will underestimate him next time, when he has the incentive of desperation and revenge.

When the teams are not evenly matched, when the outcome is not in doubt, the symbolic power of the metaphor of life and death is lost; the risk has evaporated. One contents oneself with the formal aspects of the play: the brilliant execution, the perfect design, the masterful movements. A championship team that allows itself to look ragged earns displeasure. The connoisseurs of the art want perfection every time. Champions should look like champions. Sloppiness is an aesthetic affront.

Yet the heart of sports is contestation. A test. A trial. A match. On the surface, significance resides in competing excellences: who is better? But deep down, the contest means more than that. A game is not a kind of measurement. If that were the only thing at stake, a computer could point out every relevant statistic and assign superiority in cold printed fact. An athletic contest introduces elements that go beyond measurement: on the one hand, Fate; on the other hand, spirit. About the first, we have perhaps said enough already. Two teams compete, not only by matching talent for talent but also by competing for the favor of the Fates. They compete as good or evil, death or life; they are beloved of the gods or damned. No matter how well the teams or individuals perform, a bad bounce, a fumble, an errant pass can turn the tide of play. Even the team that is statistically playing better—getting more hits, enjoying superior pitching, gaining more yards, containing the other side, shooting better, working a tighter defense—can lose a game. Even a team that nine times out of ten can beat its antagonist may lose the most important game. To win, one must defeat both the other team and Fate. Coaches war against mistakes, complacence, inattention, lapses in concentration—the ghostly extra players employed by Fate.

But the most satisfying element in sports is spirit. Other elements being equal, the more spirited team will win: the one that hits the hardest, drives itself the most, runs the swiftest, plays with the most intelligence. Even a team seriously outmanned can play with greater concentration or devise more wily tactics. Half the pleasure of football is the contest between wit and brawn. Jim Thorpe of the Carlisle Indians, perhaps the greatest runner the game has ever seen, said his secret was to "show the man a leg, and take it away"; his reflexes and shifts of direction were wilier than any of his opponents, however big or swift, could master.

There is nothing more satisfying in sports, especially for a player, than to face a team more highly rated, catch them when they are playing at their best, yet still refuse to yield to them. Nothing is ever so sweet as victory under such circumstances. It is, one knows, a triumph of spirit. One will concede that the other team is better, *should* have been favored, under most circumstances *could* have beat one's own team. But not today. "We knew what we had to do. We did it." It is for this sort of victory that sports were invented.

Sports are creations of the human spirit, arenas of the human spirit, witnesses to the human spirit, instructors of the human spirit, arts of the human spirit. Spirit is not always visible in sports; is not always actualized; is often dormant. But at any moment it may flash through. Athletes often store their energies, wait, coil, spring. They love to dare the impossible. They love to be given challenges no one has a right to expect them to beat, and to prove by deed that the impossible is possible. They have to prove to themselves that their capacities exceed their past accomplishments. Sometimes, deliberately, they will set themselves at a disadvantage, tempt their opponents to test them, move in a step or two and dare them to try to hit behind them—and then go racing back to pull in a line drive with a running over-the-head arms-outstretched catch. In any one game, a man cannot count on being given opportunities for greatness; over a season, or over a lifetime, the opportunities are finite, can be numbered, come at their own pace. Thus, one must be ever alert to grab greatness as it passes by—to seize every risk, accept every dare. The great ones attempt what the good ones let go by. This, too, is a window to the spirit.

If I had to give one single reason for my love of sports it would be this: I love the tests of the human spirit. I love to see defeated teams refuse to die. I love to see impossible odds confronted. I love to see impossible dares accepted. I love to see the incredible grace lavished on simple plays—the simple flashing beauty of perfect form—but, even more, I love to see the heart that refuses to give in, refuses to panic, seizes opportunity, slips through defenses, exerts itself far beyond capacity, forges momentarily of its bodily habitat an instrument of almost perfect will. Perhaps it is a form of Slavic masochism (we should never discount it), but all my life I have never known such thoroughly penetrating joys as playing with an inspired team against a team we recognized from the beginning had every reason to beat us. I love it when the other side is winning and there are only moments left; I love it when it would be reasonable to be reconciled to defeat, but one will not, cannot; I love it when a last set of calculated, reckless, free, and impassioned efforts is crowned with success. When I see others play that way, I am full of admiration, of gratitude. That is the way I believe the human race should live. When human beings actually accomplish it, it is for me as if the intentions of the Creator were suddenly limpid before our eyes: as though into the fiery heart of the Creator we had momentary insight.

10

The Sixth and Seventh Seals: Competing, Self-Discovery

SOME PEOPLE, one-sidedly Protestant in temperament, approach sports as a means to an end: exercise, physical fitness. It is not the contest that attracts them. For myself, the prospect of shooting baskets endlessly, or jogging, or doing calisthenics seems far from the mark. The joy of sports is the competition. The essence is the conflict. But competition is not a simple concept. There are many ways of approaching it.

For some people, there is, indeed, a need to be number one. Not being on top is a blow to their self-image. This is especially true in tennis. Men (and women) in the top ranks of American society go on putting one another down in the courtly game of smashes, kills, and annihilations. Political leaders, foundation executives, and professors—by no means all such, but of a certain disposition—hate to lose. Not only because defeat is death, but also because being number two does not suit them. Upwardly mobile America is fiercely competitive, in an abstract way: what matters is not substance but competitive position. Leo Durocher once said, "Win any way you can." There are people who approach sports with that in mind. But even that injunction has two senses. One is lit-

eral. The other recognizes that a sport is a deliberate channeling of energies and possibilities, and is characterized
by limits, forms, rituals; *within these*, "any way you can"
depends on wile, guile, and energy. The first interpretation uses the game as an instrument of ego; the second
submits the ego to the limitations of the game, and makes
of every game an exercise in the exploration of possibilities within these limits. Finding new ways to lull, trick,
and outwit an opponent, especially an opponent of superior abilities, yields considerable pleasure; and affords, as
well, an exact appreciation of how games differ from mere
measurements of skill.

The most important distinction, however, is that the ultimate competition in sports is not with others but with
oneself. The distinction seems obvious in individual
sports like swimming, high jumping, long-distance running, or other track-and-field events. In many such
events, measurement is everything. The athlete ac-
cumulates best *times* or *distances*. "Competition" in such
sports provides both stimulation and the pressure of producing on demand. The presence of other good athletes
forces one to "outdo" oneself, to push oneself to new accomplishments. Still, one does not quite so much defeat
one's rivals as defeat one's old self. Both in training and in
the meet, one's attention is ultimately upon one's own
performance: one's own best time, one's own best distance. One keeps trying to extend one's achievements further. To have record-setting athletes as one's peers is a
spur and an incentive. One must try to better their marks,
but the essence of that struggle is to exceed one's own
previous limits.

This same distinction operates in baseball, basketball,
and football, although in somewhat different form. In
such sports, achievement is not so precisely measured.
These sports have all sorts of measurements—batting and
earned-run averages; passes completed and yards gained;
shooting percentage and total points scored, among
others—but true achievement in a game is more intangible than these statistics reveal. A brilliant, impossible
catch in baseball goes into the record book exactly like the
catch of a routine pop fly. Yards gained by extraordinary
effort and will, in crucial situations in football, are lost

among the more routine gains. Clutch shots made in basketball show up in the statistical totals without the characteristics that made them significant. In such sports, measurements are not the essence of achievement; they provide a sort of abstract, objective guide to one's overall comparative skills. A miler who has run a mile in 3:51 can be precisely identified with his achievement. Of course, a passer whose completion record is 63 percent also commands respect, but one feels that a great deal has been omitted: how was he on third downs, in calling plays, in the clutch, in surprising his opponents, in bringing home the big victories?

The career athlete keeps in his mind an image of his own ideal performance. I remember that Sandy Koufax, in a torrid pennant race in one of the last years he was pitching for the Dodgers, hurled two brilliant games in September, back to back. As I recall it, the first game was a one-hitter, which the Dodgers lost. The second was a no-hitter, which they won. The radio announcer was congratulating Koufax effusively for his no-hitter, but Koufax made a comment of considerable detachment (I quote from memory): "Actually, I pitched a better game Saturday, even though we lost. I had better stuff, and kept the ball just where I wanted it. Tonight it was a struggle all the way. I'm just happy we won." The win, the no-hitter, was not in his eyes as good a performance as the loss, the one-hitter.

The good athlete does not judge by external standards. He measures his performance against his own ideal. Whatever others may say—whether they praise him in prosperity, or neglect or damn him in adversity—he knows for himself the difference between performing well and performing poorly. He sets his own goals for each season. He sees his career as a whole. He takes his eyes off how others are doing, and even off outcomes, and limits himself to playing each game with maximum concentration.

In team sports, however, and in the heat of actual competition, two new dimensions are added to the contest. It remains true that the essential competition is with oneself. But two new questions probe further into the nature of an ideal performance: how does one behave under fire?

"Suppose you were an
anthropologist from Mars . . . .
Flying over the land
in a rocket,
you notice great ovals
near every city."

Sacred Space: "All the hours
of practice, all the years,
of discipline, all the frustrations
of getting ready,
have their focus here."

"Arenas are like monasteries; individual games imprint on memory single images blazing as if from an illustrated text. Awesome places, a familiar, quiet sort of awe. Our cathedrals."

"Baseball is designed like the federal system of checks and balances."

"Football is a celebration of a not innocent and not rational and not liberal human condition."

"It is a quiet game of fairness and precision, of control and discipline, of private hurt and aching limbs."

"Basketball is jazz: improvisatory, free, individualistic, corporate sweaty, fast, exulting, screeching, torrid, explosive, exquisitely designed for letting first the trumpet, then the sax, then the drummer, then the trombonist soar away in virtuoso excellence."

"Each feels himself to be acting at his very best, better than his individual best; and not submerged, but lifted up—up out of some of the limits of the single self."

"The batter faces the pitcher in utter solitude, depending on no one but himself."

"Football is essentially a corporate game, a game of solidarity, an almost socialist experience."

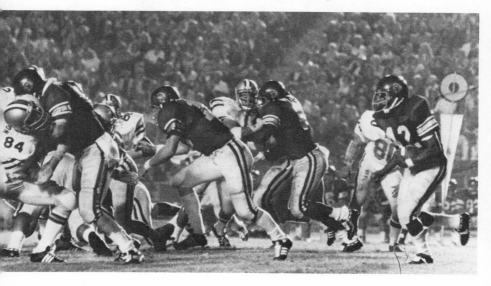

"Deep in the resources of each of us may be ripening
one, supremely lovely act."

how well does one become one with the team? There are players who in practice seem sleepy and unimpressive, who can't seem to find themselves except in the excitement of a game; there are players who seem to have every talent and perform efficiently in practice, yet in the pressures of a game they do not sparkle, or seize opportunities, or press their opponents. This is, perhaps, why coaches and scouts seek out *desire*. Athletes with lesser talents but great desire are better fitted for actual contests than men of vast ability but psychological reluctance.

Desire may be a purer gift than talent. Physical skills may be improved by hard work, but there may be no way of improving one's desire. A good training program and hours of practice can convert physical weaknesses to strengths; but if a man lacks desire, it may be impossible for him or anyone else to rouse him to play to his capacity. Shame, incentive, anger, threat, argument, persuasion, friendship do not succeed with everyone. Coaches, indeed, may spend more time trying to awaken desire than trying to improve physical skills. On the day of an actual contest, being "up" for the game—fit, passionate, and totally attentive—is indispensable. Sometimes, oddly enough, being thoroughly relaxed, even a little ill with fever, is the best way to be "up." One doesn't try too hard; one lets oneself "flow," perfectly in groove.

Now, perhaps the hardest thing is to learn one's own potential—of body, wit, heart, emotions. One has to learn to push oneself and to pace oneself, when to keep loose and easy and when to make demands. How each player does these things is unique to him. No rule covers all cases; exact insight into individual cases is both required and difficult to attain.

Yet baseball, basketball, and football are also contests. Without the keenest possible struggle to win, a contest is meaningless. But "win" is an ambiguous concept. Under conditions of highly organized play, whether in professional leagues, colleges, or high schools, winning has extrinsic importance. The coaches, at least, are hired or fired for their records; the costs of stadium, uniforms, training, travel, etc., must be paid for by admissions; often the football revenue, in particular, is necessary to pay for the costs of intramural, women's, and other sports in the col-

lege or high school. A losing team offers too few challenges to Fate, while a winning team keeps raising the
stakes higher and higher. Fans are not wrong to come out
for winning teams and to turn away from losing teams.
The former carry a kind of magic with them. On one level,
then, winning has extrinsic financial significance.

For professional players, naturally, sports are no longer
pure. Sports are a business, a craft, a way to earn a living,
a specialization. Of course, the same point may be made
about philosophers, poets, novelists, essayists, and academics; the instant they hire themselves out on the
strength of their crafts, they, too, cease to be as free, unfettered, and pure in their interests as the slogans of their
professions claim. Like them, the athlete is a hired hand,
a "pro"; also like them, the athlete may struggle, despite
financial necessity, to keep alive the freedom and the
cold, swift-running currents of pleasure native to his
craft; he may refuse to let commerce corrupt the essential
spirit of the sport. Thus, the athlete may feel some tension
between the desire to win in order to be at the top of his
profession commercially and professionally, the desire to
win in order to fulfill the aim of any contest, and the
desire to win in order to feel as though he is on the side of
being, abundance, good fortune and has played at the
highest pitch of his ability. These are three quite different
motives, and they are not always in harmony.

Sometimes a player will say, truthfully, whether his
team won or lost: "We didn't deserve to win." This sometimes means: "I'm disgusted with our performance." It
sometimes means: "They outhit us, outhustled us, out-
played us." On other occasions, a player will say ruefully,
meaning it truly but not wishing to use it as an excuse:
"We're as good as they are—or better—but today they got
the breaks. We'll take them next time." Sometimes a
player might say: "We won the goddamn pennant. The
wife and I are $15,000 richer. But by God, we were lucky. I
don't think we could do it again, if we tried. I'm gonna
enjoy it while we have it."

Thus, there are at least five levels to winning. The deepest satisfaction comes when all five are present. Individuals differ in depth and generosity of spirit, of course,
and so some may not care about all five levels; in other

professions besides sport the same variations can be seen. The five levels are:

1. Forget the emotional stuff. Winning means $15,000 instead of $8,000. It means a raise next year (which means a higher salary base the rest of my life—by the time I'm sixty-five, it may mean hundreds of thousands of dollars more in lifetime earnings). *Or:* This means a chance to make All-American and go as a high draft choice. It means I made an impression on the scouts.

2. Winning means we're number one—the best in the world, better than number two or three, on top of the mountain—and today I want to crow. We're the best. It's like living in a sphere above the heads of everybody else. Heady.

3. Winning is like living more abundantly, and like avoiding death: so the fact that we played well, took advantage of the breaks, and came home with the victory is very satisfying; now we have to knuckle down and show improvement before next week, next year, etc. Winners drink champagne; losers sip gall. I'd rather win.

4. The game is decided by the breaks, chance, Fate; and today Fate was on our side. We won, and that's the point of playing. In the long run, the breaks even out, so we'll take a victory any way we can.

5. The competition brought out in me the highest level of play I'm capable of. It was a great game, and in the struggle with myself, I won.

In France, once, an American watched two local soccer teams, the best in their district. After a magnificent contest, the American congratulated the captain of the winning squad on his team's superiority. The Frenchman was confused. He was happy, he explained, that the other team played so well; it forced his team to play better than they ever had. A contest, in his view, was an occasion for rising to heights—being *forced* by good opposition to rise to heights—never reached before. The point of the contest was to see how high one's level of performance could be pushed. To attain this goal, his team needed and was grateful for stiff opposition; that is why contests were invented. It is said that in China similar views about competition obtain.

Such notions are not unknown to American athletes. A truly great team suffers if it is never sufficiently tested. Schedules are drawn up years in advance; when the event finally arises, teams may not have the stiff competition they hunger for. It is not much fun to beat opponents handily. The deeper satisfactions come from defeating by narrow margins teams given at least an equal chance or even favored. Best of all is to be the underdog, consistently underrated but able every time out to defeat the favored team. That is perhaps the underlying myth of sports in America: a kind of democratic spirit, favoring desire, wit, and pluck over pedigree, birth, and favor.

The ultimate aim in sports is to give as flawless and as spirited a performance as possible. And yet, to face the risks of a fair contest *and* to emerge the victor is even more deeply satisfying, placing, as it seems, both good performance and Fate in their intended harmony. Those who deplore (and secretly dread) the intense competitiveness of American life might observe: (1) that during a lifetime, as during a career, one must expect to lose often; to die many times with grace is excellent preparation for reality; (2) that there is a difference in desiring harmony between one's best performances and the laurels of Good Fortune and desiring to vanquish an opponent; and (3) that every once in a while, the humiliation of an arrogant opponent is an immensely satisfying and highly democratic pleasure, not to be ascetically declined. Just because George Blanda said "I had Cleveland exactly where I wanted them" and purposefully swung his foot and drove the football through the distant goalposts (and through a dozen painful memories), one ought not to think too unkindly of him. The Browns deserved it.

In sports, dynasties rise and fall. No one dares to be too arrogant too long. *Hubris* and *nemesis*, veritable fountains of youth, churn as noisily in the veins of sport today as in the days of the discus throwers, the runners of the marathon, and the wrestlers of ancient Greece.

THE SEVENTH SEAL: SELF-DISCOVERY

The combats of sport are intended to prove and to try the athlete: to push his body to the uttermost, to probe his emotions for weaknesses, to winnow and to harrow his spirit in the dry soil of injury, defeat, and unaccountable discouragement. When the lungs burn, when old injuries throb, when the muscles tighten and the bone-wearying pace dulls the brain, when drops of sweat curl like points of fire into the eyes, when the chest heaves and the greatest efforts are yet to come, then we see what naked will can do. Then we discover who is a quitter, who cannot bear the intensity, who panics, who is frail of heart.

More prosaically than that—for most of an athletic career is prose, not poetry; boredom and discipline, not drama—every athlete soon discovers that he cannot imitate his heroes. His skills are not the same as theirs, or in any case his body and spirit have rhythms of their own. For most athletes, the experience of sport is an experience of discovering limits. The mind's eye can see a perfectly level swing, the fat of the bat hitting the small white ball, center against center, the ball then soaring swiftly to distant open spaces across the shimmering green. Yet the hands, hips, and shoulders—yes, and the flash of eye and the all-too-uncontrollable distillation of the spirit into perfect grace—fail to execute. One swings and misses. Or the mind's eye sees the center of the orange-rim basket, and the mind's ear already hears the nets *twang* as the hand dribbles; but in pushing up the ball, the body, or hand, or spirit wavers and the spinning ball *clangs* on the rim and drops away. In will and intention, each athlete knows perfection. The vast majority cannot come close to attaining it. Each athlete in every sport discovers very early that others, in this way or in that, are his superior. Each finds what he can do best. Each picks his level. Each labors to learn all that he has talent, endurance, and will to learn. Each must, sooner or later, cease pretending to be what he is not, cannot be, and rejoice in playing up to the limit given him. Life is not equal. God is no egalitarian. Prowess varies with every individual.

God fell in love with variety, and the fields of sport are ample enough to house most of it. Not all, it is true, can play football, basketball, or baseball. There are many other sports. Each sport is for most a teacher of humility and reconciliation. The formal structure of the games is virtually the same at every level. Every kid on the sandlot can be in every danger Joe Namath has ever faced. Every kid, by analogy, must at his own level exercise the same instant judgment, courage, and attempt to make his body—and the ball—do as his will directs. Occasionally, less frequently than Namath surely, he has the pleasure of a perfect act.

I recall as a boy of twelve practicing every day, by the hour, with my best friend, Barry Balint. Barry had short stubby fingers, and he wore thick, horn-rimmed glasses, but he could buzz a spiraling pass like an angel. (His younger brother Joey would later play for Navy.) No one in our class, no one in our small town in western Pennsylvania, could throw as well as he could. Barry and I decided to make ourselves ready to play for Indiana High (Billie Hunter, later of the Yankees and the Orioles, was then our hero, a three-letter man and quarterback of the football team). Something was wrong with my arm and shoulder; I never could learn to pass, and perhaps I had certain self-doubts, too. But even at age eleven I had fingers longer than most grown men, could almost pick up a basketball with one hand, and I was as fleet of foot as any kid around. It was easy to decide: Barry would pass, I would be the end.

There was a vacant lot a block from Barry's house, and every day for hours it belonged to us. The grass was wiry and uncut, but we kept it trampled down. A worn dusty path cut diagonally across, to save passersby the corner. We marked off a line of scrimmage, and picked certain spots downfield at which Barry, on count, would throw the ball. We planned the routes that I would run, and timed them. We called "plays," naming the spot and the count on which the ball would be thrown. I would run anywhere except directly at the spot. I would keep my head, shoulders, and feet aiming anywhere but at the spot. Counting first aloud and then, after several weeks, mentally, when we had unfailingly internalized each other's rhythms, Barry would fade back with the ball and I would run my pattern. He would throw. I would give a last feint, turn, step, and there waiting for my rushing fingertips, more often than not (in the gilded memory of middle age), would be the spiraling ball. Barry practiced throwing it high above my head, in front of me, and behind me; throwing it at my chest; throwing it at my knees. He practiced looping it and burning it like a rifle-shot. He practiced swift 2-yard bullets, and long 30- or 40-

yard bombs. His trick in every case was never to make me wait, always to keep the ball at the farthest possible spot in front of me that I could reach in a dead run and without breaking stride. My trick was to deceive imaginary opponents, to retain the secret spot of contact with crystal-clear concentration in my mind, and to use flying feet to power extra speed, if needed, and "sticky fingers" to pull in any pass within a yard or so on any side of the intended target. The two of us breathed, thought, counted, acted as one. Barry could put the ball through a tire swinging on a tree. He made things easy.

It is difficult to express the sheer beauty I experienced, facing leftward, feeling the blazing sun upon my head, feeling the weedy field fly beneath my feet, listening mentally for the assigned count, feinting, then suddenly facing rightward, looking back, and spotting it, falling out of the silvery blue sky, glinting in the sun, the burning pointed oval that my outstretched fingers so desired, touched, held, pulled in, and then the fantasy of the white yard stripes gliding into one another as without breaking stride I crossed the goal line. The beauty, the precision, the discipline of the thing is one of the loveliest memories of boyhood.

Accidents of personal history—my family moved away; other kids, slower to develop, overtook Barry's skills—prevented us from playing our appointed roles on a real team. (We could beat any kids around in pickup games.) Barry, I believe, ended up playing tackle or end at Indiana High. Johnny Dubinsky, who at twelve was shy and fey, became, I think, the quarterback and poised star of the team. None of us played in college. We had had our day, met our limits.

Yet I would be astonished if Barry and John, and all the millions of others like us, didn't still watch Blanda, Namath, Unitas, and all the other Sunday heroes with exquisite pleasure, admiration, and beauty-scorched memory. What we wished to do, strove for—what do I mean? *still* strive for, *still* emulate—they do as gracefully as gods. We were for a season gods, or at least boys with dreams; we still are. We went to our limits, as they go to theirs; and if theirs exceed ours, we regard them not with envy but in brotherly participation. The spirit, the beauty, are greater than any one of us, are the air in which all of us soar, sea in which all of us swim, sun in which all of us share the power and the glory. The superstars are not brilliant solely for themselves; what we could only dream, they do, but as dreamers they belong to us as much as to themselves, brothers of the same holy grail.

I relate this memory, indulge these dreams, only to indicate the pleasure that recognition of limits brings. So long as an athlete is a rival, so long as we are in a contest, I am entitled to hate him, to envy him, to defeat him and pull him down a peg in any way I can; and he is out to deflate me. One should not underestimate the murderous sort of hatred contests draw upon. Each great deed of his forces higher the pressures on my lungs, muscles, nerves, will, wit, endurance. One hates one's tormentors, justly. But hate is the other side of love. A great rival is a great gift. How can one extend oneself into fresh heights if there is no one to force one higher? An artist of any sort who has no peers suffers from the lack. Great peers make one greater than one could become in solitude. When I have tried and tried, again and again, and still cannot keep abreast of my rival, there comes, perhaps, disappointment, even grief, but finally reconciliation. My limits have been extended to the breaking point. I can go no further. Thanks, friend; otherwise, how would I know?

Yet the recognition of limits is not the only form of maturation taught by sports. There comes also, at least to some, a sense of their own bodies and attitudes, a sense as it were *from the inside out,* quiet, subtle, full of luminosity and peacefulness, beaming from deep within until its rays at last reach consciousness: a sense of inner unity. One can distinguish yet hold in unity. *Distinguer pour unir.* Muscles, sinews, ligaments, nerves, juices, bones. Concentration, relaxation, tension, sweetness, turmoil, rage, desire, envy, humiliation, panic, calm, steel, confidence, anxiety. Each has an effect on the bat, the ball, one's every movement. In certain combinations, one's body and heart and soul seem to move as one, and one's performances improve. Learning how to listen for the fertile self, the united self, is as important for the athlete as for the writer.

To those who have not acutely and clearly experienced the unity of hand, heart, and mind, these words may sound mystical, yet they are matters of experience. Discipline, time, and perhaps a special grace (since many things we wish for do not come when bidden but at a time of their own choosing) make them part of our familiar world, as friends and recognized allies. For example, I once noticed in splitting logs, at least the slightly green, large logs left in our yard over a single winter, that there was a clear relationship between my consciousness and the successful splitting, in a single stroke, of each log. The trunk of one log was well over 18 inches in diameter; it had been cut in sections of the same length. Standing these logs on end, I would swing the heavy sledge-ax Bob Streiker at the hardware store had recommended to me, and most of the time the ax would bury itself in an inch or two of wood, and only heaving and shoving could pry it loose. Then I tried to concentrate on the wavy lines of the wood's grain. I soon learned that my eye, conscious mind, and clear intention were not steady enough to allow me consciously to direct my blows; the ax still stuck.

I then remembered an incident from several years earlier. Once I was shooting baskets in a school playground. A little boy of nine sat against the wire mesh of the school window, watching me. I had a hot hand that day, and basket after basket dropped pleasantly into the waiting net, uttering the sensual *snap*. The boy stood and approached me timidly. "How do you do that?" he said. "You make everything. Can you show me?" Overcoming a rush of pleasure, I cleared my throat and began rather formally. "Well, you see, you hold your feet like this, take the ball so, bend, jump . . ." and suddenly I found I couldn't do it. I tried three times and couldn't put one in. "Sit down, kid," I said. "Wait till I get it back. Watch." I dribbled a few times, tried to forget *how*, thought about the ball, its weight, the center of the basket, and cleared by mind of everything else. The shot came back.

I decided to try the same thing with the ax. I felt its weight, mentally felt the arc of its swing, and concentrated on the log's sweet invisible center. Along the wavering lines of the grain, a crack had jagged its way to the core of the tree. That center was too weakly visible for my conscious mind to direct my hand to the exact point of tension on the crack. I had confidence that a smooth swing, guided by restful concentration, might detect it; I remembered that a smooth lifting of the basketball, left to instinct and concentration and will, had found the basket's center far more often when I didn't try to guide it than when I did. My mind was at peace. I visualized the central fault of the log, I swung with mind as empty of control as I could—and the ax went through the log as swiftly and smoothly as a hot knife through butter for the August corn. The twin sides of the log fell neatly at my feet.

So long as I could hold anxiety and conscious mind at bay, my instincts were at one with the wood and the logs split as gently to the touch as perforated crackers. When I too much marveled at my skill, worried whether I had really got the knack, *tried* to concentrate, made mental adjustments during the downward swing—with a rude jolt the ax stuck. Only when I could relax, when I had confidence, when I felt a certain harmony and relaxation, did the ax penetrate from top to bottom sweetly and without jarring blow.

This is one of the great inner secrets of sports. There is a certain point of unity within the self, and between the self and its world, a certain complicity and magnetic mating, a certain harmony, that conscious mind and will cannot direct. Perhaps analysis and the separate mastery of each element are required before the instincts are ready to assume command, but only at first. Command by instinct is swifter, subtler, deeper, more accurate, more in touch with reality than command by conscious mind. The discovery takes one's breath away. A democratic harmony seems to exist in the recesses of the self. The mind should be no tyrant; will should not be authoritarian. Rather, one listens to the humblest parts of oneself, allows them to express themselves, concentrates quietly, without forcing or pressing, on the desired end, and lets the constituent assembly of the many parts of self and world work their consensual will. When all work together in implicit harmony, the center of the self meets the center of the focused world: the fat of the swung bat meets the inner secret of the ball in unmistaken sweetness and grace, and the inner will of the swing and the inner will of the ball fuse like a single streak of light. The sound of the meeting tells no lies: an unforgettable sound. The ball soars swift and true, direct or in parabola. Unless the defenders stand directly in its path, the sound means "hit."

The same is true in football. The instant he releases them, there are passes the passer *knows* will reach their mark; passes the receiver knows, no matter how improbable it seems, that he will catch. It is not so much a matter of conscious thought or conscious will; highly disciplined, prepared, and tutored instinct—like some swift computer—does the job.

Sometimes, and here perhaps some readers will begin to doubt me, the mysticism is even deeper. I can swear that once, in a championship game of touch football, on the last play of the game, I felt an unfamiliar moment of panic. I was the only freshman on the team, a defensive back. I had played well the entire game. But it seemed plain the play would be directed at me. I diagnosed the play, guessed the intended receiver, the ball was thrown directly at him, within the range of my hands. I jumped. Somehow it eluded me; my timing was poor, something. But it seemed to me then that when I jumped, the ball jumped with me. It seemed they *willed* to win, and that I had somehow surrendered to panic in my heart.

In the game with Denver mentioned in Chapter 1, when Blanda threw one of his "miracle" passes, he "looked down" one of the defenders, froze him, threw past him for the touchdown. After the game, the defender, an old acquaintance, explained to Blanda ruefully that he knew exactly what was happening but he couldn't move, he felt helpless.

John Brodie of the San Francisco 49'ers is certain that, under certain conditions, when passer and receiver purely *will* a completion, then, no matter what the obstacles or how tightly or well the defenders play, the pass will be complete. The ball will pass right through perfectly placed hands, or seem to jump just over or under them, or bounce from them directly to the receiver. Every athlete knows experiences of this sort, in which *wanting* something badly enough, in a moment when hidden forces seem to be on one's side, makes it happen: a long chase after what seems to be a triple, but one hauls it down; a throw to second base to cut down a runner; a determined hit; a basket under impossible conditions when time is running out; a one-handed catch one could never duplicate. The human will is unfathomable. One need not believe in miracles. Only in the twin miracles of instantaneous instinct and sheer don't-accept-no determination.

The year after my debacle as a freshman, our team was again in the intramural championship, against the same squad as the year before. Because of a delay in the physics lab, I arrived at the game late. We were losing by a touchdown. For a year I had waited for this day. My blood was pounding, but I felt a deep and certain calm inside. A favorite pass play was called, but the passer threw a yard behind me. I wanted that ball so bad. I stuck out one hand at a crazy angle. The defender had left me and was moving for the interception. The ball stuck by its point in my crazily cupped hand, I pulled it in, the defender ran at empty air, and no one stood between me and the touchdown. Another play later in the game, not unlike the first in improbability, won the game. It felt to me as though sheer will had done it. Planning had not, could not, have been effective. Luck, perhaps, but not luck alone; an absolute determination to seize the slightest possibility and convert it into fact. Afterward the other team teased me, calling me "lucky." I laughed with them, but I did not believe it was luck. I wanted victory so *much* more than they did. It seemed so plain to me that *wanting* to make those plays had made them. They couldn't know my desire, but I did. Desire so strong it dominates events (although it doesn't, can't, always do so) is as the world ought to be. When desire and event thus meet as one, there is a harmony in the self rarely sounded, a chord, a melody, for which one cannot always find the notes. The music when one finds them is ineffable.

SPORTSREEL

The Century of Myth and Symbol—Ours

A thousand years from now, anthropologists may be arguing that life in our century wasn't nearly as rational, desiccated, and analytical as most of the writers of our time described it. They will point out that 32 million persons in the United States in 1975 admitted believing in astrology. Great mythic hungers made millions of others ache for psychic food. Many intellectuals believed in a "socialism" without empirical content, not Russian socialism, or Eastern European socialism, or North Korean socialism, or even Swedish or British socialism, just in *socialism*, a socialism, as they imagined, without bureaucracy or system. Others found historical meaning in "liberation" and "revolution" without a clear idea of any state in history more liberated than the one they already had. Everywhere, future anthropologists will note, enormous appetites for meaning and identification wandered loose, seeking objects upon which to attach. As traditional religions lost their heat, empty hearts sought in social change, politics, the stars, the pursuit of sexual pleasures, and dreams of glamour something to make them seem important, beautiful, and good.

Even the automobiles people drove showed strong mythic content: Cougar, Maverick, Cutlass, Monte Carlo, Vega, Mustang, Grand Prix, El Dorado, Fury, Beetle, Hornet, Dart. Scholars might even come to believe that twentieth-century America was one of the most luxuriant makers of symbols the human race has ever known, a people drenched in mythic life, attuned to the symbolic universe as few humans since the cavemen. It will count as a high achievement.

These experts will also observe that the names of sports teams tried to crystallize the attitude of cities toward themselves, to express a certain attitude or spirit, to try to draw from the symbol a certain energy and focus. Every state, they will notice, officially chose an animal and a flower to typify it. Every team—often after great deliberation in which the entire populace became involved—chose a name.

It will be fascinating for them to categorize the myths that govern the major professional football, baseball, and basketball teams in the United States. Some names grow simply from an item of the uniform: White Sox, Redlegs, Red Sox. Others derive from the mythic power of industrial life: Oilers, Steelers, Jets, Brewers, Expos, Astros, Supersonics, Bullets, and Mets. Others reach back to historical human types with special powers: Giants, Angels, Saints, Raiders, Pirates, Chiefs, Redskins, Indians, Braves, Yankees, Warriors, Royals, and Athletics (or A's). Some have names based on local peculiarities: the Dodgers because of the Brooklyn trolley cars outside Ebbets Field, the Bums because of an eminent local cartoonist; Browns because of a coach's name; Bills because of Buffalo Bill. Others suck symbolic strength from the animal kingdom: Lions, Bears, Cardinals, Eagles, Rams, Falcons, Bengals, Dolphins, Colts, Broncos, Chargers, Orioles, Tigers, Cubs, Bulls. Others try to catch in a single myth the historical or patriotic energies of their origin: Vikings, Cowboys, 49'ers, 76'ers, Patriots, Padres, Celtics, Knickerbockers, Lakers, Capitols. Some use geographical derivatives: Twins, Phillies, Texans. One uses a name to rhyme with its cousins: Nets. A whole set of other names flickered briefly in the World Football League: Flame, Fire, Sun, Stars.

The human imagination did not wither in a scientific age. Science and secularity were only temporary myths within a surrounding jungle of myth, clearings painfully hacked out, always encroached upon by Apollo, Gemini, and Lodestar. Poetry and myth, they may conclude, finally proved more vigorous than reason in what they may (mythically) describe as the Age of Enhumanment.

STOP THE REEL

Belief and Unbelief

The Seven Seals occur as a metaphor in The Apocalypse of St. John. Around the edges of those seals arise images of evil and destruction. In Ingmar Bergman's *The Seventh Seal*, the figure of Death reaches across a chessboard toward the knight. Life and death, goodness and corruption, faith and doubt, civilization and barbarism all engage in age-old combat. It is not plain whether civilization is a triumph over savagery, or whether savagery is the stronger force over which civilization is suspended like a fragile fabric. The question torments American literature from Herman Melville to John Barth. Is ours a civilization or a mask? And which, then, is the originating spirit of our sports?

Themes of belief and unbelief, darkness and light, are vivid in many recent comments on sports, especially in America. A sampling of such themes retrospectively illuminates our investigation to this point, and opens up questions we must next consider. Some regard sports as a source of hope; others see them as metaphors for all that ails society. An adequate theory of sports must account in some fashion for all such opinions. Medieval theology arose as a speculative effort to comment on, and to reconcile, the "Sentences" gathered by Peter Lombard from the opinions of the early Fathers. Here, then, is a sampling of the diversity of views: "sentences" that stimulate the inquiry so far pursued, and yet to be pursued.

In the sports world, as in society at large, individuals representing an authoritarian, anti-life force are lining up in opposition to those representing a creative, humanistic life force. . . . These two positions represent fundamentally opposed views of life. When we enter the sports world to do our research and applied work, we have to make the choice of which of these two forces we are going to support. —JACK SCOTT (1971)

Well-meaning people often ask sportswriters, even middle-aged sportswriters, what they are going to do when they grow up. —ROBERT LIPSYTE

Sports, athletics, games are too important to be just for the varsity. In fact, our professionalizing of sports, down to the high school level, is the greatest enemy of general health and fitness that we have. —JOHN HOLT (1970)

Pro football is a sick society's projection of itself into public spectacle. . . . Football comes closer to political fascism, I think, in its cultivation of mass hysteria and its fawning idolization of the powerful. The correlation between the growing importance of political authoritarianism in North America and the increasing popularity of big-league football should not be overlooked. —JOHN McMURTY (1971)

Thousands of people who don't know me use my participation on a Sunday afternoon as an excuse for nonaction, as a fix to help them escape their everyday problems. The toll of providing that experience is beginning to register on me. —BILL BRADLEY (1971)

Society, and its sports, are polarizing rapidly. We still have the choice of either fighting to preserve the neo-colonialist profits of our bosses or fighting together with the peoples of the neo-colonies to abolish the system of bosses entirely. —PAUL HOCH (1972)

No press, no interest, no baseball, no twenty-two-year-old shitkicker making thirty-five grand a year at an animal occupation.   —LEONARD SHECTER (1969)

Most of the sportswriting in the Twenties and Thirties was written for dolts. Grantland Rice mixes metaphors about twenty-four times in "Outlined against a blue-grey October sky." Today's sports pages have more style and more art than any other part of the paper. Look at Dalton's anthology of sports writing each year and you'll see the steady improvement. . . . The other day I was interviewing a player and found myself forming his answers before I asked my questions. I was about seventy-five percent accurate. A friend of mine says you've heard it all in sports when you reach thirty-five. I'm three years over the limit. Eventually, I'm going to have to get out.
                    —WELLS TWOMBLY (1974)

You see, in the spoon-fed, Alice in Wonderland world of sports broadcasting, the public was not accustomed to hearing its heroes questioned. . . . What was it all about, Alfie? Was football more important in this country? Was it a moral crime to introduce objective commentary to the transmission of a sports event? If so, how did the people get this way? Remember, this was 1970—an endless war was raging in Vietnam. The economy was in trouble. Unemployment was high. Racial problems were still in the news. The fact that there could be such outrage against a sports commentator [Cosell, for lightly criticizing a black player] after one football telecast, had to be a reflection on the values of many Americans.
                    —HOWARD COSELL (1973)

. . . we are marks for every hustler with a couple of jocks in tow. None of it has contributed to our civilization.   —LEONARD SHECTER (1969)

"But, still, aren't sports the toy department?" "Of course."
                    —JIM MURRAY (1974)

Sport was the main occupation of all of us, and continued to be mine for a long time. That is where I had my only lessons in ethics.   —ALBERT CAMUS

Never in the history of this country, with the exception of V-J Night, has "God Bless America" been played as many times as it has been played on televised football games beginning that fall. . . . This came at a time when the President and his people were out hitting hard. If you opposed the war, you opposed America. Now, translate that to, if you opposed America (which you didn't in the first place) you opposed football, and if you opposed football, well, my God, where will it all lead? . . .

Conversely, during the 1970 season ABC chose not to televise the University of Buffalo's half-time show, which reflected a different view of America. The show dealt with matters like ecology and pollution, and it did, indeed, deal with the Vietnam war. The decision not to carry the show was made by Roone Arledge, the American Broadcasting Company's vice-president in charge of sports programming. He dropped it on the theory that it was antiwar and, therefore, political.

—JERRY IZENBERG, *How Many Miles to Camelot?* (1972)

There are probably more really committed Christians in sports, both collegiate and professional, than in any other occupation in America.   —BILLY GRAHAM

The Anglo-Saxon sport, par excellence, is golf, a game in which a player at any time has the opportunity to cheat at will, but in which the game loses all interest from that point on. It should not be surprising that this may be correlated with the attitude of the taxpayer to the treasury and the citizen to the state.

No less instructive an illustration is provided by the Argentine card game of *truco* in which the whole emphasis is upon guile and even trickery, but trickery that is codified, regulated and obligatory.

—ROGER CAILLOIS, *Man, Play, and Games,* (1958)

But it was the Freudians who made the colossal blunder. You could argue that they overlooked football on the grounds that it was just too big to be noticed. . . .

Obviously, football is a syndrome of religious rites symbolizing the struggle to preserve the egg of life through the rigors of impending winter. The rites begin at the autumn equinox and culminate on the first day of the New Year with great festivals identified with bowls of plenty; the festivals are associated with flowers such as roses, fruits such as oranges, farm crops such as cotton, and even sun-worship and appeasement of great reptiles such as alligators.

In these rites the egg of life is symbolized by what is called "the oval," an inflated bladder covered with hog skin. The convention of "the oval" is repeated in the architectural oval-shaped design of the vast outdoor churches in which the services are held every sabbath in every town and city. . . . These enormous roofless churches dominate every college campus; no other edifice compares in size with them. . . . .

Love of mother dominates the entire ritual. The churches, without exception, are dedicated to Alma Mater, Dear Mother. (Notre Dame and football are synonymous.)

The ceremony begins with colorful processions of musicians and semi-nude virgins who move in and out of ritualized patterns. This excites the thousands of worshipers to rise from their seats, shout frenzied poetry in unison and chant ecstatic anthems through which runs the Oedipus theme of willingness to die for love of Mother.

—CHILDE HERALD, *Rocky Mountain Herald* (1955)

Even in athletics, the traditional bastion of *ésprit de corps*, individual aspiration appears to be gaining the upper hand as superstars leave their championship teams for momentarily greener pastures. Selfless commitment to a group goal, we assume, is an outmoded value, obsolete in business firms where the only thing members have in common is their employer.

—THE EDITORS, *Psychology Today* (1974)

Education, said William James, is a process by which we are able to distinguish what is first rate from what isn't. Sport, more often than not, shows us the elements of what is first rate.

It does this because it is the long-sought moral equivalent of war, not as an outlet of aggression and violence, but as an arena where man finds the best that is in him, a theater that reveals courage and endurance and dedication to a purpose, our love for our fellows and levels of energies we never knew we possessed. And where we see, if only for moments, man as he is supposed to be.
—DR. GEORGE SHEEHAN, *New York Times* (1974)

My apologies to Dr. Sheehan for failing to see how Bill Bradley and Larry Csonka have contributed more to this country than the scientists seeking a cure for cancer. It is hardly fair to see some of America's bright young people barely scraping out a meager existence when Bill Walton is earning upwards of half a million dollars per year to run around in his underwear before a packed house of raving fanatics.   —FREDERICK J. POMERANTZ (ibid.)

This is a university, not a circus.   —ROBERT HUTCHINS

Not enough young men and women who come to a university have ever had a punch in the nose, not enough have ever had a black eye, not enough have ever been involved in contact sports or personal physical combat. . . .
One thing we saw when we had student violence on campus a few years ago was that riots started because of the most relatively innocent incidents—a kid with a bloody nose was enough to start a riot because many of the young men and women had never seen anybody bleeding on an important scale before. They interpreted a bloody nose as a sign of brutality. I think it would be good for us if we had some of those participant activities where everybody gains a sense of his own physical feelings—what it feels like to hurt a little, what it feels like to get bumped, what it feels like to be able to run faster, or to get caught, or to lose.
—MAURICE B. MITCHELL, in *College & University Business*
(1973)

[We should deplore] what universities with a major sports program and particularly a major football program

do to their coaches. We put them in a position where we say you must win because the university has said we are not going to put any funds into the athletic program and it must earn its own way. Now, if intercollegiate athletics are worthwhile, if the university has decided that it wants a major program, then there is little logic in saying it must earn its own way. When a university does that it forces the intercollegiate athletic program to be commercial.
—JOHN FUZAK, in *College & University Business* (1973)

Those who had not won their letters had a higher degree of sportsmanship than those who had. Football players scored lowest in sportsmanship of all the teams represented; baseball players, basketball players, and track and field athletes scored highest. Of all the athletes, subsidized athletes (the better ones?) demonstrated the poorest sportsmanship attitudes. An overwhelming number of all the respondents approved of breaking rules if they would not be caught or penalized.
—ROBERT N. SINGER, *Coaching, Athletics, and Psychology* (1972)

In the field of conduct and morals, vociferous proponents of college athletics have claimed for participants far greater benefits than athletics can probably ever yield, and in attempting to evaluate these supposed benefits, have hailed the shadow as the substance. The workings of commercialism have almost obliterated the non-material aspects of athletics. And yet such qualities as loyalty, self-sacrifice, courage, and, above all, honesty, can be more readily and directly cultivated through the activities and habits of the playing field than in almost any other phase of college life.   —SAVAGE (1929), cited by Singer (ibid.)

. . . sports (again, especially professional sports) remain one of the few areas of our national life and culture relatively uncontaminated by the erosion of standards. There is still a fairly clear notion of what constitutes excellence in sports and there isn't much argument about the nature of the criteria. In baseball you know that somebody who hits .330 is likely to be a better hitter than someone who hits .260.

The public for sports is an educated public. In the arts with which I have a closer professional concern, we do not have as discriminating a public as sports do. We have millions of people who really are connoisseurs of many different games, so that what you've got here is a kind of passion for a world in which the standards are clear, excellence is relatively uncontroversial as a judgment of performance, and in which the major preoccupation (despite reserve clauses and despite all the gimmicks and commercial gimmickery that we associate with professional sports) is to do something supremely well, in which everyone has agreed that this is the major objective and in which the better the person or team does something the more honor and the more and greater riches are likely to accrue to him. We want that kind of world, we see it in less and less pure form in other areas of our national life. The need and the hunger for such a world is what accounts for the passion that so many people, including me, feel about professional sports.

—NORMAN PODHORETZ, in *Yale Reports*
(radio transcript; 1972)

I had a bartender friend in Philadelphia years ago, a devoted baseball fan, who told me, and he said this with tears in his eyes, that the most beautiful thing in the world, more beautiful than any blond, more beautiful than a mountain lake at sunset, was bases filled, two out, three and two on the hitter and everybody moving with the pitch.   —RED SMITH (ibid.)

The energy, the grace, the tactical brilliance and the precision that these huge creatures can command and in the case of my team, the New York Knicks, the capacity for selfless teamwork does present a spectacle that I find beautiful, exciting and exhilarating and, if I may be pompous, . . . spiritually exhilarating.

—NORMAN PODHORETZ (ibid.)

Thus was founded what came to be called the Chipmunk School of Sports Journalism. It came by its name in an era when some electronic genius was mixing voices at different speeds on recording spools and peddling the result as the warbling of a trio called the Chipmunks. It was more chatter than music.

One afternoon at Yankee Stadium, the late and deeply missed curmudgeon, Jimmy Cannon, noticed that the youngest and most irreverent authors in the press box cared not a whit for the heroics in progress out there on the field. They were all clustered in the back, making insulting remarks about those noble athletes and their personal habits. They had absolutely no respect, and it showed.

"You guys sound just like those damn chipmunks on that record," Cannon snarled. "That's what you bums are, chipmunks. Why don't you shut up?"

In their relentless desire to destroy all icons and bring all athletes down to an earthly level, writers have produced a landslide of unflattering articles, columns and books.

They are all designed to show how shallow athletes truly are. There is not a stain-glass window unshattered. No tombstone has been left unturned. One gets the impression at times that the place where the vice squad ought to start is not the tenderloin, but the dugout.

—WELLS TWOMBLY (1974)

People tend to look at life—and at sport—through their own experience and mental categories. When a person looks at a game of football, he tends to see a reflection of his own life. If it's mainly violence and getting ahead and winning at all costs, he'll tend to see that in the game. . . .

But many of the players—most of the ones I know—resent those images. They know there is more to the game than that. And I think there are many fans who see past those images and get glimpses of something more. . . .

Often, in the heat and excitement of a game, a player's perception and coordination will improve dramatically. At times, and with increasing frequency now, I experience a kind of clarity that I've never seen adequately described in a football story. Sometimes, for example, time seems to slow way down, in an uncanny way, as if everyone were moving in slow motion. It seems as if I have all the time in the world to watch the receivers run their patterns, and yet I know the defensive line is coming at me just as fast as ever. I know perfectly well how hard and fast those guys are coming and yet the whole thing seems like a movie or a dance in slow motion. It's beautiful. . . .

Pressures that used to get me down don't affect me to the same extent now. I've learned to shed certain destructive attitudes when a game is under way. A player's effectiveness is directly related to his ability to be right there, doing that thing, in the moment. . . .

Call it mystical if you like. For me it is simply one of the elementary facts of experience. Here-and-now awareness, clarity, strong intention, a person's "tone level"—these are things a lot of people who don't know anything about Yoga or mysticism talk about. . . .

One place in which you see the principle of self-knowledge work most clearly is with injuries. Two years ago I had a problem with my arm; I couldn't lift it above my shoulder—which is not good for a quarterback. Dealing with that sore arm led me into a process of self-discovery. . . .

It wasn't enough anymore to simply play a better game of football. I had to change the way I perceived the world, the way I thought and felt, and the way I treated others. Life was a larger and more interesting affair than I had ever dreamed. . . .

It's important to win—there's nothing quite like it. It's important to go all out during a game. But there is a lot more to football than that. . . .

Life can feel like a box after a game. You can get into another order of reality when you're playing, a reality that doesn't fit into the grids and coordinates that most people lay across life—including the categories coaches, fans and sportswriters lay on the game. . . .

Sport is so important in creating values in America, it would be great if it could open up these inner dimensions for people. It's really what many coaches and players want to do, after all. They want sport to be more than winning at any cost, more than beating people up and making money and getting ahead over somebody else's dead body. But we have got to break out of this conspiracy to belittle sport and human nature.

—JOHN BRODIE with Michael Murphy, in *Intellectual Digest* (1973)

In the great days of pro football, the game spoke for itself; the rise of the broadcaster is a sure sign of the decline on the field. . . .

We are fairly good specimens of the madness—men who were 21 or 22 and just out of college when the boom began, in our late thirties or early forties now. I know that we do not watch as much, and—this is crucial and far more important—we do not watch the same way, with the same passion. . . .

Equally significant: we do not gather anymore on Sundays for the game. It is just not that important, and it has lost its awesome pull.

—DAVID HALBERSTAM, in *New York* (1974)

Sport: If you want to build character, try something else. . . . We found no empirical evidence that sport builds character.

—BRUCE C. OGILVIE and THOMAS A. TUTKO, in *Psychology Today* (1972)

Hence the notion that athletic glory could be shared in by the neighbors of the glorious athlete, or team, gained early acceptance and has survived, largely unexamined, to the present. . . .

Thus endures the foundation stone of nearly every variety of spectator sport now flourishing: the linking of the participant's destiny with the fan's, in terms of a common city, nation, race, religion or institution of higher learning. In short the whole system depends on *granfalloonery*, a Kurt Vonnegut word, to express "a proud and meaningless association of human beings." . . .

According to a sociologist, people who live in Columbus, Ohio, are "not free" to admit indifference to the Ohio State football team. Nonenthusiasts who dwell in Columbus are categorized by normal folk as "freaks." Respondents to a poll overwhelmingly listed the Buckeyes as their most frequent topic of conversation and also ventured that a sound, working knowledge of the team's activities was a *sine qua non* for doing business with fellow townsmen. Most subjects agreed, furthermore, that a lack of interest in the team could be termed "downright unpatriotic."

—MICHAEL ROBERTS, in *The New Republic* (1974)

Identification is a degraded and diluted form of mimicry, the only one that can survive in a world dominated by the combination of merit and chance. . . . From this is derived the worship of stars and heroes, especially characteristic of modern society. . . . This superficial and vague, but permanent, tenacious, and universal identification constitutes one of the essential compensatory mechanisms of democratic society. The majority have only this illusion to give them diversion, to distract them from a dull, monotonous, and tiresome existence. Such an effort, or perhaps I ought to say such alienation. . . .

—ROGER CAILLOIS, *Man, Play, and Games* (1958)

. . . even radicals who consciously reject all those values somehow find themselves at Jet games or glued to the TV Knick game, and I myself will find it difficult to resist the temptation to open tomorrow's *Times* to the sports page. . . .

If the link between sports and "maleness" is as deep as I think it is, it is not surprising that male radicals find themselves unable to liberate themselves from the paralyzing hold of sports. Nor is it surprising that homosexual or bi-sexual men are probably less caught up in sports than the average male heterosexual. Ultimately the fight for liberation from sports is a fight for liberation from sexually defined social roles.

—ISAAC D. BALBUS, in *The Nation* (1973)

In examining the pro football explosion of the 1960s and 1970s, for example, we must look at more than the economic infrastructure of the teams and the number of viewers; we must also look at the way the games are experienced—e.g., how many people watch games in bars and social clubs, how many in homes; how important betting

pools and other forms of gambling are in sustaining interest in the games; what kind of struggle exists within families over the use of the TV set and how the growth of
women's consciousness has affected it; how many people
who watch the games play football themselves; what the
differences are between the generations or the sexes in
their response to the sexist nature of the advertisements
and the commentary, to the patriotic rituals and ceremonies, to the actions, on the field and off, of black players.
We have to know something about these questions,
which speak to the impact of football on daily life, to determine whether the sport is in fact serving as a "fortress
that is holding the wall against radical elements," as one
college coach suggests. My own experiences suggest that
precisely the opposite might be happening. . . .

—MARK NAISON, in *Liberation* (1973)

1. Baseball is not a game to professionals. Baseball is
only a game when you can wake up on a Sunday morning, lie back comfortably, and decide whether or not you
feel like going down to the park. A professional doesn't
even think in terms of "a game of baseball," he thinks in
terms of a day's work of baseball. . . .

2. I now have to add very quickly that you are not really
playing for money any more than a writer writes for
money or an artist paints for money. Pitching to me is an
art in the sense that the driving force, the original motivation, is the pride you have in yourself. When an artist
paints a portrait, he does it for himself. Once the canvas is
complete, he tries to get the best price he can, just as a
ballplayer lays his record on the table at the end of the
season and tries to negotiate the best contract he can. But
that comes after the fact. . . .

3. Baseball is not the simple game so many people
seem to think it is. There is a misconception—and for
some reason a growing one—that there is nothing happening on the field that is not visible to the naked eye.
That isn't so. The subtleties of positioning on each batter
are observed by very few fans; the pitcher's success or
failure in getting the batter to hit according to the positioning of his fielders, by even fewer.

If baseball becomes boring to a fan, it isn't because he

can see everything that's going on; it is because you have almost had to play big-league ball yourself to have an understanding of what is taking place beneath the surface. . . .

I think I've made it fairly clear by now that I don't like to see my profession degraded unnecessarily. I don't want to exalt it unduly either. I do not think the ballplayer is of any extraordinary importance in our national life. We do not heal the sick or bring peace and comfort to a troubled world. All we do is provide a few hours of diversion to the people . . . who identify their fortunes with ours through the season.

And yet, though the game of baseball itself is an entertainment, I don't think ballplayers are really entertainers. An entertainer works directly with his audience, adjusting his performance to its reactions. The audience is the second party. We are in a contest—every one guaranteed to be a bit different—and we adjust ourselves not to the reactions of the spectators but to the actions and reactions of the opposing team. . . .

The customers come to hear the entertainer perform; they come to watch us live a part of our lives. By its nature, it is a brief, self-liquidating life. It is a temporary life, really, a period between the time of our youth and the beginning of a lifetime career. If there are those who think it is a frivolous life, an essentially meaningless life, I cannot agree with them.

—SANDY KOUFAX with ED LINN, *Koufax* (1966)

[There is] a new female recognition (something men have always known) that there are important lessons to be learned from sports competition, among them that winning is the result of hard, sustained, serious training, cool, clever strategy that includes the use of tricks and bluffs, and a positive mind-set that puts all reflex systems on "go." This knowledge, and the chance to put it in practice, is precisely what women have been conditioned to abjure.

—SUSAN BROWNMILLER, *Against Our Will* (1975)

Part Three

IN
SPORTS WE
(SHOULD NOT)
TRUST

MUHAMMAD Ali reads a sentence as though he were being tortured and has an army IQ rating of 85, but who could deny the sharpness and clarity of his brain when he is under fire in the ring? Joe Namath might never have qualified for Oxford as a Rhodes scholar, but who will deny that in his craft he is an artist of analytic power? Recognition of the different orders of intelligence, Aristotle once wrote, is the first mark of a well-developed mind.

A new class of fan—and athlete, too—is involved in the passions of sports. College-educated, professional in a special part of life, sophisticated through travel or the media, the new fan is a thinking person. Not necessarily a *better* person. Nor even, necessarily, a *deeper* person. ("A little knowledge is a dangerous thing.") Older persons who have not gone to college, who are decidedly not "well-informed," who do not try to keep up with changing fashions in thought, honor the enthusiasms of the new fans with skepticism. The new class boasts of its own intelligence, probing, criticizing. The occupational hazard of the new class is a passion for utopia, a disrespect for institutions and traditions. It is a two-edged passion, needlessly destructive sometimes, at other times creative.

A certain cynicism is in order. In sports we trust—no one. Questions must be raised. Establishments need criticism. Criticism of the critics is also necessary. The critics are numerous, complacent, and now conventional. One joy in sports today is its engagement of intellect: criticism and countercriticism.

To uncover the meaning of sports for men, we must also consider sports for women. The relation of sports to politics and morality, to the press, to regionalism, and to money is, in each case, complex and tangled. The intellectual task—the sport of intellect, perhaps—is to make two or three distinctions that allow light to stab in unaccustomed places. Money and an entertainment ethic sicken sports today. A lover of sports is driven to propose a reformation; in my case, Burkean in style.

SPORTSREEL

The Newest Sport

THE NEWEST SPORT in America is revolution. The new sport conducts irregularly scheduled "big events"; it has developed minor leagues, support bases, and arduous training programs; it has already attracted enormous fan interest. The national newsmagazines and television networks give it breathless attention; public television has paid money for opportunities to film the "underground." The heroes and heroines of the new sport appear on T-shirts and posters. Movies are made about them. Little children everywhere dress like them, mimic their speech, practice their moves.

The teams so far attracting most fan support are the SLA "Cobras," the National "Weatherpersons," the Manson "Family," and the New World Liberation "Front." Fan interest is enlivened by the "Soliah Sisters" and the "Berrigan Brothers." The sport has been played by college students since about 1967, and although it shows some signs of internal weaknesses like those which destroyed the World Football League, there is already talk of forming a National Liberation League. Some desire a playoff to determine each year's national champs. Few sports match revolution in excitement.

Playing this sport is not, however, all fun and games. Aficionados distinguish clearly between the serious players and the dilettantes, the heavies and the light-weights. The sport is sufficiently advanced to have become professionalized; a few thousands make their living from it. Post offices carry pictures of the heroes and heroines. The FBI has kindly volunteered to keep the most accurate possible statistics. The real pros work out constantly; there is no regularly scheduled off-season.

Patty "Tania" Hearst and William and Emily Harris, for

example, allegedly whiled away the hours at their hideout on a farm near Scranton in the summer of 1974 by making an obstacle course out of furniture in the dining room and taking indoor training courses. Bombers and terrorists draw up raiding plans in precise detail, practice them in advance, and try to execute them on the scheduled day with precision. Then they sit back and wait for cheers, applause, and, sometimes, illegal succor. According to *Rolling Stone*, it cost Jack Scott, whose "athletic revolution" suddenly became a little more literal than he had intended, more than $20,000 to support Hearst and the Harrises in the summer of 1974. That is more money than some fathers of five have to spend on their dependents for an entire year, or even two years. In addition, Scott reportedly devoted at least fourteen working days to crossing and recrossing and rerecrossing the continent in an automobile, ferrying his team to new events. Coach Scott objected, it appears, to the use of weapons, but not to the crimes that constitute the heart of the new game.

A crime is a serious event. It is almost always a team event. The troops need to be "up" for the challenges they face. The stakes are high. Often, the action has profound liturgical and ritual significance. Revolutionaries do not pick on any bank, but on one that is an especially loathsome representative of capitalism. Capitalists vs. Socialists. Radicals vs. the Pigs. Revolutionaries vs. the System. Women are allowed in this league as equals with men; often, indeed, it seems mainly to be a woman's sport. Women seem to give the orders. In many cases, the bombs that go off in buildings seem to have been planted in ladies' rooms.

Think of the excitement on the day of the game, the intensity as the hands of one's watch move closer to the hour. Reflect on the dangers. Imagine the look on the faces of one's parents, one's friends, one's teachers, if they could see one now. Profanity presses joyously against one's lips. And as one has seen it happen in a thousand movies, one waves a gun imperiously, orders terror-stricken bank officials to do one's will, feels fingers tighten on warm steel. Can there be a pleasure keener than to have been brought up to be middle-class, "nice," gentle, and then prove oneself capable of violent crime?

Revolution yields delicious revenge on the discontents of being civilized.

For revolutionaries, losing isn't the main thing; it's the only thing. Were they to win, they would be the establishment. All the guilts for injustice and illiberty and inequity would rest upon their heads. One cannot be a martyr without fighting on the losing, hopelessly losing, side. Getting even with one's parents and their surrogates—the system—requires that constantly one stay outside it.

Endless restlessness is the most desirable characteristic in new recruits. Those who might one day sell out are a team's most grievous weakness. The logic of the game of revolution is to dissolve all rules of civilization; the logic is absolutist. Once one is willing to attack property, the logic of rebellion requires conflict with persons, in an escalating pattern of violence in which initiative is not wholly within one's own control. Attacks on persons— kidnapping, holding a person hostage, shooting by accident, murdering by design—are the next stage. The ultimate logic of the game is suicide; best of all, death in a conflagration under conditions of bitter battle. For then one dies as a soldier, as a martyr, in the symbolism of heaven-aspiring flame. Then one does not have to hide any longer, wear disguises, eat cold hamburgers, or live with the actual mediocre workings of the society of one's dreams. One disappears into one's dreams, like heat and smoke into the sky. The heroes of the revolutionary game are heroes who, in failing, die. The point of the revolutionary game is to contrive a situation in which one may die for illusions. Or, as a poor substitute, a situation in which the truly sensitive and intelligent persons in society both sympathize with and applaud one's supposed seriousness, courage, and daring.

The players of the new revolutionary game must claim to be working for all humankind, especially the poor and the oppressed, while having as little as necessary to do with pigs, honkies, and pig-supporters. That reduces rather drastically the number of humans one needs to love.

On the day of a big game, it is permissible to have a nervous stomach, not to eat in advance, to speak to one another harshly and nervously. The exultation of emerging victorious must be experienced to be believed. Other athletes will understand it.

Television is so interested in the new game that even now it will pay to put on every foot of film it can obtain. It paid for interviews with Abbie Hoffman from hiding, and eagerly used photos of Daniel Berrigan's occasional appearances before his capture. The people "underground" want all the attention that, considering their condition, they can get.

As the best players are rounded up by the police and FBI, the new sport could be introduced to even wider audiences if the courts would sentence the young revolutionaries, not to jail, but to endless repetition of their crimes. Imitation banks might be built in stadia in major cities, and fans by the thousands could come to watch Patty Hearst, the Harrises, and others carry out a holdup. Imitation federal buildings could be constructed in the infield, which they could bomb in the sight of thousands. At the end of the performance, the fans would rise and cheer. The revolutionaries could doff their caps in recognition. Television could carry live the more significant reenactments. Loyal citizens all around the nation could tremble at the shaking of foundations. The pictures of revolutionaries could be printed on bubblegum cards.

The new sport has blood, disaster, heartbreak, sex, youth, villains, romance, and cultural significance. It has found a number of promoters worthy of its possibilities, and is already a multimillion dollar business.

11

Of Women and Sports

DURING the famous tennis match between Billie Jean King and Bobby Riggs, September 20, 1973, at least one woman I know was so nervous she couldn't bear to watch. The defeat of Billie Jean would have been, for her, excruciating. She dreaded the probability that a woman would crack under pressure. She had seen it happen too often to too many women. When Billie Jean won, decisively won, she was elated. All around the nation, reports later showed, in restaurants and at parties, in homes and in bars, many women of America felt a wave of emotional release such as they have seldom collectively experienced. There were cheers, clapping, exultation. Billie Jean, having offered a gift of a little squealing pig to Mr. Riggs and having been borne into the arena like a Roman goddess, had defeated the lion, driven him from the court, *killed* him. Tiring, he rubbed his aching arm.

Billie Jean later shared a television talk show with John Unitas and Henry Aaron. She liked their company. They understood each other. "That was really great. We really got into it," she said afterward.

Is Billie Jean King the wave of the future? Since I have two daughters, ages eight and three, in some regards I devoutly hope so. In others, I am not so sure.

In her work for a master's degree thesis at Arizona State University, Doloris K. Suddarth discovered striking differences in personality traits between male and female athletes involved in interscholastic gymnastics competition in 14 high schools in Tempe and Tucson. The male gymnasts were high in ego strength, somewhat reserved, dominant, adventurous, tough-minded, liking group action, self-sufficient, relaxed, and unfrustrated, according to Miss Suddarth. The female gymnasts were lower in ego strength, somewhat warmhearted, submissive, timid, tender-minded, zestful, liking group action, group dependent, tense, and frustrated. "Many traits expected of the successful athlete by coaches and sports psychologists are in direct conflict with traits associated with females by parents, teachers, and peers." She reportedly contends that a woman athlete has, in effect, a split personality. "On the field she needs an athletic personality; in the social situation, she cannot be successful without a complete reversal of traits."

Culture, many of our contemporaries would say, is the villain. Women have been conditioned by culture to be what they are. Two assertions usually follow from this diagnosis: first, that it is *desirable* to change female characteristics; second, that culture *can* be changed easily. Are these assertions sound?

There is, of course, a prior question. Perhaps culture is not, in fact, the reason for personality differences. Some, at least, would argue that a woman's body is so different, not only outwardly but also genetically and in its glandular, neural, and physiological base, that women may be expected to exhibit quite different personality traits from men. Body and spirit are ultimately at one; each deeply affects the other. Not just in culture but in nature, women are quite different in personality from men. Culture may modify the natural inheritance of women and men, but slowly and indirectly, under laws of irony. For culture is a long-term, subtle, and semiunconscious choice of options. Cultures express the variety human liberty introduces into nature. There is a range of freedom for cultural choice, but that range is finally limited by nature itself and by previous history. Since the present intellectual climate leans so heavily to the view that nature is wholly, or almost wholly, malleable by culture, I think it the better part of wisdom to lean against this tendency. It is probably true that nature is far less malleable than our desires lead us to believe. It is probably also true that culture has roots extremely deep and is itself subject only to relatively slow and superficial adaptation. Neither nature

nor culture is as easily altered by individual will as contemporary *hubris* holds.

Yet there is no way of deciding the elementary issue—
that is, whether nature is the root of important personality differences between men and women, taken statistically. It is an issue worth arguing, and a good argument
requires stout defense of both sides. It may be assumed
that neither side possesses the entire truth. Nevertheless,
here is not the place for such an argument. Let us concede
the point that culture is vastly more powerful than nature,
and simply argue, on the basis of the two assertions mentioned above, whether it is desirable to change female
characteristics; and whether such change can be achieved
by will and effort.

To begin with the second first: One of the most simplistic mistakes of the modern era is belief in the easy manipulation of culture. The cult of education and information
seems to assume that *opinion* is the main motivating force
of human beings. Change minds, change lives. It seems
to turn out, however, that minds are complex, sinuous,
ironic, and only partly conscious. It is not unusual for lis-
teners at a conference called for some new form of "con-
sciousness-raising" to ask: "But what *should* our attitudes
be?" In a "radical" society, attitudinal hygiene is given
great importance. Opinions are properly formed. Correct,
germ-proof words are chosen. It does not follow that the
mind has changed, only the mental superego. An enlightened person would never admit an unenlightened opinion. Tides change, so the sophisticated must acquire
nimblemindedness; they must always know "where it's
at." Racism, sexism, classism, imperialism, and other sinful attitudes must never cross their lips.

Censorship is socially enforced, in radical society as in
any other, and righteousness is publicly upheld. The ancient Puritanism of America is quite capable of adapting
itself from the forms of Protestant culture to the forms of
radical culture. And that is the fascinating point: the more
"mind" seems to change, the less it changes. Cultural values, particularly the deeper and less fully conscious cultural values, are protean. They assume the shape of whatever conventional wisdom rules the day. Conventional
causes come and go, the deeper values remain—not quite

unchanged, but all the more vigorous precisely because of their capacity for surface adaptation.

Thus, even when we wish to change the culture in which we live, or any culture, it is doubtful whether we can do so. I have heard learned men say that Mao's China is not so much Marxist as it is Confucian and Taoist; that the ancient Chinese love for collective behavior and elaborate bureaucracy has found new release and vigor under modern conditions; that Mao has been original precisely in recognizing the ancient desires of his people and giving them a contemporary form. So it may also be in the United States. The more we change, the more we remain the same. In particular, it may turn out retrospectively that what is now called the women's movement or women's liberation is, in fact, one more example of male dominance and the weak ego strength of women. What is called equality may turn out to be regarded as one more capitulation of women to the male ideal. I do not assert this here. My point for the present is that culture is far deeper than our common biases allow us to suppose. We like to believe we are masters of our destiny, creators of ourselves. This belief may be a frail conceit.

The first proposition—that it is *desirable* to change female characteristics—is more interesting. I would like my daughters to grow up self-assured and self-possessed, athletic, poised, and an equal, in their fashion, to any man they meet. Actually, I have few doubts about that. Both of them already seem more self-assured than my son. *He* faces mainly female authorities at home and at school, from the time of birth until at least high school. He is surrounded by a chiefly female culture. It seems to me that the effort to civilize him, make him polite and courteous, instruct him in peaceableness and the avoidance of conflict, is rather heavily enforced. Almost solely in the company of other boys, and in male sports and in the combats of male play, do his and their wilder, meaner, and more aggressive instincts receive exercise. Tomboys in the neighborhood, until about age thirteen or so, share in these activities, this roughness, not only equally but often as superiors.

Since it is the object of many civilized and enlightened people to eliminate these instincts from the human repertoire, boys at their instinctual play are often regarded as barbarians in need of stronger inhibitions; girls are already more thoroughly taught in these respects. In the old days, inhibitions were enforced around sex. Today, they tend to be enforced around conflict, hostility, aggression, and violence. I take it as a sign of the civilizing, Christianizing, and feminizing of our culture that so many males now wear their hair long again. The spirit of women has won the West, I judge, watching Peter Fonda in *Easy Rider* riding eastward through the same canyons through which his father Henry, in a score of movies, rode westward, one with a gun, the other under the signs of peace. The schoolteachers, librarians, and ministers' daughters, brought out to civilize the young ones, have finally succeeded. A new era has been born. With as bloody an ending, according to *Easy Rider,* as in the old.

Would it be a good idea to discipline the boys to greater "femininity," and to force the girls out of the old cultural forms into a new aggressiveness, under the general program heading of "androgyny"? Actually, plan things as we might, individuals will still, blessedly, resist our disciplines. Like the tomboys of old, who could beat up any boy on the block, hit and field and catch as well or better, swear as pungently, and take command in any situation; so, in the future, some individuals will take one path, and some another. Just as some boys endured taunts of "sissy," "grind," and "apple polisher" en route to the power, status, and wealth of their present social positions, so in the future some boys will prefer more peaceful ways. The cultural enforcement of androgyny, we may be sure, will stimulate rebellions.

Nonetheless, I wish my two daughters had greater opportunities to play baseball, basketball, and football than they do at present. While the boys on our block are playing their rather vicious games of stickball, football, and basketball, most of the girls at present go for long chatty walks. Perhaps they should. Yet I see my son developing qualities that most of the girls do not seem to acquire. I wish my daughters had equivalent institutional support. Institutions are critical for individual growth.

The first time I came home from work early enough to see him play, my son had just been put into center field in the last inning of the game. The youngest player on the team, he wasn't very good. His team was ahead by two runs. Two men were on base. A long fly came out to him. He ran in. He should have run out. The ball sailed over his hopelessly waving glove. The other team won. No words could console him. He felt every ounce of responsibility for the loss. Neither coaches nor players blamed him. I tried to say something kind as we walked to the car. He choked out, "I just missed it, that's all. I lost the game. Now they'll *never* let me play." The tears finally came. It was a silent ride until I could change the subject. Needless to say, he felt around for excuses to quit. He didn't like the game, he said. But he kept going back. By the end of the spring, his team was miraculously in the finals. Losing by 10 runs in the last inning, the team caught up and went ahead in another miracle of recovery. In that last inning, he hit two weak grounders, was safe on errors, and scored twice. Playing shortfield, between first and second base, he cleanly fielded all three outs in the last half of the inning and threw the hitters out. From bum to hero in a single season. The range of his emotions, his self-confidence, his capacity to accept failure, and his easy familiarity with the desire to quit increased dramatically.

In most places, I gather, sensitive people complain about the Little League, its ambitious, aggressive fathers, and demanding coaches. In our village, the village leagues are focal points for the community. At halftime, or between innings, the coaches are careful not to blame the boys or pressure them; they point out errors; they jump on the good athletes who are being lazy; I haven't seen them humiliate or wrongly drive anybody. I like their attitude. On the other hand, I wish the girls could play. At least two who have lived on our block could outdo all but the biggest boys. Perhaps, if there are more openings in the near future, more girls will have the experiences of conflict, aggression, and team competition that the boys now monopolize.

The little girls in our village begin becoming cheerleaders, with uniforms and pompoms, at age eight. I'm glad my daughter Tanya finally decided not to join, although she debated it almost to the last minute. She and I stood her brother Rich and his nine-year-old friend Charley in a game of touch football the day after her decision. She doesn't catch well, lacks a certain coordination in her hands, and she fumbled a first lateral, fell down, was fallen on, got up crying. She wanted to rejoin her mother and the baby on the sidelines, said she didn't like the game; just as Richard had that first bad day. As usual, she wiped her tears indecisively. In her indecision, I called the next play. She executed a perfect fake and made a brilliant long touchdown run, her thin legs loping in long strides as gracefully as a deer's. The boys couldn't catch her. All afternoon, she kept calling the same play—"I like that play," she said—and scored five satisfying touchdowns. Richard wanted to keep playing until they could tie the score, but we had to leave. "Let's let them score," she said near the end. "They're good enough to do it on their own," I said. "Keep playing hard." "We could just play *almost* hard," she said seriously. "They'd know," I said. "They can do it without us, so watch them close." They did score at the end, but we were still a touchdown ahead.

Tanya cannot possibly continue to compete against the boys in football. When she reaches her teens, the probabilities are high not only that the boys will be bigger and stronger but also, perhaps, that their physical competitiveness and aggression will be different. My thoughts turn, therefore, toward the invention of new games especially suited to girls, particularly to the many who are not tomboys and are not likely for generations to receive the kind of encouragement in the home that most boys receive very early: sports equipment, lessons, practise sessions, roughhouse with the father. I saw a little of women's rugby at Aspen, and learned a new respect for the sheer physical durability, bravery, and toughness of young women. Russian women, many will recall, have long had, with other Eastern European women, a reputation for physical strength and skills. On the other hand, such games as rugby and football seem to me too harsh for women. Flag football is quite possible, however: instead of tackling the runner, the defenders try to pull one (or both) of the thin strips of cloth worn under the belt on each hip. Touch football retains enough of the essence of the game to give enormous satisfactions. I watched college women play football of this sort at Avila College in Kansas City; they relished it as boys do. Their moves were instinctive, learned, admirable.

Basketball is already well adapted to women. The girls' high school championships in Iowa have long matched the boys' in statewide interest. Baseball and softball are also accessible to women. Volleyball might come on strong. Soccer, lacrosse, and field hockey are already played in many schools.

But the invention of games is not at an end. Baseball, basketball, and football as we presently play them have, after all, been invented in the last 100 years. There is nothing to prevent us from designing new games, suited perhaps both to men and women. Games do not spring like Venus fully formed from the sea. Intuition and age-old rituals nourish them; the unconscious—not so much of the individual as of the collective—nudges the inventive mind.

We know in advance what some of the ingredients must be. First, there should be a contest, a struggle. Second, there should be teams, collectives, thoroughly united organisms. Third, a certain degree of "violence"— of hard physical challenge, of being hurt and taking pain—is exceedingly important. Fourth, victory should symbolize something profound in the culture, probably something repressed, and something that the explicit rituals of the culture do not already symbolize.

Consider football for men. Some interpret it as an example of territoriality, of acquisitiveness, of grasping for possession. This explicitly capitalist ideology is already amply exemplified, even exhausted, in the world of work. What is original and unique in football is that you do *not* win a game by amassing yardage or territory; you win by crossing the goal line. Any territory that you have gained, after a score you immediately surrender. Victory comes from crossing the end line—by outmaneuvering, outwitting, or out-lucking the opponent. The pleasure is the pure one of defeating obstacles, not of acquiring possessions. The obstacles to "life, liberty, and the pursuit of happiness" in the United States are a well-kept secret of civics books and liberal rhetoric. Conflict and violence are a critical part of the freedom and energy of our system. This secret enhances the private pleasure of football. Football seems *truer* than the official ideologies. It mirrors the culture, not in some simple sense, but as a kind of counterimage. The very reason the new radicals and lovers of nonviolence hate it so gives it its power, too: *their* ideology says that revolution is moral and desired by the "oppressed." On the contrary: football dramatizes the sacrifice, discipline, and inner rage of collective behavior, including socialist behavior. Football yields a socialist, not a fascist, metaphor. Women require an equivalent.

Tackle football seems to be an exclusively male preserve. That is part of its meaning. That is part of its pleasure. The violence of tackle football, the aggression, and the physical force are insuperable obstacles to women; they are so for most boys and men, too. A few women might play the game, but the numbers of women who could compete with men in it must be very small indeed. One can imagine women becoming as skilled in softball as men, and even as skilled in basketball (admittedly, one would have to wait a generation or two for skills to improve, even if differences in size did not obtrude). Yet only a utopian of very high enthusiasm can imagine women in full numbers competing against men in tackle football. It is, perhaps, good to have at least a partial preserve for males. It is a pleasure when women, as well as men, enjoy participating in the liturgy: actively and intensely watching games together, respecting their basic difference. What liturgy would do this for women?

In *Against Our Will*, Susan Brownmiller has recently made, in hidden form, a point well known to the ancient Greeks: women are not equal to men in the fundamental logic of the human body but live, rather, in danger of men's physical superiority, in necessary trust of men's better instincts. It was for this reason that Aristotle argued, despite his own friendship with his wife, that in the general case a woman could never be a friend to a man. In his eyes, friendship depended on radical equality. Women were not equal to men, in his experience, not at least in this most earthy, direct, and fundamental sense.

Only if a man is willing to set his physical power aside,

and to treat a woman on the level of civilized respect and intelligence, are men and women equal. But what a man sets aside, he may again call upon. Thus, the whole relationship between a man and a woman depends upon so deep a meeting, so deep a tacit commitment between the two, that appeal to physical superiority would seldom, if ever, be explicit. (There is no point in saying that such an appeal would be unthinkable; it is always possible. Physical superiority is a reality of which one need not be conscious for its effect to be established.) A civilized man— informatively, the English word is "gentleman" —sheathes physical power in gentleness. But the sheer steel stiffness of the hidden blade, however cushioned, is important; its absence would invite contempt.

The symbolism of tackle football reminds women of realities that many would rather pretend do not exist, but which some respect. It dramatizes clearly a world they cannot enter. It is a world beyond their experience. In this respect, it is for men what childbearing (and perhaps other activities) are for women; a sexual boundary beyond which one can peer with vicarious pleasure, across which one cannot venture in experience. For such reasons, women announcers or interviewers at a football game seem out of place (just as some women feel a jarring reaction against male obstetricians or male police in cases of rape). It is the present nature of those symbols to exclude women, just as plainly as it is the nature of the uniforms to heighten, even to caricature, the male physique: the tight pants, exaggerated shoulder breadth, tapered waist and straight hips, and the enlarged metallic cup as phallic vessel.

A certain kind of woman does enter successfully into the symbolism of football—a man's woman, the sort who does not try to make men other than they are, who takes male aggression as matter-of-factly as men do, who thinks tactically, strategically, and even physically as men do. There are such women. In real life, they are often those who love being women, who think the culture of men is a little crazy and certainly not for them; and tomboys, who feel at home among men and master the skills men master. In movies, they are often bar girls or prostitutes, gambling casino operators or widows who have raised children alone; they are contrasted with ministers' daughters, librarians, schoolmarms, or the emissaries of Christianity and higher civilization. If more women play the game (even as touch or flag football) and increase in excellence, they will rapidly command respect in a hitherto largely male preserve. For a decade or so, for example, universities could field women's teams and have them play in conjunction with each stadium's regular Saturday games. The attention might stimulate millions of girls.

In the name of androgyny, in recent years, feminists and their sympathizers have wanted to civilize, enlighten, and humanize fundamental instincts in the male. They have wished to feminize the male, in order to "humanize" him. They will extirpate, they say, machismo, militarism, fascism. Football has become for many the symbol of everything they loathe. In the name of pacifism and peace, they wish to cut out everything in their lives that involves them in aggression and violence.

From afar, one can admire such a project. Yet it seems based upon doctrines in whose power many of us lack sufficient faith. Irredeemably heretical, we do not believe some myths of the new radicalism, pacifism, and enlightenment. Despite efforts to censor them scrupulously from consciousness, aggression and violence are permanent concomitants of civilized existence, repressed but ever-present and powerful, and never more so than when confined to the unconscious. Beware of arguments with pacifists. If looks and tones could kill, many moralists would be murderers. A new game for women might be built around an image of controlled physical force—involving pushes and shoves; demanding strategy and tactics; and drawing upon repressed materials.

Football, in this sense, reveals important and perennial truths about the male, and perhaps the human, animal. No wonder it seems to so many males a liberating and joyous game, even under the disciplines and frustrations of extreme physical exertion, rigorous conditioning, the daily chafing of team play and organization, the grinding of the coaches. Men know—even lazy men know—that only hard work and discipline make excellence. The liberty required to use one's talents with precision, without error, and with grace is won only by frequent and demanding work. The quarterback who misses several games or practices is seldom sharp. "The more you work," playboy Joe Namath has said, "the more perfectly you play."

And so men submit to the grueling *ascesis* of the football season. And so, as well, they taste the honest taste of bodily aggression, violence, rage, hatred, and the ecstasy of danger. A rational, enlightened person would not praise football. That is precisely what marks the game as springing from the inner human spirit. So long as rationalists dominate the public symbols of society, football will have the added delicious taste of necessary counterbalance: the taste of forbidden fruit. The more rational and organized society becomes, the more linear, glassy and chromed our corporate offices become, the more profoundly our souls will reverberate to the symbols of football. Football gives the lie to those who believe that the human being is fundamentally rational, liberal, peaceable, sweetly cooperative. In football, the dream of many a first-grade teacher for her darling little boys is shattered.

Until age thirteen, girls are often taller, stronger, faster, and smarter than boys. Proceeding modestly and self-critically, we might try to develop more and more competitive team sports for them, while not slighting those sports—like precision team swimming—in which competition is of a different order from that of football, baseball, and basketball.

To be sure, a vast social experiment to involve girls and older women in new sports might not be successful. It is of the nature of experiments that some fail. One needs to have enormous confidence in the wisdom of our own generation to believe that our passions and convictions have the power of human history, nature, and enduring culture behind them, and will not one day seem to have been a trifle silly and extreme. So we must be vigilant, not coercive, and alert to our own deficiencies. Still, I feel strongly in the case of my own daughters that they are being cheated of advantages that have brought me in my lifetime enormous pleasure. I want them to love being women, and to push their bodies and spirits to the utmost. I hope our age is creative and inventive in their behalf.

New games for women (and perhaps for men) should express precisely those values important to the development of women that run *counter* to the other rituals of the culture. Not necessarily anger, aggression, hostility. For all the talk about women being inhibited in such expression, I have not met a woman who couldn't stand off any psyche standing in her way. Women seem dramatically to underestimate their own power, both of intellect and of emotion, and they seem especially vulnerable in failure and humiliation. (Dr. Suddarth's "lower ego strength"?) Too many women seem to dread failure, do not seem to be accustomed to it, do not seem to realize that failure is as ordinary as a baseball team losing twice (at least) a week. So a truly good game for women might demand high wit, arrogance, boldness, risk, and involve the experience of many failures.

Some say that women need competition; but it sometimes seems that women are already under great social pressure to compare themselves with others. The legitimation of failure, along with the strengthening of the will to persist and not give up, is a more important ingredient. Baseball, basketball, and touch football provide ritual learning opportunities for experiences like these. They make an individual responsible to a team. They provide high standards of excellence, public testing, and the discipline of submitting to the verdict of victory. Victory springs from an admixture of excellence, intuitive decision, and Fate. The verdict exceeds one's own capacities to control it, yet provides clear, visible evidence of the state of one's preparation.

In some respects, our culture already provides for women more than for men a kind of toughness, intuitiveness, and public testing. Perhaps it is chauvinistic and deeply erroneous to wish that the training of women were more like the training of men—that competitive team sports should come to play as large a role in the childhood and growth of women as they do in those of men. Yet I love very much the pleasures sports afforded me, and I wish my daughters could share in them to the full extent of their desire and their talent—not just in tennis, or swimming, or riding, or those other individual sports in which women already excel, but also in combative team sports, familiar or newly invented. On the other hand, perhaps it is better that women should be as different from men as possible. Perhaps it would be better for the human race to have sharp sexual differentiation, a male culture and a female culture. But since some in our midst want to experiment in exactly the opposite direction, it may be assumed that the women who wish to be more like men will never succeed until they live through the sports that have so much to do with making some men what they are.

SPORTSREEL

Redeemer of the Boxing World:
Muhammad Ali!

"Boxing," Jimmy Cannon once wrote, "is the swill of sports." More than any other sport, boxing, it appears, made prostitutes of journalists. In the old days, promoters used to slip a hundred bucks for an exciting buildup or a good postfight account. A boxing match is no surefire combat. The fellows in the ring have to be careful of each other's best punch, and too much boxing, too little hitting, can appear to be a fraud. Not to mention the ease by which one fighter or the other, or both, can execute a practically undetectable fraud, even after having drawn considerable blood. The public has to believe they hate each other. Even they may have to believe they hate each other.

A fight is the easiest sport in the world to promote. Its symbolism is transparent. It is the most fundamental metaphor of conflict. "The manly art." (Contrast: "The womanly art of breast-feeding." Men fight. Women nourish. Such symbolism underlies even the claims of some women political leaders that the entrance of women into politics will bring the peace, justice, and love the "boys" have not. Golda Meir and Indira Gandhi, and Bella Abzug in her fashion, have dented that myth.) Unlike team sports, a fight does not need to be personified; it *is* personified.

Nevertheless, the more America became middle-class after World War II, the less attractive boxing grew. Its ambience had always been working-class, and below that the shady world of racketeers, thugs, and bookies. If the better element came to the great fights in top hats, tails, and minks, driven by chauffeurs, it was as a delicious form of slumming. Come affluence for many, fade boxing. The shadiness affronted many. The direct violence—less and less visible in daily suburban life—affronted others.

The first fight I ever saw was Foreman-Quarry, in the Garden. The splash of sweat and blood in the brilliant lights when blows crashed the head startled me a little; the camera and television had never caught them. The primitive, animal directness of the conflict—the, I suppose, brutality—stirred both sickness and attraction in my stomach. Close-ups, in the flesh, of football line play do the same, except that the equipment seems to provide at least a little distance, cover, justification. One is obliged in boxing to confront the animality of human nature in a way that modern life would like to hide. My feeling there was much the same as my first experience of a battlefield, on a morning in Vietnam, hours after a pre-dawn Viet Cong attack on a Vietnamese naval station in Quang Ngai. The bodies of dead V.C., blue and stiff, lay frozen in the exhilaration of a hot-blooded charge. Cold blood dried on their naked flesh, which had been torn by barbed wire and shrapnel.

I had grown up listening to the bitter Conn-Louis fights. Billy Conn was a local boy, but my favorite was Louis. Later, in college, Rocky Marciano, doing his daily runs near Brockton, used to stop by at the seminary for a chat. His incredibly brave fights with Ezzard Charles were the stuff of local and immediate legend. Rocky wasn't my idea of a brilliant man. He seemed small and vulnerable in street clothes or jogging sweats, until, after coaxing, he matched his clenched fist with ours.

The sport was plainly dying. Then Cassius Clay came along, and later changed his name to Muhammad Ali. Suddenly, boxing became the sport of the literate. The class structure and the excitement around the sport changed. Why? How?

It would not have changed, I believe, if Cassius Clay had been a right-wing, flag-waving conservative, a Catholic, a docile and pious believer in hard work, daily Mass, and chastity. Ali was what the times demanded. He took a Third World name. He violated the codes of modesty, humility, and love for mother. He skipped practice sessions. He worked out lightly. He was lippy, boastful, argumentative, ideological, and non-Christian. He became a draft-resister, and suffered repression by losing his crown and serving time. He spoke the language of resistance and rebellion, used a speechwriter to help him with his soon nearly patented versifying. In the ring, he danced and jibed just as he spoke. He was for real. And he came to symbolize an attitude. He carried with him in the ring all the electricity that Spiro Agnew also conveyed. They were, in a sense, foils for each other. Agnew and Ali were mutually matching alliterates.

Howard Cosell had an outsider's sympathies for Ali, just as he had, at the other end of the symbolic scale, for Vince Lombardi. Cosell and many others rode with Ali into a new age of sports reporting. Ali was not fisticuffs alone, he was sociology and defiance and irreverence and "up the establishment." He turned his fights into cosmic tustles not seen since Lucifer met St. Michael on the plains of heaven. For many, Ali was the Archangel of Deliverance; for others, the most beautiful of all the liars, the evil angel of our nature. In a culture famished for myth, he fed.

Nearly all reporting on Ali wandered in the mists of myth. Faint praise seemed like opposition; criticism aligned one with establishments. In the name of the new truth and new accuracy in sports reporting, in the name of digging deeper into the hows and whys of sports, those who loved Ali seldom dug deep, into facts at least. He said he would give his riches to the ghettos. Did he? How much? Where? We never learned. He said he lived by new disciplines, by chastity, by a strict Muslim code, as a model for the ghetto young. Did he? We heard in 1975 about a young model, not his wife, in a hotel room with him in Manila. Then we were told that such goings on had been observed for several years, and had been flamboyantly displayed but little reported in Zaïre the year before, and that before that Ali in Harlem had pulled girls out of the crowds into his limousine and sped away.

Then came the great silver bird bearing his true wife from Chicago to Manila. In the hotel, reporters heard loud words, later saw broken furniture, and chronicled the swift departure of his wife for Chicago. Front page stories. Joe Frazier mocked Ali's infidelities. More front page. Still, the arena wasn't sold out. Later, weeks later, Ali tells the press: "I arranged it all. Tickets weren't going so good. I couldn't have paid for all that publicity. And my wife had to go home anyway."

Say it isn't true, Ali: say it isn't true.

He fought Frazier in the third fight like an angel. For fourteen dramatic rounds both men seemed to take a beating. Frazier, in his prefight negotiations, was said to have bargained only and solely for the loser's share. Toe-to-toe, they took each other's worst until Frazier's manager, before the beginning of the fifteenth round, said his man could take no more. The hero of the Islamic world concluded negotiations with the President of the Philippines, a leader embattled by Muslim rebels but lifted up by world attention to his highly visible state courtesies to Muhammad Ali. Then Ali flew back to America, a wealthier and now more highly fabled man among men. The redeemer of the boxing game.

12

Sports Are Not
"The Game of Life"

THE TREE was coming up fast. Inside his gleaming metal auto, John Brodie was too drunk to react, too sullen to care. With a loud smash that shook the entire area, the great tree held its ground against the onrush of metal and glass. Blood was all over the inert quarterback of the San Francisco 49'ers when they found him and pulled him from the silent smoking wreckage. He had hit the windshield, two huge flaps of skin flayed open on his head and face. It wasn't certain he would live, let alone walk again, as they sped his limp body through the darkness to the hospital. This was not the first time the police had found him drunk, nor the first time he had smashed a car. A hero at Stanford, son of a wealthy man, handsome quarterback, Brodie at his best looked like a slick ad in *Playboy*. At his worst, that night, he looked bloody, drunk, and almost dead, perhaps an object of disgust even to himself.

Sports are best understood as a religion. But they are not Christianity. Sports inculcate important moral values. But an athlete is not necessarily a moral man in other spheres of life.

Sports are lovely for their own sake. We should not be naïve about how much of their value is transferable to the rest of life. Brilliant artists, geniuses, have been wrecks as human beings; some have been decadent, immoral, petty, avaricious; some have been fascists and totalitarians. The arts demand their own intrinsic kind of morality, parallel to but not identical to a complete human morality. They are special crafts, with their own laws, disciplines, and their own purgative, purifying, and mystical stages. They provide images, metaphors, analogs for human morality. But they are not the same as human morality. They lie upon another plane, occupy a different field, reach to a quite different range. Sports are like the arts.

Babe Ruth—on the diamond the hero of little children, the model of fidelity and team loyalty and perseverance and courage and recognizable integrity—was off the field a buffoon, a boor, a sot, a mouth-stuffing, insatiable pig. Some athletes take drugs, are sadistic, egotistic, childish, immature, stunted in their development. John Brodie has written a book about the mess he was making of his life. He describes his drunkenness, his isolation in the shell of his own hollow ego, his unconscious plan to destroy himself. With luck, with help, he began to see what he had been doing to himself. But it was rather late in his career. He says frankly he was like a little boy, had not grown up.

Human beings cannot forever live their lives in separate compartments. There is *bound* to be some transfer from one set of our activities to another. When John Brodie began to mature as a man, he gained new powers as an athlete, too. The insight and analytic power he gained over his destructive urges in the rest of his life he began to apply to the way he approached football. A sharp and clear direction of his intelligence and desire in one part of his life became a sound approach in the other. Y. A. Tittle, whom for years he had hated, returned to the 49'ers and taught him a new mathematical system for analyzing the field of possibilities: positions, formations, angles, patterns, and plays. This new numbering system increased many fold Brodie's mental ability to diagnose opportunities and to give precise verbal instructions to his team. The combination of fresh mental clear-sightedness and a new technical vocabulary liberated Brodie to perform with his team as he and they had never performed before. It was their best year.

So it is impossible to speak as if there were *no* transfer between life and sports, or sports and life. "Life is not like a football game," Brodie writes in his book. "But by play-ing football you can learn a whole lot about life." Every participant in sports feels certain increases in mental and physical powers, even in the self-confidence that comes from a well-prepared body. To bolster one's internal con-fidence one gains an inner sense of accomplishment; to bolster one's external confidence one gains status in the eyes of others. By contrast, think of the humiliations borne by those who as young boys were weak, or overweight, or uncoordinated, who could not publicly perform in gym classes the simple exercises that others did easily. Not a little of one's own self-image as a human being derives from the powers and beauties of one's own body.

Still, it is worth knocking down once-and-for-all (as if one could) the old saw that athletics "prepare one for the great Game of Life." They do and they don't. They may and they may not. The Nazis exulted in physical fitness, pagan athleticism, games, and contests. Mussolini tried to recreate the glories of the classic Roman athleticism; his statues still stand, muscles rippling, tendons stretched, as embarrassing monuments to empty dreams. Common sense and experience teach us early in life that the superb physical fitness of the muscle boys exhibiting themselves on the beach, or riding motorcycles, or playing rugby at Aspen is often coincident with moral flabbiness, intellec-tual mush, and lassitude of spirit.

College catalogs and commencement addresses make great claims for the "humanizing effects" of the liberal arts and the humanities. These claims are much to be disputed. Professors of the humanities—several leap be-fore one's mind's eye—are often far from being highly de-veloped human beings. To call some of them humanists is to add a deceitful honorific to a description of their caste. Some "do" humanities the way a skilled mechanic takes apart V-8 engines. The man who teaches Tolstoy, or Blake, or Wittgenstein may be a pigmy in comparison to the giants he "teaches," and have as little humanism in common with the objects of his love as a pedant with a poet. Geniuses come by ones, but PhDs are graduated by the thousands.

Teaching the humanities is no guarantee that human-ism will be transferred from the objects of study to the students. Participation in sports does not guarantee that the moral values implicit in sports will be transferred to the athlete. When Franny of *Franny and Zooey* receives an A— for a paper on Tolstoy, she faints away in despair at the gulf between academic excellence and the life of the human spirit. No closer is the star athlete to being a moral hero.

There are three veins of thought a lover of sports ought clear-headedly to oppose. One identifies sports with narrow politics. The second sees sports as a serious duty, a moral mission. The third relates sports to knowledge of the world, rather than to self-knowledge.

A heavy-browed manipulation of the metaphors of sport still weighs on us years after the Nixon administration, which conducted a public pilfering of the good coin of sports for political purposes. All those invocations of *game plans, options, the will to win, team spirit,* and the rest were thefts from the offertory plate. They made profane what is sacred. Sports are sports, not politics. The bearing of sports on politics is deep, not partisan; attached to order and constitutional law and fair play, not to a single side.

Nixon and the radicals he so detested had in common the narrow politicizing of everything they touched. They had a Midas touch; and they left greasy whatever their fingers rested on. What could be more drab and creepingly totalitarian than to turn sports, religion, and even the relations between the sexes into politics? Were all of life to become politics, we would be mad within a generation—diseased, confined within a "total" society presided over by our elected keepers. The only hope of sanity is that *not* everything is politics; *not* everything is a game of one-upmanship, petty power, and "oppression." Sometimes, somewhere, there are peace, equality of rules, contemplation, reciprocity, the roaming of the free spirit, delight in diversity, inequality of talents and results, the comfort of rough edges, animal passions, comradeship. In a word, play—the opposite of politics, of issues. Confidence in contingency and in Fate. Delight in creation as it is.

The Duke of Wellington claimed that victory at Waterloo was won on the playing fields of Eton. The experiences of the ruling class of Great Britain in the highly individualistic sports of the Crown were held to be a precondition of imperial rule. The concept of fair play—of justice as fairness—was born in those matches, was celebrated and solidified as a basic expectation of British life. Almost every nation has recognized that the physical fitness of its subjects, the channeling of their animal energies into sports, and their shaping by the inner forms of certain sports are an enduring interest of the state. In the Soviet Union, in underdeveloped nations, and indeed in most parts of the world, great government subsidies, direct or indirect, are poured into athletic programs. In Sparta, in Athens, in Rome, in medieval Europe, in almost every culture, power has been recognized in the health of the human body, particularly in the young warriors and in the ruling class. And not only in health, but also in the habits of courage, teamwork, and wit that athletic contests sharpen.

There is nothing sinister in the connections between sports and the well-being of the state. Any state worthy of its citizens would be foolish not to try to perfect the human body and the human spirit through athletics. The human animal (and traditionally the male) must in most social circumstances, not least in those climatic zones relatively hostile to human survival, be aggressive, confident, and as highly developed as possible. Whether in the name of empire or in the name of liberty, the strength of the human body and the human wit have often made a difference between victory and defeat, annihilation and survival.

The human animal is a warlike animal; conflict is as near to the truth about human relations, even the most intimate, as any other feature. Sports dramatize conflict. They help us to visualize it, imagine it, experience it. The logician Morris R. Cohen once tried to persuade William James that the nation already had, in baseball, "the moral alternative to war" that the latter said was the highest priority for intellectuals to invent. According to Cohen, the austere James didn't seem to grasp the point. Cohen attributed James's blindness to the fact that James unfortunately lived in Cambridge, which despite its "100,000 souls (including the professor) is not represented in any baseball league that can be detected without a microscope." Greek drama purified only fear and pity, the philosopher continued, but "baseball exercises and purifies all of our emotions, cultivating hope and courage when we are behind, resignation when we are beaten, fairness for the other team when we are ahead, charity for the umpire and, above all, the zest for combat and conquest." Some, he wrote, may have regrets for an error that lost the game, but "there is always the consolation that we have had our inning, and though we have lost, there is another game or season coming. And what more can a reasonable man expect . . . ?" International baseball, he felt, could arouse "far more national religious fervor than the more monotonous game of armaments and war." He didn't add, but could have, that it would be cheaper and more fun. What he wished most to point out, however, is that sports are finally larger than any nation-state. Men are, of course, rooted animals, loyal to one culture and state. But a contest requires a larger frame of reference; another culture and society must be included. An international league would include all. "National rivalries and aspirations could find their interest expressed in a close international pennant race, and yet such rivalry would not be incompatible with the establishment of the true Church Universal in which all men would feel brotherhood in the Infinite Game."[*]

Almost sixty years after this vision, one cannot help thinking that a *baseball* League of Nations might have succeeded. Much as I admire Daniel Patrick Moynihan, I can't help thinking more fondly still of sending Tom Seaver against the world. And yet, to be fair, a truly international sport would more likely be soccer, in which the U.S. would, deliciously, begin as an underdeveloped nation. It would be exciting for Uncle Sam to be the underdog again, and to fight his way to the top. For today, at the UN, America is indeed an underdog. There are not two dozen democracies in a world of over 140 states.

In this respect, my vote for one of the most self-contradictory books on sports ever written would go to Paul

---

[*] Morris R. Cohen, "Baseball as a National Religion" (1919); reprinted in *The Faith of a Liberal*, (New York: Holt, 1946).

Hock for *Rip Off the Big Game* (1972), who bows in awe before the greatness of "monopoly capital," the villainous creator, source of power, and manipulator of sports in America. The book is useful just because Hoch reduces the whole process of world history to a single cosmic game. It eats his heart out that working people love sports so, that they "are being asked to identify with every team but the real team, the only team in the only contest that can really make a difference—workers versus capitalists." And he ends his book on this theme: "We still have the choice of either fighting to preserve the neo-colonial profits of our bosses or fighting together with the peoples of the neo-colonies to abolish the system of bosses entirely." Compared to the real world, sports offers a simple, lucid vision. But compared to Hoch, the world of sports is complex. Yet even he, in his nonviolent, brotherly, loving, and anti-machismo moments, might agree that an athletic contest between workers and capitalists, or bosses of neocolonial powers and peoples of "neo-colonies," might be morally superior to war.

Hoch's book is useful because it reduces the wisdom of critics like Dave Meggysey, Chip Oliver, Bernie Parrish, Leonard Shecter, Robert Lipsyte, and Jack Scott (who says in his extraordinary introduction that Hoch's book "just may be the most important book written on American Sports") to the absurd. Sports, Hoch holds, undergird monopoly capitalism, militarism, racism, sexism, competitiveness, sexual repression, and counterrevolution. ("I was happy to discover," Scott writes, "that this book is not an attack on sports. . . . *Rip Off the Big Game* is an attack on monopoly capitalism, not sports. . . . It attacks the rulers of American society and the barons of the American sports industry, not the American people or athletes.") Hoch's Chapter 5 is "Molding the Modern Militarist," Chapter 8 is "School for Sexism," and Chapter 10 concludes with "Cultural Revolution: Socialism or Fascism?" He characteristically refers to athletes as jocks or beefsteaks, indeed, as "a beefsteak pseudo elite of brawn not brain, myth without power, and one completely under the thumb of the real bosses." Images of Bill Bradley, George Blanda, Frank Gifford, Sandy Koufax, Fran Tarkenton, and even Bobo Newsome, who used to visit relatives next door to me in McKeesport, make Hoch sound bush.

Religious power was inherent in sports well before "monopoly capital" arrived fresh and pink in this blooming, buzzing world. Missing this, Hoch falls into endless self-contradictions: he talks about huge profits in franchises, then about how many franchises lose money; about how capitalists rushed to embrace sports, and how hard it was for sports to attract investment; about how unfair it is for colleges to put so much money in major sports for males, and how often the profits from these sports support all other sports on campus; about how television is making Americans athletically passive, and how hard it is for sports companies to keep up with the demand for athletic equipment, since more people are participating than ever before. Hoch turns everything he sees into a political sermon and misses the dynamism within.

Sports are deeper than politics—deeper than any single political system, and deeper in the human heart than political authority. Sports lie at the very root of liberty and law, in the free play of intelligence and imagination, and in the animal (and the spirited) zest for self-perfection. If politics withered away tomorrow, which it won't, there would still be sports. (In heaven, it is rumored, the angels play in the presence of great love and light. Sports yield our metaphors for paradise.) Who imagines that the completely good life would entail *working,* pursuing means toward ends? Utopia, paradise, the passing away of proletarianism, the ultimate vision in every culture known to history consists in everlasting play. Which is to say that sports already are in end time. Participation in sports is a foretaste of the eschaton. Sports constitute the one place in life where the revolution is already *here.* Sports show what it is like to perform perfectly, with full attention, at the peak of body and spirit. What more could anyone ask? Except that, being human, we aren't completely satisfied. We desire further struggle. We need further tests. Which is why there is no end to sports, dramatizing as they do our inner life.

Hoch speaks of sports as an opiate. He has it wrong: sports are the real thing. Work is the opiate—work and revolution and politics. *Those* are the drugs for killing time, making a living, acquiring power, place, and possessions. Sports lie in a different realm altogether, a freer realm, a realm of ends, a point at which time, compressed and self-contained and instantaneous, is transmuted into eternity. O! the long hours, the timeless summers, the instants lifted free from the track of work and history.

Market experts find that 30 percent of those who buy newspapers buy them solely for the sports pages, and that many others read the sports pages first and longest. It is a sign of a healthy spirit. To read about sports is not to read about history but about actions in a world outside of time. Reporting on sports is not like reporting on politicians, academics, or corporate executives in their clanking, greasy worlds. Reporting on sports is like bringing back a Rembrandt: food for the imagination. The political reporter is an investigator; the sportswriter is an artist. The latter nourishes the life of the spirit.

There is no greater sacrilege than politicizing sports; nothing more imperceptive, more crippled in intelligence. To fail to recognize in each thing its own uniqueness is a sin of intellect.

The second vein of thought a clear-headed lover of sports must oppose is the cult of the "Christian athlete," invocations of "athletics as the School of Life," and banquet addresses about the "Game of Life." One must pay sports the compliment of skepticism. Those who cultivate the preposterous cult of the ultimate athlete—a grotesque parody of the world Mussolini wished to build—may like to think that games are the secret to the Great Game of Life.* But their very effort, spelled out in capital letters, groans with Weighty Seriousness; it sinks like a boulder in an Alpine lake. They are trying to moralize sports, to inflate them with baggage of which it is precisely the liberation of play to strip us. Sports are fun because they are *not* the Game of Life. Sports are a delight because they are an aside. They are our liberty. They are our bursting of the shackles of conscientious suffering. They are, deli-

---

* See George Leonard, *The Ultimate Athlete* (New York: Viking, 1975).

ciously, ends in themselves. Even cads and cheats and decadents can play. There are no moral entrance requirements, no tests for High Seriousness. All are called.

There is not even any heavy imperative: *Be Spontaneous!* You may play games with strict rules, if you care to. Here there is no command: *Be Anti-Establishment!* You may play games with thousands of years of traditions and rituals within them, the sports of kings, if you care to. Here hang no signs insisting: *Be Revolutionary!* You may delight in the order, organization, and precise execution of a collective that moves to the command of a single will, if it pleases you.

The point of games is that they lie outside of ordinary life. They belong to the world of imagination. They are pledges of our ultimate liberty of spirit. And *that* is how they hold "a mirror to life"—flashing their illumination upon a secret hidden underneath the pretensions of ordinary serious life. Ordinary life commands us to pay attention, to take our duties seriously, to be responsible citizens and somber revolutionaries, to march in with others when the saints march in. But the spirit of play suggests that underneath the weight of Calvinism there is nothingness.*

The spirit of play is Catholic, Latin, Mediterranean. The spirit of work is modern, Protestant, Northern, Marxist. Worry about the future is work. The time of play is present time.

Protestant writers, discovering play, often get things backward. I say this in all kindness, trying, in a Protestant culture, to sound a distinctive note. Protestant writers, by and large, exalt play in a way that makes it *important*. They make it seem like a moral obligation. Through always being serious, some take things to extremes. They are for work and against idleness; then suddenly for celebration and against uptightness. From Calvinism we rush to Esalen. Always seriously, of course. Yet play is to be played exactly because it *isn't* serious; it frees us from seriousness. One plays with intense seriousness, freely, because play isn't serious.

It is not surprising that Catholic writers, steeped in the

* *The Experience of Nothingness* (New York: Harper and Row, 1971) specifies my meaning.

pre-Calvinist era of the medieval festival, have been the first and most profound writers on play. Johan Huizinga's *Homo Ludens*, Josef Pieper's *Leisure, the Basis of Culture*, and Karl Rahner's *Man at Play* are the classics in the field. Protestant writers of the last decade, fed perhaps by the general cultural attack on America's "uptight, puritan, acquisitive and aggressive past," have more lately entered the fray: Harvey Cox's *Feast of Fools*, Robert E. Neale's *In Praise of Play*, George Leonard's *The Ultimate Athlete*, and, in symbolic range the deepest of all, David Miller's *Gods and Games*. Neale remarks that "praise of work is the ruling spirit of contemporary society." He fears that even his own vision of play will be infected with "implicit praise of work," since an author cannot "escape the presuppositions of his society." Accepting his cue, we may call one approach to play "Protestant," another "Catholic." Insofar as Protestant, specifically Calvinist, assumptions have contributed most to the shaping of America, the "presuppositions of our society" are generically "Protestant." "Catholic" and "Jewish" revisions of the bases of our culture are only slowly becoming felt.

In this sense, "Protestant" theories of play tend to make play a *means* to work. Play is a pause that refreshes—for harder work later. Play prepares us for later life. Play teaches us serious values. Play is an opportunity to retreat, recoup, and then reenter "real" life with purer spirit. Play is diversion. Play "celebrates," and celebration is important—one fulfills one's religious obligations by celebrating. One *should* play. This is one approach to play.

Tony Schwartz, author of *The Responsive Chord*, has a piquant phrase that may be used in rebuttal: "Don't should on me!" Play lies outside the realm of *shoulds* and *musts*. Play is an expressive activity. It flows. It reveals outwardly the inner energies of the human being. One doesn't play *because* it is good to play. The natural activity of human beings *is* play. Play is good in itself. The proper category for play is not moral but natural. Play is a pagan part of the human beast, our natural expressiveness. It flows from inner and perennial energies, and needs no justification.

Protestant traditions tend to link goodness to duty, obligation, command, and will. Catholic traditions tend to link goodness to beauty, proportion, fitness, achievement. The Greek word for good, *kalos*, is not a word for duty. It describes the attainment of natural beauty: the achievement of an individual in realizing, if briefly, the ideal possibilities of its type. Catholic traditions tend to link the moral life to the artistic life. Protestant traditions tend to link morality to obedience to principle, to conscience, to the commands of God.

These are rough approximations, of course, but differences between a Catholic culture and a Protestant culture become quite dramatic. The development of capitalism depended on the underpinnings of Protestant attitudes; Catholic countries for generations bore the reputation, in the face of industrial modernity, of being backward, lazy, hedonistic. Visualize the cultures of Southern Ireland, Spain, Italy, the Balkans, and Latin America. Contrast southern with northern Germany. Contrast, even, the sensibility of France with that of Scandinavia. The more easygoing, fleshly, less serious Catholic undercurrent is broadly distinguishable from the progressive, orderly, hardworking Protestant current of the modern age.

In the United States, this contrast is muted for two reasons. First, the poorer Calvinist cultures of the American South are almost as different from Ivy League Protestantism as Catholic cultures are. There are several different Protestant cultures in the United States. "Redneck" culture shares with "ethnic" culture a sense of being put down and mocked by a superior culture. The sense of family is similar. There are parallels—but also differences—in the respect accorded authorities. The passion for sports and for hard-hitting competition is similar, however. Sexual patterns are at least analogous—heavy emphasis on chastity, on the one hand, but a lot of good old backseat screwing on the other. The differences between, say, Alabama and Notre Dame will be remarked on at a later point. Here it is only necessary to warn that the rough category "Protestant" has more than one variant; and that Southern Protestantism has at least some similarities to Northern Catholicism.

The second distorting factor is that Irish Catholics,

while constituting only 17 percent of American Catholics, set the Catholic tone; and the *ecclesiastical* tradition of American Irish Catholicism is not very Celtic, after all, but rather "Jansenistic": severe, disciplined, moralistic, quasi-Protestant. Artists have not had a happy time in Ireland; the pagan Celtic strain in Joyce or Yeats, while very "Catholic" in cultural sensibility, was out of tune with a rigid ecclesiastical structure. Epithets like "the fighting Irish," or "Pat and Mike, the Irish drunks," suggest the non-Calvinistic, ebullient, earthy strain in Irish life. The games of the Kennedy family, their zest for fun and frolic, their splashes in the White House swimming pool, illustrate essential cultural difference from Northeastern Protestant sobriety. There is a trace of the outlaw in every Catholic puritan. Pete Hamill, Jimmy Breslin, and Eugene McCarthy can never be counted on to be entirely proper.

Dave Meggysey, before his conversion, used to give inspirational talks in the off-season: "The competitiveness of football is excellent preparation for the competition of life." As John P. Sisk * has noted, this makes play "a discipline ordered to worldly success." Sisk adds: "The field of play was a place of serious business, a school of character-building, in which the Old Coach was a harsh schoolmaster who never had any doubts about the adult sanction for his apparently childish activity." Many a Catholic coach has adopted this perspective. For coaches, play *is* their business; their livelihood depends on it. And, for Catholics, play was indeed one field open for upward mobility. Vince Lombardi confided that his Italian name, he felt certain, closed to him for many years a shot at being a head coach anywhere; when he finally landed his job, in Catholic Green Bay, at age forty-six, it was with a kind of repressed fury, an intense drive for respectability, a deep desire to prove that he could instill "basic American values" as well as the next man.

And yet, the Catholic (and not least the Italian) heart knows that devilment and things done "for the hell of it" are best. Lombardi loved Max McGee and Paul Hornung, the wild ones and rule breakers on his squad, the best.

---

* Sisk's article, a small classic, is "Hot Sporting Blood," *Commonweal*, March 2, 1973, pp. 495–498.

When Lombardi went to Washington, the press specu-
lated that Lombardi would "crack down" on the bon-
vivant, high-living, and fat-bellied Sonny Jurgensen.
Lombardi did no such thing. He was Catholic enough to
go along with a certain hedonism, provided only it wasn't
hurting the team. Joe Namath attributes his own high living and flaunting of the rules to his "gypsy" nature; but
Catholic cultures have a way of winking at infractions of
Puritan rules. "Human nature," Catholics shrug. (Southern Protestants resemble Catholics here, too.)

Nevertheless, in the Catholic scheme, play has *its own*
seriousness and even fanatic passions. Some games are,
literally, to the death. Even little children, one observes,
do not play as adults glowingly remember, in carefree innocence, but with bitter and combative intensity. The
whole human being pours self into play, nothing held
back. Indeed, asceticism, the ancient word which Catholics use in talking about all forms of religious life, was
originally the Greek word for discipline, the conquering
of body, and the training of the single-minded will that
prepared the athlete for competition. The danger of fanaticism, of course, is great.

A Protestant culture often seems scandalized by what it
perceives as a waste of energy and care. Shouldn't these
be saved for "important" things? The Olympic marathon
runner Kenny Moore told *Sports Illustrated:* "For two
weeks every four years, we direct our kind of fanaticism
into the essentially absurd activities of running and
swimming and being beautiful on a balance beam." Absurd compared to what? Implicit in Protestant culture is a
metaphysics of progress. *Progress is our most important
product. The March of Time.* We are going somewhere,
achieving something, *building a better world.* Since human
existence is loaded with so much metaphysical
meaning—all anchored in the work we achieve—sports
must necessarily seem like the "toy department."

A Catholic sensibility, however, is attuned to the ultimate absurdity of everything in human life. The ex-
Catholic Hemingway imagined that against the nothingness, against the *nada,* a lone human can create forms and
rituals within which perfect acts can be achieved. Such
achievement, he thought, was the highest kind of grace to

wrest from absurdity. In this perspective, concern about making history is bush; a desire to contribute to meaningful progress is the "toy department"; a naïve faith in the betterment of the human race is proof of childishness. *Do. Train. Act. Be perfect. Achieve such beauty as ye might. While the juices run.* These would be the adult imperatives.

The realm of play is not the realm of work. It is human destiny to create objects in the world through the application of vision and intelligence to work. To work is to share in the creativity of God. We are not "condemned" to work. Work is our liberation, our opportunity to be creative. Even "meaningless" work may be redeemed by the intention, intensity, and perfection with which it is done. *No* work is in itself meaningful. Everything is equally absurd. Meaning is largely *conferred* by human intention and human love; it is not totally discovered waiting in the world. And so even the athlete, the artist, or the star of screen or stage confers meaning on millions of painful, detailed, grinding, harrowing, preparatory tasks. "Genius is 99 percent perspiration, 1 percent inspiration," said someone, whom every writer of books for generations has mentally thanked. To play with excellence is a craft. One does not play for the sake of *work;* one plays for the sake of excellence. The point of the excellence is that there is no point. Against the darkness, it is all we have.

Oh, how I would like my own words to cross the darkness, standing against the rush of time! It seems like that for athletes, too. During an evanescent youth, for a brief number of years, they have a chance to create *meaning,* a moment of excellence-in-act, of an order they may never attain in any other field. One ought not to mock the sagging, middle-aged athlete who is already beginning to reminisce about his most glorious and vivid deeds. Those are his defense against the night, his great deeds. And what are ours?

"Holy Mary, Mother of God, pray for us sinners, now and at the hour of our death," is the prayer of Notre Dame. Now and the hour of death are seen as one. The fruit of the Virgin's womb, even in the womb, hangs already *sub specie aeternitatis* upon the cross. We who are living are already, in God's eyes, dead; and so the most perfect deeds we are to achieve in life may already, like an aging athlete's, be behind us.

Patty Hearst, the kidnapped heiress and fantasizing urban guerrilla, is said to have held Jack Scott in contempt because of his retrogressive love of sports. He should, she thought, have embraced the "serious" work of revolution. But revolution, too, provides a series of exhilarating great deeds, in a world of ritualized behavior, played by rules described with loving care in revolutionary handbooks, and demanding an *ascesis* of revolutionary disciplines. So engrossing, however, become the revolutionary games that the projects of humble politics are soon forgotten: too messy, too complex, too corrupting.

We may expect increasing numbers to learn, slowly or rapidly, that politics is also a game, not in the way that football is a game, but in its own way. All things serious, given enough time, corrupt human purposes. The great Protestant delusion is that human existence is shaped by human will. Only when human will has destroyed this planet will many serious and well-meaning persons recognize, in the flames, that the game they are playing can be lost. It would be entirely fitting if the biblical prediction of the coming destruction of this world were to be carried out through the hands of those who thought they were improving it.

To grasp that sports is an essential, salvific religion in our present madness is to begin to be a skeptic about the religion of making the world better by our work. Through sports, we save our sanity.

In God's house are many mansions, many athletic fields. On some of those fields, in Catholic and Jewish and Greek traditions, for example, there is no contradiction between spontaneity and strict adherence to seemingly petty rules. Observe toddlers at play, how they establish rules. "This is water. This is land. You can't step on those. Step only on the magazines." The spirit of play is the invention of rules. At the heart of play is love for the finite, the limited, the bounded. "Out-of-bounds" is the primal cry of play. The description of a fixed universe is the first and indispensable step of every free act. For human beings are embodied spirits. The free spirit is not pure spirit, pure will, pure intellect, pure desire; it is incarnate in hands and legs and lungs and sinews, in a place, at a time, in a culture, among others like oneself. To choose to move in *this* direction is to choose against going in *that*. To step forward is to place one foot on a limited bit of sod. Without limits, no act. No act, no freedom. Freedom is the art of limits. Play is the exercise of freedom.

Baseball, basketball, and football—like tennis, soccer, hockey, and countless other sports—are constituted as possibilities by bounded universes. Their liberties spring from fixed limits. Limits concentrate the players' acts in forms of high definition, in luminosity, in brilliance. What thrills the observing heart in play is form, so rare in our formless and chaotic lives. We live—our spirits live— by form, as our bodies live by bread. Without sports, millions would wither inwardly.

If sports are the "School of Life," it is *not* because in sports we learn lessons in how to live. Rather, it is because in sports we learn that there is something more important, more basic than moral seriousness: liberty of spirit, achieved through form. Many Americans seek liberty of spirit *apart from form*, in chaos and formlessness and undisciplined spontaneity; the overtense Protestant spirit may require temporary lawlessness. (Esalen is Protestant liberation.) True liberty is achieved *through form*.

Put otherwise, Dionysus is the god of an overorganized Protestant society. Wagner was its celebrant. In messy Catholic countries, Apollo is the striven-for god. Where there are large, squawling families, political and social disorder, a freer rein to passion, there the beauties of clear form, brilliant as a pike in the noonday sun, excite the heart. Where skies are somber and duties firmly clarified, the cries of chaos torment nighttime dreams.

One notices in athletic circles in the American South an almost Catholic sensibility. Southern life is almost Mediterranean in its underlying myths, scented heavily with sin, rains, madness, decay, chaos. On the surface, in well-scrubbed faces, one sees intense respect for order; young men speak with astonishing respect and affection in the startling phrase "my daddy," and Christian athletes extend a vigorous hand in greeting and talk in well-controlled, courteous, and friendly cadences, like gentlemen. When Dionysus is too well known, Apollo rules the sur-

face. Catholic and Southern sensibilities are unlike in
this: the Protestant spirit flirts ever with Dionysus, re-
senting its own severe controls; the Catholic spirit knows
Dionysus on more familiar terms ("the fighting Irish,"
"drunken papists") and ever aspires toward Apollo, seldom secure in its striving. When Notre Dame plays Alabama—or North Carolina, or Texas, or Oklahoma—you
can feel the underlying myths crackle in the conflict.
There is passion in the Southern breast, which the men
from Notre Dame must tame. To defeat Notre Dame, the
Southern men must explode.

The third vein of mushy thought a clear mind should
oppose is the notion that there is some simple transfer of
values learned in sports to other areas of life. It is a mark
of wisdom, Aristotle wrote, to see in every sphere of life
its proper measure. Each sphere is unique. Each has its
own proper conditions, laws, and contexts. The secret to
sound moral wisdom is to note precisely the differences
between realms.

The skills a quarterback learns in swiftly "reading" the
patterns set in motion by the defense are limited skills.
He knows that there are eleven opposing players; he
knows the other team's most effective defensive formations; he knows most of the possible variations they can
use; he knows—at least abstractly—several other possible
formations teams in history have tried. Rarely will he face
a formation he has never seen before. In corporate bureaucratic life, the quarterback may be inclined to use the
same schematic vision to grasp the obstacles arrayed
against him. But the number of players in front of him is
seldom so clearly arrayed, and the span of time during
which obstacles may be set in motion is not nearly so instantaneous as the formations he faces on the gridiron.
The rules in the real world are not so clear, nor so closely
refereed. The scope for ambition and other motivations is
infinitely vaster. And so forth.

At best, sports provide clear, well-defined forms. It is
their clarity that makes these forms valuable. However
complex they may be—and many quite intelligent persons cannot at first follow even an abstract diagram of the
movements of all the members of a team on a given play—

these forms operate within such narrow and concentrated human limits that they are, compared to other parts of life, simple. From such complex simplicity spring their beauty and their power. One sees through their complexities with a single illumination. Insight in more complex fields of motivation and behavior can, in the end, be equally singular and luminous; but a great many other insights into their component parts must lead up to the penetrating vision.

Perhaps what one learns best in sports are habits of discipline and poise under fire. Having faced often the prospect of the death that comes through defeat, one tends not to panic when things go badly. Having experienced often the deep, groaning desire to quit under pressure, to yield, to admit that one cannot bear the pain or the intensity of the struggle any longer, one knows that there are always hidden resources yet to be called on. Perhaps one recalls, as well, that cunning just at the point of maximal weariness has more than once been one's salvation; and one thinks through the situation coolly just one more time, and tries yet one further daring move. One knows what it is like for some companions to slough off and let the few stouter hearts bear the heat of the game. One remembers occasions when a comrade wilted under fire, then recouped and redeemed himself. One remembers one's own weak knees, nervousness, and failing heart. One recalls the hatred one felt for opponents, and the rage at a flagrantly unjust ruling by officials—and one remembers how important it is at such moments to channel one's passions toward the immediate end in view. One knows defeat and also exaltations—and how both soon recede. One is painfully reminded of foolish boasts and subsequent humiliations, and also of moments when one sold oneself far too short and confidence untimely failed.

In a word, in times of stress in later years, the symptoms of one's own reactions under stress are thoroughly familiar. One need not pay much attention to them. One is free to concentrate upon the matter at hand.

These are the qualities of heart most to be esteemed in the experience of sport, and most easily transferred into other spheres of life. For they regard, not so much the field of play external to oneself, as one's knowledge of oneself under pressure. They release a kind of grace.

Those who have not known the rigors of competitive team athletics do not easily find other social and institutional frameworks in which such skills in self-knowledge may be experienced and perfected. That is why there is a special comradeship among former athletes, a bond of trust within which athletes understand one another swiftly and with few words. And why there is a silent tension between athletes, who have known these fires, and nonathletes, or anti-athletes, who have not. The latter seem not to live as gracefully with defeat, humiliation, or self-betrayal; they seem less conscious of their own complicity in weakness—in other words, with their own sense of being sinners. They *pretend* more. They have been defeated less.

George Leonard describes a little fat boy, waiting nervously in line at a corner of an athletic field, who knows he cannot do the chin-ups the gym teacher expects each lad to do. When his turn comes, he waddles to the bar, reaches up for it hopelessly and with clammy hands, tenses slightly. "UP!" says the smirking instructor. Humiliated, the boy tenses but, of course, can't lift his feet off the ground. He shrugs and walks away with what small dignity the titters of the others, and their biting jokes, allow. Leonard would have us feel the lad's resentment, nourished well into middle age; his fierce hatred for the athletic establishment, his vengeful feelings about the jocks.

It is a good example of the essential humiliation every athlete in the school—All-State back or little fat kid— sooner or later must suffer, from self and especially from others. There are many ways of coping with humiliation. One includes the loss of weight; the fat kid can come back next year as the whiz. Another includes a certain wisdom; the lad who chins himself with ease and snickers now will later burn behind the ears when teacher finds he can't get the "i" right in "believe"; then the fat boy gets to snicker.

Life isn't equal. Living with humiliation is part of not being equal to everyone. In few fields of struggle are the standards of excellence so clearly worked out for our humiliation. Being humbled is the name of—some game or other.

SPORTSREEL

Lombardi

Vince Lombardi has become a demon to some unbelievers. He is known for the sentiment "Winning isn't everything; it's the only thing" and for his supposed ruthless authoritarianism. Are these what he believed and practiced? If so, how did he believe and practice them? One of the most graceful essays ever written about him is included in Howard Cosell's *Cosell*. He calls it "Lombardi: Ask his Players." In fact, few men have won so much love and devotion from those who have worked for them.

Why, then, the antagonism?

For one thing, the enlightened seldom notice the power and authority in the games *they* play. At CBS, or at the New York *Times,* or at *Newsweek,* authority is no bowl of Jell-O. The style, however, is seldom as direct as on a practice field.

Second, a coach is a teacher. He doesn't just hire a bunch of pros and have them "do their thing." He has to give the team unity, a style, a signature. He has to bring each individual to the highest peak of his craft for each performance. Excellence is much more tightly demanded in football than in journalism, if only because there are only fourteen games of sixty minutes each in which to be as perfect as one can.

Third, class and ethnic styles of exercising authority must be taken into account. Football coaches deal with young men of many backgrounds and emotional histories. Most of the players they deal with are in their twenties; the oldest (except for a rare Blanda) are in their thirties. There are angers and furies in coaches, but the players soon learn how to interpret them, how to discern whether they are fed by personal animosity, pettiness, resentment, or only honest passion. One learns in life how to adjust to barks, epithets, and rages, just as one learns the underlying states of soul that prompt them.

Lombardi, it is said, could shed tears openly and be as tender as a child; the range of emotions open to Italian males is considerably larger than the range allowed upper-class Anglo-Saxon males. There was no need for Lombardi to be a cool, laconic Humphrey Bogart, Paul Newman, or Cary Grant.

Lombardi is also praised for the wide range of his sympathies. He treated individuals very differently. He nursed Bart Starr along, glowed with pleasure at the antics of Paul Hornung, bellowed with rage at certain hulking linebackers. His record with blacks, Cosell notes, was remarkable for its honesty and color blindness.

Finally, the record shows, few coaches had the streak of humor that often lit Lombardi's face and presence. He could laugh at himself, and mock his own intensity. His teams knew how to laugh. Can a man who laughs so easily be as cold, tyrannical, and unintelligent as his unrelievedly serious critics allege?

If life is not a football game, neither is it a morality play between the enlightened and the unenlightened. Those with conservative convictions are often, in execution, amazingly tolerant and compassionate; those with liberal convictions are often, in execution, machinelike, arrogant, and unbending. The human being is endlessly complex, immeasurably rich in variation. In particular, football coaches, whom psychologists describe as, in the main, "authoritarian personalities," may be more fair and just in their dealings with individuals than are sweetly liberal psychologists. So, Lombardi.

Of course, winning *is* the only thing—as an attitude, a desire, a spirit. In football, winning means excellence, defeating the demons of error and fate. Winning means outwitting everything that climate, occasion, injuries, opposing strategies, and chance can throw in one's way. Winning means being as perfect under fire as humans can be. Losing means somehow, through one's own fault, not having prepared enough.

"Winning is the only thing" does not mean "win at all costs, by any means, fair or foul." Nor does it mean that losing is without dignity. Every team, even the Green Bay Packers at their best, loses sometimes. It means that losing is, in the end, one's own responsibility. One's own fault. It means that there are no excuses. "Winning is the only thing" is capable of sinister interpretations. But it is also capable of expressing the highest human cravings for perfection. Winning does not simply mean crushing one's foes but being the best one can possibly be—and conquering the Fates and adversities that are stronger forces even than opposing teams. Winning is both excellence and vindication in the face of the gods. It is a form of thumbing one's nose, for a moment, at the cancers and diseases that, in the end, strike us all down, every one of us, even spirits as alive as Vince Lombardi's.

We miss you, Vince.

13

Regional Religions

CHRISTIANITY has many denominations, and Judaism many traditions. Sports, too, awaken different symbolic echoes in different areas of the nation. Not all lovers of sports love hunting. A few count demolition derbies as a sport; many fewer think dog shows are a sport; and others train dogs for savage, bloody dogfights. Tennis is the sport of a social class not likely to appreciate the grease, dust, roar, and danger of auto racing. The kingdom of sports has many mansions. The nation's three major sports have regional variants.

Football was born in western Pennsylvania, and it remains basic and well loved throughout the region. The rivalry between Johnstown and Altoona high schools was so fierce in the 1930s and 1940s that I never got to see them play. The annual riots after every game were too destructive; competition between the schools was banned for twenty years. For decades, one could predict the national championship from year to year by which college the best players from the region agreed to attend. The Southern schools—Louisville, Alabama, Miami, Kentucky—began wooing them to warmer climes just after World War II. Yet it would be difficult to say that football was a mania in the region. The predominant local cultures are mainly Eastern and Southern European, Irish, German, and black. The style was hard, calculating, driving, tough. One fullback from Windber, a mining town of fewer than 6,000 souls that specialized in defeating (or at least beating up) the major schools of the area, was famous for having sent six opponents to hospitals for a night of observation; his knees drove into opposing lines as though he were a locomotive rather than a lad of seventeen. The earliest amateur and professional clubs began with scions who had attended Rutgers or Princeton, but soon recruited the sons of miners and steelworkers. In a region of little upward mobility, young men played with a ferocity tutored by knowledge that, however violent football might be, the mines and mills were more violent still.

The passion feeding football in western Pennsylvania was the passion of chargers and hitters who gloried in their endurance of pain and punishment. There is a strain of masochism in the western Pennsylvanian character, almost a need to absorb punishment in order to prove oneself. In any case, endurance is perhaps the most highly prized characteristic—playing both ways, on offense and defense, as Johnny Lujack did with the Chicago Bears; going on forever like George Blanda; being "durable" like John Unitas; coming back operation after operation like Joe Namath; carrying four or five men with him before falling to the ground, as Leon Hart did; refusing to go down, as little Jim Mutscheller, not big for an end, used to do at Notre Dame. Not that Pennsylvania football lacked excitement. Daring passers and runners abounded. But the essence of the Pennsylvania game was physical aggression. Each team was trained to hit hard; desperate line play was the rule. Jack Ham and Pete Duranko are recent alumni of this school. Even the most explosive and brilliant players had to conquer that defensive fierceness first. The top passers specialized in quick release and long, flat bullets. The formations usually were basic, punchy, organized for power rather than flash.

A football game there, as liturgy, is not primarily a celebration of the state of Pennsylvania or of the regional culture; the larger social identity is not so highly developed. Penn State has little of the statewide glory Ohio State carries. Pitt does not glamorize the city of Pittsburgh. Loyalties tend to be diffuse and local. Notre Dame is probably more powerful symbolically than any team within the state (which is not to suggest that Pittsburghers don't feel delight when Pitt beats, or even threatens, Notre Dame, as Carnegie Tech did in the 1930s). A football game in western Pennsylvania is a celebration of local fighting spirit rather than of local institutions.

It is said that Southern and Eastern Europeans, having learned over centuries to distrust governmental or non-familial institutions, are not so civic-minded as Anglo-Americans; they do not react to the symbols of the state with unalloyed attachment. In any case, the liturgies of sports in western Pennsylvania tend to celebrate the sports and the athletes rather than a regional or civic jurisdiction. Fans were loyal to the Pirates and Steelers through long years of drought; the glory of the city was hardly to be celebrated. (Pittsburgh? Glory? The concepts hardly fit.) If there is madness and riot nowadays when the Pirates clinch the World Series or the Steelers take the Super Bowl, it is not exactly chauvinism that is celebrated; rather, a sort of vindication, surprise, astonishment, and the unfamiliar sense of being number one. The sports of the region are rugged, violent, and aggressive; so, too, are the victory celebrations. It is certainly true that labor in the mines and mills has seethed with suffered violence for generations. For generations, men have endured the worst industrialism could do to them: chopped-off fingers, broken knees, poison-coated lungs, bent backs, blackened hands, and mangled death. Sports are, comparatively, an easy way to make a living. What people there respect in athletes—and politicians—is learned from their own lives.

In Alabama, Arkansas, and Mississippi, by contrast, college football is a statewide religion; it *does* celebrate the state and the region. The poor boys of the South, white as well as black, also hit hard, glory in aggression, and value toughness; it is for them, too, a form of populism and assault on the unseen establishments that govern their lives. Bear Bryant, in particular, loves speed and wit and complex strategy. His teams play a wide-open brand of football. They run, it seems, from dozens of formations, and his recent staple, the wishbone, is remarkable for its swiftness, multiple options, and ability to open up the defense. The football of the Deep South is a rugged kind of football, but it is best described as fleet, explosive, difficult to contain. It is almost the reverse image of Pennsylvania football.

Somehow, in the South, to play a good game is to honor one's state, one's university, the South, and the true spirit of the American nation. The dominant churches, Baptist and Methodist, doctrinally so explicit about the separation of church and state, actually have forged a new *tertium quid* with the regnant society: a unity of religious values and national values that makes every liturgy of one simultaneously a liturgy of the other. A victory by Alabama is celebrated by virtually the entire state. The rivalry between Auburn and Alabama is a contest to decide who, for the year, is the established institution of the state religion. A loss by Alabama is carefully dissected by the state newspapers, the key plays diagramed for all to see, so that the "bugs" that somehow got into the healthy organism can be diagnosed and medically destroyed in time for next week's return to health. The young men are taught to play with heart, with concentration, with dedication, to be worthy of university and state and nation— and themselves. All these are grasped as a kind of unity, within a holistic culture. The liturgy of a football game is, indeed, a communal and statewide worship service, within a unitary cosmic scheme. (In professional football, Miami and Dallas most closely approach this collegiate symbolism; at a Southern Super Bowl, even national football "gets religion" in the classic style of the region.)

Football in the Big Ten is, undoubtedly, a focal point of passional religion every centimeter as deep as in the Deep South. But the style and manner are as different as a Baptist from a Lutheran liturgy. The Baptist and Methodist churches are in the "free church" tradition, and they cherish emotion, inspiration, charismatic speaking in tongues, the surges of personal conversion and sudden seizure. The churches of the Midwest—even the Midwestern Methodists—are filled by far more orderly and sober folk. They believe in orders, institutions, fixities; they distrust sudden conversions, too much talk, and flashy "show." Their faith is guarded in traditions, forms, and authorities, not left to the spontaneous spirit of the revival. In Alabama and Mississippi, the whole state is enthralled every spring by the photographs in their local papers: Bear Bryant presiding behind the kitchen table as yet another local lad chooses to accept a scholarship to 'Bama and signs, under the beaming faces of his parents, a letter of intent in the sanctity of yet another humble home. In the Midwest, Woody Hayes may refuse to buy so much as a single gallon of gas in Michigan, but everyone expects him to recruit every great athlete in Canton, Massillon, and throughout the state. A testimonial ceremony isn't necessary; you just show up in church in September.

"Three yards and a cloud of dust," they say of Ohio State football, and everyone makes fun of Woody Hayes's aversion to the pass. The forward pass was, of course, perfected in the Midwest, at Notre Dame, and Fran Tarkenton at Minnesota, Bart Starr at Green Bay, and Sid Luckman and Johnny Lujack with the Chicago Bears have thrown as well as any passers in the game. (Tarkenton and Starr were, of course, imported Southerners.) Still, the Packers, Vikings, and Bears—like Michigan, Ohio State, and Minnesota—have played essentially Midwestern football: hard, orderly, cleanly executed, disciplined, tight. The "black and blue" conference, they call it. The Midwestern spirit does not easily accept the flashy, the glamorous, the shortcut, the easy way. The fans come to cheer, and they take enormous pride in their favorites; they fill some of the most enormous stadia in the nation with the regularity of the seasons. Their form of exaltation, however, is not the intoxicating, spirit-beseeching revivalism of the cheering sections, nor the dazzling card-section displays of California; it is the large, disciplined, soul-stirring marching band. Legions of girls in cowboy boots are not the style, nor platoons of beach girls with pompoms; a single "golden girl" from Purdue is nightclub act enough. The cheerleaders are male as well as female; they perform with spirited decorum rather than with frenzy. In the Midwest, football is businesslike. The celebrity culture of East and West passes over the plains nonstop by air. Let Texas and Alabama give the nation passers and shifty-footed halfbacks; the Midwest supplies the linebackers and the hard run-

ners who believe in power. "Hopalong" Cassady, Red
Grange, Bob Griese, and others make these symbolic
statements lies, of course. Football teams in every region
absorb all sorts of talents and take talent where they find
it. But the style of play—and celebration—in the great
Midwest is built on character, solidity, and depen-
dability.

Nowhere, they say, is football more passional and
single-minded than in Texas (around Dallas) and
Oklahoma. A Notre Dame fan can hardly help being
aware that Notre Dame's past encounters with Southern
Methodist, Texas, and Oklahoma have brought Notre
Dame into a wholly different sort of world. In the Southwest, the great runners have the speed of halfbacks and
the power of fullbacks. The passers fill the air with foot-
balls. The mythic spirit there is not of miners and mill-
workers, nor farm boys, nor rebels, but of cowboys. In
Texas they play football as though the constricted field
were wide open spaces, and they seem to shoot their way
in and out of times of possession. It is as though the culture of the region were pressing in on them, pulverizing
them with the gentle terror of the huge sky; they are fix-
ing to explode. There is a charged-up energy in the Southwest that resists fencing in. They play the game in order
to break away.

When I was young and saw early telecasts from Dallas,
El Paso, and Norman, I could hardly believe the rapid
exchanges of touchdowns. Down there, it seemed, no one
respected order, patience, hard work; down there, they
went for broke all the time. They seemed to look beyond
the humble first-down markers; all they saw were goal
lines. Perhaps my image of the Southwest is colored by
the great confrontation of Notre Dame and Doak Walker
of Southern Methodist in 1947. Walker, "perhaps the
greatest player the game has ever known," according to
Esquire, was too injured to play. (We Notre Dame kids, in
the arrogant wisdom of our fourteen years, had early predicted that "Choo Choo" Justice of North Carolina and
Doak Walker of SMU would "conveniently" be unable to
face Notre Dame when the day came; and they were indeed injured.) Yet Kyle Rote, unheralded, taking the ball

in shotgun formation and firing it all over the field, ripped the greatest Notre Dame team of all to shreds, firing touchdown after sudden touchdown, and until the final gun it was impossible to believe Notre Dame could halt his unorthodox, intensely spirited, and brilliant play. Notre Dame finally won, in a game of heart attacks.

Southwestern football combines the speed of the Deep South and the power of the Midwest. The teams seem built to race toward game totals of 40 points, to see who gets there first. Big scores for big states. And Okies and small-town Texans seem to have a psychology parallel to that of northern white ethnics, with one exception. Like northern workers, they know the yoke of being looked down upon—'''rednecks''—and being given society's dirty jobs and low esteem; and they play as though their egos depended on it. The one exception is the attitude of obedience and social rectitude that governs the Southwest, as opposed to the cynicism and sullen hostility to authority that infuses the northern working classes. Vince Lombardi, coach of the Green Bay Packers, commanded obedience and bullied people to attain it; the players of Texas and the Dallas Cowboys speak of coaches Darrell Royal and Tom Landry as softspoken but ruthless machines. In the Southwest, the power of the establishment is almost unchallengeable. In northern cities, Lombardi was no establishment; he had to earn his authority by the force of personality. Players complain that the Texas coaches are aloof and impersonal; no such complaint was registered against Lombardi, hate his guts as some players did. "He treats us all equally," said one. "Like dogs." A football coach in the Southwest becomes an institution and joins the oil men; a football coach up North still faces establishments that he will never enter.

In California, football, like everything else, seems to be more fun. The weather is so good, not even rain and snow toughen character. Social repression and industrialization were never so cruel as elsewhere in the country. Chiefly settled in the last fifty years, California does not have the same entrenched ruling class as elsewhere. Blacks and chicanos have undergone the sort of humiliation rednecks and ethnics have known elsewhere; but everyone else seems to have been born above the snapping jaws of poverty. The Chinese and Japanese, so cruelly regarded on their arrival, have been spectacularly successful in business and the professions. The social order of California is easier than elsewhere. California is not a fertile soil for the rebellions of football. When restless Americans shook the dust of stiff eastern societies from their boots, they sought liberty ever westward—until, at Berkeley, the Pacific hemmed them in and there they gathered. When California radicals protest against establishments, it is not for the bare exigencies of survival but for the pleasures of a full and "liberated" hedonism. California is America's Mediterranean. California is for the history-stricken easterner what Oran was for Camus: maroon bodies in the sun, at one with the shimmering sea, just beyond the hovels of disease and poverty that history has never changed.

In California, football is the exuberance of the healthy body delighting in its talents. If one hears of a Bartkowski, one does not imagine a factory worker but a handsome beachboy. A young socialite like John Brodie can move from Stanford to the 49'ers as one would expect few wealthy easterners to do. Football elsewhere is a game of the oppressed, fed by inner rage and anger, bursting for daylight. In California, the entire game is sunny, and a pagan delight in physical contact replaces anger. Jack Snow is competitive and spirited, but it is hard to think of him as full of pent-up rage. O. J. Simpson, Anthony Davis, and John McKay, Jr., play with every ounce of energy imaginable, but they do so, it seems, from enjoyment rather than from meanness. Lew Alcindor, changing his name to Kareem Abdul-Jabbar, betrayed his New York origins in the sullenness and anger of his presence. Bill Walton, the tall, red-haired, California-born radical, did not play in order to escape a harsher fate; not knowing the system of mines, mills, and prairie towns, he found the system of *sports* oppressive. He explains that his love for the game and his inability to find suitable competition outside its organization keep him playing, not a fierce desire to find a better life.

Both John Wooden, the great basketball coach at UCLA, now retired, and John McKay, the former football coach at

USC, spoke often of making the game "fun" for their players. They recruited widely and well. Who would not like to go to school in California? The sun soaks enmity out. The social structure is uniquely open, fluid. The soft morality of the cinema lingers in the background. Flowers grow in abundance; the air is sweet. A football game televised from California is uniquely festive. Nature makes pretty girls prettier. The fans participate in elaborate and lovely card signals. The pom-pom girls dance with western Indian steps never practiced elsewhere. Fans arrive in shirt-sleeves and Bermudas. The athletes on the field seem, on the average, taller and handsomer than elsewhere, of a distinctly higher social class. Football in California is a civilized game, however grueling. Spirit rather than inherent toughness seems to play a greater role in the surging scores and quick excitement of California football.

In the Ivy League, sports are a very important symbol— but it is not considered sophisticated there to say so. Students in the Ivy League are in a very difficult emotional position. They are supposed to be "above" the rest of the population, including the cleaning ladies, janitors, and policemen from Cambridge, Ithaca, and the other Ivy towns who serve them. They are supposed to be more critical, sophisticated, and self-aware than, say, students at Ohio State. So even when they enjoy a game—like the magnificent last-minute Harvard "miracles" over Yale in recent years—they have to be slightly self-mocking and guarded. Once they have become successful alumni, of course, and can come back in camel's-hair topcoats, with silver liquor flasks and shiny family station wagons, it is all right for them to delight in a school victory and buzz about it for weeks. While they are students, enthusiasm of that sort is déclassé.

It is not that the Ivy League does not recruit seriously and hard, or that the athletes are not superb. Calvin Hill, Ed Marinaro, Chuck Bednarik, Harvard's Pat MacInally, Bill Bradley, and many others have moved quickly into stardom in the pros. It is, of course, difficult to find many young Americans able to carry the heavy load of verbal skills required of students in the Ivy League. Yet athletics are taken seriously in the Ivy League—and on the front page of the New York *Times*—and seem to arouse just as much passion in their fans as in virtually any other schools their size. In the old English upper-class tradition, of course, it is bad form to be *seen* trying too hard. (If you must study late, do it with a flashlight under covers.) Enthusiasm is all right in the free churches; in the cultural traditions of the Ivy League, it is repressed.

The Ivy religion is cool, like a clean white Unitarian church. Its passions are cerebral, like those of Brook Farm, the transcendentalists, and William James. The proper treatment to inflict on the defeated is mock mockery—the waving of white handkerchiefs from Harvard's side to Yalies across the way. The athletic event is put in "proper perspective": an excuse for a date, a drink, a fireplace, a room. It is not the athletic contest that dominates the weekend. As little as possible of life and death are invested in the game, or in anything. Detachment is the central tenet of the Ivy faith.

Moreover, the *true* life-or-death conflict in the Ivy schools is the grade point. It is, of course, bad form to wish too earnestly for an athletic team to be number one in the Ivy League or in the nation (God forbid!). It is also bad form *not* to be, perennially, as near to the top of the class as possible, *not* to be accepted in the best graduate schools, *not* to be offered the most prestigious job opportunities after graduation. True faith requires, not disbelief in the competition to be number one, but disbelief in the view that athletics is the chief avenue of competition. The Ivy League is the only league in the country in which acceptance of a professional athletic contract is silently regarded as a step *down* in social power. The scholars of the Ivy League have rarely been astute commentators on the mythic life. Cold analysis is their speciality. Power, not sports, is their religion.

In the Ivy League, a truly superb football game has the added excitement of participation in an almost forbidden passion. One should not care; one really *ought* to be above winning or losing; a truly incompetent performance by the athletes of both teams would give reassurance that one's own kind of people really aren't very good as jocks. The Ivy League style was once devoutly Puritan, and now is devoutly given to detachment. Yet every creed has its forbidden pleasures. At Harvard, Yale, Cornell, Princeton, and the rest, it is sinful to care. Nowhere else is secret caring more delicious.

The beating of the Crimson's drums outside my window on an October afternoon, as the band marched in maroon jackets and dark pants (none of those Midwestern braids or high bobbing caps), reminded me with pleasurable surprise during each year of my years of graduate school that the world was still alive. I wanted to see Harvard *cream* Yale. This secret feeling tasted almost as sweet as sin. "A sign of lower-class origins," one Professor clucked at me when he caught me waiting for a meeting with my *Times* open to the sports page.

Nevertheless, when Harvard twice in a row surprised supposedly superior Yale in the last minute—in true Frank Merriwell finishes (Merriwell having been a Yalie)—it is difficult to believe that in at least 10,000 sinful hearts a little lust for victory did not slyly creep. If Hester Prynne could not resist adultery, can all of Harvard have resisted secret consent to the delights of total triumph? I have played squash with Harvard men, and watched others, even in their fifties, playing tennis; believe me, they will *kill* opponents as pleasurably as any monster man of Michigan's front four. Being number one is the deepest of the Ivy League traditions, which other athletes imitate only from afar.

SPORTSREEL

Grantland Rice: The Statue
Made of Words

In 1924, following the Notre Dame–Army game, Grantland Rice wrote the most influential sports story in our
nation's history. Its opening lines have stirred me every
time I come upon them: "Outlined against a blue-gray
October sky, the Four Horsemen rode again. In dramatic
lore they are known as Famine, Pestilence, Destruction,
and Death. These are only aliases. Their real names are
Stuhldreher, Miller, Crowley, and Layden." Anyone who
has lived in the Middle West knows how overwhelming
the sky can be; everything is outlined against the sky. Autumn, in particular, opens up the sky; the sky brings the
cold. "Blue-gray" is one's precise memory of an Indiana
sky. "I wonder," Red Smith later wrote, "what angle
Granny watched the game from if he could see them outlined against the blue-gray October sky." But the answer
is obvious. Rice imagined himself down on the field,
prone perhaps, watching as the players watched. And,
gradually, he pulled his vision back, like a television camera, even like a camera on a Goodyear blimp, and looked
again:

They formed the crest of the South Bend cyclone before
which another fighting Army football team was swept over
the precipice of the Polo Grounds yesterday afternoon as
55,000 spectators peered down on the bewildering panorama
spread on the green plain below.
A cyclone can't be snared. It may be surrounded but somewhere it breaks through to keep on going. When the cyclone
starts from South Bend, where the candlelights still gleam
through the Indiana sycamores, those in the way must take to
storm cellars at top speed. Yesterday the cyclone struck

again, as Notre Dame beat Army 13–7 with a set of backfield stars that ripped and crashed through a strong Army defense with more speed and power than the warring Cadets could meet. . . .

Rice himself suggested in an *Esquire* article (November 1945) how the images first came to him. Brink Thorne and he were watching the Notre Dame–Army game of 1923, a year before the famous game of 1924. They were crouching at midfield along the chalk line, "when on a certain play Notre Dame's four flying backs came sweeping from the Rockne shift around Army's left end." Stuhldreher, Layden, and Miller led the way; Crowley carried the ball. None of them weighed more than 163 pounds, but "what they lacked in poundage, they more than made up for in speed, spirit, smartness and driving force. They worked with a rhythm that was unbelievably beautiful to watch. . . ." On this particular sweep, Crowley was finally forced out-of-bounds after a gain of 12 yards. "But he was moving at such high speed that he had to hurdle both Thorne and myself to keep from trampling us underfoot. 'We'd better move back,' I said to Brink. 'They are worse than a flock of wild horses on a stampede.' " The next year, in 1924, Rice was high in the press box, feeling safer than when "the back of my neck was almost impaled on Crowley's flying cleats." But he remembered the angle of the previous year.

Rice has been accused for his poetic fancy. The modern writer flees poetry in sports to find it in politics; Theodore White, Hunter Thompson, and Garry Wills are the Grantland Rices of our day. "Rice released the sportswriter's imagination," one critic says. "He convinced generations of sportswriters to give up their dull habits of accuracy and let fly. He legitimized the use of those colorful words—*smash* for hit, *turf* for field, *ripped* for ran—which endure to this day." Yet Rice did not invent this usage. It grows naturally from the sounds, sights, and sensations of the game: the noise of clashing shoulder pads cries out for onomatopoeia. The feel of a surface through one's shoes is better represented by *turf* than by *field* or (today) by *carpet;* and the sudden burst of a certain type of halfback through the line is not adequately described by *ran.*

In recent years, intimidated by television, writers have become afraid of the poetry of the English language and of its correlative in actual athletic contests. All the imagery of the medieval period persists in athletics, if not in high-rise office buildings (although even there *barons, fiefdoms,* and *serfdom* have their equivalents). Sports are played well only with spirit; without enthusiasm, effort flags. Sportswriting, matching its subject, must also reflect enthusiasm. The subject is not secular.

But medieval religion had its wholly secular machinations, too. The barque of Peter is propelled by a rather greasy engine room. The modern temper can't seem to understand the common, ordinary duality of life: the highest flights of the spirit are supported by the crassest demands of flesh, by the oiling of every wheel with money and sleight-of-hand. Behind all poetry lie prose and leg-work.

Rice remembered in 1945 how Notre Dame's "Four Horsemen" earned their name in the second period of the game in 1924. Notre Dame had the ball at its own 20 when "the swift, striking stampede started." On the first play, Crowley broke for 15; then Layden and Miller added 16, a Stuhldreher pass to Crowley went for 12, Don Miller burst away for 20, and Layden split Army for the last 10: a touchdown in seven plays. (He omitted a 7-yarder.) But Rice didn't remember a significant detail which Elmer Layden later revealed in his own autobiography, *It Was a Different Game* (1969).

Knute Rockne was getting so much press that he hired a Notre Dame student as a part-time public relations officer. The first was Arch Ward, later of the Chicago *Tribune,* but in 1924 the lucky lad was George Strickler. Strickler had seen the movie *The Four Horsemen of the Apocalypse* six times, including one screening just before the Pullman trip to the Army game. At half-time, Strickler circulated casually in the press box and mentioned off-handedly to four writers, including Rice, that the Notre Dame backs that day were running like the "Four Horsemen" in the movie. Rice's story went in the paper the next day, but even on the train back to South Bend, Strickler was planning how to get a picture of that "lightest backfield in the starring ranks of football history" on

four huge black horses. On Monday he borrowed four
horses from a livery stable, put the now famous four in
the saddle, and sold the pictures nationally—they still appear. A photograph reinforced Rice's words, which had
been inspired by a movie, which was rooted in a vision
from Sacred Scripture. Could television be far behind?

On January 1, 1925, Notre Dame, having begun to fill
stadia in the East, was on the West Coast for the Rose
Bowl game with Stanford. The "Four Horsemen" faced
the 200-pound Ernie Nevers, ranked by his coach Pop
Warner the all-time greatest back in football history,
ahead of the legendary Jim Thorpe. Elmer Layden describes the game he played that afternoon as the greatest
in his life, and indeed he flew across the field with abandon, intercepting two Ernie Nevers passes for touchdowns, one for 80 yards and one for 70, besides running 7
yards through center for another, and punting brilliantly
all afternoon. Stanford led 3–0 at the first quarter, but
Layden propelled Notre Dame to a slow, relentless victory, 27–10. Until 1949, his 18 points were a Rose Bowl
record.

"In my roving day and time," Rice wrote in 1945,
"looking back more than 46 years, I have seen a thousand
backfields, east and west, north and south, pass by in
review. No member of the Four Horsemen could be
named on an All-Time selection. But as a unit, as something to watch, they remain more vivid in memory than
any of the others I have seen." Recalling backfields in
some ways even better, Rice clarified: ". . . pound for
pound, they stand alone. They had no need for any sheer
power. If you consider such assets as speed, brains, heart,
alertness, and rhythm important, they had no equal."

Celebration in football is, finally, for the unit. Unfortunately, athletes do not leave behind statues shaped in
marble or cast in bronze, but only memories, images
etched upon the mind, recreated best in transient words.
Theirs is a fleeting beauty, as fleeting as the golden leaves
that fall in autumn across the land. And that is, ultimately, the poignant sweetness of the game: the juice of
youth stiffens and soon passes. The average playing life of
a professional football player in 1975 is 4½ years. It is, of

all games, a game for the exuberant young; a warrior's game.

And a writer, Grantland Rice, more than their own deeds, made four light young backs "immortal." Made a million see in mind what only 55,000 saw in flesh. Writing, too, is a lovely sport.

14

Jocks, Hacks, Flacks, and Pricks

YEARS AGO, the sports pages were the best-written, most lively, and most informative about the many cultures of this nation than any other pages in the paper. The writers, or at least a good share of them, were poets, lyricists, modest craftsmen. They delighted in the nation and its variety; they loved their beat. Such love is at the heart of any form of art. It forms a secret bond between the artist and his audience. Behind the words in newsprint on the page lay a secret bond of understanding. Readers met the writers in their hearts. *Cor ad cor,* went Cardinal Newman's motto, *loquitur:* Heart says to heart what words do not.

Long ago, one waited for terse accounts of great games or great fights by teletype. Line by line they came, bare, stark, to the point. In imagination, knowing the games and the images of the players, the men gathered round, animation rising and falling, as in their heads they recreated every action, every deed.

On the radio in the past, as one drove a truck or in some other circumstance (painting a bedroom) heard the play-by-play, one learned to love the basic accuracy and the single bare detail that lifted the imagination. For the Ali-Frazier fight of October 1, 1975, those who could not get to the theaters for closed-circuit TV listened for radio summaries, round by round. Not only who hit whom, but with what force and what effect, was suggested in stark

and cryptic messages. The mind flew. The inner eye recreated each detail. The stomach churned.

Late for a football game at Notre Dame, I once heard the
first half on the car radio. The terse verbal images, the
cadences of mounting excitement, the use of the half minute between plays to feed details to the imagination about
the substitutions, tempo, and mood reminded me of how
objective and to the point sports broadcasting used to
be—still is, where television is not watched. There was no
pretense that sports is entertainment. One got the basic
liturgy, the essential drama.

That one received it through an eyewitness, whose
skills and perception one had some reason to doubt (no
two witnesses being the same), did not detract from the
essential focus of the experience: the game itself. Perhaps
things never happened on the field exactly as Bill Stern or
Rosie Rosewell used to call them. Listening to a portable
radio at the game, one could see with one's own eyes
whether "racing back on the warning track" really threatened the outfielder with the crash into the wall that the
broadcaster seemed to suggest. But excitement in the
voice of the broadcaster also helped one to *see* even what
in the park's one's own eyes "saw"—added form, added
consistency, supplied a context for comparison. All the
more so when one wasn't present. Not for nothing have
millions of men had fantasies of broadcasters' voices in
their ears as they practiced shooting baskets, or even
weaving through traffic: ". . . *three seconds left to play, 1
point behind, Bradley shoots, it's up, it's good! . . . he's to
the 30, gets one block, sidesteps the safety man, he's to the 20,
only one man has a shot at him now, the 10, the 5, he's over!
Touchdown, Olivieri! . . .*" Even the great Bill Bradley,
practicing his shots "around the horn," hour by hour,
disciplining himself to make 10 out of 13 from every spot
before he moved to another, broadcast his own game with
his own lips, cheering himself on, in isolation in Crystal
River, Missouri.

The advent of television has made cowards out of many
sportswriters, mere chatty, fatuous, and complacent entertainers out of many broadcasters, and shambles out of
the religions of sports. It is true that television has given
us enormous pleasures, and taught us to watch the games

with new eyes. The "instant replay" has helped us to freeze the instantaneous ballet of a runner's moves; but it has rendered the unaided eye weak and undisciplined at a real game. It is harder to concentrate in the stadium; one has to remind oneself that there will only be one chance to see. The game looks totally different in the flesh. One regains there one's peripheral vision. One doesn't have to peer through the limits of the television box, subject to the judgments of a producer about which camera angle shows which portion of the play. One sees the whole. How large it is!

In a stadium, one feels present at a liturgy, at a kind of worship service where delight and fun are proper decorum. There is a sense of presence. Smells, touches, discomforts, the sweat and heaving of one's fellow spectators give one the sense of flesh, humanity, actuality. At home, pleased as one is to settle back and watch the vivid color in contemplative enjoyment, there is, rather, the feeling of being a voyeur; one feels a kind of distance and detachment. To be sure, the power of the drama itself is often so intense that one is drawn "into" the game. One's living-room, hotel room, or bar becomes an arena of its own. One cheers, yells, groans, gets up and walks around, whoops, hollers. It is not as though one were a million miles away. One is *there*, after a fashion.

In between times, however, the broadcasters go back to being entertainers. The game is not allowed to speak for itself. Instead of the steady beat of the radio voice, there is the mindless chatter of a late-night talk show, a Johnny Carson in a jock. Everything one loathes about the entertainment ethic now obtrudes itself in places where respect is called for. Blessed are they who can listen to the radio while watching the plays on silent television. I find no television broadcaster suited to the demands of sport. The tolerable voices among them would be Frank Gifford, who understands and has accurate sympathies for the ritual he is faithful to; Vince Scully when he is covering the Dodgers (but not at other times); and Curt Gowdy, who is endurable when he does not overpraise or gild or give us pieties. What I admire is a workmanlike performance that allows the game to come to me undiluted. The television voices are far too conscious of themselves, watching Liz

Taylor and Doris Day gaining on them over their shoulders, thinking they have to please us with their (God forbid) personalities. *I do not want to be entertained.* I want to experience the event.

Because they establish a level of patter—and what Howard Cosell calls the "chemistry" of interaction—the sportscasters trap themselves in banality; they cannot rise to the level of the high drama right before their eyes. When nothing is happening, they chatter on. When something happens, they can't escape their chatter. Their voices may get louder. Their exclamations are not different from our own. Where the radio broadcaster must describe what happened, carrying its inherent dramatic power, the television broadcaster says: "Did you see that! Did you see that!" They have a naïve faith in the human eye. In all the millions of bombardments the eye receives each second, it needs to know *which* to fasten on. The function of a broadcaster is to give us *form.* The television people have forgotten form. They do not trust the power of the word. They do not remember that Word, not vision, was the name God gave himself. In Hebrew as in Christian thought: God speaks, but is not seen.

The ear, not the eye, is the organ of human fact. And also of thought. The ear is personal (it carries tone and "voice"), holistic, stimulative. The eye distances, makes flat, kills, tames. To hear a great mind lecture is to have access to his thought—and to his heart and seat of judgment—that reading his books does not supply. The liturgy of the churches, is, wisely, centered on the spoken Word. So ought the liturgies of sport to be. Television, in trusting to the eye and renouncing the function of words except as filler, makes sports trivial. The eye is the most superficial sense. Television, the medium of the eye, cheapens us.

Still, sports triumph over television, and are enhanced by it. The use of several different cameras teaches millions about the relativity of standpoints. Was Pete Rose, awarded first base by the umpire, actually hit by the pitch? Three different camera angles show he wasn't. Was Charley Taylor out-of-bounds? Three cameras and a stop-action show he was. Multiple cameras do what the single eye cannot. Instant retrieval helps the eye to see again (but weakens concentration and memory). For those who do not know the game through long exposure, the isolation of a single player or a special match-up illustrates the atomic pieces that compose the whole. In taking one's eye away from the whole, however, these atomic pictures frequently recreate a totally different game.

Football, in particular, is a game of eleven men moving as a unit. While it is useful to understand the small dramas of which each play is the sum, to comprehend the true rhythm and the flow of play one has to grasp the whole. I, for one, would love to see television cameras snap pictures from above, and dramatize the lines of an actual play just as X's and O's diagram it on the coach's blackboard. Newspaper photos sometimes capture at least one instant of a whole play. I remember once a Notre Dame game with North Carolina in which, on a touchdown run to open up the second half, the Irish blockers left not a single opponent standing; it was the vision of the whole field that gave one pleasure. One photo caught it all, I seem to remember.

Basketball, for this reason, is exceedingly difficult for television to cover; the quality of team play and the sense of patterns on the floor are almost excised by television. For baseball, television is almost perfectly suited, in its ability to focus on solitary artistry. The problem baseball poses for television is not due to baseball but to television. Television is a nervous medium, hating '"dead" space, irresistibly urged to fill silent moments with something, *anything*. The leisureliness of baseball is one of its deepest pleasures. Television has to jazz it up. It is out of "sync" with baseball.

Television has distorted what we share. The fault is not that of the technology involved. The fault lies in the conception of the sports directors, producers, and sportscasters. They boast endlessly about their skills. The self-hawking of television is revolting, endlessly telling us, as if we did not have schedules every day, what they will do next. A particularly disgusting point was reached in 1975 when ABC used sports shows to shill for Howard Cosell's short-lived extracurricular career as emcee of a variety show. Nothing showed better the corruption of sports by entertainment than this fancy of Cosell's; having turned football into television entertainment, he moved by inexorable logic to what he may have really wanted all along. To argue, as Cosell does, that network shilling is made necessary by money already invested, as well as by the pressures of competition, is the oldest excuse for corruption known to history.

Were television to govern its approach to sports by the nature of sports, rather than by the canons of entertainment, the technology available could do the job. For dozens of years, sports did not bore Americans. Television sports have begun to bore. Iron laws of entertainment so decree. Revulsion gathers.

The most damaging effect of television, however, has been its enervation of sportswriters and their editors. Often it happens that one cannot see the televised game. Then it is almost impossible to find out in the papers the drama of the game itself. The writers take for granted that their readers have seen the game; they write about everything else. They have lost their faith in the power of the written word. For even when one *has* seen a game, either in the flesh or on the tube, the pleasure of reading about it the next day is unabated. One tests one's own perceptions against the reporter's. One rejoices in (or deplores) his way with words. One delights in the poetry of recollecting experience in tranquillity. Words direct the eye and heart. Words sort out diffuse impressions. Words contrive a permanent form for life. The power of words is far vaster than the power of television. Why have newspapers had a failure of nerve? Perhaps the sports pages can usher print media back to the center of our culture, now that the novelty of the cathode ray is wearing off.

For we have seen dozens of politicians on television now. One charismatic leader begins to look like all the others. One wearies of the pretty faces of the anchormen, experts, and politicians. One hungers for words to sink one's imagination into. So also with the parade of athletes, celebrities, and multiple sportscasters on the tube. The game's the thing. One craves words about it.

No pages in the paper used to be, and occasionally still are, such a vivid stimulus to the imagination. No pages give a writer equal scope. Weather, place, local culture, history, strategy, judgments, decisions, moods—all these are part of the reality of every contest, are focused by the contest, make up the drama of the contest. In almost every game, changes of strategy or tactics subtly influence the outcome; even if a team decides simply to "play its game," that phrase begs for analysis into its components. Television, of necessity, almost always fails us here. For two reasons.

A contest is a drama whose meaning is not clear until beginning, middle, and end are seen as one. A television sportscast is too close to the event to render an account of it as a single form. Here is where the writer has a function television does not even attempt. The writer can bring back a portrait, complete, whole, whose end is included in its beginning, whose unfolding he can clearly see. The reporter of an athletic event is rendering a drama as vividly and clearly as he can. The talent required is a craftsman's talent, an artist's talent. Collections of the great sportswriting of the past abound in craftsmanlike examples. One seldom sees them in the papers today.

Second, television sportscasters are merely guessing in advance, or from the press box, precisely what will work or is working on the field. But the writer has an opportunity to find out, and to make it part of his story. For example, a sportscaster can say from the booth, "If the Giants want to win today, they have to pass short." Then, indeed, the Giants may pass short. So said Howard Cosell on October 20, 1975, when the Giants startled everyone, including Cosell and Alex Karras, but not Frank Gifford, who predicted it, by beating the Buffalo Bills 17–14 in the last six seconds. But how many short pass plays do the Giants have? And what, precisely, is the weak spot in the Buffalo defense that will make the short pass work—and where? Which blocking patterns are emerging that allow the Giants to run around end successfully, as they had not been doing for weeks? On a football field, things don't just happen. Someone is thinking about them, probing, trying to make them happen. The writer, after the game, can formulate the critical questions and get the solid answers—if not necessarily from the principals, then perhaps from a scout observing such matters for next week's opponent.

On September 8, 1975, for example, Alabama met Missouri in a televised game. I was reading a biography of Bear Bryant that weekend, and for the first time gained a grasp of what Bear had been trying to do at Alabama and what his traditions at the school meant. The spring before, I had visited Missouri and had sharp images in my mind both of the campus on the plains, the relatively humble stadium there, and the faces of Missouri students. I knew a little of the function of the Missouri team in the state, and a little of its struggles toward greatness. For the first time in my life, my sympathies were very strongly with Alabama, which Bear seemed to hope might become his best team ever. One former Alabama player, now a coach in another league, said before the game that the Alabama squad included the greatest talent ever assembled on one team in the South. Yet Missouri totally mastered Alabama. The frustrations of obviously excellent players were tangible; one wanted, amost, to reach out and help. I couldn't figure out exactly how Missouri was doing it. Two or three offensive plays they used seemed extraordinarily interesting; they worked with such brilliance that I wanted to know the secret.

The next day, I looked in vain in the relatively long accounts of the game in the New York *Times* and *Newsday* for an account of those plays, and of the defensive formations that kept Alabama contained as they had seldom been in five years. Gladly would I have exchanged a dozen articles on trades, analyses of financial conflicts, and organizational chitchat about players' unions and corporate bosses for intelligence about the strategic insights that dominated the actual play. A friend of mine in Alabama, blessedly, mailed me the sports page of the Anniston *Star*. There, precisely diagrammed, were the plays I wanted to know about. That is the sort of intelligent reporting one longs for in the press. Football is delightful because it bears such study. More is always happening than meets the eye. The players and the coaches, appearing for television interviews, have been intimidated by the entertainment format; they seldom get a chance to say abstractly and technically what we need to know—what they would tell their own observers in the booths above.

Television, in its hunger to personalize the game, seldom deals with its abstract strategy, its formal design, its team execution. It gossips.

Yet not all the failings of sportswriters today—contrary to self-serving myth, we are unlucky in our generation—are due to cowardice in the face of television. In at least two ways the writers, some of them at least, undercut themselves. Some of them believe that they are superior to those they cover; they believe it is their function to prick the bubble of illusion surrounding sports. For convenience, we may call them pricks. They would prefer, second, to be working on some other section of the paper, covering financial or business news, or investigating city hall. There is some plausibility to their new conception of sports reporting, for it is not often that athletes or coaches in the sports world speak the idiom of our new journalists; and the growth of sports as a plaything of millionaires badly needs to be investigated. Still, it seems astonishing to read writers who do not love their subject.

In early 1975, David Shaw of the Los Angeles *Times* wrote a page-one article of 129 column inches on the new sportswriting, praising his own paper as the best in the country, and lavishly commending its publisher and editors. He had warm enthusiasm for the new breed of sportswriters, the "team" *he* plays for, so to speak. He praised the "quality of their writing," their "questioning minds" and "master's degrees." According to the new breed, to write in this way about a local football team would be to be a rooter. That is wrong. But choosing up sides among writers, and cheering for one's own, is right. Shaw names his own team, and their degree of loyalty, with serenity. The movement started with Larry Merchant, Joe McGinniss, Jack McKinney, and George Kiseda at the Philadelphia *Daily News* in 1957. It has spread to the Los Angeles *Times*, but not to its opposition (Shaw emphasizes) the *Herald-Examiner*; to *Newsday*, the Boston *Globe*, the Philadelphia *Inquirer*. "Only a few other sports sections in the United States [are] now actively moving toward the level of those already mentioned": the Washington *Post*, New York *Post*, Chicago *Tribune*, Chicago *Sun-Times*, Miami *Herald*, and New York *Times* (which has "special problems"). The new sportswriters have a

"litmus test" for their side: how a writer covered Muhammad Ali, Joe Namath, and the early New York Mets. The
good writers dealt with such symbols "on their own
terms, as representatives of a new independence and self-
awareness." The good guys saw that the early Mets
weren't serious but a diversion, and the good guys
"laughed sympathetically" with them. The way you laugh
is important nowadays, even in sports.

It is astonishing to read Shaw's description of earlier
sportswriting, however: " 'Meat and potatoes' sportswriting, it was called, and it consisted almost solely of
scores and statistics—batting averages, shooting percentages, earned-run averages, running yardage, passing percentages. . . ." Shaw must not have gained his master's
degrees in sportswriting history, nor dipped into anthol-
ogies; for the older sportswriting was some of the most
sociologically acute, colorful, lyrical, and biting in the history of journalism. What pleasure it affords, nowadays, to
read collections of old clippings.

Shaw, however, was deeply moved by "the socio-polit-
ical upheavals of the 1960's." His interest is ideological,
not historical. He writes a trifle ecstatically:

> The times—and the nation's sports pages—they are a
> changin', and it is now no longer sufficient to write sports
> stories by the numbers . . . or by the clichés. The more so-
> phisticated and literate reader of today's sports page wants to
> know more than what happened on the field. He also wants
> to know how it happened and why (or why not), as well as
> what may have happened before (or after) the event, in the
> locker room, the courtroom, the boardroom and the bed-
> room.
>
> Racism, drugs, sex, religion, gambling, exploitation, psy-
> chology, cheating, feminism, dress styles, violence, antitrust
> legislation—all these subjects, and many more, have been
> explored in detail on the sports pages in recent months.

Shaw lists several ways in which the new sportswriters
are better than the old; his claims sound either untrue or
disheartening. The athlete is not romanticized, but "ana-
lyzed, criticized, and even condemned." The sporting
event is not "treated as seriously as a holy crusade" but
dealt with "lightly, humorously, sarcastically or scorn-
fully." We now probe "the athlete's development as an

individual, his relations with others (on and off the field) and his attitude toward a whole range of personal, political, and psycho-social issues." This is supposed to be important for grasping what happens on the field (and also for one's daily dose of political education?). In addition, "Where once the sports pages contained some of the worst writing in the newspaper, now—on any given day—the best piece of pure writing in some very good newspapers might well be found on the sports page." Also, "the rooter as writer is a vanishing breed." Finally, "the biggest single change in sportswriting has been the coming of sociology to the sports page."

Shaw, above all, exalts his own new intellectual status. The sports department is no longer "the toy department . . . a sandbox peopled by the idiot children of journalism." The "new-breed sportswriter" is "socially and politically aware, motivated more by his own curiosity and need to write than by a love of sports for sports's sake." The greatest impetus to the new sportswriting, Shaw admits, however, is television. The "good" papers no longer recreate or analyze games; they look for "soft angles" not covered by television.

The new sportswriters do not actually write very well; only Roger Kahn—and he is not really one of them— writes with distinction. The late Leonard Shecter wrote with bite and wit, however, and his book is the fullest statement of the pricks to date. The title of this delightful, wry, and astringent book is itself an insult: *The Jocks*. He describes it as "a sports book by a man who hates sports." Hate, of course, is next to love, and infinitely to be preferred to indifference. Many a good book has had its origin in hate. Passionate attack is as important in writing as in football. What Shecter adds to hate, however, are arrogance and contempt. His own words convey his point: "There are two kinds of sportswriters—those with the good sense and ability to go on to other things and those with neither." He calls his classic chapter on the subject: "To Hell with Newspapermen, You Can Buy Them with a Steak." His own style around the clubhouse when he covered the Yankees may be inferred from comments like these: "The last thing a ball player cares about are the precepts by which a newspaperman is supposed to live.

. . . The only thing a ball player wants to know is what you have done for him lately. . . . Why should a ball player have the right to decide when he will talk to a newspaperman? . . . I leaned over backwards to be nice to ball players and was rewarded by arrogance. I accepted the arrogance and even began to feel it was my due. I never get angry. . . . I suppose my major problem, when I first began to cover a baseball team, was that I was more interested in being a newspaperman than a sportswriter."

There is a virulent passion for debunking in the land, one of the consequences, it is said, of the horrors of Vietnam, the sudden visibility of the depth of racism, and Watergate. Perhaps the roots of this passion lie deeper still, however, and the evils mentioned may be merely its occasion. A new class is struggling for power, in the world of sports reporting as in government; its method is contempt for all that has gone before. Its source is not our present theme, but its effects plainly are. In Shecter, as in others, the rage against sports seems overwrought, disproportionate, and off the mark. Sports are symbolic realities, but somehow in these writers sports begin to symbolize *political* evils. It is as though their rage against the nation, and perhaps against themselves, had been misdirected into sports. They do not, by and large, distinguish clearly enough between the realm of the spirit acted out in sports and the impact of mass communications and commercial interests. Rifle shots might hit their targets; they use napalm from a height.

"Nowhere else in the world," Shecter writes, "is such a large portion of the population so consistently engaged in sports and games." One wonders. It is estimated that 2 billion persons saw the World Cup championships in soccer in 1974, outside the United States. It offends him that 228 million Americans paid to attend major sports events in 1967. The figure sounds impressive until we average it out for a population of 200 million: paid attendance is approximately one per person every year. In 1973, by comparison, 112 million Americans visited a zoo. Only 35.9 million attended football games in 1967, according to Shecter; baseball games, 34.7 million; basketball games, 22 million. (These figures are for professional or college games.) Another 67.8 million went to the races. It dismays

Shecter that sports have become "a monster, a sprawling
five-billion-dollar-a-year industry." This is a large sum.
Yet many industries are larger, including the print and
broadcast media, the pet industry, and cosmetics. Out of
a gross national product of almost $1.4 trillion, $5 billion
does not seem disproportionate.

Shecter devotes most of his energy in *The Jocks* to
every example of "the dump, the fix, the thrown game,
the shaved points" he can find in the history of American
sports. He adds little new evidence to familiar allegations,
and lists few episodes that are not well known. His point
is a good one. Wherever money is involved, it is wise to
be cynical, best to be on guard. From his point of view,
however, the public gets pitifully little from the hoopla.
Sports yield, in his judgment, "a marvelous sense of the
importance of the unimportant." His prose is passionate:

> Around the simplicity which most of us want out of sports
> has grown a monster . . . which pretends to cater to our love
> for games but instead has evolved into that one great Ameri-
> can institution: big business. Winning, losing, playing the
> game, all count far less than counting the money. The result
> is cynicism of the highest order. There is no business in the
> country which operates so cynically to make enormous
> profits on the one hand, while demanding to be treated as a
> public service on the other. . . . What we get, as opposed to
> what we think we get, is what this book is about. . . . It's
> about the cynicism of American sports. . . . It's about the
> newspapers and the newspapermen who shill for sports. It's
> about television, the conscienceless and ruthless partner of
> sports. It's about the spoiled heroes of sports, shiny on the
> outside, decaying with meanness underneath. It's about the
> greedy professionals and posturing amateurs, the crooks, the
> thieves, the knaves and the fools. These are not trivial things.
> Sports have a great and continuous impact on American
> life. . . .

Shecter's passion for purity is a useful contribution.
But how will it be executed? If it means that sportswriters
will now become investigative reporters whose mission is
to prove that men in sports are as venal as men outside of
sports, we shall not learn much we don't already know.
The more they write about the sports *industry*, the more
the new sportswriters involve us in money, contracts,

deals, swindles, and a vicious cynicism of our own. With
the moral passion of the "chipmunks" (to use Jimmy Cannon's term) we can perhaps agree; everything depends on
how they execute. Here is where they contribute to the
distortion they deplore.

The main business of a sportswriter is to describe what
happened in athletic events. The contests themselves are
the forms of his craft. Everything else is secondary, in-
strumental, and to be judged in that light. The business
side of sports smells of rot; but the business side of sports
should be reported on the business pages. The politics of
sports are rotting, too; but the politics of sports belongs
on the national or the city desk. Many of the stories about
big money in sports—money made by teams or paid to
individual players—are not true; they are exaggerated as
part of the hype to attract attention. Nothing should be
hidden; everything should be reported. *But not in the
sports pages.*

When I read the sports page, I'm not interested in big
business, wheeling and dealing, money; all that is part of
the mundane world of everyday and belongs on the other,
boring pages of the paper, to be read from a sense of duty.
On the sports page, I seek clear images of *what happened;*
or, in advance, *what is likely to happen* in athletic contests.
I expect guidance in learning afterward exactly *how it happened.* I would like sports reporters to be, in this sense,
better newsmen. I would like them to give probing, intelligent, and artistic accounts of the one world that here
interests me: the events on the field. Let them be reporters. But about the contests on the field, not about the
industry. If they want to work for the financial pages, let
them; but not at the expense of the events without which
sports do not exist. The essential craft of the sportswriter
is mimetic: to recreate events, to imitate and to reveal
their form, to catch new sides to their significance. The
craft is more like that of the novelist or dramatist than like
that of the investigative reporter. The craft of the sports
columnist, and of those writers not assigned to specific
events, too, take their meaning from athletic contests.
Without the contests, there would be no sports. No matter
what is said, or done, or thought elsewhere, the essential
subject is what happens on the field in games.

It is important to our kind of civilization to keep sports as insulated as we can from business, entertainment, politics, and even gossip. Naturally, sports involve all these elements. But none of them must be permitted to obscure the struggle of body and spirit that is their center. The athletic contest has too much meaning for the human spirit to be treated with contempt. Our civilization needs sports, and it needs as well the skillful exercise of the sportswriter's craft. The narrative forms that recount athletic struggles supply millions with a sense of form. These forms express implicitly realities of law, fairness, effort, and spirit.

Who, watching the sixth game of the 1975 World Series in Boston's ancient and angular Fenway Park, as first the Cincinnati Reds and then the Boston Red Sox fought their way back from 3-run deficits and battled for four hours with brilliant play after brilliant play—Lynn of Boston lying immobile after crashing his spine into the center-field wall; Foster of Cincinnati throwing sharply from left field to make a bases-loaded double play at the plate; Evans of Boston racing back to the seats in right in the eleventh to take away a certain home run; Fisk fighting the night breeze with his hands to pull his twelfth-inning homer far enough inbounds to hit the foul pole and give Boston a 7–6 victory—who, watching this game, could not detect some of the main sources of our civilization's strength, acted out in ritual form? It is ponderous to put it this way; best if one drinks in the pleasure, imitates the attitudes, without too many words. But it is precisely in tacit and unspoken ritual forms that all religions have most effectively taught their hidden mysteries. The account of these rituals, in narrative form, is the main business of the sports page. It is being seriously neglected.

Without narrative forms, a culture flies apart; sorting out the relevant from the irrelevant becomes impossible; living loses zest. Life in its multiplicity overwhelms the brain, blows it out. The opera, the play, the cinema, the short story, the ballet, the modern dance—all these wrest form from chaos. The forms of play, including the narrative forms crafted by sportswriters, are absorbed into the psyche, become the forms through which other forms may be perceived. For this reason, above all, it is important to be vigilant over the corruptions and the range of sports.

Standards of fair play, honesty, courage, scrappiness, law-abidingness, excellence, perfect execution, etc., are all dramatized in a baseball game, in football, and in basketball. These are standards difficult to meet in the contests themselves, in the industry that makes them possible, and in the rest of life. As we have seen, these standards belong not to the players, who may not embody them, but to the inherent structure of the game. Without such standards in its ritual structure, a game could not be played; it would be meaningless. Without such standards in a culture, human beings could not complain of vice, corruption, or incompetence.

Sports are not a sufficient vocabulary of forms for a whole human life; but they are a fundament, a basic vocabulary, around which it is possible to build an ampler human structure. Many athletes and coaches find their work of absorbing interest. For others, athletics are just a job for a certain time in their lives. For most of us, they are part of our mythic world—nourishment for body, soul, and imagination.

It is not uncommon for writers in a given field, even a generation of writers, to lose sight of their essential function. Ever since Theodore H. White's *The Making of the President, 1960*, a generation of political writers has developed a mania for looking under, behind, and around the central actions of politics. There is passionate concern for "inside" stories, but far less concern for grasping clearly the economic consequences of political ideas. So, also, among sportswriters there appears to be at present a damaging and costly failure of nerve. Intellectually, sports have been treated with disdain; commercially, television has intimidated writers and editors, and led them to neglect what they do best and, indeed, what only they can do: clarify the dramatic form of each sports event. Just because people have "seen it on the tube," one ought not to cease describing the event as it occurred outside the limits of the camera lens. Repetition is no enemy of sports; nor of religion; nor of art.

In addition, there are characteristics of sports that differentiate sportswriters from any other writers on the paper. There are two pleasures in sports: first, a perception of the sheer excellence of play; second, the identification of self with the struggle and the outcome. Nourished by the latter, one can with pleasure enjoy from time to time a contest between teams one hardly knows. But true enjoyment does not begin until the self is risked, until there is a part of the self to lose. It is not absolutely essential that one become completely partisan in order to feel this risk. As a Dodger fan, I felt a relative neutrality between Boston and Cincinnati in the World Series of 1975. Or, to put it more exactly, I rooted for Boston in every game until the last. They deserved not to be humiliated, and their spirit was infectious; but after six years of steady excellence, Cincinnati deserved a championship. I wanted Middle America to win one. I would have been pleased, but a little less so, if Boston had won. Such response is more than aesthetic; I find myself identifying, acquiring loyalties, choosing sides, accepting risks, even when the grounds of choice are neither deep nor unchangeable.

One's appreciation for a game, moreover, increases with detailed familiarity with various factors that affect it. Bookmakers take even minor factors into account: the weather, injuries, morale, the place of a game in the schedule, and so forth. Athletic deeds gain part of their significance from the history in which they occur. A home run at the end of a slump, at a critical point, brings a special pleasure. If one knows that a player is hurt, and if one also knows his characteristic moves, one can watch an entire game anticipating, and then enjoying the specific pleasure of a drama adequately "true to form." One recognizes, for example, Joe Namath's relative immobility because of his bad knees, but one also knows that at any moment he can fire an electrifying pass. The long waits between his four or five moments of brilliance may be justified (but were not, really, in 1975) through the pattern they fulfill, linked to a history of previous deeds. One measures an athlete against his remembered form, his best; and one's standards for him grow as he grows. Appreciation in sports requires a grasp of local history.

History, then, is at the heart of sports. Each contest is part of a chain of others. Each is partly self-contained, but each is also linked to others. The excitement of many contests depends on rivalries from the distant past. In part, these are collective rivalries between organizations; in part, personal rivalries between coaches or players. "Last year, they murdered us." "The last three weeks we played badly; tomorrow we have to establish our rhythm, our kind of game." Each game has its stakes; no two raise the same expectations.

But we are not infinite. We cannot appreciate the full traditions of the top twenty college football teams, or of twenty-six professional football teams with one thousand-one hundred and eighteen players. The human imagination, heart, memory, and intelligence are finite. The nature of the human psyche is to proceed from what is close to us outward; we cannot without self-deception begin by embracing everything. To claim to love humanity is to carry a very large and thin pane of glass toward a collision with someone you can't abide.

Thus, a sportswriter becomes a folklorist of sorts, steeped in detail and anecdote, practicing a form of intellect from which all others spring, the lore of the wise man of the tribe. Like Arthur Daley and Red Smith, Dick Young and Jim Murray, virtually every veteran writer learns this craft. Knowledge in sports is exceedingly concrete. Great theories and general rules don't carry athletes too far. Each must tailor principles to his own individual circumstance. Particularities, quirks, eccentricities, peculiar preferences, habits, and customs loom large in sports—as everywhere in life except where the rationality of bureaucracy extends, its rules snarling and tangling one another up. The most highly prized form of intellect is concrete.

All these characteristics of the sports world draw the sportswriter into an unusually close relationship with the subjects of his work. Even independently of his need to keep on good terms with his sources, or to avoid friction between his paper and the teams he covers, the attitude of a writer to his subject normally involves ties of long standing, profound loyalties, and deep personal identification. Some critics deplore such developments and speak with contempt of "shills" or "house flacks." Such contempt seems, most of the time, misplaced. For an atti-

tude of love for the subjects of one's writing and even a
deep loyalty and rootedness in a particular team are
uniquely appropriate in sports reporting. The readers of
sports stories in the local paper read from a point of view,
with a sense of identification, and also with a passion for
perfect play on the part of their team. As they are critical,
so the writer may be. Scrappy, independent loyalty is
best. I do not find it shocking to imagine sportswriters in
the press box shouting hoarsely for the home team and
pounding their desks in excitement. The cool modern
types may do it differently; in the world of sports, there
are many styles. The essential point is to get the drama
right for one's readers.

Many readers are intelligent. They are inured to the
stupidities of journalism. They delight in craftsmanship
lovingly performed. They like to read a writer who challenges and defies them. They want him often, in their
stead, to sock it to errant players, management, owners,
television, industry, the world. They recognize the difference between loyalty based on love for excellence and
sycophancy. They are tolerant, endure a great deal of mediocrity. But work of quality has a way of winning recognition, being cited in conversation, reread, and given
thanks at first in private, later perhaps more publicly. Bill
Veeck, flamboyant owner of several teams, says he prefers
the sharp, pesky, argumentative writer who takes a poke
at management. He's interesting. He's reacted to. He does
in his craft what the players do in theirs. And he helps
both his paper and the team, much as the biggies may
dislike the names he calls them.

The writers of the new breed—Shecter, Larry Merchant,
Wells Twombly, Robert Lipsyte, as well as the ex-athletes
Jack Scott, Dave Meggyesy, Chip Oliver, Jim Bouton, and
others—often picture themselves as the first frank, critical, and abrasive sportswriters in the nation's history. Yet
lovers of the game have always known how to barb,
skewer, and roast a charlatan, a fake, a quitter, a ten-
derskin. Boston writers rode Ted Williams hard; he
kicked back. Writers in Atlanta tried to drive Bear Bryant
out of football. Years ago, Frank Leahy was the target of
vicious criticism, some of which helped force his resignation. Rosie Rosewell used to want the Pittsburgh Pirates

to win so bad it hurt to hear him when they made mistakes. (The broadcasters, of course, are hired by the team; they are not exactly "press.")

Since at least the age of nine, I've received one clear message from the papers: that sportswriters would make better managers, and maybe better players, than the fellows on the field. Half the pleasure of the connoisseur is trying to outguess events. His imagination swiftly runs ahead, with keen expectations, and the poor fellows who have to play the ball seldom attain the perfect form anticipation craves. So it is not new for sportswriters to be critical.

What is new is the relatively recent surge of hostility so total it is puzzling, a kind of global disappointment and resentment, as if America and life and sports had let some writers down. It is as though one had a right to expect a nation to be just, true, good, compassionate; as though liberty and justice were easy to attain, and failures to attain them due solely to slack will; as though an intense will for goodness were sufficient. Yet I am not sure the hostility of which I write springs from innocence. It may be futile to try to guess its motives. It has given prominence and power to the pricks, with mixed results.

A prick is a writer who is out of place in sports. He really wants to deal with a world of Serious Subjects. Enlightened, bright, able, interested in facts (without necessarily uncovering many), the prick thinks himself incorruptible. He also writes well, or tries to. The flack, by contrast, is a company man, not in the sense that he is, say, an announcer paid by a ball club, but in the sense that he is sycophantic.

A flack has no independence of mind. A "house announcer" or "house writer" is different from the flack in this respect. His loyalties are plain. Yet he is faithful, as well, to standards that transcend both him and his employer. He does not bite the hand that feeds him; he has room for self-respect; he does not wear a leash. He does not expect sports organizations to operate by a higher morality than newspapers, universities, or other human organisms. He has learned a certain tolerance for human frailty. He often calls himself, self-deprecatingly, a "hack": seldom setting the world on fire; doing a decent job; establishing a solid, if modest, reputation; workmanlike; like most players on most ball clubs or, for that matter, like most human beings. The type, as Lincoln put it, that God loved to duplicate. The sports department of the *New York Times* numbers 53. They can't all be rising stars.

"A baseball club, the public has been brainwashed into thinking, is like a city's army going out to do battle with the mercenaries of another city," writes one prick. Another writes: "Sports act as an important socializing agent for misdirected elitism, nationalism, racism, and sexism, thus tending to turn jocks into proto-fascists." A third writes that he applauds the breakdown of local loyalties by television, as on the *Game of the Week* and *Monday Night Football*. He praises the universalization of sports, although he finds himself less interested than formerly. Even though he is a New Yorker, he writes, he would believe Joe Namath great even if he were playing for the Los Angeles Rams.

These attitudes seem noble and large-spirited. Yet they run counter to the human heart. Intense group loyalties are part of being human. They are important to the survival of the race. They teach forms of fairness, justice, and fellow feeling on which other moral forms are based. In every sport, these local loyalties are transcended by the rules of play. The game is larger than the local passion. Sports help to show how one can be particular and universal at the same time; partisan, yet not self-enclosed; loyal, yet rule-abiding; attached to one's own, yet capable of recognizing worth in others. Babe Ruth was an idol for millions who weren't Yankee fans. "All-America" teams command respect from all sections and factions. Even those who despise Alabama, or Notre Dame, or Ohio State can—and do—recognize their frequent greatness. To love the Dodgers is not inconsistent with recognizing that the 1975 Cincinnati Reds were a better team, that Oakland and Boston played more exciting baseball, and that the Pittsburgh Pirates were explosive and underrated. Sports fans are often quite objective about the strengths and weaknesses of various teams and players, despite their loyalties. Their judgments are, or can be, settled on the field. I would much rather argue the merits of Notre Dame with an ardent Alabama fan than argue politics with extremists of the right or of the left. Any day.

The pricks, in sum, tend to have large, even global souls. The hacks have humble loyalties. The pricks are strong on principle. For the hacks, morality is rather more familial; their deepest moral bond is likely to be a loyalty between persons, as in the family, rather than a morality of principle, or duty, or universalizable rule, or moral imperative. The prick doesn't trust the easy tolerance of the hack. The hack believes that pricks, like other men of principle, will in the name of moral principles betray their friends every time. The war between pricks and hacks is an ancient war. Often, each has something good to say. It would be silly to be a flack for either one of them.

For all who report sports, however, at least this much can be demanded: a passion for excellence in covering the heart of the matter, the actual contests on the field. Today not many have it. Lacking that, the rest is beside the point.

SPORTSREEL

An Unrehearsed Classic:
Vince Scully

The tape recorder gives us a chance to test the "verbal dexterity" of broadcasters as well as writers. The wielders of colorful words do not always read so well in print. The following *verbatim* transcription of one of Vince Scully's accounts of a Dodger game is as perfect a jewel as if it had been imagined, written, corrected, polished. None of these has been done to it. The words are printed as they were delivered on the air. It is as worthy, in its way, as the deed it voiced: the fourth career no-hitter, first perfect game, by Sandy Koufax.

September 9, 1969

Chicago Cubs	0	0	0
Los Angeles Dodgers	1	1	1

W. P., Koufax
L. P., Hendley

The live broadcast by Vince Scully, top of the ninth:

Three times in his sensational career has Sandy Koufax walked out to the mound to pitch a fateful ninth when he turned in a no-hitter. But tonight. September 9th, 1965, he made the toughest walk of his career, I'm sure, because through eight innings he has pitched a perfect game. He has struck out eleven, has retired 24 consecutive batters.

And the first man he will look at is catcher Chris Krug—big, right-handed hitter—flied to center, grounded to short.

Dick Tracewski is now at second base, and Koufax ready—and delivers: curve ball for a strike—0-and-1 the count to Chris Krug.

Out on deck to pinch-hit is one of the men we mentioned as a "possible": Joe Amalfitano. Here's the strike-one pitch: fast ball, swung on and missed, strike two.

And you can almost taste the pressure now. Koufax lifted his cap, ran his fingers through his black hair, and pulled the cap back down, fussing at the bill. Krug must feel it too, as he backs out, heaves a sigh, took off his helmet, put it back on, and steps back up to the plate.

Tracewski is over to his right to fill up the middle. Kennedy is deep to guard the line. The strike-two pitch on the way: fast ball outside, ball one. King started to go after it but held up, and Torborg held the ball high in the air trying to convince Vargo, but Eddy said. "No, sir."

One-and-two the count to Chris Krug. It is 9:41 P.M. on September the ninth. The 1-2 pitch on the way: curve ball tapped foul off to the left of the plate. The Dodgers defensively in this spine-tingling moment: Sandy Koufax and Jeff Torborg—the boys who will try to stop anything hit their way: Wes Parker, Dick Tracewski, Maury Wills and John Kennedy—the outfield of Lou Johnson, Willie Davis and Ron Fairly.

There are 29,000 people in the ball park and a million butterflies: 29,139 paid. Koufax into his windup and the 1-2 pitch: fast ball, fouled back out of play.

In the Dodger dugout Al Ferrara gets up and walks down near the runway, and it begins to get tough to be a teammate and sit in the dugout and have to watch.

Sandy back of the rubber now, toes it. All the boys in the bullpen straining to get a better look as they look through the wire fence in left field. One-and-two the count to Chris Krug. Koufax, feet together, now to his windup, and the 1-2 pitch: ball, outside, ball two. [*The crowd boos*]

A lot of people in the ball park now are starting to see the pitches with their hearts. The pitch was outside. Torborg tried to pull it in over the plate, but Vargo, an experienced umpire, wouldn't go for it. Two-and-two the count to Chris Krug. Sandy reading signs. Into his windup, 2-2 pitch: fast ball got him swinging! Sandy Koufax has struck out twelve. He is two outs away from a perfect game.

Here is Joe Amalfitano to pinch-hit for Don Kessinger. Amalfitano is from Southern California, from San Pedro. He was an original bonus boy with the Giants. Joey's been around, and as we mentioned earlier, he has helped to beat the Dodgers twice. And on deck is Harvey Kuenn.

Kennedy is tight to the bag at third. The fast ball for a strike: 0-and-1 with one out in the ninth inning, 1 to 0 Dodgers.

Sandy ready, into his windup, and the strike-one pitch:

curve ball tapped foul, 0-and-2, and Amalfitano walks away and shakes himself a little bit, and swings the bat. And Koufax, with a new ball, takes a hitch at his belt and walks behind the mound. I would think that the mound at Dodger Stadium right now is the loneliest place in the world. Sandy, fussing, looks in to get his sign; 0-and-2 to Amalfitano—the strike-two pitch to Joe: fast ball, swung for and missed, strike three!

He is one out away from the promised land, and Harvey Kuenn is coming up. So Harvey Kuenn is batting for Bob Hendley. The time on the scoreboard is 9:44, the date September the ninth, 1965. And Koufax working on veteran Harvey Kuenn.

Sandy into his windup, and the pitch: fast ball for a strike. He has struck out, by the way, five consecutive batters, and this has gone unnoticed.

Sandy ready, and the strike-one pitch: very high, and he lost his hat. He really forced that one. That was only the second time tonight where I have had the feeling that Sandy threw instead of pitched, trying to get that little extra, and that time he tried so hard his hat fell off. He took an extremely long stride toward the plate, and Torborg had to go up to get it. One-and-one to Harvey Kuenn. Now he's ready: fast ball high, ball two.

You can't blame the man for pushing just a little bit now. Sandy backs off, mops his forehead, runs his index finger along his forehead, dries it off on his left pants-leg. All the while, Kuenn just waiting.

Now Sandy looks in. Into his windup, and the 2-1 pitch to Kuenn: swung on and missed, strike two. It is 9:46 P.M. Two-and-two to Harvey Kuenn—one strike away.

Sandy into his windup. Here's the pitch: *swung on and missed, a perfect game!*

[*Long wait as crowd noise takes over.*]

On the scoreboard in right field it is 9:46 P.M. in the city of the angels, Los Angeles, California, and a crowd of 29,139 just sitting in to see the only pitcher in baseball history to hurl four no-hit, no-run games. He has done it four straight years, and now he capped it: on his fourth no-hitter, he made it a perfect game.

And Sandy Koufax, whose name will always remind you of strikeouts, did it with a flourish. He struck out the last six consecutive batters. So, when he wrote his name in capital letters in the record book, the "K" stands out even more than the "O-U-F-A-X."

SPORTSREEL

Humble Howard

"Look, there is no damn way you can go up against Liz Taylor and Doris Day in prime-time TV and present sports as just sports or as religion. Sports aren't life and death. They're entertainment."

—HUMBLE HOWARD

No sports commentator in recent years has stirred the juices as much as Howard Cosell. Why? Commentators are to sports what prophets and theologians are to religion. Howard is the nation's first major non-Christian sports prophet. He never had to learn all those inhibitions that young Christians, particularly those in the heartland of sports, the Bible Belts of the land, drink in with their mother's milk and relearn from their pappy's strap. Every culture carries with it distinctive ideals, and in the case of the Christian athlete, these usually involve a ritual form of modesty, self-effacement, team-consciousness, and oft repeated loyalty. In America, individualism reigns and associations are fluid; hence, assurances of loyalty and conformity are precious. In public, at least, the pieties fall as thick as snowflakes.

Cosell describes himself as a "needler," and he admits frankly to a certain abrasiveness. That he is no great practitioner of self-effacement is obvious, and that modesty is not a virtue he carries to extremes may be glimpsed even in the titles of his books: *Cosell* and *Like It Is*. Cosell gives good reasons for every boast he makes. The usual Christian fashion, not least in the world of sports, is not to boast in public, with or without good reason. Cosell is under no obligation to bow to pieties that inhibit others. He has helped to raise the degree of abrasive frankness in our national discourse. He has added to the repertoire of future sports commentators one more style, one more approach to the subject. For his exaggerations, self-promotions, and violations of cultural taboos, he has paid a certain price—not unlike that paid by other ethnic types in sports (like Namath, Billy Martin, and Muhammad Ali) who do not share the classic pieties.

One recalls Cosell, on his very first regular Monday night broadcast, saying in his own inimitable tone of voice: "Leroy Kelly has not been a *compelling* factor in this game." Cleveland won 31–21. Howard thought the first night a great success. Then the flood of letters and editorial protest startled him. "You see," he explains in *Cosell,* "in the spoon-fed Alice in Wonderland world of sports broadcasting, the public was not accustomed to hearing its heroes questioned." But this is nonsense. The Boston sportswriters used to tear Ted Williams apart. Nothing is a more common experience of athletes and coaches than criticism in the press—considerably more accurate and ferocious than Cosell's. Yet thousands of letters came. More than half the mail was about Howard and Muhammad Ali. "I knew instinctively what [it] meant. It was a pattern with which I was painfully familiar: 'Get that nigger-loving Jew bastard off the air. Football is an *American* game.' " Cosell doesn't stop to recognize that half the mail was in defense of Leroy Kelly, a black man. He does not see that his tone says far more than his words, projects his sense of his own superiority. Some of the mail, he is told, "says you can't criticize the players, you never played the game." It is a question of tone. His tone belittles others. No one doubts he can *talk* better than most ex-athletes; has, in his own words, "great verbal dexterity." His tone needn't indicate that he is also better in every other way. Humble Howard!

The second reason for Cosell's capacity to enrage is not so much a question of style as a question of substance. Granted that he is so damn sure of himself, that he pronounces his judgments in a tone of voice that makes him seem almost papal in complacence ("papal bull," one almost wants to say), Cosell also diagnosed the existence of a new constituency for sports. Studies have shown that high numbers of professional people—from managers and executives to lawyers and intellectuals—follow sports with passion. Some 89 percent of managers regularly attend football games or watch on television. The "average sports fan" includes not only drivers of beer trucks or construction workers, but a large majority of the new and swelling professional class. Cosell decided to give them sociology as well as sports. He broke with conventional ideas.

Cosell describes sportscasters tearing copy off the wire machine and reading the results verbatim:

> That was their idea of a sportscast. Not mine. I had my own notion about the business. I felt that the field was wide open for anyone willing to develop the sources and get to the scene. . . . I wanted to explore the issues. The world of sports was about to explode in America. Great changes in technology were coming; an increase of leisure time; the exodus to the suburbs to escape from the great cities. The whole pattern of society was changing, and sports would become ever more important. The influx of black athletes had begun. A whole new set of smoldering problems would emerge. Could we keep giving the country line scores as news?

Cosell tended to side with "change," with the new professional classes, with the advance, so to speak, of New York liberalism across the countryside. In this way, Cosell won the reputation—a valuable one as time went on—of being antiestablishment. The transformation of Cassius Clay into Muhammad Ali was almost perfectly suited to dramatizing Cosell's career. A black man, a dissenter, a colorful and lippy violator of the same pieties of modesty and self-effacement Cosell himself was violating, Ali was also a brave and bold champion. Call him a fraud, if you wished. Call him a coward. Call him all sorts of names— the more you became preoccupied with him, the more valuable he became as a draw. Then in his fights he took the assaults of his enemies' best blows and, while absorbing some defeats, most of the time came back to win. His bouts with Joe Frazier and George Foreman were classics. Ali talked big. But he delivered big, too. His style gave credibility to Cosell's. Their careers benefited each other. At critical stages, each helped the other.

Yet Cosell, as an immigrant outsider, was always deeply involved in his own family; his wife Emmy figures often in his writings, and he remembers that his father was disappointed every day until his death in 1957 that Howard didn't continue as a lawyer. Thus, Cosell had complex sympathies. His essay on Vince Lombardi is a poignant answer to Leonard Shecter's vicious assault on Lombardi in *Esquire*. Cosell understood the intensity of Lombardi's attachment to family values and to the old immigrant ways of excellence. It was as if Cohen (Cosell's original name) well understood Lombardi, rising as they did off the same streets of New York, with a passion for excellence fed by resentment of false pieties. Both of them endured no little abuse from those whose preferred style was different.

On the plus side, then, are Cosell's attack on less than truthful pieties and his insistence on being himself—"integrity" is one of his favorite words, a word one imagines him sticking out his chin to say, his eyes flashing a certain defensive arrogance, his lips already set for counterattack to any challenge. Nevertheless, I hold his influence on the nation's conception of sport to be negative. Cosell grants that sports are not *merely* entertainment, but entertainment and something more. He has wanted to bring "honesty" to sports, he says:

> It must be realized, once and for all, that sports are not separate and apart from life, a special "wonderland" where everything is pure and sacred and above criticism. A football game is not a holy sacrament, and baseball does not truly equate with apple pie and motherhood and the American flag. I suggest that in American society today, it is time to tell it like it is—and that includes sports.

Cosell's critics said he and Don Meredith were making *Monday Night Football*, which changed the social habits of millions of Americans, "entertainment, not football." But Cosell had clearly recognized that sports is *both* news and entertainment. He explains that ABC had to attract 30 million viewers, and each paragraph he wrote needed to earn back "$100,000 a minute." It was big business, a risk; it had to compete, and it had to succeed. The other networks predicted failure, having failed themselves. Against his critics he would reply: "ABC will not be like the others. We'll be number one because we make football entertaining."

For Cosell, the debate is between news and entertainment. He confuses the false pieties of the Anglo-American style with religion. In rejecting sports as something like a sacrament, sacred, profoundly rooted in the human spirit and in a particular people, he thinks he is rejecting a "wonderland" where everything is "pure and sacred and above criticism." Religions aren't like that. Everything in a religion is subject to criticism; people have gone to war over such criticisms. And in treating sports as though they were part news, part entertainment, he misses half the true passion, excitement, and "hot sporting blood" in sports. Cosell's memory about individual players, teams, and even particular plays is truly remarkable, and his ability to draw upon the past often adds enjoyment to a particular deed upon the field. Yet often his comments seem to be either occasions for him to show off or beside the point. He usually doesn't add much to our comprehension of which plays, formations, and strategies are working or not working. He seems to miss the dimensions in which football is like chess. One misses in him the pleasures of connoisseurship. Above all, one finds in his commentary too much flair for the personal grudges, anxieties, career turning points, etc., of the individual players and coaches. He runs the commentary along the lines of gossip, as do journals like *Sport* and the *Sporting News*. Such comments make the game personal. No doubt, they are successful for some, and he knows they will be. But they do change the experience of watching the game, for the worse.

I like to know the specific drama of each contest, for each is different, and on this point Cosell is helpful. His excitement about excellence is contagious, particularly when he supplies the narrative at halftime for the swift review of the previous day's games. His respect for the athletes' endurance, effort, and zest for perfection is also winning. Yet, still, he somehow leaves us with a certain emptiness about the games, an emptiness he himself seems to feel. Often in *Cosell*, he complains about "the disproportionate emphasis placed upon sports in America in which people get so bound up with an event, with winning or losing, that their whole sense of values is discarded in the transitory escape from real life that the event provides." He has a certain contempt for the fan, for

Middle America, and it often shows. The day after Robert
Kennedy was shot, Cosell said in his morning broadcast
that he could not speak of sports, and talked instead about
"the three assassinations in a decade and why I had to
think about what I do and why I do it, and I suggested
that it might be the time for everyone to do just that because there was a terrible sickness in the society." He was
surprised by the volume and bitterness of the resultant
mail, telling him, in effect: "Don't tell me how to live, just
give us the scores." Cosell was stunned. "My instant reaction: What hope is there for the country if this is the
thinking?"

A great deal of hope. The politicalization of almost everything is a form of totalitarianism. The preservation of
parts of life not drawn up into politics and work is essential for the human spirit. In the well-ordered world of
baseball, an assassination is a grievous, savage, and blasphemous intrusion. By recounting the meaning of conflict
and competition, as these are acted out in sports, Cosell
might have made an overpowering point about the
murder of Robert Kennedy—the equal of the point Kennedy himself had made, citing a Greek dramatist, when
Martin Luther King was brutally gunned down. Kennedy
loved sports. Cosell need not have preached, but only
used the resources of his métier to make his point. Instead, his political and moral lecture—on the "sickness"
he imputes to "our society"—was out-of-bounds, a viola-
tion. Under the emotion of the moment, he might be
forgiven. But those who reacted with outrage at his words
were moved, perhaps, by a good, deep, sound, and true
instinct. To politicize sports is to contribute to the politicalization of everything, the blaming of everything on
politics, and the despair of many naïve persons with the
human condition—which they falsely seem to believe
politicians can wave away. I myself was sick at heart that
day, devastated, and did not want to hear the scores; but I
was glad the world was still going on, the scores were still
coming in. My essential faith is not in politics, which is a
brutal, ugly business.

Cosell was not alone in departures of this sort. Later,
Wells Twombly did the same thing in the San Francisco
Examiner, and so did the young editor of the *Daily Cal* at

Berkeley: "It has been a custom for sports columnists and editors to be to the right of Genghis Khan politically, and to be behind Spiro Agnew in insight. The sports world must not sit back and watch everything go to pot all around it. It cannot, as some of its backers would prefer, exist in a vacuum unrelated to the world."

At all times and in all places, sports do have a relation to politics and culture; it would be foolish to believe that sports are apolitical. But the relationship of sports to politics is not simple, nor is it direct. Sports provide elementary metaphors for certain conceptions of fair play and justice, for a sense of constitutionality and due process. These things, too, are rituals and have a sacred quality. Even during and after an assassination—which violates them—they retain their force. They go on. Life goes on. To turn to sports, as some did on those days, is not necessarily an escape. The pretense that life will *not* go on, the attribution of the foul deed to a curable "sickness"—*that* may be the escape. The glimpse into the abyss of brutality is an insight into everyday reality.

That there is evil in the world to be fought; that injustice is relentless; that death unfairly defeats us all and with special cruelty takes the young—all these are deeply written into the laws of sport themselves. The metaphors of sport would be cheapening on such occasions, for actual death exceeds symbolic death, and actual injustice symbolic injustice. But the essential points are no different. Young athletes have died in their prime; great stallions have come up lame at the threshold of victory and had to be "put away" before their promise was fulfilled. Handsome bullfighters have, grotesquely, accidentally, felt their stomachs torn apart by the unpredicted twist of a maddened animal. Outrageously unfair mistakes of judgment have cost teams World Series games. Cheats, frauds, and unfair tactics have brought about defeat for the worthy. If sports do not permeate the sports commentator's mind with images like these, he has not seen beneath the surface entertainment. And that is sad.

At the heart of sports there is a deep aloneness, a silence, in which one faces extremities. The cold tearing of the tissues of one's lungs, the strains upon the fibers of one's heart, the blackness threatening one's brain, are so

intense that it sometimes seems impossible to will another step. One's whole self groans against defeat.
Against death. Yet death comes.

For revolutionaries as well as for those who defend the
liberties they have won, sports are not a poor preparation
of the spirit. Jack Scott offers a key to the real emotion
behind the sermons of the new commentators: "The new
breed of college sports writer is also attempting to dispel
the stereotype image of all athletes as being crew-cutted,
dumb jocks." One does not dispel this image by pulling
cheap politics over one's superficial metaphysics. Cosell,
in particular, is better than that.

Yet it comes as no surprise when at the end of *Cosell*,
Cosell confesses slyly: "The one thing that would take me
out of broadcasting would be the opportunity to serve in
the Senate of the United States"; and, later, when Cosell
replies "jocularly" to a questioner about his ambitions for
the Senate, "I doubt that there are ten better qualified persons in the United States." (The precedents he cites are
Ronald Reagan and George Murphy.) Cosell too much
believes that politics is the real world, and sports an escape, to be a reliable theologian of sports. He treats them
as escape. I think I am not alone among lovers of sports in
turning to them for something far more substantial,
something much more basic to my life than that. Just as
clergymen sometimes suffer from being too close to holy
things, from handling them in their daily work and as a
matter of routine, thereby losing their touch for transcendence, so also many athletes, coaches, and commentators
have too much of a good thing and lose their touch for its
mysteries.

Having done so well in cracking the crust of unreflec-
tive pieties, Cosell fails at the most radical level to "tell it
like it is." He leaves out the inner power of sports, the
power of the human spirit, without which crowds could
not be attracted and so much love and energy could not be
inspired. In trying to be secular, dry, abrasive; above all,
in trying to entertain, he neglects the living roots. Left to
his care alone, therefore, one would expect sports to
wither on the vine, to begin to bore him, and many others
with him.

15

The Universities and the Professionals

ONE OF THE THEMES of the new sportswriting concerns abuses in college recruiting. Another is more basic: the use of college teams as a free "farm system" for professional teams. Let me make a proposal outright. Professional teams should pay for the services so provided. A mandatory contribution to a National Collegiate Athletic Association (NCAA) sports fund of, say, $250,000 by each professional team every year would go a long way toward reducing the deficits of college athletic departments. These moneys, fairly distributed, would allow the universities and colleges to direct a portion of their budgets into new programs, especially those for women, without weakening already thinly stretched money-making sports. The colleges provide an invaluable service. Just as great industries in chemistry, metallurgy, aerodynamics, tobacco, agriculture, and other fields contribute to the universities that train their personnel, so should professional sports.

College sports do not need the professionals. Long before professional basketball and football leagues became publicly acceptable, the college game was highly organized, held the allegiance of a fervent public, and reached a high level of excellence.

There were 634 college football teams in 1973, but only 26 professional teams. Not all the players, by far, entertained the ambition of making football their profession. Years ago, Gerald Ford didn't.

But should the universities allow themselves to be used as training grounds for the professionals? Well, there are schools of journalism and television, political science and agriculture, chemistry and engineering, law and medicine, business and accounting, teaching and nursing. Is sports the only profession that ought to be excluded? It is not the least spiritual profession, nor the least mythic, nor the least central to a culture. The athletic programs of certain schools are likely to make as great a contribution to the life, vitality, imagination, and moral unity of a given region as any other school programs. It will pain professors in other fields to admit it. The president of Kent State tried to jolt the citizens of Ohio with this declaration in 1973: "The people of Ohio have a deeper love of football than they do of the classics." Because of a shortage of funds, he had to fire as many as sixty professors; he could not cut back, he complained, on the commitment to sports made by the university before he took the job. During the early days of the energy crisis that same year, a source at the Federal Energy Office told a reporter: "The surest way to start a revolution in this country would be to shut down night football, baseball, or basketball games." To "serious" observers, these are scandalous priorities. I think them sound.

Colleges and universities exist for intellect, of course. But intellect has many tasks, not the least of which is the creation of narrative and dramatic forms by which the people live. Most of the faculty and graduates of universities engage in quite pedestrian and workaday intellectual tasks. Even those relatively few whose own preoccupations came closest to the ideals of "pure intellect" are also remarkably pragmatic, empirical, and highly specialized in their own working practice. The vast majority of faculty members in a university are intellectual *workers*, specialists, professionals, whose work is as grubby as that of other workers in society and just as practical. There are not many who love ideas for the sake of ideas, whose approach to their work is, in the ancient and medieval sense, "intellectual." There are few, in short, who treat ideas as a field of play. Most, indeed, think their work is more important than that of coaches and players. Economically and socially, however, it would be difficult for them to prove that their work does have larger public significance. Indeed, that difficulty is the source of much resentment.

Surprisingly, I have discovered, those intellectuals who are truly intellectuals, who respect the playfulness and freedom of intellect, who do not regard intellectual exercise as work but rather as play, passion, and delight, are almost invariably those with the greatest appreciation for sports. Not all are believers, of course. Some, especially those with more austere European roots, find it difficult to allow the experience of baseball, football, and basketball entrance through their rather closely meshed intellectual armor. But a surprising number find joy—usually a secret joy, about which they speak little except to other believers—in the myths, metaphors, and tangible experiences of the great American games.

For they are fascinated by the secrets of the life of the spirit, and they are accustomed to seeking gold in what heavier minds regard as slag. They can scarcely prevent their roving minds from asking: What *is* so gripping about these contests of imagination? How could so many millions be so intensely aroused by them? They themselves absorb secret, forbidden sweetness from sports. As they walk across their campuses, they note that the grandest monuments of the university are built for the liturgies of sport. As they read the paper, they are pleased that the fullest, best-read sections concern sports. They do not need to be clever to separate what's important from what official rhetoricians say is important. They long ago ceased listening to the Serious Persons of our age.

Nevertheless, many university people feel embarrassment about sports. The new president would like to have his university known for its nuclear reactor, its agricultural experimentation, its high-level economics department, its top-ranked law school; he's tired of hearing it called "a football school." The serious students want the university to do relevant things, fight racism, sexism, and maybe capitalism, too (a little ambivalence about that), and disenthrone the fundamentalist pieties of the gods of sport. The faculty, absorbing budgetary cuts, looks sourly at the liquidity of the department of athletics. (The cultural differences between departments of a university may exceed the cultural differences between some nations.) The intellectual onslaught against varsity sports is overwhelming. Except that the people of the state, the alumni, and a rhetorically subdued but intuitively supportive student opinion *want* sports.

Human beings cannot live without rituals. What would faculties be without cocktail parties, committee meetings, and pregnant pauses as they lecture? Where would a city, state, or nation be without the life of the imagination, without a focal point for passions and loyalties and humor and risk? In varsity sports, universities give the nation the most profound and nourishing popular arts accessible to all our citizens. Our other religions are all, despite their universal aims, sectarian; their symbols and liturgies cannot unite as many as sports do. The liturgies and rituals of the democratic state—its Memorial Days, Independence Days, Election Days, State of the Union Messages, presidential press conferences and Dedications, its flags at half-mast, and its parades and appeals—run very thin. You cannot celebrate the state or its leader without running the risk of unbalancing democracy, as we have already done in the rituals and liturgies so heavily focusing on the President. There is sex—but sex is, after all, a private rather than a public ritual. Where, then, can a secular society turn, if not to sport, as the chief communal ritual of its citizens?

Intellectually speaking, Americans are naïve about the symbolic and mythic necessities of the human animal. We try to deny these necessities, to regard them as unenlightened and unworthy. We repress them in ourselves, try to expunge them, and pretend that we are not possessed by them. Hence, symbol and myth flourish in our midst. Heroines of cinema like Marilyn Monroe, heroines of rock like Janis Joplin, and political heroes of every type of movement live luminously in our minds and lives. We have invented mass media as the most enormous engines of myth the world has ever seen, and we transmute each person, event, and idea that enters their giant maw into "image." Our Lions' Clubs, moon shots, participatory democracies, political movements, causes, issues, trends, and celebrities are saturated with mythic materials. We, the pragmatic, nonmythic, purposive doers of the world, are as myth-devouring as any people on the planet. Outsiders recognize how thick in myth and symbol our lives are. *Reality* does not force us to be as we are.

Consequently, being ill equipped to diagnose our own mythic needs and satisfactions, struggling to purify our minds of myths, we speak poorly about the myths by which we live. We are inexpert in the realm of myth; this is our greatest intellectual weakness. Expert at criticizing and knocking down the myths of others, we can scarcely bring to consciousness, articulate, and give good reasons for our own. In pluralistic societies, in addition, the fear of being riduculed withers the capacity for affirmation. Better to be silent about one's loves than to have them laughed at. Under the pretext of keeping private what is private, a pluralistic society undercuts its loves and enshrines mockery as the sophisticated style. The only invulnerable position is to hold none publicly, to ridicule all others.

Pluralistic societies need to learn a *positive* pluralism: to encourage each person to articulate his or her loves, and to give them reasonable defense; and to encourage everyone else not to mock but to listen. Plenty of nonsense is uttered in America, and each of us needs a strong, durable, and uncorrodable (if I may quote Ernest Hemingway) shit-detector. Nonsense proliferates because we do not train ourselves to voice our inner loves exactly, intelligently, and critically. We content ourselves with acceptable generalities we do not hold, hiding our loves in private. Thus, we drown in each other's platitudes.

I said once at the University of Notre Dame—and a young man who heard me reported it next morning to Father Hesburgh, the president, who received the word with (so I am told) a certain horror—that the creation of the myth of Notre Dame football may have been the most brilliant social achievement that university has made, or ever would make, no matter how great or illustrious its contributions in the invention of synthetic rubber, its nuclear experimentation, its civil rights efforts, and so on. Many at Notre Dame, especially among its new and quite brilliant faculty, are somewhat abashed by the attention given Notre Dame football. They minimize football, and try to maximize the university's intellectual stature. Well they should. The point remains that their perspective is far too narrow. The life of imagination, the life of the spirit, needs nourishing if intellect is to flourish. And few phenomena in American life compare with the mythic power of Notre Dame football.

The very words "Notre Dame" mean a certain kind of spirit; a spirit of never quitting, of using one's wit, of playing with desperate seriousness and intense delight, of achieving not just excellence but a certain kind of flair that must be thought of as gift and grace. When John F. Kennedy was about to give the most important address of his electoral campaign, before the Baptist ministers of Houston, a technical difficulty delayed his entrance for a long and nervous several minutes. A quite secular aide leaned over to the Catholic layman who had written Kennedy's address and whispered: "If you know any of those nuns who pray for Notre Dame, call them quick." You can't think of Notre Dame without invoking a world in which grace and the miraculous are as linked to human excellence as atmosphere to earth.

Almost anywhere I have ever been in the nation (*except* in the state of Indiana outside South Bend), from Texas to California to Nebraska, I have been able to find a radio station that carries Notre Dame football games live. In many parts of the country, one can also see every Notre Dame game in a delayed television rebroadcast. The NCAA usually leads off its television schedule with Notre Dame, and gives Notre Dame at least two major appearances. (Indeed, the NCAA had to make serious threats to keep Notre Dame from televising *all* its games, thus disrupting the NCAA's own television plans.) This is not because someone is *promoting* Notre Dame. It is because the Notre Dame mystique already exists. For at least sixty years, Notre Dame has struck deep chords in the American imagination.

Some Protestants and Jews and Catholics *hate* the school ("Send *that* one to your Pope!" a drunken Purdue fan once turned around to tell me, when I was fourteen, after a Purdue touchdown). But millions of Catholics and others passionately identify with its ups and downs.

Many want to beat Notre Dame; many want Notre Dame to win; all expect that a Notre Dame game will be uniquely spirited. There is an intensity, a communality, a passion for victory in the Notre Dame student body that must be experienced to be believed. The school is small enough, the stadium and field house compact enough, and the social, ethnic, religious, and economic fate of everyone sufficiently linked to ensure that more than "school spirit" is involved. There is at Notre Dame a single wave of desire.

Suppose that an institution wanted to communicate to 40 or 50 million persons a certain set of attitudes with respect to the struggles of life, or to teamwork, wit, perseverance, courage, invention, desire. I doubt whether any institution, whatever its resources, could have set out intentionally to fulfill such a goal or accomplished it as deeply, for so many millions, as has Notre Dame. Not all human values are communicated through the liturgy of football, but those that are present are important and quite beautiful enough. It is an enormous accomplishment to have nourished so many on the spirit of Notre Dame.

In the liturgies of schools like Notre Dame—at Ohio State, USC, Texas, Georgia, and others—all can come together: the governor of a state, corporate executives, alumni of every rank, students, and their parents, players, townspeople, citizens from every walk of life. Television carries the images into hospitals and taverns, factory commissaries and police stations, prisons and old folks' homes. Were I the president of a new state university or private college, or a member of the faculty, I would strongly encourage the development of a high-level athletic program within the realistic means of the school. The costs are great, but so are the returns—the rejoicing of the human spirit, the unifying of many.

Some will argue that it is wrong to encourage varsity sports in which, at most, 200 or 300 males of the student body can compete. To be sure, an athletic program should be made to pay a very large share of its own way, more so than other departments; and this is usually the case. A full range of intraschool competition should be encouraged, for women as for men. The development of intercollegiate sports competitions for women should be placed on a realistic, long-term basis. The building of a program that will not become a mockery but will hold the allegiance of many for many years requires planning, time, and money. But a program of maximal participation by all students—even including, perhaps, mandatory athletic requirements for all who matriculate—is properly capped by a first-rate varsity program for the relatively few men and women of highest talent. For every school is a corporation, a persona, and it almost cries out to be personified in mythic conflict with other schools.

College sports like football are exceedingly expensive, but not much more so than a good department in almost any academic field. It would not be right to say that an athletic department, even at the largest schools, is a "big" business; even with a budget of $2 million, it is actually a relatively small one. Football is virtually the only sport to turn a profit, and only on a few campuses. A few basketball programs may also break even or earn a little. Only twenty teams in the nation command an average attendance at football games of more than 50,000, usually for six home games.* In 1974 Michigan drew the most, an average of 93,894; Ohio State (87,552) and Nebraska (76,341) were next. There are 120 NCAA football teams in the South, and average attendance at games in 1974 was 14,210. In the East, for 137 colleges, average attendance was 6,644. The national average was 10,073. For 3,101 college games, the total number of fans was 31,234,835. Ninety-one teams were shown on television broadcasts under NCAA policies, but about a third of these were shown only locally. ABC-TV paid $16 million to the NCAA in 1974, including funds to cover Division II and III playoffs and five championship events. Approximately $490,000 is paid for each national broadcast, and $355,000 for a regional appearance, most of it to each participating conference or school—the lucky 54 to be broadcast. (An appearance on television is a great boost to recruiters.)

Twenty-five million two hundred thousand TV sets

---

* The statistics that follow came from the *NCAA Annual Reports 1973–74*, the *1974 NCAA Television Committee Report*, and Mitchell H. Raiborn, *Financial Analysis of Intercollegiate Athletics*, 1970 (P.O. Box 1906, Shawnee Mission, Kansas, 66222.)

(36.9 percent of the audience) tuned in for at least five minutes of the Note Dame–USC game of 1974, which the Trojans won in the second half, 55–24, after falling behind by 24–0; in 14.3 million homes the set was on for the entire game. For the great Michigan–Ohio State game that year, won by Ohio State when Michigan missed a last-minute field goal, the figures were, respectively, 26.3 million and 11.5 million. Despite television, attendance at college games has doubled since 1954.

Attendance, however, does not pay all the bills for coaches' salaries, grounds, equipment, travel, and accommodations away from home. The average NCAA school in 1969 received 59 percent of its football income from ticket sales, 5 percent from student activity fees, 16 percent from guarantees or options, 7 percent from broadcasting and television fees, 2 percent from alumni contributions, 2 percent from programs, advertising, and sales, 2 percent from concessions and the rest from other items. The average total income from all sports was $571,000. (The range, however, was from less than $1,000 to $3.6 million). Average total expenses in class-A institutions were $1,322,000; in class B, $247,000; and in class C, $102,000. Average expenses for class-A teams were $308,000 for grants-in-aid, $247,000 for guarantees and options (to visiting teams), $421,000 for salaries and wages, $155,000 for travel, $64,000 for equipment and uniforms, $36,000 for building maintenance, $27,000 for athletic dining hall, $33,000 for athletic residence, $22,000 for taxes, $12,000 for medical expenses, $21,000 for stadium and other rentals, $15,000 for printing, $12,000 for telephone and postage, etc. It costs class-A schools an average of $668,000 for football, or 51 percent of all expenses, compared to $130,000 for basketball, or 10 percent of all expenses.

The average class-A school had 41.1 full-time employees in intercollegiate athletics, including 22 coaches. The average total of coaches' salaries was $184,000 or about $8,400 per coach. (Many coaches are not full-time.) The highest-paid coaches in the nation are not paid as much as the highest-paid professors (many professors earn more than $30,000, a sum only a few coaches top). In most athletic departments that turn a profit, the profit comes almost entirely in football and is used to subsidize other sports. (In the 118 largest football programs, football provides 68 percent of all revenues, basketball 9 percent.) Football is the most expensive sport. It requires between sixty and eighty players on the team, compared to basketball's twelve or baseball's twenty-five. Its stadium is rarely in use, yet it must be maintained. An excellent basketball program can be maintained with only a dozen or so scholarships each year (an average total of $38,000). A good football program maintains five times as many scholarships each year (an average of $193,000). In 1974, the average class-A school gave out 149 full scholarships and 69 partial grants, a total of 218, for all sports. In 1973, Notre Dame used 31 full and 4 partial scholarships for football.

It is relatively easy to see that athletic programs are costly, and most are not self-supporting. The NCAA report of 1969 discovered only 40 class-A respondents whose revenues exceeded expenses, by an average of $188,000. In 21 class-A schools, expenses exceeded revenues by an average of $176,000. Most class-B schools were losing an average of $103,000; most class-C schools lost an average of $69,000. Class-A schools earned an average of $1,000 in basketball and $292,000 in football, while all other schools, on the average, lost money in both. All other sports lost money in all schools.

Funds spent on intercollegiate athletics are spent on a relatively small number of athletes. The average class-A school numbered 6,650 students in 1969, but only 396 athletes participated in intercollegiate play in all sports—about 6 percent. The Harvard-Dartmouth football game in 1975, however, drew 31,000 fans. Thus, for the dollars spent, it is likely that as many students, alumni, and friends of the college participate in the rituals of intercollegiate athletics as in any other programs of the college, including its theater arts, film series, and public lectures.

At Harvard in 1974 there was talk of retiring the jersey (84) of Pat McInally, the first time such an act had been contemplated since football began at Harvard in 1876. Then one of the Harvard professors said: "We've never retired a scholar's examination blue book. Until we do that, I don't see how we can retire No. 84." George Plimpton wrote of that approvingly: *"Priorities."* Honors and privileges abound for young scholars at Harvard. Just as the other Ivies scorn the Cornell marching band because it steps like Big Ten bands, so the Ivy schools always want to show that they are not like all the others. It is not a matter of priorities; it is a conceit. Harvard, Yale, and Princeton scores are carried in the major headlines of the Sunday *New York Times.*

The Ivy schools do see to it that all their athletes receive degrees at graduation. Recruitment and lack of follow-through are, together, the place of maximal abuse in college sports. It seems flagrantly unjust to recruit players, allow them to represent the college, and not insist that they qualify for graduation. Some 30 percent of athletes, apparently, never get their degrees; 62 percent of the players in the NBA never got their degrees. This problem is especially acute for poor blacks. Of course, it is a problem for poor blacks who are not athletes too, and indeed as many as 50 percent of all students who enter college as freshmen do not complete degrees. Still, a school that uses athletes to represent it for four years should be obligated by NCAA ruling to make provision for full academic credit.

Colleges and universities in the United States play a special symbolic role in our society. Although any region that wishes to expand its base for modern industries requires universities to provide trained personnel and to attract research monies from the government, universities are not only organs of research, science, technical innovation, and industrial advancement. They are also symbols of regional character, pride, and assertion. Education itself is a religious institution in this country; its role is considerably more than pragmatic or dryly secular. The professional class of a state—the pharmacists, farmers, lawyers, doctors, engineers, chemists, accountants, teachers, and others—owe their training to local land-grant or other universities. Intercollegiate sports provide a happy and light-serious opportunity for ritual demonstrations of loyalty and rivalry. Arkansas–Texas, Alabama–Auburn, Michigan–Ohio State, California–Stanford, Harvard–Yale, and other sectional contests provide a delicious opportunity for trips, taunts, and happy times. If there were not such ritual occasions in sports, they would have to be invented elsewhere.

Universities like Chicago that have turned away from intercollegiate sports seem to suffer from a lack of lightness and fun; a kind of stuffiness and arrogance surround them. The symbolic climate of such schools becomes severe, workmanlike, and internally divisive: department separate from department, school from school, town from town. There are not many activities that can unite janitors, cafeteria workers, sophomores, and Nobel Prize winners in common pleasure.

Actual physical participation in sports—in tennis, golf, jogging, swimming, squash, handball, and others— seems everywhere on the rise, among both men and women. Intercollegiate competition should be seen as a felicitous capstone upon this broadening base, an occasion for celebration and delight.

The most important contribution of universities and colleges at the present time might be the encouragement of scholars from various disciplines to grasp the genius of our American sports, to study their bearing upon our culture, and to incorporate their cultural reality into the legitimate investigations of their disciplines. In anthropology, economics, sociology, psychology, literature, history, philosophy, religious studies, and many other fields, there is much to be learned about one of the most impressive realms of experience in our national life. Here stands the stadium and there the basketball arena, competing in visibility with the library and the laboratories. It is not a happy thought that their reality is so often unnoticed, as if the faculty wore blinders. The diminution of academic prejudice in this regard might go far toward bringing the department of athletics into the center of academic discussion, not simply for condescending put-downs but also for praise, admiration, and the enlightenment of all. In this context, the necessary reforms might more easily be carried out in an atmosphere not of *ressentiment* but of mutual high regard.

SPORTSREEL

The Ivies Do Fight Fiercely

In 1968, in a breathtaking finish, Harvard tied highly favored Yale, 29–29. In 1974, with Harvard again losing (16–14) and less than five minutes to play, at its own 5-yard line, while the sun was setting sadly behind Harvard stadium, quarterback Holt pitched to Curtin, who lateraled to McInally, who passed to Dart at the Yale 42. A jumble of plays later, with only seconds remaining, Holt faked to McInally right, rolled left, faked, and dove into the end zone: 21–16 Harvard. Yalies who earlier, after *The Star-Spangled Banner*, had jumped and waved their upraised index fingers, now felt hot tears on their cheeks as they received the kickoff, with twelve seconds left to their vanished dreams of championship. The Harvard fans mercilessly waved a sea of white handkerchiefs. Francis Whiting Hatch '19 celebrated the event for *Harvard Magazine* *:

> *Harkness dough (Yale dough at that)*
> *Built Harvard's modern look,*
> *While Widener gave a library*
> *To house the treasured book.*
>
> *But it remained for Andover*
> *To deal old Yale a jolt*
> *By shipping Harvard luscious fruit:*
> *A pineapple named Holt.*
>
> *With fifteen seconds on the clock*
> *'Twas McInally right;*
> *Holt scampered left, with fuddled head,*
> *And found a speck of light.*

A tiny crack in Yale's defense,
And with a daring dive,
He lost, for Yale, five million bucks
In their endowment drive.

Let's face it, older graduates
Have pigskin in their hearts,
With victory as sharply barbed
As Cupid's lethal darts.

16

Money Changers in the Temple

EVERY RELIGION has problems with money changers.

The problems of professional sports, however, are especially severe because of the peculiar character of owners. The owners of professional teams may be divided into three classes. Some, after gathering enough capital elsewhere to purchase ownership, make sports their basic business; Walter O'Malley and his son Peter, owner of the Dodgers, are in this class. Others are wealthy persons, who run sports clubs as a kind of hobby; Wrigley, Payton, Yawkey, and others come to mind. A third class is composed of businessmen who invest in franchises, whether alone or in syndicates with others, to complement their main business interests elsewhere. A majority of owners belongs to this class.

Most professional franchises, it appears, are not profitable in themselves. The collapse of the World Football League in 1975 shows that the upper limit has been reached both of cities able to support franchises and of television dollars. Professional teams can be profitable to their owners even when they lose money, however, because the owners can use their losses to offset taxes they would otherwise have to pay on their profitable businesses. Thus, ownership of a professional team often comes "free" to those with capital. In addition, however, they can pay themselves salaries out of the club's funds, so that their team's "losses" actually represent personal income; they can also charge off a wide variety of expenses. Along with ownership, they receive millions of dollars worth of publicity, local social status, and sideline benefits for their other businesses. It is not necessary to believe that any owner is in the game for a self-sacrificial love of sports. Or that any has actually risked his economic survival. True, many businessmen lose sound judgment when they invest in the odd business of sports; some lose their shirts. Investors in the World Football League and in marginal franchises elsewhere can lose large sums of money. Sports is a business. Those in it for money are in it for money. When they say it isn't the money, it's the principle—it's the money.

Everyone I know these days seems to be a socialist, or at least an anticapitalist. (They are not for *Russian* socialism, or *North Korean* socialism, or for bureaucracy or discipline; but they *do* hate American business, the profit-motive, capitalist morality, etc.) So I feel constrained to say that I am *neither* a capitalist *nor* a socialist. The near-bankruptcy of liberal New York and virtually socialist England, and the actual quality of life in "socialist democracies" (including Sweden) dishearten me. On the other hand, the range of sinfulness open to capitalist systems attracts my libertarian side, but the social results offend my humanistic side. I wish there were an alternative to modified capitalism and modified socialism. I approach the question of the financing of sports from a certain ideological neutrality, born of double despair.

Sports owners are not only capitalists; they also tend to be, by and large, particularly retrograde capitalists. For one thing, the traditions of the sports business and the short career span of the players (an average of $4\frac{1}{2}$ years) gives players' unions far less power than other workers' unions. Furthermore, the players' contracts are not like contracts anywhere else; the owners "reserve" their "rights" to a player's services forever (or until, for a price, they surrender them), with or without a contract. Even the modified reserve rule in baseball and football, which allows players to "play out their option" and to seek employment on another team, binds players to owners in ways not seen in any other business. Moreover, the exemptions sports owners have from competition give them imperial rule in their home regions and over their own squads. They have been able to keep detailed profit-and-loss statements secret; the figures which from time to time become public are full of discrepancies, disguised categories, and basic ambiguities. Finally, owners of sports teams are, for businessmen, unusually attracted to public notice, notoriety, and assertion. They tend not to be highly cultivated men, interested in funding symphonies or museums. They tend to be autocratic, imperious, and something less than public-spirited. They seem to have toward their managers and players a fairly heartless, vindictive, and hair-trigger eagerness to show who's boss.

In a word, the owners of sports franchises are as easy to hate as the Borgias or Sforzas: arbitrary, cruel, total in their power. The question is, what can we do about it? The first task is to review some basics.

There would be no money in sports if people did not love sports, if sports did not *draw*. A kind of religion underlies the gross business superstructure. It can be suffocated. The lifelines of that religion are identification of fans with players, and the rootedness of teams. The callousness of the owners has treated these lifelines with contempt, cutting them at whim, crudely, compulsively.

Second, the world of professional sports has grown enormously. The night has been invaded, even for World Series games. Attendance at professional football increased from 6 million in 1964 to 10 million in 1974; baseball from 21 million to 30 million; basketball from 4.8 million to 11 million; hockey from 2.8 million to 13.6 million. (By comparison, in 1974, more than 78 million attended horse races; more than 50 million auto races; and over 65 million bowled at least occasionally.)

Third, salaries to professional players have swollen. The *average* salary to the National Football League in 1975 was $42,338; in baseball, $41,000; in basketball, $65,000 in the NBA and $80,000 in the ABA; and in the National Hockey League, $70,000. (The *minimum* salary is $15,000 or so in each league.) These are not full-year salaries. Those earning above $40,000 rank in the top 0.5 percent of the population by income. It grows increasingly harder to identify with them. They have joined *the other side*. It may be time to *send them a message*.

Violence grows among the fans. They do not sympathize with their own team when it makes errors. Why should they? The players are now, by income, bosses. The players stand among the privileged. The players are not *us*. They are *them*. One has a right to hold them to perfection. A fellow making $40,000 a year doesn't have a *right* to let us down. Such sentiments, I believe, reflect accurately the contempt—possibly the envy, certainly the sense of betrayal—fans have toward the players. The central figure in the decay of sports is probably Joe Namath; we must return to him.

Fourth has come television. In 1960 there were 679 hours of sports on network television. By 1974 the total had increased by over 60 percent, to 1,102. The 12 teams and 432 players of football had swollen to 37 teams and 1,640 players—although the collapse of the World Football League in 1975 reduced these figures promptly to 26 teams and 1,118 players. Baseball grew from 16 major-league teams and 593 players to 24 teams and 887 players, basketball from 8 and 96 to 28 and 326; hockey from 6 and 114 to 32 and 622. Television financed this growth. Television permitted this overload on our sensibilities, thereby changing the substance of our experience of sports. The blow inflicted by television could be fatal; it is still too early to predict.

Baseball is, by far, the oldest professional sport, at least in terms of the leagues we now know and in terms of national significance. Football came into its own, professionally, in the late 1950s. Basketball hit its stride in the 1960s, with the Cousy-Russell era of the Celtics and the impression made by the Knicks on the New York media in the late 1960s and early 1970s. Hockey came on strongly late in the 1960s and then faded, on television at least. *Everyone* aims at television: soccer, even cricket. Narrow is the gate. It is conceivable that we have reached the end of an era. "The easy-money, apparently endless, expansion era is over, and the major league scene, which has doubled in size during the last 15 years, is now headed for contraction," Leonard Koppett predicted in the New York *Times*. Within months of his writing, the World Football League went out of business, stranding hundreds of players, and the American Basketball Association was riven by dissension, as its teams began petitioning for admission into the NBA.

For a professional franchise to succeed today, one economist has projected, an initial capitalization of some $16 million over a five-year period is required. Only after a large investment and a period of time can one hope for a return. In an earlier period, the Oakland Raiders spent some $5 million in the first years, and only later saw this money grow to a franchise worth $15–25 million. But the number of metropolitan regions that could support such expansion is much more limited than dreamers once imagined. There are not more than 25 or 30 such markets in the nation, it now appears, and maybe the lower figure is more exact.

There can be no argument that *someone* must subsidize sports. Like the other fruits of civilization, sports are not productive; they are expressions of liberty. They are "play." When they become professionalized, of course, they are no longer play for those who participate. They are a form of work. As Prince Hal says in *Henry IV, Part 1*: *"If all the year were playing holidays,/To sport would be as tedious as to work."* For baseball players traveling through a season of 162 games, and basketball players playing three times a week from late October until April, the traveling and the jading cannot be play, however playlike some moments of that time remain. For those who participate vicariously, however, through their working vicars, sports remain moments apart from work. The "clergymen" may work; the congregation plays.

From the very beginning, when colleges were barely subsidizing sports, modern professional sports awaited patrons. In socialist countries today, the patron is the state. In the United States, the patron is the capitalistic owner. In the beginning, however, the hope of profit was slim. The organization of sport precedes the sport, in the sense that a game cannot develop high excellence and full potential until its financial underpinnings have been established. Church, state, philanthropy, or private business—*someone* has to set aside, construct, and maintain the playing space, training facilities, and patterns of organized and regular competition. Someone has to pay for the uniforms. Someone has to plan the attendant festivities (or at least their preconditions—bathrooms, water, commissaries, etc).

The struggles and the scandals involved in the growth of organized baseball from 1865 to 1900 are fascinating from this point of view. Baseball players of the early days were wild, unruly men, often crooked, corrupt, and thieving vagabonds, barely restrained and loosely held together as teams. To have a game—especially a game for which spectators were willing to contribute to the costs—a great many individual lives had to be interrupted, rerouted, redirected, concentrated within a narrow frame of space and time. The families of the players had to be supported.

On Tuesday, June 15, 1869, for example, the Cincinnati Redstockings arrived in Brooklyn to play the New York Mutuals. For hours before the 2 P.M. game time, the streets of Brooklyn began to fill with fevered and excited fans. Cincinnati won 4–2, but they demonstrated that the game could draw crowds. Could a regular schedule be carried out? Baseball waited as a new national rail transportation system was perfected. All the attendant difficulties had to be financed. No player could give a season to baseball indefinitely without provision for at least subsistence. No entrepreneur could count on crowds large enough and frequent enough to be certain of his investment. For years, baseball was not a money-winning proposition. It was an expense, justified by love of the game, a flair for self-advertisement, some small hope of eventual return, and civic chauvinism: for the honor, for example, of Cincinnati. (The Redlegs in 1869 won 65 games in a row as they toured the country, facing all comers.)

Young children sometimes believe that everything happens spontaneously, by nature, without cost. In the beginning, there were large costs to those associated with organized baseball, football, basketball; these costs were especially noteworthy because there was almost no hope of reward. Sponsors, administrators, managers, players—all took part for marginal financial but pleasant psychological rewards. Fame was one reward. Status. And the pleasures of the game itself. Alex Karras, the great tackle of the Detroit Lions and later a television commentator, explains that until a very recent era most players played "to prove something" to the world: that they had value. Most were poor; most were looked down upon socially. It was not money that drove people, and it wasn't precisely a love for sports, or at least not that alone. It was the opportunity to excel in public, to establish one's ego in a society in which the unknown ego is disvalued. It was to "make something" of oneself. Joe Namath, George Blanda, John Unitas, and John Lujack—all raised within a 30-mile radius—had one sentiment in common: "Anything rather than the coal mines."

There was a certain toughness about it all in the beginning, a rather Spartan self-discipline. One could not in those days treat one's body like a million-dollar investment. It wasn't worth much to anybody. No use saving it. One dared, gave all one had, took one's chances, satisfied oneself. The huge salary paid to Joe Namath to sign with the New York Jets—and the advent of television—changed these early patterns.

The New York Jets—as only New Yorkers would or could—built an entire franchise around a single human being, for whose services they paid a (then) staggering $400,000 for a three-year contract. An ordinary American worker, who works from age 25 to 65 for $8,500 a year (the average factory wage in 1974) makes only $340,000 in his lifetime, for 40 years of work. Joe Willie Namath's father netted perhaps $200,000 in his lifetime. Son Joe did as well in his first year of work. Alex Karras started at $9,000 in his first year as a Lion; George Blanda started at $5,500: better than the mines, for a half year's work. At the peak of his fame, Bob Cousy was earning $20,000 from the Boston Celtics, as the greatest draw the game had ever seen until that time.

Building their team around Joe Willie, the Jets started a revolution. Joe eventually led the Jets to a stunning Super Bowl victory over the highly favored Baltimore Colts, in the days when the Jets and the other teams in their American Football League were thought to be vastly inferior to the teams in the older National Football League. The Jets' investment in Joe Namath, more than any other factor, won equality for the American Football League and

changed the structure of organized football. But it also altered the financial structure of every team in that league
and every other.

Higher salaries for players at first seems like liberation.
But is it? How hard can Joe Willie play—how hard can the
Jets play him—when he represents so high an investment? For half a decade after their championship the Jets
lost and lost, and game after game Joe was absent from the
lineup with injuries. Courageous, cocky, he was hobbled
by gimpy, painful knees. Brilliant, a joy to watch, he was
so often injured that even when he played, he was as
often as not just beginning to recover game-level
sharpness when he was out again. Yet the franchise was
built on him. Without him, the Jets were a bore.

In this sense, built on Namath, the Jet game was
skewed, off center, cockeyed. Namath loves the game and
has enriched the lives of millions who have followed his
exploits; there is a radiance around his presence in almost
everything he does; a halo of inner confidence and recognized self-worth surrounds him, as if he were some secular saint. And yet, Namath was a drag upon the team and
upon the game. A player is, or ought to be, more than a
few moments of brilliance in a season; Namath's injuries
did not allow him the day-in, day-out excellence the game
demands. The high salary paid to Namath—in 1975 about
$15,000 per playing week—injured the game. Just as too
much hero-worship of the President injures democracy.

I would just as soon see Namath receive a half million
dollars a year as executives like Harold Geneen of ITT, or
the owners of the Jets. My objection is not to Namath's
ability to draw such money. Why shouldn't he? My point
is that it has altered the game. CATFISH SIGNS FOR $3.5M.
PELE WILL PLAY IN U.S. FOR $4.7 MILLION. WILT WANTS $5
MILLION. These headlines are ominous.

Such high salaries paid to the professionals shift the financial structure, the motivations, and the systems of
identification that gave the game its inner power. The
payroll for a football team of 43 players, not to mention
the administration staffs and coaches, now runs into millions of dollars. Syndicates, for the most part, put up the
money. The players play, in essence, for "the organization"—not for the city, the state, or the public. And not

for the game. It is not surprising that many franchises lose money, and that the World Football League was built on hype, deception, and self-destruction. On its business side, sports now spin off center; noises and rubbings portend destruction. The game is top-heavy in its financial structure, torn apart by inner greed.

The attitude of players toward themselves is now more calculated. If they have a business sense about themselves, they must compute their annual value times the length of their playing careers. They represent a commodity to be invested in and also to be protected: Pete Rose, Inc. They think like executives. They invest. All well and good. They exploit themselves, and who can be against exploitation of one's own resources? But the money grabbing kills the game.

On the part of the public, a different sort of identification with the players results, a different attitude toward their injuries and grievances. More American workers are injured on their jobs each week—eyes burned out, fingers lost, knees smashed, lungs corroded past the point of healing, toes mangled—than on any of the weekly casualty lists of any of our wars, and for far less money than ballplayers receive. The workplace in America remains for many millions a violent place. The violence inherent in modern machinery and modern living patterns (traffic, distances, chemical substances, lifts, etc.) too often goes unnoticed. A child from New Guinea confronting downtown Pittsburgh for the first time would have every reason to be terrified and to prefer the safety of the jungle.

When football players were working-class kids like everybody else, one had a cultural identification with them that is largely lacking now. They all seem now to go to college. They make a mint. They don't talk the same kind of English workers do. They go out with movie stars. Their wives and kids dress like bankers' families. *They've joined the enemy.* When some players talk about "slavery" to the owners, the fellows who work for Jones and Laughlin Steel or in the mines or for the railroads snicker.

Watching sports is more and more like watching wealthy mercenaries do what they get paid for doing. The power of the cultic symbols has been altered. In medieval times, church towers dominated the towns. To thrust those towers into the sky, ordinary people made many sacrifices and often gave the labor of their hands and the best fruit of the land. The churches were built with a certain purity and pride—even today, relatives in rural Europe will show you with pride what they've added in their generation. In American towns, the banks are invariably the most modern, stylish and expensive buildings. Far from being simple, utilitarian, spare, and frugal, they provide every town's most lavish architecture, the temples of our civilization. (Abroad, American civilization will be marked for future historians by hotels.) As a logo of our civilization, the cross has been replaced by the dollar sign.

So in sports, the new symbolism is how much is paid to whom, not how local heroes have contrived a new design upon the championship. Barter has risen in interest. Rootedness has fallen in importance. You can't, they say, stop "progress." As surely as day to night, the medieval order yields to money-making. In the early days of organized sport, the crassness was simpler. Hired hands skipped from club to club, sometimes under aliases, several times a season. Ringers sold their services, and accepters of bribes lurked greedily under many uniforms. America was lusty, in love with confidence games, and deliciously sleazy then. We watched *The Sting* with pleasure in the season of the Watergate.

Still, the age of the contemporary organization casts a special pall. The money comes legally enough. But there is too much of it. It drowns the sensibility. It makes the spirit wither. It suffocates the life of sports.

Contemporary organizations are run by functional reason, bureaucracy, and specialization; they are models of human ingenuity. Creating such an organization can still be an adventure. Yet once they have been created, such organizations, so necessary to our way of life, are ugly organisms. Their scale is not a human scale. Bureaucracies may aspire to be teams, or even families, but they never are. Teams that congeal, that beat with a single heart, are the model each collective would like to imitate, but cannot. A team bases itself upon the heart. An organization calculates which of your services it can buy and for how much. The money-grabbers want it both ways: they have turned teams into organizations, but want them to continue to act like teams. This contradiction may be fatal.

The disease that rots our sports today is not intrinsic to sports; it is intrinsic to modernity. To do things today means to do them "big," to lavish tons of money in order to buy oneself teams and championships. You buy the coach, you buy the players, you persuade the city fathers to put up the stadium, you build huge promotional campaigns—and *presto!* in three or four years you can bring a world championship to Miami, or Oakland, or wherever. Many try to do it; only one a year succeeds. So one ought not to picture it as simple. The point is, you need lots of capital, the tax breaks that permit the absorption of huge initial losses, a crisp organization, a slick sense of public relations and promotion. Building a franchise has become an even more absorbing sport than the sports themselves. The sport of tycoons has become big team hunting.

It is *this* sport that the modern sportswriter is tempted to cover. He, too, likes the flow of money and power. These are sacred and highly honored passions in America. To those who are moralists at heart, the urge to describe the grubbiness and sleaziness of the world of power is an irresistible temptation. And so the sports pages have been taken over by the new sportswriting, by investigative reporters on the trail of the big team hunters. But this is to report the world of work, not the world of play; the world of power, not the world of myth; the world of capitalistic life—or socialistic life—not the world of sports. No doubt the two worlds intersect. No doubt the money angle holds some interest for the fans. Money is used in the United States as an attention getter. But due proportion has been violated.

For there would be no business at all if there were not a spiritual power to undergird the business structure. I marvel each time I enter a Catholic church in the United States, recalling the poverty of our grandparents who built those structures with their dimes and quarters, when they could not even send their children to college or pay their mortgages or feed the family "well-balanced" meals. I marvel when I see the crowd at the 7:30 Mass on

Saturday evening, and again three times on Sunday morning; the parking lot at our neighborhood parish, ample as it is, overflows four times every single weekend. The sermons one hears all across the country are not given by golden-tongued preachers or teachers of brilliance, God knows, and the services often have a perfunctory character. And yet the people come, by the millions. Entertainment does not draw as spirit does.

We are expected to sympathize with Larry Csonka when he abandons the Miami Dolphins for the World Football League and $3 million. "I have to think of my family," he says. His family was not starving. If ballplayers cannot say no to money, if they will take the highest offer they can get and move away accordingly, they invite contempt. What they do is understandable enough, but wrong. It flies in the face of the rootedness and the fan's identification with them which gives their profession inner power. If they think so little of their profession, why shouldn't fans?

The fault, of course, is not the players' alone. If the structure of sports were more fair—if the owners didn't have their own cynicism and their own imperial powers over contracts—perhaps the players would have greater security and a greater sense of fairness. Sports are too important to the life of the spirit to be left to the free market alone. The players, of course, want a freer market. They want to be free to auction their services year by year. Their playing lives are short. They run great physical risks. They want to maximize their returns.

Suppose that the Congress nationalized all sports leagues, designated the metropolitan areas that could support a major league team (and in which sport), established various maximum salary grades and criteria for meeting them, set generous medical guarantees and pensions, and carefully limited television exposure. We might, then, have more orderly and credible organized sports. But since most franchises lose money, who would bear the expense? The tax base of the region? (New York needs new taxes?) The federal government? Would congressional committees wrangle over pork-barrel legislation bringing home teams to their district, or slyly negotiate trades for popular players? Do we need a regulatory commission for major sports?

The system we have needs revision. The worst abuses are: (1) *migratory teams*—Philadelphia A's to Kansas City A's to Oakland A's and *still* not drawing a million fans a year, after three world championships, and now threatening to move again (maybe to Chicago, while the White Sox go to Seattle?); (2) economically senseless and imagination-stupefying *expansion;* (3) the lack of *contractual freedom* for players; (4) the identity-destroying *high salaries* paid to players; and (5) the failure to *indemnify the colleges* for their services in preparing professional athletes.

Since sports organizations have special status under the law, government should see to it that these abuses are corrected. To be sure, each sport is a little different from the others. Yet remarkable analogies obtain. Thus, in any sport, before a team can establish itself in a region, it ought to be made to operate there, even at financial loss, for at least seven years. Its franchise ought to be renewable at seven-year intervals. Such a requirement would help end cynical migrations; it would protect the rootedness of sports. Further legislation might require an owner to divest himself of the local team, and to reinvest in another, should his emotional interests lead him elsewhere; an owner could not simply move his team away. In other words, sports organizations ought to be viewed as semi-public organizations in which the public has rights to be protected. Should a region prove unable to support a team in lean years as well as in good during the initial seven-year trial, then and only then would an owner be free to seek governmental approval, as well as league approval, for a transfer or for dissolution of the team.

The rights of owners simply to draft players from college, without any choice on the part of the players, seems illegitimate. Even modest modifications might help. For example, upon their graduation from college (not merely their completion of four years), all prospective players might be permitted to apply to the top three professional teams of their choice, ranked in order of preference. They would apply to the league office by a certain date. Their own motivations would be various: some would prefer certain regions; others would choose weaker teams in the hopes of speedier advancement; some would choose to work under a certain coach; others would want to play with a proven champion. The league would forward these choices to the teams concerned. A week later, a modified draft would be held. The team that finished lowest in the standings the preceding year would be allowed to make its first selection first, from those who named it as one of their top three choices. The other teams would proceed in order, each choosing one name from among those on its list. There would be twelve rounds to this draft. If no team had twelve applicants, or if it did not want to offer a contract to any of those who did apply, it would simply lose its turn. After twelve turns, any player not chosen could seek out any team, and any team any player.

This system would strengthen the individual player's freedom of choice, but still give great latitude to the choosing teams. The most sought-after players would be on at least three lists. The lowest-ranking team among the three they list would have first chance to choose them. None of them, in some years, might gravitate toward the worst teams; then again, those eager to start quickly probably would. Nevertheless, this system might not balance the league as well as the present arrangement. O. J. Simpson, for example, would almost certainly not have chosen Buffalo among his top three, but rather a team already laden with talent, like the Rams. The main point is that the proposed system would give some voice to the players, at least to those who are most likely to be chosen first. A player might not get his first choice; but some, at least, would get one of three.

A ceiling might also be set on the salaries paid to players, and on the value which the owners would be permitted to count in their depreciation schedules when establishing their business expenses. These limits could be ample, and could differ in different sports. Since a player would be free to seek a contract with another team when his contract ran out, mere salary considerations could not lure him away if he were already at the top level. In order to prevent one team from paying *everyone* at top level, and thus buying out the best players, each team might be limited to paying no more than three top-level salaries.

This limitation would enable teams without three such salaried players to bid for the services of stars not yet at that level. Short-lived contracts would enable teams to renegotiate such salaries on an annual or biennial basis.

We have lived through an era in which sports were made as secular, materialistic, crass, and cynical as owners and players and commentators could make them. Hostility, violence, and ugliness are increasingly visible among the fans. Cynicism earns its own reward.

SPORTSREEL

A Sense of Evil

The mythic tissue surrounding sports has always suggested that sports are "clean" and "All-American." This mythic world owes much both to Great Britain and to the Anglo-American spiritual sensitivity. The "fair play" of the playing fields of Eton, but also the scouting movement, the Temperance Leagues, the Chatauqua camps, and other American movements of individualism, self-improvement, and progressive thinking—these sanctified certain ideal types as truly American, compared to others. In the stories of Frank Merriwell, Garry Grayson, Tom Swift, and other heroes for red-blooded American boys, the most highly prized qualities were wit, pluck, clean-living and implacable enmity against ever-present "bullies." Sports were imagined to be a realm of muscular Christianity—of maleness on the one hand and purity of heart on the other. If in other climes a certain shiftiness, sensuality, sheer physical aggression, duplicity, and trickiness were deemed appropriate, the true American hero was pure of heart, candid, straight, true, plucky, modest, and full of boyish charm and manly courage.

These traditions were not, be it noted, precisely British. The British are an older, wiser culture, given to a certain matter-of-fact toughness and pragmatic amorality. By contrast, those of the British who came to New England tended to be enthusiasts, dissidents, saints, passionately religious. The Anglo-American is quite different from the Briton: more democratic, more active, rougher, less formal. "Phlegmatic" would not be an apt description of his national character. "Moral" would be closer.

In a peculiar way, as a result, the American mythology of sports has moved on two separate levels. On the higher plane march Frank Merriwell and all the legions of straight-shooters and Christian athletes, self-effacing, gutsy, and victorious: the clean-living, true-blue gentlemen athletes. On the lower plane carouse the avaricious, sexy, aggressive, hedonistic Texans of *North Dallas Forty* and *Semi-tough*—the heavy-drinking, womanizing, masculine hell-raisers of the early days of baseball history, and of today: men like Max McGee, Paul Hornung, Joe Namath, and the horny hero-villains of contemporary sports fiction. In Babe Ruth, the high road and the low road ran as parallel as a modern urban street with elevated highway overhead: Babe Ruth visiting the orphans in a tuberculosis asylum in the newspaper story, and carousing late at night with the prostitutes in the parlor car, unknown to the public.

The moral pretenses of Anglo-American civilization demand a public standard of rectitude, while permitting a private standard of individual choice. Attacks upon "hypocrisy" are one of the most consistent patterns of our cultural life. "Muckraking" is possible only because the public rectitude is prescriptive rather than descriptive, and the gap between the two is never closed. We are not even sure we want it closed. We hate Puritans. Yet our allergies inflict on us Puritan itches.

Liberal, radical, and (in general) progressive thinkers commonly undertake a double mission. First, they engage with gusto in the unmasking of hypocrisies. They attempt to reduce the gap between public myth and private practise by a stream of steamy exposés. Thus, they scratch the itch. Second, they hold aloft new standards of moral progress, idealism, and moral striving. "See," they say, "many athletes are horny, vulgar, racist, sexist hedonists. Frankness and candor are required of a truthful generation. Debunk the myths. For our society must *not* be racist, sexist, or nihilist. It must be just, egalitarian, brave, self-sacrificing, generous and truthful. It must live up to its ideals." Our muckrakers are not immoralists. On the contrary, they are busy setting up a new mythology which their children, carrying the endless project forward, will then debunk. Whatever we are allergic to, they inject into the nation's system. Saintly to the bitter end.

But the true practise of sport goes on, beneath the moralistic mythology of virtue and clean-living. Basketball without deception could not survive. Football without aggression, holding, slugging, and other violations—only a few of which the referees actually will censure—could not be played. Baseball without cunning, trickery, and pressing for advantage would scarcely be a contest. Our sports are lively with the sense of evil. The evil in them is, to be certain, ritualized, controlled, and channeled. But it is silly to deny that the disciplines of sport include learning how to cope with the illegal aggressions and unbounded passions of one's opponent and oneself. Sports provide an almost deliberate exercise in pushing the psyche to cheat and take advantage, to be ruthless, cruel, deceitful, vengeful, and aggressive. It is "good sportsmanship" not to let such passions dominate; it is naïve not to see them operate in others and oneself.

In football, defensive players hold, illegally, on almost every play. In basketball, a "non-contact game," the violence under the boards is fierce. In baseball, intimidation by pitchers, baserunners, and defensive players is straightforward and expectable. Morality on the athletic field is not a Pollyanna morality. It is controlled by more rules and referees than is any other part of life. Coaches devise ways to get around the rules (players change jerseys; feign injuries to stop the clock; call signals to draw the other team offsides, etc.). The many roles of bluff, feint, intimidation and trickery are so important in sports that they are codified and rendered classical. (There are similar codes and classic moves in scholarship, journalism, politics, and every other field.)

Sports, then, are no escape from evil and immorality. They are designed to teach us how to live in a world that is less than moral. That, too, is one of sport's pleasures. To be an American is to be obliged to indulge in certain moral pretenses. The "American way" is to be decent, moral, trustworthy, law-abiding, tolerant, just, egalitarian, and so forth. Which is fairly heavy. To give a fellow an elbow when the referee isn't looking, just before the ball comes off the rim, is profoundly satisfying to the un-American, unregenerate, unsaintly self.

It is "good sportsmanship" to see to it that the basic structure and procedures of the contest are fair. A good contest, by its nature, requires fairness. The outcome should hang uncertainly between evenly matched opponents, playing under similar rules. A false conception of good sportsmanship, however, prevents many players from giving themselves fully to the competition. Instead of concentrating on the excellence of their own performance, many amateurs, in particular, begin to worry about the psyche of their opponents; they hold back. They lack the instinct for the jugular. They don't want to "humiliate" their opponents. Their condescension toward the frail ego (as they imagine it) of their opponents prevents them from playing as well as they might. They "let up." When they do, commitment and fire leave the contest. The true morality of sport is absent.

It is necessary to be objective about games—to play every one as though it were one's last, seriously, with purpose, at full alert. The point of games is to propel oneself into a more intense mode of being. Not to play hard is to kill time, but not to transcend it. To concentrate on the game is, in a sense, to be indifferent about one's opponent or oneself. It is to refuse to be distracted by wayward passions. If an opponent plays unfairly, the sweetest revenge is not revenge but victory; one avoids striking back in kind in order to concentrate on the one thing necessary: perfect execution. Concentration on the game itself is the best safeguard against indulgence in ugly, errant passions. It is the highest form of sportsmanship. It is not so much a moral as an ontological attitude. One isn't trying to "be good," but to act perfectly.

Recently, the moralistic impulse has uncovered homosexuality in sports. Muckrakers have informed us that homosexuals appear in professional sports at about the same frequency as elsewhere in our society. Writers used to leer about fanny-patting, celibate training camps, nudity and team showering, and wrestling matches on the soapy floor. The new muckrakers seem to want to give a double message: "See, the world of sports is corrupt and hollow, a world of fake machismo, infested by gays. But it's all right to be gay, it's great, it's fine." They want it both ways. In the pagan world, in Greece and in Nazi Germany, athleticism and homosexuality went (so to speak) hand-in-hand. As did art and homosexuality. Machismo and homosexuality are not opposites. Sport favors neither one.

Sports are natural religions. All things human are proper to them. In pushing humans to extremities, they push virtues and vices to extremities, too. The world of sports is no escape from evil. Nor is it an escape from virtue, excellence, and grace. In sports, we meet our humanity. Assuming one begins with limited hopes, there is more to admire in sports—and in our humanity, and in our nation—than to despise.

17

Some Burkean Reforms

GET READY for a lecture.

There are two ways of looking at reform. One [at the blackboard] is based on a passion for justice. The other is based on realism. Number one holds it is more moral to demand justice now. We may call this view Jacobin [writes on blackboard]. The other holds that life cannot bear instant justice without exploding into worse injustice. We call this the Burkean view [chalk squeaks]. The difference is not a difference between "radical" and "conservative." The Jacobin *may* uphold old and conservative ideals. The Burkean *may* argue for a sharp change of policy. The Jacobin, for example, argues that busing is based on constitutional principles, and that *he* is the true conservative. The Burkean argues that *new* policies of racial integration must be invented, because the present ones effect the opposite of their intention.

The Jacobin tends to judge by moral visions. He is willing to start all over. To experiment. The Burkean tends to look for institutional resistances and institutional possibilities. He thinks institutions are hard enough to build— and to control—without starting new ones prematurely.

The Jacobin tends to criticize severely any falling off from moral ideals. The Burkean tends to look on institutions kindly. Not because they are perfect or even good, but because he suspects that alternatives may be worse. The Jacobin thinks the Burkean timid, afraid to try new things. The Burkean studies the history of experiments rather closely. He believes the Jacobin well intentioned but usually self-destructive.

The Jacobin is fond of declaring his love for true ideals—for the *real* values of the nation, or the *true* ideals of sports—while criticizing the actual embodiments of those values and ideals, the jocks, the authoritarian coaches, the racist and sexist organizations, and so forth. The Burkean expects most concrete institutions and persons to fall far short of the highest moral ideals, and he is pleasantly surprised by *any* signs of virtue. The Jacobin believes virtue easy, the Burkean believes it hard.

The Jacobin is easily fooled by those who pass clear "litmus tests" of moral purity or ideological correctness. The Jacobin attaches great importance to having and voicing morally correct opinions. The Burkean doesn't trust opinions, attitudes, or litmus tests very much. The Burkean smells corruption in every scheme for human improvement and every manifesto for reform. It doesn't surprise the Burkean that Jack Scott lost his job at Oberlin College for alleged authoritarian and doctrinaire positions; or that Dave Meggysey tried to make a "comeback" with the Oakland Raiders after claiming to be out of their league; or that George Sauer, one of Scott's dropouts from the New York Jets, tried to return to football in the WFL. He doesn't believe the Jacobins thoroughly reason out the institutional and concrete applications of their abstract ideas. They want too much too fast, and make themselves unhappy. The Jacobins think the Burkeans are at best curmudgeons and at worst "running dogs of the imperialists."

The favorite tactic of the Burkeans is to create new checks and balances in old institutions. They seldom counsel a single program of reform or revolution. Experience has taught them that programs of revolution or reform are soon ensnared in fresh corruptions, often worse than those they set out to rectify. They hold to the commonsense view that human beings are never to be trusted. A Burkean approach to the reform of sports in the United States, therefore, begins by granting that all the accusations made by the Jacobins are probably true. The owners are unusually authoritarian? A corrupt sense of "winning" has invaded sports? Drug use is too heavy? Signs of racism and sexism linger in the sports world? Television holds sports captive? Probably. Even if all these and other accusations are true, still, it is remarkable how much beauty and excellence are still created in sports, and how many millions still delight in them. In every other human institution—in the university, the church, journalism, government, business, the foundations, and the rest—the situation is not better than in the world of sports, and often it is worse.

The Burkean, nonetheless, judges institutions harshly. There are ugly sicknesses in the contemporary world of sports, as in the modern approach to life generally. The problem is to become as clear as possible about the sources of the spiritual power in sports themselves, and then to recommend checks and balances that might allow these sources room to gather strength.

The time for fundamental change, however judiciously conceived and slowly executed, is riper now, the Burkean believes, than at any time in recent decades. (Yet such unaccustomed optimism makes a Burkean nervous.) For one thing, the financial fever has abated. Whole leagues have collapsed, or threatened to collapse. Many franchises are in financial trouble. Attendance at football games shows slight (5 percent) but worrisome declines. The number of "no shows" exceeded a million in the NFL in 1974. The treatment of sports on television has prompted boredom and signs of satiation.

Whatever the deficiencies of a market system, and they are many, the slow-moving market does have a way of enforcing a certain reality. Dozens of promoters have lost a million dollars or more. Waiting lists for season-ticket holders in Kansas City, which used to contain 5,000 names, have dissolved. Owner H. L. Hunt worries that the television base for football can be washed away: "When the tide shifts, things can go downhill very fast."

The Internal Revenue Service has moved to close the right to depreciate players' salaries for the sake of windfall tax losses. If this move by the IRS succeeds, the speculative fun will go out of sports. Franchises could drop in value from $20 million to $2 million virtually overnight. We could go back to the days when owners nourished teams along, as did Art Rooney of the Steelers and Tim Mara of the Giants, or as Connie Mack did with the Philadelphia A's from 1901 to 1950, never earning much money, never losing much. A downward pressure will then be exerted upon salaries. All these marvelous signs of business decline may not continue, but their trend is favorable to true sport.

For we do not need to worry about the resistance and longevity of *sports* if the business goes to hell. Even if greed and superficiality should sicken an entire generation with the sports we now see, and even if the present organization of the sports world should collapse, the human longing for sports will express itself again. But the sports we have are good ones. My proposals for reform assume a long view, and are intended to awaken discussion from which actions may grow with a sort of naturalness. With forethought, advantage may be taken of events as they occur.

(1) *The number of professional leagues and teams in the United States should be carefully regulated by a governmental commission, so as not to overwhelm human emotional capacity.*

More is not better. Sports depend on our capacities for sympathy and identification. These capacities are not infinite. When the list of competitors grows too long, the mind is overloaded. Contests can only have significance when one knows the history and character of the contestants. Most people stop caring when the number of teams gets too high. How many men can a girl have before she becomes "that kind of girl"? Lou Grant of the *Mary Tyler Moore* show has an answer: "Six." In a sports league, sixteen, I believe, is the maximum number the affections reach. Twenty is a long stretch. Twenty-four generates indifference to several teams, and not just indifference: contempt. The New Orleans *Jazz?*

Sixteen or (grudgingly) twenty teams in a sport (divided in two separate leagues, the champions of the two leagues meeting in a final contest) is ideal. In this case, the design of a season can be simple. Mind and affections can gain a grasp on all the teams and even many of the individuals. One can juggle many comparative performances simultaneously. Major League baseball has grown too large; shrinkage by four teams or more, if it occurs naturally, would be a blessing. The National Football League is too large; its twenty-six teams could shrink to twenty, to the benefit of all. The existence of rival basketball leagues is an anomaly, too taxing to the imagination and affections. Basketball, moreover, is a sport cheap enough to operate on very little money, and could quite adequately develop a system of minor leagues intermediate between college and the major leagues.

When there are more than twenty teams in any one league—more than ten in a division—one finds oneself ignoring eight or ten teams almost totally. Nature itself imposes such restrictions. Even the journals which must cover sports sag under the burden, like branches with too many apples. Who cares who ranks 27th? In a conference of eight teams, four or five may have a shot at the title; two or three may be spoilers; one or two may flounder at the bottom as patsies for everyone. Mind and heart can manage that. When each league has divisions, and each division has conferences, and only the computer knows who is to play whom and in what order, a certain clean rationality has been lost. All three of our major sports exceed human scale. The fact that a city wants the status of having its own franchise is not an imperative, only a desire. The limitations of the human imagination must be respected.

It is comforting to a Burkean that a town like Green Bay could support a team capable of defeating New York, Chicago, Los Angeles, Dallas, and Washington. This apparently anomalous fact is rooted in the accidents of professional football history. It is a sample of the way history achieves its own concrete goods, unimposed by abstract conceptions. In the same way, we can applaud the gradual shrinkage in the number of professional teams.

Expansion was produced by three impulses: (1) greed; (2) the then untested limits of television support; and (3) the desire of the established leagues to preempt plausible locations of rival franchises, and the desire of outsiders to muscle in on potential wealth. *Hubris* normally has its fall. Above a finite number of teams, the human being cannot possibly find enough affection to distribute.

(2) *The number of nationally televised appearances ought to be cut down to proportions consistent with human caring.* So far, of course, television has been providing virtually all the events the market can bear. Over 200 football games, professional and collegiate, were broadcast on national television from late August 1975 through January 1976. No one should have to go to church that often.

There is nothing wrong with allowing the free market to find its own saturation point. Yet the quality of being an almost sacred event—which gives sports their awesome pull—is not indestructible. The appetitie for sports is kept alive by a tremor of excitement, awe, and even fear that comes near the beginning of a contest: *mysterium fascinans et tremendum.* The sacred can be trivialized by too much use. For a time, virtually a whole generation could cease to care.

A distinction may be drawn between nationally and locally televised games. The practise of televising all the sold-out games of the local team is sound. Local roots are important. It is also a pleasure, especially when the local teams are having poor years, to watch a significant game between top teams, at least occasionally; as on Monday night or an occasional Sunday doubleheader (before or after the local game). The institution of *Monday Night Football* is a happy one; blue Monday is not so blue when the evening holds so pleasant a reward. Other games should be kept off the air in order to keep alive the sense of special occasion.

In basketball and baseball, the present system seems appropriate; the whole thing is lower key, and mostly focused on the locals. The only major flaw is the *Game of the Week.* The producers of the *Game of the Week* in all three sports and the schedulers of *Monday Night Football* have introduced an extraneous set of considerations. They seem to strive for regional balance, some relative equality in number of appearances, and other considerations aimed rather at the good of member organizations than at the pleasure of the fan. No doubt, these considerations have roots both in financial rewards and in factors of status. (The appearance of his team on television certainly helps a college coach to recruit future players.) But they run counter to the long-run tastes, expectations, and interests of fans. Surely, there is some method for settling the financial rewards equitably behind the scenes. It is far better to watch the best game featuring the most highly ranked teams each week, or the classic rivalries, than to be subjected to "regional balance." Quotas are a drag.

But my real objection is more profound. Care needs to be taken on national television not to injure the identification of fans with their local teams. It is tedious to watch a game between teams whose players one does not know. The contest becomes a bare exhibition of athletic skills, like a circus act. The pleasure of watching a star athlete of whose reputation one has heard can await the appearance of that star against the local heroes. At playoff times, there is ample occasion to watch the best of the nonlocal teams. Until then, the *Game of the Week,* in whatever sport, lacks the crucial ingredient of identification of the self with one team or the other. Such broadcasts fall to the level of mere entertainment. One watches without attachment or participation. The habit of lesser intensity soon spreads to other occasions.

A sturdy farmer and feed seller in Iowa, a Packer fan, replied to these theories of mine with some contempt: "Ain't no such thing as too much football." There may be millions like him. They must be weighed against the other millions for whom enough is enough, whose level of disgust, once summoned up, might not recede. Both television executives and owners of franchises ought to calculate rather carefully, in advance of a sudden surfeit, the optimal limit of exposure, national and local.

A good many of the late-season bowl games should be eliminated, or limited to regional and local transmission. Fake games like Pro Bowls and All-Star games ought to be cut entirely. Exhibition games should be drastically reduced in number to two at most, and banned from television. The closer television hews to the real thing, the more long-run trust and excitement it will build.

In professional football, a televised season of fourteen weeks, plus the playoffs, would permit the most faithful fan to watch plenty of football every season (the local team and/or one national game each Sunday, and one game each Monday night), plus the championship contests. If the NCAA were to broadcast the top game in the nation each Saturday, plus an additional championship playoff between the top four teams at the end of the season, a determined fan could see fifteen more games. The major bowl games would still be on. Fifty games or so is enough devotion for a season.

Each viewer can, of course, turn off the dial, find other things to do; and most people often do. Still, television is a public presence, not just a smorgasbord. What is too readily available loses a large part of its attraction. A special sense for sports, once lost, will leave an emptiness the nation does not need.

(3) *Sports leagues should establish rules for television broadcasters.*

Sports organizations have placed themselves in a position of dependence on television. When a sport is not useful to television, television will drop it. Moreover, television sucks the spirit out of everything it touches. It trivializes what it hypes. Its conception of entertainment is to wave flags of action and gimmickry to catch the slumbering attention of its audience. Sooner or later the audience, aroused and then bored, treats entertainment as entertainment: seeks something new.

The case of hockey is a warning. For six years, television brought hockey to the public. Whether the fault was that of NBC, the second three-year sponsor, or that of the National Hockey League, whose thick-skinned policies discouraged skepticism and controversy on the air, ratings fell by 40 percent. Hockey sank from sight. No immutable law decrees that football, in particular, will never have a major falling off.

The professional game is most likely to suffer a dropoff. Professional football is a less imaginative and inventive game than college football, too tightly controlled by specialists, too protective and self-regarding, too efficient and machinelike. Its perfection leads to some brilliant and explosive confrontations, particularly in the playoffs. The Super Bowl, however, is almost always a dud.

The television coverage of the professionals is also particularly garish and technically flashy. TV specialists cover sports specialists. City-slickness prevails. The mythic quality of the game is diminished. The crassness of the television producers cannot, of course, totally crip-ple the power of the sport. But unless all those concerned think more carefully about the source of that power—the mythic content of the essential drama—they may well find themselves facing both falling attendance and falling ratings.

Football prospered on television because even the most ardent fans had never experienced the close-ups made possible by television. Now the novelty is wearing off. The camera close-ups prevent one from seeing the game whole. One of the greatest pleasures of the game is to see receivers get open on one play, and to anticipate a later call in which the passer will try to find them again. On television, however, one almost never sees receivers breaking into the clear; one never gets a downfield view. The camera is focused on the passer or the runner. The complementary patterns of the several receivers are lost. The "isolated camera" shots give us only the solitary run-ner, not his relation to the whole. A game of strategy requires a strategic vision. Television has given us atomic particles.

In addition, when a game does not crackle with excite-ment, announcers become anxious. Most games are in-tended to be played in a quiet and workmanlike way. They were not scripted for television. Brilliant play en-livens almost every game, but at its own pace, in its own way. Most sequences are, and ought to be, patient, plodding, and slow. Games have their own integrity, and are in part contemplative. Their steadiness suffuses indis-pensable music through the soul.

Basketball players, constantly in motion, pride them-selves on a certain coolness, poise, unflappability. They seem to be playing super-calmly, in a mode of conscious-ness quite different from that of ordinary life. Thus, even so apparently active a game is at heart meditative. Each team, moreover, has its own rhythm and tries to impose it slowly on the routines of the other. The underlying drama of the game is slower and less visible than the frenetic surface.

In a perfect game in baseball, one side never even gets

on base. A high-scoring game, full of hits and runs, seems somehow sloppy. ("Well, we saw a lot of action anyway," I apologize to the children, after an 8–5 game, as if in unconscious recognition that it was not baseball at its best.) In football, most plays are line plays, in which the drama is that of strength, position, and team coordination—not a highly exciting drama.

In an odd way, therefore, the drama of sports is the reverse of the sensationalism that is the staple of television. There is in sports a lot of boredom of a certain sort, a kind of quiet that is not a flaw but a strength. Contests without high drama or heroics yield subtle pleasures, sometimes the best of all. Of course, occasionally, for some teams or for a series of games, every contest is electric with the unforeseen and the extraordinary. These are exceptional events. A "good" game is often not, by television's standards, "good entertainment."

It would be in the interest of sports authorities to give thought to the mythic component of the games they hold in trust. After more than a decade of experience, both television and sports have an opportunity to reconsider. *What* is it they are communicating? *Which* techniques are faithful to the underlying intention? Which obstruct it?

The mythic quality in sports is not a hype. It has nothing to do with color or excitement. It has to do with the clean lines of the contest as described by the rules and traditions of each game. Baseball is a game of solitary artists working together to circumnavigate the bases; each advance is decided by inches, and the calculations are minute and almost "scientific," based on well-known probabilities. Football is a game of team coordination. In set and formal plays, one team attempts to break through the formal defenses arrayed by the other. Basketball is a game of subtle team movement, held together by strong melodic lines, along which constant deception and instant improvisation are indispensable: a game of establishing authority and rhythm, and of exciting "moves." Baseball is rural in its pace. In two-and-a-half hours of football, play-action consumes twelve to fourteen minutes, usually less than six seconds per play. The rest is preparation. Basketball is especially difficult to televise, for it is a team game requiring a perception of patterns and flow embracing the entire movement on the floor.

The trained eye looks at all these games abstractly, as an artist looks at a painting, seeking out the abstract structure and relationship between the parts. In each of these cases, television at present defeats the trained eye. The eye almost never sees the whole, is *prevented* from seeing the whole. Visual images are inherently exciting (the eye has a madness of its own), and so television often mesmerizes us and pleases us, even while diverting our eye from the essential contest. But that is exactly the problem, to which no one seems to have given thought.

What does television do with the "dead" spots in baseball and football? It fills them with television tricks. These soon become boring. The deepest hold that sports events have on the hearts of their participants is the symbolic power of the contest itself. Falsifying this, burying it under cloying clutter, television slowly sickens us. Its broadcasts have become talk shows with athletic backdrop. If cancer is formed by slow doses of polluted foods, perhaps sports are slowly being killed by television.

There is enough hot sporting madness in Columbus when Ohio State plays, or in Dallas for the Texas-Oklahoma game; there are sufficient anticipation, delight, and awed suspense, before almost any contest. A self-effacing, quiet intrusion of television as a report on what the eye can see, the senses feel, would do the job. Television ought to try letting a contest speak for itself, as it did down the generations before TV. Less show biz, more event. Television must be taught respect, must be taught not to falsify.

Rules insisting that television cover the full scope of play, allowing us to see its basic patterns; that the commentators curb their chatter and put in words what is happening on the field, in expository and analytic form; that the auditory portion of telecasts use the power of words to accompany the visual images, so that words may add to what the viewer sees; that a sharp distinction be observed between the style of a talk or "action" show and the style of an athletic struggle—such rules might help to restore a basic integrity to sports broadcasting.

I confess to a certain skepticism. People involved in

television seem to be unusually gimmicky in their approach to life. The eye fascinates them. The eye is the most deceived and deceptive organ of sense, the one most easily seduced by surfaces and motion. Athletes are not trying to present pleasing visual images. They are engaged in contests of considerable self-punishment and danger. Their art is a difficult art, and it demands of them considerable interior concentration and self-discipline. Television is a particularly surface-oriented medium, in a certain way dry and secular and cynical. It is always promising to "probe," and then delivering nothing more than new "angles" or fresher gossip. Hence, television almost never catches dimensions of the human soul, neither in politics nor in drama nor in sports. Perhaps the medium itself is limited by its very nature; we do not learn about soul from the eye. Perhaps it is only the entertainment ethic that governs television which corrupts everything it touches (including the evening news). In any case, the world of sports had better exert itself *against* television, offer television *dignified resistance,* and *reduce its dependence* on television.

For television is a fickle lover. What it promises, it does not deliver. When it wearies it goes away. Sports do not need television for survival. In the past, sports excited national audiences through ticker tape, newspapers, and radio. They can do so again. The human imagination is considerably more powerful than the tube. Television needs sports more than sports need television. Sports might withhold themselves from television and be the better for it. Short of that, sports should have at least the dignity of a quarterback under the rush of giant tackles; or of a pitcher refusing to be intimidated by the best bats of the opposition; or of a strong forward clearing the boards with authority at a crucial moment. Lack of courage in the sports world is the clearest proof that while the mythic structure of sports calls for virtue, those who participate in the game may be among the last to learn its lessons.

(4) *Coaches and players should voluntarily set limits to the seductions of money.* It is difficult in America to ask certain persons to limit their lust for money. We do so, however, in other fields of public service. A President of the United

States is not admired for becoming rich in office. A priest in a Cadillac is regarded with disdain. There is something deeply incongruous in the temptation of athletes, or coaches, by deals designed to awaken an itch for affluence. At the very heart of sports is commitment to *ascesis*, discipline, and training of the body and the mind. No doubt, talented persons deserve to be singled out and honored with higher salaries than less favored mortals. I have no envy of the fortunes made by athletes; like other fans, I share in the pleasure of the recognition their high salaries provide. Yet there are limits beyond which rewards become sickening. It is not envy that moves the stomach to rebellion. It is disdain.

Sports fashion a world of form. They teach proportion. To see greed running loose, each person out for the maximum he can get, far beyond any sense of need arising from our communal experience of daily life, is to feel spiritually betrayed: $3.5 million for Catfish Hunter, $4 million for Joe Namath, $4 million for a single fight of Muhammad Ali's, $400,000 every year for this giant and for that. The offering of insurance policies, options, three cars, a share in the franchise, real estate, businesses— these are offerings to lust and greed. They are not evidence of a healthy human spirit.

"Why not?" some will object. "You only live once. You only play for so many years. Who would take the punishment an athlete takes without getting all he can?"

No moral argument, not in the form of commandments or principles, yields a reply to such questions. The moral argument against these sentiments is, perhaps, essentially aesthetic. Such conduct is inherently ugly, disproportionate, and out of scale with the values celebrated in the craft of sports. It is disgusting to one's fellow citizens. Go ahead and accept what you can get. But do not be surprised if you are loathed for it, not because others are envious, but because others believe you have betrayed what you seemed to stand for. The *mythos* of sports cuts across the grain of promotional hype and unchecked greed. Like the little boy said: "Catfish Hunter stinks." Asked why, he does not hesitate: "He's only in it for the money."

Talent comes for free. It is a gift. No athlete is the cause of his own talent. There is a line somewhere at which public recognition of his talents, including high compensation, passes over into indulgence in greed. Joe Namath started the trend, sowing a sickness at the heart of the very things he loves most, or claims to. Tragic errors of this sort have brought down many heroes of the human race. The highly paid heroes, after all, do not deliver more than those who preceded them and who accepted considerably less. The deeds of the latter live after them with just as much solidity, and with clearer, cleaner lines, like perfectly placed bunts on the velvet surface of the diamond. In the future, today's highly priced athletes may be regarded as "robber barons," who got what they could and corrupted what they claimed to love.

As sports are not entertainment, neither are they business. Naturally, they are *in part* entertainment and *in part* business. When their essential spirit is corrupted by either the one or the other, the pain of loss is accompanied by disgust.

(5) *Newspaper and magazine writers, regaining their faith in words, should describe the contests on the field as if no one watched television.* The poetry and the drama of sports are best caught in words. The written word has a power television cannot touch. It is a power, in particular, over form. For reasons expressed above, the human spirit needs words, needs the irony, the subtlety, and the bite of words, and above all the capacity of words to go beneath surfaces, their power to pull aside veils and uncover unsuspected dimensions of human striving. Many regions of athletic experience have scarcely been explored.

(6) *In football, the degree of specialization should be reduced.* One of the sources of injury in football is an extreme use of specialists. When most players play only during a small part of the game, the game becomes for each of them increasingly abstract. They do not keep in mind the need to go an entire game. They go in "to do a job," rather than to play a rounded game. Their way of thinking both about themselves and about their opponents is narrowly focused. "Abstractions kill," Camus

said; in sports they also injure. A tight end brought in to deliver a single block on a single play imparts a mechanical quality—and a ferocity—that alter the nature of the game.

Players like John Lujack and Chuck Bednarik used to play on both offense and defense; no one does so today. The contemporary use of two platoons (offensive and defensive) and specialty teams (for punts, kickoffs, passes, runs, goal-line situations, etc.) adds variety and high efficiency. But the cost is high. Members of a "suicide squad" covering kicks have only a handful of opportunities each game to vent their passion and to impress their coaches. A gradual return to the earlier form of play, in which at least a certain number of men play almost continuously, would add to the human struggle, to the role of chance and surprise, and to the general level of interest. The games would seem less mechanical.

The number of injuries in football, especially to the knees, also suggests the need for some new designs in equipment or changes in the rules. The pleasure of the game does not depend on high levels of ferocity. Violence is inherent in the game, but it is a controlled, ritualized, and restricted violence. One can check the amount of violence, particularly of an abstract quality, without undermining the pleasure of a hard-hitting physical contest.

Some critics call *all* violence dehumanizing. Their conception of "human" seems false. Others harp upon the violence in football, without noticing the more hidden forms of violence throughout modern life. Are more college youngsters injured in football than suffer from mononucleosis, nervous breakdowns, and other illnesses that arise from academic competition? Many ulcers, heart attacks, nervous breakdowns, and other forms of disorder afflict office workers, managers, and others throughout our highly mobile and impersonal system. For the gains our society makes through specialization, bureaucratization, mobility, and impersonality, the cost in psychic and physical damage is high. Football makes its own violence direct and explicit, and in this sense yields a feeling of honesty and relief not afforded by the more diffuse violence of modern life.

Football serves, we have noted, as a mythic representation of modern corporate life. Yet not all the vices of such life need afflict football. Efforts to reduce the amount of specialization would lead players to pace themselves and to respect others in ways that are discouraged by the abstract way in which the game is presently conducted. Players executing only blocks are too like doctors concentrating on kidneys. When the game becomes technical and mechanized, it gains a measure of heightened intensity but also falls into patterns of predictability and boredom. Judicious changes, therefore, might result in at least an equal measure of excitement, although perhaps of a different order.

(7) *All athletes who are awarded scholarships and who complete their years of athletic eligibility ought to be bound by strict rules to complete their academic degrees; and the colleges ought to be rigorously obliged to matriculate every athlete who competes.* The NCAA ought to supervise carefully the fate of all students who are given athletic scholarships, to see to it that none are peremptorily dropped from school if, through injury, a failure to make the team, or personal choice, they do not complete their athletic eligibility. Colleges that grant athletic fellowships should be regarded as conferring on such youngsters a *right* to full matriculation, with provision for continued scholarship assistance should they drop out from sports. The college rather than the athletic program might be held responsible for continuing such scholarships. But the rights of the youngsters involved should be firmly protected. Of course, not all students who enter college elect to finish college. The financial possibility of doing so ought to be available to all who enter because of sports.

(8) *Professional teams ought to be obliged to reimburse colleges for the costs of the education of the players who enter professional ranks.* This reimbursement could take the form of an annual assessment on each professional team, to be paid into an NCAA scholarship fund. It could also take the form of a direct payment from the professional team to the college in compensation for each player chosen in the draft or later hired as a free agent. These assessments could be levied by law, as part of the cost for the

privilege of a franchise. Or they could be granted by agreement between the professional leagues and the NCAA. Red Smith put the argument this way:

> Where could colleges find financial support for their athletic programs? Well, there are thousands of corporations and foundations in this country that endow scholarships or make gifts in other form to help develop the physicists, chemists and geologists they will need tomorrow. If American Can and the Nabisco Foundation deem this a wise investment, shouldn't self-interest suggest something to the National Football League?
>
> Owners of professional baseball clubs are not noted for philanthropy, yet baseball has supported its own farm system for a century. Professional football and basketball are practicing parasites fed by the colleges. It has been suggested that if the function of a college is to prepare students for postgraduate life, then perhaps a school can fulfill its purpose by teaching young men how to be linebackers for the Dallas Cowboys. And if that is so, perhaps it is time the Cowboys bankrolled a few scholarships.

I would not leave the matter to philanthropy. The NCAA should so insist, and so should the federal government (which provides so many favors to the clubs).

(9) *Professional leagues should be made by law to respect the rights of professional players as free individuals to contract freely with the teams of their choice.* Teams should not own "rights" to players, beyond the actual contracts they have entered into with the players as individuals. The benefits of freedom should inhere in the players. Constraints upon this freedom should be clearly spelled out and carefully limited. There are four such constraints:

(a) Balance in the league must be observed.
(b) Wealthier teams must not be permitted undue advantage.
(c) Owners must be able to make trades to improve their teams.
(d) As much stability and fan identification as possible should be permitted.

None of these constraints need undermine the basic principle of the liberty of the individual player to contract for his services. Presently, the athlete is considered as an asset purchased by the owner and traded by him as a commodity independently of the salary paid the player. The owner owns rights to a player in addition to the services for which he contracts. Conclusive justification for the assertion of such rights does not seem to be available. Since they are respected in the present structure of tradition and law, however, these rights will be difficult to take away. Yet, in truth, the owners did not exactly pay for these purported rights. In the ordinary case, all they did was sign the player to a contract for services. In baseball, of course, the owner assumed the risk of training a younger player in the minor-league system. Teams that invested best in minor-league prospects usually reaped dividends in later championships. The modern picture, because of the role assumed by colleges and universities, is quite different.

The rationale behind the concept of the owner's rights to a player's services is that it protects competitive balance. If players were free to sign with the highest bidder, the argument goes, the wealthiest owners would buy up all the best players, without compensation to the poorer owners. At present, the new owner has to compensate the former owner for the rights to a player's services; thus, the former owner gains resources for finding a replacement. A recognition of the importance of competitive balance could, however, be achieved by other means; neither logic nor reality decree that the present system is the only one possible.

For example, if no one owned rights, then no owner would have to compensate another for signing one of his players to a new contract at the end of the old one: each would face only the salaries to be paid directly to the players. No one would have to "buy" players; owners would simply contract with them. (It would be possible, as well, to put an upper limit on salaries.) One could eliminate the category of rights to a player's career and limit teams to contracting for the player's services directly with the player or his agent.

Wealthy teams already have advantages over poorer teams, as they would have under virtually any system. Yet building a championship team requires more than money. Some very lavish purchases do not work out.

Some highly priced players do not play well in certain environments. Some relatively poor teams, financially speaking, develop the best, most cohesive, and most highly spirited teams.

One proposed modification of the present system provides a modest step forward. After the expiration of his contract, any player would be free to sign a contract with a new team. Then the two teams involved would agree on compensation. If they could not agree, the matter would go to binding arbitration outside the commissioner's office. Each team would make a final offer. The arbitrator would have to accept one offer or the other, without modification. In this way, the bargaining would be realistic and its outcome (at least in its parameters) known in advance. This system would be an improvement because it would take the decision about compensation out of the league commissioner's office; it would eliminate arbitrariness and uncertainty: it would take the onus off the player.

In addition, according to this plan, a player under contract could not be traded without his approval. Players would be better able to build some stability into the lives of their families, and to plan their futures. On the other hand, because they have not been playing enough or for whatever reason, some players might willingly move, if requested, before the expiration of their contracts.

One objection to this plan is that too much free bargaining by players would result in salary wars and constant movement. The stability of no-trade contracts would seem to cut down on movement, however; and the workings of a free market would seem to keep any salary "wars" within bounds. For there are many more players than there are openings; and the most highly paid stars are already at the upper limits of their possibilities.

The main point is that the freedom of the individual athlete to make contracts with the team of his choice seems more decent, right, and appropriate to sports than the present system. The pressures of an athlete's short playing life and the possibilities of injury would probably lead him, in most cases, to prefer long-term contracts. Owners, presumably, would prefer a number of short-term contracts, allowing themselves flexibility, and some

long-term contracts, assuring themselves of the services
of certain players for several years. Since the average playing life in the NFL is 4½ years, each team would seem to
have sufficient flexibility.

There are, in a word, several possible ways of organiz-
ing the business structure of professional sports. The
issues are many, and the legal technicalities are properly
the concern of experts. The present practices, however,
were not inscribed by God on tablets of stone, nor even
by the Founding Fathers on Philadelphia parchment.
They have developed through custom, scheming, and
special privilege under law. They can be amended by the
same methods. Major consultations of lawyers, econo-
mists, and others should be held under private auspices,
in order to think these problems through and work to obtain changes in the law, in order to protect the public interest. Cult is the center of culture, and sports are close
enough to the heart of American life to need the constant
attention of acerbic intelligence and fearless reform.

In this sphere, above all, standards should be high.
Conservatives, radicals, libertarians, reactionaries, or
moderates, we can all gather in the stadium—and even
root for the same teams—and yet we should not assume
that all will have the same ideas about the meaning of
reform in sports. Let there be argument, then. But let the
arguments be clear, with all the evidence laid open, and
the public permitted to enter in. As our sports are fair and
rule abiding, so should our discussions be.

Such discussions should be conducted on page one,
with the national news, and on the editorial page. They
must not be permitted to interrupt the more important
business on the sports pages.

(10) *Sports for women should be more realistically encouraged, and new sports invented.* Baseball, basketball,
and football (in its nontackle versions) may be played by
women, and in due time may be played with an excellence analogous (allowing for size) to men's. Still, all
three of these sports were invented primarily for men.
Games might be invented which are more perfectly suited
to the physical and cultural needs of women, sports perhaps in which both men and women could compete. It is

likely that, in future decades, opinion leaders will be more willing than those at present to notice and to define perduring differences, on the average, between men and women, culturally and intellectually as well as physically. If so, special games might better express the special genius of women. In any case, American women should not be deprived of the physical rigors, disciplines, defeats, and team experiences provided by athletic competition.

In colleges and universities, in particular, athletic opportunities for women should certainly be expanded. The two most expensive sports in most programs—football and basketball for men—are at present those that most frequently pay their own way, or at least a large share of it. For almost 100 years, traditions of competition between males in these sports have nourished the present levels of interest. Analogous competitions among women may one day be of equal symbolic power, both to women participants and to huge audiences. The success of girls' basketball in Iowa may offer a model for other regions. Such success does not come handed on a platter. It has to be earned, against significant odds.

Such a challenge may or may not be worth picking up. It is not certain that women will—or ought to—build up a structure of competitive sports. Despite the ideology of the moment, it seems plain to me that in virtually every known culture, athletic competition (as distinct from athletic activities) plays a significantly lesser role for women than for men. Perhaps past traditions *can* be overturned. Perhaps they *should* be overturned. But perhaps they testify to realities more important and enduring than present ideologies.

Women are the equals of men, in value and in dignity and in personhood. But perhaps what they are about, and what their lives mean, and the ways in which they express themselves in action are and will remain significantly different, and all the more valuable for that. Perhaps, then, their sports will be different. Creativity and invention are not at an end. What we may hope for is the triumph of authenticity and integrity: the expression through sports of the best that lives within the self. Time will winnow experiments.

It seems only fair that a due proportion of funds, authority, and access to facilities should be made available to women. However, just as men struggled to build what they now have (and athletic departments of the American type were a novel development in history), so women will have to struggle. In addition, men's basketball, baseball, and football have special public status, which they have earned. They will continue to draw upon levels of support that new sports, whether for men or for women, will require time and effort and great inner power to match. Women in sports face an imposing challenge. It will rejoice the spirits of all if they prove equal to it.

(11) *A semipublic National Sports Commission should be established by the Congress, with clearly specified powers of regulation, arbitration, research, and supervision over the major national professional sports leagues.* This commission should be semipublic, partly governmental and partly private. Its budget should be for five years, half supplied by the federal government, half supplied by assessments on each professional team. Its governing board should be composed of representatives of the players' associations, the owners, the coaches or managers, the Congress (representing the public), players now in retirement, the sportswriters and broadcasters' associations, and the universities. Three members from each of these seven categories would provide a board of twenty-one members. The commission would have a full-time executive director and appropriate staff, including a special panel of trained and experienced arbitrators. It would have responsibilities for record keeping and for complete annual reports to Congress on the status of professional sports.

The positive justification for such a commission is the critical role of sports in the imagination and spirit of the nation. The negative justification is the string of scandals, corrupting practices, and serious grievances now afflicting the disordered and haphazard institutions of sports. Insofar as sports are public services, they have claimed special legal treatment. The logical extension of this conception is special legal oversight. The public interest is substantially involved, for sports are an educational institution of enormous power.

The commission should be partly public and governmental, because of the importance of this public interest. It should be partly private, so that the world of sports is given adequate separation from governmental control.

Once established by the Congress, such a commission could be formed by the legitimate election of representatives from the participating categories. This governing board could then choose an executive director for an appropriate term of office.

The exact responsibilities of the commission should be clearly specified. In my judgment, such oversight would include at least the following activities:

(a) Reviewing the size of leagues and mobility of franchises;
(b) Defining the rights and contractual responsibilities of players and management;
(c) Arbitrating disputes between leagues, between leagues and broadcasters, and between management and players;
(d) Specifying the responsibilities of broadcasters of sports events;
(e) Conducting research into significant aspects of professional sports in America;
(f) Keeping records of the business side of professional sports, and making appropriate public disclosure;
(g) Exercising supervision over ethical practices.

Within the clearly specified limits of its charter, the commission would have legal, binding powers.

The commission would have jurisdiction over the major established national sports: baseball, basketball, and football. At a later date, hockey leagues might also be placed under its jurisdiction. In the beginning, it would be better not to attempt too much. Hockey is not yet a truly national and well-established sport. Its future is less secure. On this judgment, of course, there is room for argument.

The commission would recognize that the traditions, legal status, needs, and structures of the three major professional sports differ from each other. Yet much would be gained by considering their different problems in a context of correlation and coordination. For they serve the same public.

These reforms are proposed for purposes of stimulating discussion and careful thought. They grow naturally, I believe, out of present trends and possibilities. But in order to take root in reality, they must be refined, revised, and bent to fruitful shape.

The main intuition suffusing them ought to be obvious. Sports are not merely entertainment, but are rooted in the necessities and the aspirations of the human spirit. They should be treated with all the intelligence, care, and love the human spirit can bring to bear. It is a corruption, not only of sports, but also of the human spirit, to treat them as escape, entertainment, business, or a means of making money. Sports *do* provide entertainment, but of a special and profound sort. They *do* depend upon a financial base, and it is not wrong that they should repay investors and players decent returns. Yet sports are at their heart a spiritual activity, a natural religion, a tribute to grace, beauty, and excellence. We ought to keep the streams of the spirit running clean and strong.

AFTERWORD

THE READING and reflection required for this book—and also the field work in stadiums and arenas—provided unusual pleasure. They also fit a life plan. Aristotle once said that young men cannot understand ethics or metaphysics until they reach the age of fifty. The young philosopher's problem, then, is what to do until he's fifty.

Aristotle himself learned about the arts; served in the government of his place and time; had economic, cultural, and political experiences of a most subtle and fascinating kind. The same was true of another idol of mine, Jacques Maritain. I have tried to accept their hints as best I can.

The concept of greatest interest to me from the beginning (*Belief and Unbelief*, 1965) has been "intelligent subjectivity"—the role of sensibility and imagination in insight and judgment. This interest has led me to experiment in fiction and drama. It has also led me into the practice of politics, including studies of ethnicity and of symbols in presidential politics. In *Choosing Our King*, I described several "civil religions" that form the symbolic horizons of American politics. In this book, I have carried the same sort of investigation into the realm of sports. In the future, I hope to study the field of television and, perhaps, the cinema.

In the end, my goal is to present a sort of rounded philosophy or theology of culture. (I do not believe there is a sustainable distinction between philosophy and theology; the distinction is an accident of history.) My hope is that, ultimately, my work will have the ring of sound experience.

A concrete philosophy, redolent of actual living, will surely have a perishable quality. The more concrete it is, the more thoroughly it will date. On the other hand, a well-constructed concrete philosophy should provide a rich set of analogies for thinkers in other places and times. Creative thinkers will know how to lift out from the ashes of departed worlds what is of value for their own.

Religion is the intensity of the human spirit in its deepest and most general form. It finds many outlets and expressions. It lives in politics, in morals, in sports, and even in the dreary enterprise of economics. Cult is the living spring of culture. So the pursuit of religion in its many guises has been basic to my enterprise, particularly in those fields of experience which scholars have usually neglected. Karl Barth once said, after many volumes of his *Church Dogmatics,* that a systematic theologian *ought* to begin with ethics—that is, with life as it is lived. His advice seems valuable.

I am grateful to friends who have long encouraged me in my idiosyncratic ways: to David Tracy and David Burrell, above all. Thanks, too, to my hardworking secretary, Cheryl Parlatore; to Eileen Zanar, whose early research and well-organized files proved so valuable at later stages; to Elizabeth Russell, who typed the first draft of part of the manuscript; to Judy Lally who typed the last two drafts, as well as all the false starts of the preceding year; and to Susan Minicozzi, too.

Thanks, as well, to the Aspen Institute for a summer as a "visiting scholar" at Aspen, where this book at last began to take shape.

Above all, thanks to Donald Cutler, who kept pressing me to outline the book, then to try again. And again. And to Midge Decter, a shrewd and good-spirited editor.

To my children and wife, once again, apologies for not being all I ought. Did you really believe that all those hours watching television were "research"?

Bibliography

Eileen Zanar and Michael Novak

The following books have been especially helpful. The bibliography is not complete—some important titles are not on it—but it does provide, at least, a starting place. Only a few magazine articles have been included, simply to suggest the range, and to recognize our special debts. The boundary between "Hagiography" and "Theory" is not hard and fast. Those books that try to evoke experience we placed in the first category; those that seemed to go beyond that, and to add elements of theory, we placed in the second. Some especially good books left in the first category indicate that the field is far from exhausted even experientially.

HAGIOGRAPHY

Allen, Maury. ed. *Voices of Sport*. New York: Grosset & Dunlap, 1971. 239 pp.
Anderson, Dave. *Countdown to Super Bowl*. New York: Random House, 1969. 247 pp.
Asinof, Elliot, *Seven Days to Sunday: Crisis Week with the New York Football Giants*. New York: Simon & Schuster, 1968. 318 pp.
Barry, Rick with Libby, Bill. *Confessions of a Basketball Gypsy: The Rick Barry Story*. Englewood Cliffs, New Jersey: Prentice-Hall, Inc., 1972. 216 pp.
Berger, Phil. *Miracle on 33rd Street: The New York Knickerbockers' Championship Season*. New York: Simon & Schuster, 1970. 256 pp.
——— *Great Moments in Pro Football*. New York: Julian Messner, 1969. 189 pp.
Brodie, John & Houston, James D. *Open Field*. Boston: Houghton Mifflin Company, 1974. 230 pp.

Brondfield, Jerry. *Woody Hayes and the 100-Yard War*. A Berkley Medallion Book. New York: Berkley Publishing Corp., 1975. 245 pp.

Bryant, Paul W. and Underwood, John. *Bear: The Hard Life and Good Times of Alabama's Coach Bryant*. A Bantam Book. New York: Bantam Books, Inc., 1974. 367 pp.

Butkus, Dick and Billings, Robert W. *Stop-Action*. New York: E. P. Dutton & Co., Inc., 1972. 158 pp.

Chapin, Dwight and Prugh, Jeff. *The Wizard of Westwood: Coach John Wooden and His UCLA Bruins*. Boston: Houghton Mifflin Co., 1973. 322 pp.

Chelland, Patrick. *One for the Gipper: George Gipp, Knute Rockne, and Notre Dame*. Chicago: Henry Regnery Co., 1973. 212 pp.

Cosell, Howard. *Cosell*. New York: Pocket Books, 1974. 421 pp.

Cousy, Bob, with Ed Linn. *The Last Loud Roar*. Englewood Cliffs, N.J.: Prentice-Hall, Inc., 1964. 272 pp.

Davis, Mac. *Basketball's Unforgettables*. A Bantam Book. Toronto/New York/London: Bantam Pathfinder Editions, 1972. 137 pp.

DeBusschere, Dave, edited by Paul D. Zimmerman and Dick Schaap. *The Open Man: A Championship Diary*. New York: Grove Press, Inc., 1970. 267 pp.

Devaney, John. *The Baseball Life of Johnny Bench*. New York: Scholastic Book Services, 1974. 108 pp.

Dowling, Tom. *Coach: A Season with Lombardi*. Eagle Books Edition. New York: Popular Library, 1970. 319 pp.

Fleisher, Jack, compiler & editor. *My Sunday Best*. Tempo Books. New York: Grosset & Dunlap, 1972. 186 pp.

Flood, Curt, with Richard Carter. *The Way It Is*. New York: Pocket Books, 1972. 208 pp.

Frazier, Walt and Berkow, Ira. *Rockin' Steady*. Englewood Cliffs, N. J.: Prentice-Hall, Inc., 1974. 158 pp.

—— and Jares, Joe. *The Walt Frazier Story: Clyde*. Tempo Books. New York: Grosset & Dunlop, 1970. 248 pp.

Freehan, Bill, ed. by Steve Gelman and Dick Schaap. *Behind the Mask*. Popular Library. New York: Popular Library, 1970. 223 pp.

Garagiola, Joe. *Baseball is a Funny Game*. A Bantam Book. New York: Bantam Books, Inc., 1962. 151 pp.

Gemme, Leila B. *The New Breed of Athlete*. Washington Square Press. New York: Pocket Book, 1975. 190 pp.

Gelman, Steve. *The Greatest Dodgers of Them All*. New York: G. P. Putnam's Sons, 1968. 191 pp.

Goldman, Richard P., ed. *Sportswriters' Choice*. New York: A. S. Barnes & Co., Inc., 1958. 332 pp.

Golenbock, Peter. *Dynasty: The New York Yankees 1949–1964*. Englewood Cliffs, N.J.: Prentice-Hall, Inc., 1975. 394 pp.

Gottehrer, Barry. *Giants of New York*. New York: Van Rees Press, 1963. 319 pp.

Hollander, Zander, compiler and editor. *More Strange But True Football Stories*. New York: Random House, 1973. 153 pp.

—— *Great Moments in Pro Football*. New York: Scholastic Book Services, 1974. 174 pp.

—— *Basketball's Greatest Games*. Englewood Cliffs, New Jersey: Prentice-Hall, Inc., 1971. 242 pp.

Holmes, A. Lawrance, ed. *More Than a Game*. New York: The Macmillan Co., 1967. 192 pp.

Holmes, Tommy. *Baseball's Great Teams: The Dodgers*. New York: Macmillan Pub. Co., Inc., 1975. 192 pp.

Holtzman, Jerome, ed. *No Cheering in the Press Box*. New York: Holt, Rinehart & Winston, 1974. 287 pp.

Holzman, Red and Lewin, Leonard. *Defense! Defense!* Warner Paperback Library Edition. New York: Warner Books, Inc., 1974. 267 pp.

Hornung, Paul, as told to Al Silverman. *Football and the Single Man*. Garden City, New York: Doubleday & Company, Inc., 1965. 252 pp.

Izenberg, Jerry. *The Rivals*. New York: Holt, Rinehart and Winston, Inc., 1968. 284 pp.

Jenkins, Dan. *Semi-Tough*. A Signet Book. New York: New American Library, 1973. 216 pp.

———— *Saturday's America*. Boston: Little, Brown & Co., 1970. 292 pp.

Kahn, Roger. *How the Weather Was*. A Signet Book. New York: The New American Library, Inc., 1975. 184 pp.

Katz, Fred, ed. *The Glory of Notre Dame*. Hong Kong: Bartholomew House, Ltd., 1971. 334 pp.

Kaye, Ivan N. *Good Clean Violence*. Philadelphia & New York: J. B. Lippincott Co., 1973. 288 pp.

Klein, Dave. *The Vince Lombardi Story*. New York: Lion Books, 1971. 154 pp.

Koppett, Leonard. *The New York Mets: The Whole Story*. New York: The Macmillan Co., 1970. 383 pp.

Koufax, Sandy, with Ed Linn. *Koufax*. New York: The Viking Press, 1966. 294 pp.

Kramer, Jerry, ed. *Lombardi: Winning is the Only Thing*. New York: The World Publishing Co., 1970. 174 pp.

Layden, Elmer with Snyder, Ed. *It Was a Different Game: The Elmer Layden Story*. Englewood Cliffs, New Jersey: Prentice-Hall, Inc., 1969. 175 pp.

Libby, Bill. *The Walton Gang*. New York: Coward, McCann & Geoghegan, 1974. 285 pp.

Liston, Robert. *The Pros*. New York: Platt & Munk, 1968. 275 pp.

Lombardi, Vince, with W. C. Heinz. *Run to Daylight*. Tempo Books. New York: Grosset & Dunlap, Inc., 1963. 189 pp.

Marsh, Irving T. and Ehre, Edward, eds. *Best Sports Stories, 1963*. New York: E. P. Dutton & Co., Inc., 1963. 336 pp.

———— *Best of the Best Sports Stories*. New York: E. P. Dutton & Co., Inc., 1964. 480 pp.

———— *Best Sports Stories 1965*. New York: E. P. Dutton & Co., Inc., 1965. 368 pp.

———— *Best Sports Stories 1966*. New York: E. P. Dutton, Inc., 1966.

———— *Best Sports Stories 1968*. New York: E. P. Dutton & Co., Inc., 1968.

———— *Best Sports Stories 1974*. New York: E. P. Dutton & Co., Inc., 1974.

Mays, Willie, as told to Charles Einstein. *My Life In and Out of Baseball*. A Fawcett Crest Book. Greenwich, Conn.: Fawcett Publications, Inc., 1973. 287 pp.

McPhee, John. *A Sense of Where You Are: A Profile of William Warren Bradley*. New York: Farrar, Straus & Giroux, 1965. 144 pp.

Meggyesy, Dave. *Out of Their League*. Warner Paperback Library Edition. New York: Warner Books, Inc., 1971. 222 pp.

Mokray, William G. *Basketball Stars of 1963*. New York: Pyramid Books, 1962. 160 pp.

Mosedale, John. *The Greatest of All: The 1927 New York Yankees*. Warner Paperback Library Edition. New York: Warner Books, Inc., 1975. 254 pp.

Namath, Joe, with Bob Oates, Jr. *A Matter of Style*. Boston: Little, Brown & Co., 1973. 196 pp.

———— with Dick Schaap. *I Can't Wait Until Tomorrow . . . 'Cause I Get Better-Looking Every Day*. New York: Random House, 1969. 279 pp.

Newcombe, Jack. *The Best of the Athletic Boys: The White Man's Impact on Jim Thorpe*. Garden City, New York: Doubleday & Co., Inc., 1975. 250 pp.

Oliver, Chip, ed. by Ron Rapoport. *High for the Game*. New York: William Morrow & Co., Inc., 1971. 149 pp.

Padwe, Sandy. *Basketball's Hall of Fame*. Tempo Books. New York: Grosset & Dunlap, Inc., 1973. 171 pp.

Parrish, Bernie. *They Call It a Game*. A Signet Book. New York: The New American Library, Inc., 1972. 302 pp.

Parseghian, Ara and Pagna, Tom. *Parseghian and Notre Dame Football*. Garden City, New York: Doubleday & Co., Inc., 1973. 319 pp.

Paxton, Harry T., ed. *Sport U. S. A.: The Best from the Saturday Evening Post*. New York: Thomas Nelson & Sons, 1961. 463 pp.

Pepe, Phil. *Kareem Abdul-Jabbar*. Tempo Books. New York: Grosset & Dunlap, Inc., 1970. 203 pp.

———— *The Wit and Wisdom of Yogi Berra*. New York: Hawthorne Books, Inc., 1974.

Perkins, Steve. *The Drive to Win: The Making of the Dallas Cowboys*. Tempo Books. New York: Grosset & Dunlap, Inc., 1973. 275 pp.

Plimpton, George. *Paper Lion*. New York: Pocket Books, 1967. 303 pp.

———— *Mad Ducks and Bears*. New York: Random House, 1973. 421 pp.

Rappoport, Ken. *Wake up the Echoes*. Huntsville, Alabama: Strode Publishers, Inc., 1975. 464 pp.

Rathet, Mike, with the editors of *Pro Quarterback Magazine*. *The World of the NFL: Pro Football*. Chicago: Henry Regnery Co., 1972. 314 pp.

Reed, Willis, with Phil Pepe. *A View from the Rim: Willis Reed on Basketball*. Philadelphia: J. P. Lippincott Co., 1971. 208 pp.

Sample, Johnny, with Fred J. Hamilton and Sonny Schwartz. *Confessions of a Dirty Ballplayer*. A Dell Book. New York: Dell Publishing Co., Inc., 1971. 290 pp.

Schaap, Dick. *Quarterbacks Have All the Fun*. Chicago, Ill.: Playboy Press, 1974. 261 pp.

Schoor, Gene, ed. *A Treasury of Notre Dame Football*. New York: Funk & Wagnalls Co., Inc., 1962.

———— *Football's Greatest Coach: Vince Lombardi*. New York: Pocket Books, 1975. 229 pp.

Scotch, N. A. "Magic, Sorcery, and Football Among Urban Zulu," *The Journal of Conflict Resolution*. V(1961), pp. 70–74.

Shapiro, Milton J. *Jackie Robinson of the Brooklyn Dodgers*. An Archway Paperback. New York: Pocket Books, 1973. 250 pp.

Shinnick, Don, as told to James C. Hefley. *Always a Winner*. Grand Rapids, Michigan: Zondervan Publishing House, 1969. 223 pp.

Shula, Don, with Lou Sahadi. *The Winning Edge*. Popular Library Edition. New York: Popular Library, 1973. 255 pp.

Silverman, Al, ed. *The Best of Sport: 1946–1971*. New York: The Viking Press, 1971. 615 pp.

———— *The World of Sport*. New York: Holt, Rinehart & Winston, 1962. 358 pp.

Smith, Ken. *Baseball's Hall of Fame*. Tempo Books. New York: Grosset & Dunlap, 1972. 282 pp.

Smith, Robert. *Pro Football: The History of the Game and the Great Players*. Garden City, New York: Doubleday & Co., Inc., 1963. 230 pp.

———— *World Series: The Games and the Players*. Garden City, New York: Doubleday & Co., Inc., 1967. 310 pp.

———— *Sports: The American Scene*. New York: McGraw-Hill Book Co., Inc., 1963. 283 pp.

Sobol, Ken. *Babe Ruth and The American Dream.* New York: Ballantine Books, 1974. 269 pp.

Sullivan, George. *Bart Starr: The Cool Quarterback.* New York: G. P. Putnam's Sons, 1970. 192 pp.

Twombly, Wells. *Blanda: Alive and Kicking.* New York: Avon Books, 1973. 287 pp.

—— *Shake Down the Thunder: The Official Biography of Notre Dame's Frank Leahy.* Radnor, Penn.: Chilton Book Co., 1974. 328 pp.

Unitas, Johnny, and Ed Fitzgerald. *Pro Quarterback: My Own Story.* New York: Simon and Schuster, 1965. 188 pp.

Vare, Robert. *Buckeye: A Study of Coach Woody Hayes and the Ohio State Football Machine.* New York: Harper's Magazine Press, 1974. 243 pp.

Vecsey, George. *Pro Basketball Champions.* New York: Scholastic Book Services, 1970. 159 pp.

Wallace, Francis. *Notre Dame from Rockne to Parseghian.* New York: David McKay Co., Inc., 1966. 300 pp.

Webb, Bernice Larson. *The Basketball Man: James Naismith.* Lawrence/Manhattan/Wichita: The University Press of Kansas, 1973. 381 pp.

West, Jerry, with Bill Libby. *Mr. Clutch: The Jerry West Story.* Tempo Books. New York: Grosset & Dunlap, 1969. 230 pp.

Weyand, Alexander M. *Football Immortals.* New York: The Macmillan Co., 1962. 290 pp.

Wolf, David. *Foul! The Connie Hawkins Story.* New York: Holt, Rinehart & Winston, 1972. 400 pp.

Wooden, John, as told to Jack Tobin. *They Call Me Coach.* Waco, Texas: Word Books, 1973. 194 pp.

THEOLOGY

Angell, Roger. *The Summer Game.* Popular Library Edition. New York: Popular Library, 1972. 320 pp.

Axthelm, Pete. *The City Game: Basketball in New York from the World Champion Knicks to the World of the Playgrounds.* New York: Harper & Row, 1970. 210 pp.

Barber, Red. *The Broadcasters.* New York: The Dial Press, 1970. 271 pp.

Beer, Tom, with George Kimball. *Sunday's Fools: Stomped, Tromped, Kicked and Chewed in the NFL.* Boston: Houghton Mifflin Co., 1974. 204 pp.

Billings, Robert. *Pro Football Digest.* Chicago: Follett Publ., Co., 1973. 288 pp.

Bouton, Jim, ed. by Leonard Shecter. *Ball Four.* New York: Dell Publishing Co., Inc., 1971. 371 pp.

—— *I'm Glad You Didn't Take it Personally.* New York: Dell Publishing Co., Inc., 1973. 249 pp.

Boyle, Robert H. *Sport-Mirror of American Life.* Boston: Little, Brown & Co., 1963. 293 pp.

Brasch, R. *How Did Sports Begin?* New York: David McKay Co., Inc., 1970. 434 pp.

Brosnan, Jim. *Pennant Race.* New York: Harper & Brothers, 1962. 249 pp.

—— *The Long Season.* New York: Harper & Brothers, 1960. 273 pp.

Bukata, Jim. *ABC's Wide World of Sports Record Book.* ABC Series, Sept. 1974, Vol. 1, No. 3. New York: Stadia Sports Publishing, Inc., 1974. 224 pp.

Caillois, Roger, translated by Meyer Barash. *Man, Play and Games.* Free Press, 1961.

Cohen, Marvin. *Baseball the Beautiful.* New York: Links Books, 1974. 120 pp.

Cord Communications Corp. *Pro Football 1974.* New York: Pocket Books, 1974. 279 pp.

Cosell, Howard. *Like It Is*. New York: Pocket Books, 1975. 319 pp.

Cox, Harvey. *The Feast of Fools: A Theological Essay on Festivity and Fantasy*. Cambridge, Mass.: Harvard University Press, 1969. 204 pp.

Cratty, Bryant J. *Psychology in Contemporary Sports*. Englewood Cliffs, New Jersey: Prentice-Hall, Inc., 1973. 304 pp.

Dulles, Foster Rhea. *America Learns to Play: A History of Popular Recreation 1607–1940*. Gloucester, Mass.: Peter Smith, 1963. 441 pp.

Durso, Joseph. *The All-American Dollar: The Big Business of Sports*. Boston: Houghton Mifflin Co., 1971. 294 pp.

Edwards, Harry. *Sociology of Sport*. Homewood, Illinois: The Dorsey Press, 1973. 395 pp.

Einstein, Charles, ed. *The Third Fireside Book of Baseball*. New York: Simon and Schuster, 1968. 511 pp.

Eskenazi, Gerald. *A Thinking Man's Guide to Pro Hockey*. New York: E. P. Dutton & Co., Inc., 1972. 223 pp.

Fleming, Alice, ed. *Hosannah the Home Run: Poems about Sports*. Boston: Little, Brown, & Co., 1972. 68 pp.

Gallwey, W. Timothy. *The Inner Game of Tennis*. New York: Random House, 1974. 141 pp.

Hoch, Paul. *Rip Off the Big Game: The Exploitation of Sports by the Power Elite*. Anchor Books. Garden City, N. Y.: Doubleday & Co., Inc., 1972. 222 pp.

Izenberg, Jerry. *How Many Miles to Camelot? The All-American Sport Myth*. New York: Holt, Rinehart and Winston, 1972. 227 pp.

Jenkins, Dan. *The Dogged Victims of Inexorable Fate*. A Berkley Medallion Book. New York: Berkley Publ., Corp., 1973. 286 pp.

Jordan, Pat. *The Suitors of Spring*. Warner Paperback Library Edition. New York: Warner Books, Inc., 1974. 174 pp.

Kahn, Roger. *The Boys of Summer*. New York: Harper & Row, 1971. 442 pp.

Kiely, John. *This Sporting Life, That Sporting Death*. Cranberry, New Jersey: A. S. Barnes & Co., Inc., 1973. 170 pp.

Koppett, Leonard. *All About Baseball*. New York: Quadrangle/The New York Times Book Co., 1974. 400 pp.

———— *The Essence of the Game is Deception: Thinking about Basketball*. A Sports Illustrated Book. Boston: Little, Brown & Co., 1973. 274 pp.

———— *The New York Times Guide to Spectator Sports*. New York: Quadrangle Books, 1971. 259 pp.

Leckie, Robert. *The Story of Football*. New York: Random House, 1965. 177 pp.

Lipsyte, Robert. *Assignment: Sports*. New York: Harper & Row, 1970. 157 pp.

———— *Sportsworld*. New York: Quadrangle, 1975. 292 pp.

Loy, John W. Jr., and Kenyon, Gerald S. *Sport, Culture and Society: A Reader on the Sociology of Sport*. New York: The Macmillan Co., 1969. 464 pp.

McIntosh, P. C. *Sport in Society*. London: C. A. Watts & Co., Ltd., 1963. 208 pp.

Merchant, Larry. *. . . . And Every Day You Take Another Bite*. Garden City, New York: Doubleday & Co., Inc., 1971. 191 pp.

———— *The National Football Lottery*. New York: Dell Publishing Co., Inc., 1974. 346 pp.

Miller, David L. *Gods and Games: Toward a Theology of Play*. Cleveland, Ohio: The World Publishing Co., 1969. 209 pp.

Morgan, William P., ed. *Contemporary Readings in Sport Psychology*. Springfield, Illinois: Charles C. Thomas, 1970. 460 pp.

Morton, Henry W. *Soviet Sport: Mirror of Soviet Society*. New York: Collier Books, 1963. 221 pp.

National Collegiate Championships 1975. Shawnee Mission, Kansas: National Collegiate Athletic Association, 1975. 233 pp.

Neale, Robert E. *In Praise of Play*. New York: Harper & Row, 1969. 187 pp.

Neville, Richard. *Play Power: Exploring the International Underground*. New York: Random House, 1970. 325 pp.

Noll, Roger G., ed. *Government and the Sports Business*. Washington, D.C.: The Brookings Institution, 1974, 454 pp.

Perkes, Dan, ed. *The Official Associated Press Sports Almanac, 1974*. New York: Dell Publishing Co., Inc., 1974. 924 pp.

Raiborn, Mitchell H. *Financial Analysis of Intercollegiate Athletics*. Kansas City, Mo.: The National Collegiate Athletic Assoc., 1970. 127 pp.

Ralbovsky, Martin. *Lords of the Locker Room: The American Way of Coaching and its Effect on Youth*. New York: Peter H. Wyden, 1974. 236 pp.

Sapora, Allen V. and Mitchell, Elmer. *The Theory of Play and Recreation*. Third Edition. New York: The Ronald Press Co., 1961. 558 pp.

Scheter, Leonard. *The Jocks*. Indianapolis-New York: The Bobbs-Merrill Co., Inc., 1969. 278 pp.

Scott, Jack. *The Athletic Revolution*. New York: The Free Press, 1971. 242 pp.

Shaw, Gary. *Meat on the Hoof*. New York: Dell Pub., Co., Inc., 1973. 285 pp.

Singer, Robert N. *Coaching, Athletics, and Psychology*. New York: McGraw-Hill Book Co., 1972. 374 pp.

Slusher, Howard S. *Man, Sport and Existence: A Critical Analysis*. Philadelphia: Lea & Febiger, 1967. 243 pp.

Somers, Dale A. *The Rise of Sports in New Orleans, 1850–1900*. Baton Rouge: Louisiana State University Press, 1972. 320 pp.

Talamini, John T. and Page, Charles H., ed. *Sport and Society: An Anthology*. Boston: Little, Brown and Company, 1973. 493 pp.

The New York Times Book of Baseball History. New York: An Arno Press Book, 1975. 327 pp.

U. S. Bureau of the Census. *Statistical Abstract of the United States, 1973*. 94th edition. Washington, D. C., 1973.

U. S. Congress. House Committee on the Judiciary. *The Antitrust Laws and Organized Professional Team Sports Including Consideration of the Proposed Merger of the American and National Basketball Associations*. Hearings before a subcommittee of the Committee on the Judiciary, House of Representatives on HR 1206, HR 2305 HR 10185, HR 11033, 92nd Congress, 2nd session, 1972.

U. S. Congress. Senate Committee on Commerce. *Blackout of Sporting Events on TV*. Hearings before the Subcommittee on Communications of the Committee on Commerce, United States Senate, on S4007, S4010, 92nd Congress, 2nd session, 1972.

———— *Federal Sports Act of 1972*. Hearings before the Committee on Commerce, United States Senate, on S3445, 92nd Congress, 2nd session, 1972.

U. S. Department of the Interior. Bureau of Outdoor Recreation. *Selected Outdoor Recreation Statistics, 1971*. Washington, D. C.: Government Printing Office, 1971.

———— *The 1970 Survey of Outdoor Recreation Activities Preliminary Report*. Washington, D. C., February, 1972.

Vanderzwaag, Harold J. *Toward a Philosophy of Sport*. Reading, Mass: Addison-Wesley Publishing Co., 1972. 261 pp.

Vanek, Miroslav and Cratty, Brant J. *Psychology and the Superior Athlete*. London: The Macmillan Co./Collier-Macmillan Ltd., 1970. 212 pp.

Wallop, Douglass. *Baseball: An Informal History*. New York: Bantam Books, Inc., 1970. 246 pp.

Weiss, Paul. *Sport: A Philosophic Inquiry*. Carbondale: Southern Illinois University Press, 1969. 274 pp.

ARTICLES

Angell, Roger. "The Sporting Scene: Four Taverns in the Town." *The New Yorker*, October 26, 1963, pp. 184, 187–89, 190, 194–97.

Arens, William. "The Great American Football Ritual." *Natural History*, October 1975. p. 72.

Blanchard, Kendall. "Run, Jump, and Shoot: Basketball and the Ramah Navajos." 1973, mimeograph (13 pp.). Middle Tennessee State University.

Blanda, George with Olsen, Jack. "A Decade of Revenge." *Sports Illustrated*, July 26, 1971, pp. 36–38, 43–45.

—— "I Keep Getting My Kicks." *Sports Illustrated*, July 19, 1971, pp. 26–31.

—— "That Impossible Season." *Sports Illustrated*, August 2, 1971, pp. 30–36.

"George Blanda is Alive and Kicking." *Time*, Nov. 23, 1970, p. 74.

"A Kick in Time." *Newsweek*, Nov., 23, 1970, p. 114. (on Blanda)

Maule, T. "Let George Do It and He Does." *Sports Illustrated*, Nov., 23, 1970, pp. 30—32+ (on Blanda)

College & University Business, Sept., 1973. "Academics Vs. Athletics: Two Views," pp. 15–16, 18, 20, 66–68.

Balbus, Isaac D. "The American Game of Life," Review of *Rip Off the Big Game: The Exploitation of Sports by the Power Elite*, by Paul Hoch. *The Nation*, May 7, 1973, pp. 600–602.

Bergin, Podhoretz, Smith. "Sports in America-Larger than Life." *Yale Reports*, Nov. 26, 1972.

Deford, Frank. "The Last Drop in the Bucket." *Sports Illustrated*, May 12, 1969, pp. 22–24, 29.

Deford, Frank. "This One Was Worth Shouting About." *Sports Illustrated*, May 13, 1968, pp. 34–37.

Flaherty, Joe. "Dick Young: The Sultan of Syntax." *The Village Voice*, April 28, 1975. p. 8f.

—— "Howard Cosell, You Will Self-Destruct in About Two More Seasons." *New York*, December 9, 1974, pp. 58–63.

Furlong, William Barry. "The Psychologist on the Sidelines." The *New York Times Magazine*, November 13, 1966, pp. 56–57, 153–55, 157, 159–60.

—— "What Ever Became of Football?" *TV Guide*, October 4, 1975, pp. 3–6.

Halberstam, David. "Sunday, Boring Sunday: A Farewell to Pro Football." *New York*, December 16, 1974, pp. 65–70.

Hano, Arnold. "Winning with Nice Guys and a Pyramid of Principles." *The New York Times Magazine*, December 2, 1973, pp. 31, 134, 136, 138–39, 141–43, 145–46, 154.

Hesburgh, Theodore M., C.S.C. "The True Meaning of the Game." *Sports Illustrated*, Dec. 12, 1966, pp. 56–57.

Koppett, Leonard. "A Strange Business, Baseball." *The New York Times Magazine*, Sept. 2, 1973, pp. 10–11, 38, 39, 41.

Koufax, Sandy and Olsen, Jack. "Sportsman of the Year: Koufax on Koufax." *Sports Illustrated*, pp. 34–42.

Kostelanetz, Richard. "The Artistry of TV Football." *The Humanist*, January/February, 1973, pp. 24–26.

Lipsyte, Robert. "That Championship Season." *[More]* Magazine, 1975.

Mandell, Arnold, M. D. "A Psychiatric Study of Football." *Saturday Review World*, October 5, 1974, pp. 12–16.

Murphy, Michael and Brodie, John. "I Experience a Kind of Clarity." *Intellectual Digest*, January, 1973, pp. 19–22.

Naison, Mark. "No Joy in Mudville." Review of *Rip Off the Big Game: The*

Exploitation of Sports by the Power Elite, by Paul Hoch. *Liberation*, June, 1973, pp. 38–41.

Ogilvie, Bruce C. and Tutko, Thomas. "Sport: If You Want to Build Character Try Something Else." *Psychology Today*, October, 1971, pp. 61–63.

Poe, Randall. "The Angry Fan." *Harper's Magazine*, November, 1975, pp. 86–95.

Roberts, Michael. "The Vicarious Heroism of the Sports Spectator." *The New Republic,* November 23, 1974, pp. 17–20.

———— "The NFL Strike: Athletes as Chattel." *The New Republic*, August 10 & 17, 1974, pp. 14–16.

Segal, Jonathan. "Sports." *Esquire*, May 1974, pp. 60–63.

Shaw, David. "Look Ma! No Decimal Points." The Los Angeles *Times*, February 7, 1975.

Sisk, John P. "Hot Sporting Blood." *The Commonweal*, March 2, 1973, p. 495f.

Weiner, Jay. "The High Cost of Big-Time Football." *College & University Business*, September, 1973, pp. 35–42.

Wenkert, Simon, M. D. "The Meaning of Sports for Contemporary Man." *Journal of Existential Psychiatry*, Spring, 1963, pp. 397–404.

Wind, Herbert Warren. "The Sporting Scene: West of the Wabash." *The New Yorker*, March 22, 1969, pp. 93–96, 98–101.

Wray, Jerome A. "Costs of Secondary School Athletic Programs." *School Management*, Nov., 1972, pp. 26–28.

A mimeograph newsletter is also published by the Association for the Anthropological Study of Play, Dr. Alyce Cheska, Editor. Dept. of Physical Education, University of Illinois, Urbana, Illinois, 61801.

In October, 1974, *Esquire* devoted most of an entire issue to "Super Sports" and in October, 1975, to "The Joy of Sports." Several of these articles are among the best in the field.

Index